D0146257

Rethinking Global Political Economy

This important volume presents innovative approaches to fundamental issues in global political economy. Together they provide multiple arguments and avenues for rethinking global political economy in a time of turmoil and system transformation.

The authors collected here consider similar problems from a wide variety of perspectives. In particular, the authors survey the vicissitudes of globalization, the processes of global capitalism, and the building of progressive social theory, answering questions such as:

- What are the defining concepts in contemporary international political economy (IPE)?
- Why has mainstream theory in IPE so far failed to give rise to policies able to bring prosperity to more than a fraction of the world's people?
- How can we re-conceive these concepts to produce better theories and more equitable and effective policies?

Rethinking Global Political Economy contains analysis of history, linguistics, class, culture, empirical data, and normative concerns. It will appeal to those interested in seeing new perspectives and a healthy heterodoxy in the study of political economy.

Mary Ann Tétreault is the Una Chapman Cox Distinguished Professor of International Affairs at Trinity University, USA.

Robert A. Denemark is Associate Professor in the Department of Political Science at the University of Delaware, USA.

Kenneth P. Thomas is Associate Professor of Political Science and Fellow of the Center for International Studies at the University of Missouri-St Louis, USA.

Kurt Burch is Associate Professor in Political Science at St Olaf College, USA.

The Routledge/RIPE Series in Global Political Economy

Series editors: Louise Amoore (*University of Newcastle, UK*), Randall Germain (*Carleton University, Canada*) and Rorden Wilkinson (*University of Manchester, UK* and *Wellesley College, US*)

Formerly edited by Otto Holman, Marianne Marchand (*Research Centre for International Political Economy, University of Amsterdam*) Henk Overbeek (*Free University, Amsterdam*) and Marianne Franklin (*University of Amsterdam*)

This series, published in association with the *Review of International Political Economy*, provides a forum for current debates in international political economy. The series aims to cover all the central topics in IPE and to present innovative analyses of emerging topics. The titles in the series seek to transcend a state-centred discourse and focus on three broad themes:

- the nature of the forces driving globalisation forward
- resistance to globalisation
- the transformation of the world order.

The series comprises two strands:

The *RIPE Series in Global Political Economy* aims to address the needs of students and teachers, and the titles will be published in hardback and paperback. Titles include:

Transnational Classes and International Relations
Kees van der Pijl

Gender and Global Restructuring
Sightings, sites and resistances
Edited by Marianne H. Marchand and Anne Sisson Runyan

Global Political Economy
Contemporary theories
Edited by Ronen Palan

Ideologies of Globalization
Contending visions of a new world order
Mark Rupert

The Clash within Civilisations
Coming to terms with cultural conflicts
Dieter Senghaas

Global Unions?
Theory and strategies of organized labour in the global
political economy
Edited by Jeffrey Harrod and Robert O'Brien

Political Economy of a Plural World
Critical reflections on power, morals and civilizations
Robert Cox with Michael Schechter

A Critical Rewriting of Global Political Economy
Integrating reproductive, productive and virtual economies
V. Spike Peterson

Contesting Globalization
Space and place in the world economy
André C. Drainville

Global Institutions and Development
Framing the world?
Edited by Morten Bøås and Desmond McNeill

Routledge/RIPE Studies in Global Political Economy is a forum for innovative new
research intended for a high-level specialist readership, and the titles will be available
in hardback only. Titles include:

* Also available in paperback.

Rethinking Global Political Economy

Emerging issues, unfolding odysseys

**Edited by Mary Ann Tétreault,
Robert A. Denemark,
Kenneth P. Thomas, and
Kurt Burch**

Routledge
Taylor & Francis Group

LONDON AND NEW YORK

First published 2003
by Routledge
11 New Fetter Lane, London EC4P 4EE

Simultaneously published in the USA and Canada
by Routledge
29 West 35th Street, New York, NY 10001

Routledge is an imprint of the Taylor & Francis Group

© 2003 Mary Ann Tétreault, Robert A. Denemark, Kenneth P. Thomas
and Kurt Burch for selection and editorial matter; individual contributors,
their contributions

Typeset in Baskerville MT by
Newgen Imaging Systems (P) Ltd, Chennai, India
Printed and bound in Malta by
Gutenberg Press Ltd, Malta

All rights reserved. No part of this book may be reprinted or reproduced or
utilised in any form or by any electronic, mechanical, or other means, now
known or hereafter invented, including photocopying and recording, or in
any information storage or retrieval system, without permission in writing
from the publishers.

British Library Cataloguing in Publication Data
A catalogue record for this book is available from the British Library

Library of Congress Cataloging-in-Publication Data
Rethinking global political economy: emerging issues, unfolding
odysseys/editors, Mary Ann Tétreault ... [et al.].
    p. cm.
Includes bibliographical references and index.
1. International economic relations. 2. Globalization – Economic
aspects. 3. Globalization – Social aspects. 4. Globalization – Political
aspects. I. Tétreault, Mary Ann, 1942–

HF1359 .R475 2003
337–dc21   2003004036

ISBN 0–415–31293–0

To our families, partners in our odysseys

Contents

Illustrations

Figures

Table

Contributors

Kurt Burch received his PhD from the University of Minnesota. He is the author of *"Property" and the Making of the International System*, and coeditor, with Bob Denemark, of *Constituting International Political Economy*. His work develops innovative theoretical frameworks to explore conflicts and issues at the intersection of IPE and International Organization. His latest work investigates how changing conceptions of property rights and intellectual property rights help shape the organization, character, and content of the global political economy. More broadly, Burch explores how social rules are a medium through which power arises and social change occurs. As social change often sparks conflict, Burch, an award-winning mediator, also explores means for successfully managing international conflict.

Alejandro Colás teaches International Relations at the University of Sussex, England. He is author of *International Civil Society: Social Movements in World Politics* (Polity Press, 2002) and is an editor of the journal *Historical Materialism: Research in Critical Marxist Theory*.

Robert A. Denemark is coeditor of *World System History: The Social Science of Long-Term Change* (Routledge, 2000). His work in the area of international political economy, international relations theory, ethnic violence, and terror has appeared in edited volumes and journals in political science, sociology, and economics. Denemark is coeditor of the *International Political Economy Yearbook* and associate editor of *International Studies Perspectives*.

Hartmut Elsenhans, born in 1941, teaches International Relations in Leipzig, Germany. He has also taught in New Delhi, Salzburg, Lisbon, Dakar, Konstanz, Marburg, Frankfurt, and Berlin. He has field research experience in France, Algeria, Senegal, Bangladesh, and India. He has published widely on problems of development, and on political movements in countries of Asia and Africa, especially India and Algeria. At the moment, he is working on a comparative analysis of new political movements in different cultural contexts, Algeria and India. He is codirecting a program for European Studies in New Delhi.

Barry K. Gills is Reader in International Politics at the University of Newcastle upon Tyne. He is the editor of *Globalizations*, a new journal sponsored by the Globalization Research Network and published by Taylor and Francis. In 2002/3 he served as Director of the Globalization Research Center of the University of Hawaii at Manoa. He is the 2003/4 program chair for the International Political Economy section of the International Studies Association and a member of the executive board of the Global Studies Association. He received his PhD in International Relations from the London School of Economics and Political Science and his research concerns the processes of globalization(s) both historically and in the contemporary period. Among his recent work is a co-edited special issue of the *Annals of American Political Science* on "Globalization and Democracy."

Barbara Jenkins is Associate Professor of Communication Studies at Wilfrid Laurier University in Waterloo, Ontario, Canada. She is the author of *The Paradox of Continental Production* and various articles focusing on the relationship between cultural production and global power structures.

Clark A. Miller is Assistant Professor of Public Affairs and Science Studies in the La Follette School of Public Affairs at the University of Wisconsin-Madison. He is the editor (with Paul Edwards) of *Changing the Atmosphere: Expert Knowledge and Environmental Governance* (Cambridge: MIT Press, 2001). His current research focuses on the contribution of scientific and technological change to processes of social and political globalization.

Jonathan Nitzan teaches political economy at York University in Toronto. He has written on various aspects of "capital as power" in the global political economy. His recent publications, coauthored with Shimshon Bichler, include *From War Profit to Peace Dividends* (Jerusalem: Carmel, 2001) and *The Global Political Economy of Israel* (London: Pluto Press, 2002). He is presently working, together with Bichler, on the theory of financial capitalism.

V. Spike Peterson is an associate professor in the Department of Political Science at the University of Arizona, where she also holds courtesy appointments in Women's Studies, Comparative Cultural and Literary Studies, and International Studies. She is the editor of *Gendered States: Feminist (Re) Visions of International Relations Theory* and the coauthor (with Anne Sisson Runyan) of *Global Gender Issues*. She has published numerous journal articles and book chapters on the topics of feminist international relations theory, global political economy, nationalism, democratization, and critical postmodernist and feminist theory. Her new book, *Rewriting Global Political Economy: Structural Hierarchies and the Intersection of Reproductive, Productive and Virtual Economies*, introduces an alternative analytics for analyzing inequalities of race, gender, class, and nation in the context of today's globalizing dynamics.

Peter J. Taylor is Professor of Geography and Co-Director of the Globalization and World Cities (GaWC) Study Group and Network at Loughborough University and is Visiting Research Professor and Associate Director of the Metropolitan Institute, Virginia Tech. Founding editor of Political Geography and Review of International Political Economy, he is the author of numerous books and articles in which he takes a world-systems perspective on geohistorical, geopolitical, and geoeconomic topics. His books include *The Way the Modern World Works: From World Hegemony to World Impasse* (Wiley) and *Modernities: A Geohistorical Interpretation* (Polity). His latest book is *World City Network: A Global Urban Analysis* (Routledge). In 2001 he was elected an Academician of the Academy of Scholarly Societies in the Social Sciences (UK) and he has been selected to receive the Distinguished Scholarship Honors of the Association of American Geographers for 2003.

Mary Ann Tétreault is the Una Chapman Cox Distinguished Professor of International Affairs at Trinity University in San Antonio, Texas, where she teaches courses in world politics, the Middle East, and feminist theory. Her recent books include *Stories of Democracy: Politics and Society in Contemporary Kuwait* (2000); *The Kuwait Petroleum Corporation and the Economics of the New World Order* (1995); and edited volumes, among them *Partial Truths and the Politics of Community* (2003); *Conscious Acts and the Politics of Social Change* (2000); *Gender, States, and Nationalism – At Home in the Nation?* (2000). Her current research interests include Kuwaiti politics and society; international energy issues; and constructions of public and private space in the context of globalization.

Kenneth P. Thomas is an Associate Professor of political science and a Fellow at the Center for International Studies, University of Missouri-St Louis. His work centers on the control of capital mobility and competition for investment. His most recent works are *Competing for Capital: Europe and North America in a Global Era* and, coedited with Timothy Sinclair, *Structure and Agency in International Capital Mobility*.

Peter Uvin is the Henry J. Leir Chair of International Humanitarian Studies and the Director of the Institute for Human Security at the Fletcher School of Law and Diplomacy at Tufts University. His research interests include development aid, NGO scaling up, hunger and food policy, the African Great lakes region, and post-conflict assistance. His most recent book *Aiding Violence. The Development Enterprise in Rwanda* received the African Studies Association's Herskowits award for the most outstanding book on Africa in 1998.

Series editors' preface

Given the sea-changes that have been occurring in the study of International Political Economy (IPE) since the mid-1980s, it is hardly surprising that the discipline is now at a crossroad. For one thing, the political and geo-strategic map of the world has been drastically transformed. Major events such as the end of the Cold War, symbolized by the fall of the Berlin Wall and the implosion of the former Soviet Union, and the 1991 intervention in the Gulf War (under the auspices of the United Nations (UN)) were presented as the triumph of economic and political liberalism, the advent of a "New World Order."

How things have changed barely a decade later. The world has now been witness to three more military interventions, one in Kosovo, one in Afghanistan, and one in Iraq, which were not approved by the UN Security Council. The latter intervention appears to have further cemented a new geo-strategic divide; one that no longer finds the United States and the Soviet Union opposite each other but which seemingly confronts the West, in particular the United States, with the Islamic world. In political terms this new divide is being compounded by the fact that severe disagreements exist within the Atlantic Alliance.

These geo-strategic changes have not been happening in a political, economic, or sociocultural vacuum. Encapsulated by the term "globalization," a number of "sea changes" have been transforming both the practice and constitution of world (power) politics and many people's everyday lives. For all these reasons, the need to keep developing new analytical and theoretical frameworks for grasping these various transformations in IPE/Global Political Economy (GPE) has not lessened. In this regard this latest volume in the RIPE Series in GPE, *Rethinking Global Political Economy: Emerging Issues, Unfolding Odysseys* is a much needed contribution to the field.

The volume brings together a range of critical perspectives on the aforementioned "global shifts" from a variety of scholarly, political, and analytical perspectives. The volume editors have also opted to dispense altogether with the term "International Political Economy," substituting with that of "Global Political Economy." Reasons for this change in terminology is underscored in the contributing chapters' themes, which range from culture and the market, the role of environmental movements in civil society, structural, and acute violence, a new class analysis, to an entirely different frame for understanding the GPE by way of the interconnection between reproductive, productive, and virtual economies. All the contributors show a healthy concern with the twin issues of injustice and inequality, two issues that are all too often swept under the carpet in the name of "scientific" rigour and "objective" analysis. Furthermore, the contributors all aim to rethink (the practice and study of) GPE by moving theory and research out from beyond the state/market dichotomy and by integrating analyses of the various dimensions of civil society.

This volume fits into the Routledge/RIPE Series in GPE very well in that it is one of the growing number of titles that actively look to radically rethink and reframe GPE. Even more importantly, Odysseys defies suggestions that there is also a growing Atlantic divide in academic scholarship. The volume editors show that scholars of many disciplinary and geographical hues can be, and still are engaged in constructive conversation and dialogue about contemporary issues and events in (the study of) world politics. By providing a refreshingly clear view in the field and by sidestepping many sacred cows, this passionate and pithy volume continues in the spirit of the RIPE Series in GPE.

Marianne Franklin, Otto Holman,
Marianne Marchand, and Henk Overbeek

Part I

Introduction

1 New odysseys in global political economy

Fundamentalist contention and economic conflict

Mary Ann Tétreault

This volume brings together a set of essays each of which seeks to launch or elaborate on innovative approaches to fundamental issues in global political economy. Half of them had their start in a series of International Studies Association panels that I organized over a five-year period along with Dimitris Stevis. The panels looked at shifting boundaries between actors and sites of interaction among a variety of participants in the post-Cold War global political economy. The various papers examined basic premises for conceiving and analyzing world systems and global governance. In addition to essays developed from these panels, this collection includes invited contributions from scholars whose substantive expertise complements and whose normative and theoretical interests parallel those of the boundaries group participants.

Taken together, the writers argue from different theoretical and normative points of view, and perhaps from different worldviews as well. Their chapters provide multiple arguments and avenues for rethinking global political economy at a time of turmoil and system transformation. What are the defining concepts in contemporary international political economy (IPE)? How should we frame the models we build from them? Spike Peterson (Chapter 2 this volume) finds recurrent patterns of domination along conventional boundary distinctions such as "first world/third world," "capitalists/workers," "male/female," and "core/periphery," and cross-cutting patterns signifying the drawing of less conventional lines. In several chapters, the "state" surrenders its centrality as an organizing concept, but for most it remains key whether it is explicitly addressed or not. "Hegemony" is another concept that appears in these chapters, most openly engaged as the contestation among ideas in theory and in policy (Jenkins, Chapter 4 this volume). Perhaps most significantly, these chapters reflect an enlarged vision of class and its priority as an independent variable, one that incorporates identity along with relations of production (Colás; Nitzan; Peterson; Uvin, this volume). Whether the construction (or perhaps the recognition) of identity owes more to agency, ontology, or contingency points up its plasticity and indicates a "Goldhagen problematique" for understanding its social production and reproduction (Goldhagen 1996; Uvin, Chapter 7 this volume).

Several chapters look explicitly at problems of justice and equality, reflecting the concerns of many contributors with the welfare and happiness of human beings (especially Elsenhans; Peterson; Uvin, this volume), relations among persons and peoples (especially Colás; Uvin, this volume), and the troubling question of whether and how we can envision the joint survival of human beings and the rest of the planet over the long term (Miller, Chapter 10 this volume). As I discuss below, these concerns are becoming more salient, along with conflicts that don't quite fit into the old categories and problems that the crumbling "Washington Consensus" had promised to solve but merely made worse. The latter have reached such proportions that even neo-liberal Nobel laureates and famous financiers have begun to question this model as an appropriate template for guiding the global political economy (e.g. Soros 2002; Stiglitz 2002).

The relatively new interest in social justice from "enlightened" neo-liberals arises from empirical evidence that the implementation of globalization is destabilizing, and not only because of widening inequality between and within states. The most profound impact of globalization might well lie in its erasure of the boundaries that made control and containment of dissatisfaction and dissent easier to achieve before mass tourism, television, the Internet, and other democratizing technologies took "desire management" out of the hands of states. At the same time, the power of multinational firms and multilateral financial institutions to bestow wealth or inflict poverty on individuals, countries, and regions feeds perceptions that "the state" is an ineffective bulwark against the far greater power of "the market." Yet "the market" is, fundamentally, a construction of states – not "the state" in the sense of a disembodied unit composed of territory, a government, and "legitimate means of coercion," but governing units and elite groups, all composed of real human beings influencing and making decisions, and the many others carrying them out (Domhoff 1996; Panitch 1996; Nitzan, Chapter 6 this volume). Could what many interpret as state collapse actually be just state collusion or, more specifically, rent-seeking coalitions of government officials and owners of capital willing to sacrifice if not actually deny the existence of national interests in their pursuit of differential accumulation?

The most powerful coalitions between state agents and economic actors are found in liberal political economies (Lindblom 1977). The Soviet Union offered an alternative to capitalism that theoretically emphasized economic justice and material welfare, one that intertwined economic and political power even more closely together than elites are thought to be in liberal capitalist states. Even so, the power of the economic agents of the Soviet state was more structurally constrained than the power of capitalist states and their agents. The Soviets had fewer nonviolent means for siphoning resources from abroad and labored under excessive centralization and the limits imposed by pervasive top-down thinking and action on state policies. Unfortunately for the world's poor, the Soviet system collapsed during an era of especially rapacious capitalist excess – one also dominated by Neo-Liberal/Social-Darwinist theories in the social sciences. This accident of history fueled triumphalism in major capitalist democracies and a withering contempt for those who would try to tame "the market" rather than allowing it to regulate itself.

In the context of what Craig Murphy (1994) named "liberal fundamentalism," explanations for the mechanisms driving the current widening of global inequality vary. Some are so radically fundamentalist that they assert that rising inequality is the inevitable outcome of natural processes (e.g. Hernstein and Murray 1996). Others leave room for individual and institutional responsibility, arguing that states have surrendered their authority to protect their populations against the ravages of "the market" (e.g. Panitch 1996). Reasons range from shortages of analytical capacity (Elsenhans; Gills, this volume), to ethical obtuseness (Colás; Peterson; Uvin, this volume), and self-centered decisions of various kinds (Palen 1997; Jenkins; Miller; Nitzan, this volume). Globalization conceived in this larger context pervades the concerns of all the authors represented here.

Déjà vu all over again

The conventional wisdom, at least since Marx, envisions globalization as a development of "the market" in its incarnation as an element of modernity (Giddens 1990; Taylor 1999a and Chapter 3 this volume). Some go so far as to advise the governments and citizens of obsolescent states to stop trying to hold the tidal wave back, and just get out of the way (e.g. Ohmae 1996). Others have noted for some years that globalization also is a function of state–society relations. Rather than being overwhelmed by an automatic juggernaut, states choose globalization/ "interdependence" as a preferred method for achieving status over "mercantilistic" approaches offering direct control over domestic production and employment (Gilpin 1981). Well before globalization became a household word, Jane Jacobs (1984), in her fine and undervalued *Cities and the Wealth of Nations*, connected contemporary urban decay to *state-mediated* de-skilling of labor and dispersion of production processes by multinational firms. She showed how "normal" backward and forward linkages that underpin vibrant, multi-class urban neighborhoods and national economies are snapped or fail to form as various stages in production processes are spun off to low-wage, low-regulation jurisdictions. Americans have experienced this process domestically since World War I, when factory owners took the opportunity presented by the temporary replacement of skilled, male, union workers by less skilled, female, unorganized employees to Taylorize workplaces and begin a still-continuing process of de-skilling, reorganizing, and deregulating production (Greenwald 1980). This same pattern, including automation and the feminization of unskilled and semi-skilled jobs, marks the strategies of giant international firms under globalization (Park 1994; Peterson, Chapter 2 this volume). It is reinforced by the eagerness of states to attract investment by following a kind of Gresham's law of social policy, competing to offer the cheapest labor, the most "business-friendly" regulatory regimes, and even pieces of sovereignty itself (Palan *et al.* 1996; Palan 1997; Thomas 1997).

Yet the poor have their own optimistic visions of globalization, which helps to explain its pervasiveness and its myriad "bottom-up" qualities (Sen 2000; also Elsenhans; Taylor; Uvin, this volume). This vision includes the anticipated joys of rising material welfare – having plenty of "stuff."[1] The desire for stuff is deeply human and widely shared. Jared Diamond (1997: 14) tells of the genesis of his book, *Guns, Germs, and Steel* in a query from Yali, a New Guinean friend of many years, who wanted to know why Diamond and his people had so much stuff while he and his people had so little. Cargo cults (ibid.; see also Tierney 2000) are poignant evidence of the longing of the materially impoverished for stuff. Stuff is valued for more than material comfort. It may be the coin of status competition by the materially surfeited (e.g. Veblen 1934; Jardine and Brotton 2000), but it also is a means of self-expression (e.g. Fox and Lears, ed. 1983; Bordo 1993), self-respect (e.g. Appadurai, ed. 1996), and self-protection (Sen 2000; Elsenhans; Uvin, this volume). Attractive clothing, comfortable homes, nourishing and tasty food, books, art, and the gainful employment that make them possible preserve and enhance life, life chances, and life expectancies for people and their families.

Self-actualization and personal autonomy are top priorities on individual and family globalization agendas, and it is these aspects that are most vulnerable to structural and opportunistic derailment. Gilbert Rist (1997) notes that a majority of those living in low-capacity states which rely primarily on "the market" for "development" have experienced little, if any, of its promised benefits, whether or not they also receive state-of-the-art foreign assistance. Critics like Rist have come to doubt that significant improvement in the social, political, and psychological, much less the material conditions of life for most residents of presently un(der)developed areas is even possible. To attain that would require far stronger measures than unprotected exposure to "the market." It would take policies able to halt if not actually reverse the net material resource flows to "Europe"[2] from the non-European world, a pattern that has characterized exchange between them for five hundred years (Wolf 1982; Blaut 1993; Gunder Frank 1996).

Yet it is precisely the continuation of this differential accumulation that lies at the core of the top-down globalization agendas of client entrepreneurs and their patron governments in dominant capitalist states (Nitzan, Chapter 6 this volume). Hartmut Elsenhans (Chapter 8 this volume) sees the ideological dominance of international economic policy by neo-liberal fundamentalists as the biggest threat to the achievement of decent living standards by the vast majority of the world's poor. Others also note that among the stuff demanded by bottom-up globalizers is citizenship, an entitlement to democracy which includes rights to stuff along with more conventionally emphasized rights such as elections and civil liberties guarantees (Gould 1988). Yet democracy itself is attenuated by globalization, and not only in the developing world (Panitch 1996; Thomas and Tétreault, ed. 1999).

Bottom-up globalization as a psychological reality is a direct outgrowth of science and technology. This extends beyond the Internet, which is so widely touted as the primary substrate for the spontaneous development of a new "global civil society." Other elements of globalizing technology are the graphic images of global integrity generated by widely distributed satellite photographs of the earth from space, impressions of participation in a global culture through mass media such as television and popular music, and the science that explains the systemic linkages that produce ecosystems transcending state boundaries and jurisdictions. As Barbara Jenkins, Peter Taylor, and Clark Miller emphasize in their contributions to this volume, these components of bottom-up globalization reflect an imaginary based on a "map" of the world differently organized from the neat, four-color display of bounded nation-states. This new world map assumes greater mobility and also highlights global vulnerability, one reason why environmental non-governmental organizations (NGOs) have assumed a prominent role among the most vigorous contemporary claimants of global civil society status (Miller, this volume; also Stevis and Assetto, ed. 2001). Their activities, usually devised and undertaken by small elite groups, illustrate both the growing authority of global civil society and the defects in its reach and capacity which arise from de-democratization. This erosion of democratic theory and practice – the "democratic deficit" – in the developed West has proceeded with little notice by triumphalists, although critical theorists and social activists are increasingly concerned by its deleterious effects. These range from rising economic inequality to bad social policy and, given the current level of "anti-terrorist" hysteria (actually orkheia, since the overwhelming majority so affected are men), a significant diminution of civil liberties and human rights. Yet attempts to reclaim popular agency by elements of civil society should not automatically be assumed to be benign or even democratic. Rather, each must be examined and evaluated individually.

Paths of resistance and retribution

In the West, civil society is conceived not in the Aristotelian sense of citizen membership of the state but as an independent social force (Keane 1988; but see Colás 2002 for a more fully developed model). Historically, the development of an oppositional civil society traced two different paths as Europe and its settler colonies made their collective though not always coordinated transitions to modernity. Less often analyzed in these terms, the first path was religious dissidence led by "saints" (Walzer 1965); the second, more frequently examined pathway was a class-based assertion of autonomy led by "entrepreneurs" (Keane 1988; also Habermas 1991; Murphy 1994). Claims to civil rights and protection were reactions to the concentration of power in states and the denial of political participation, economic and social protections and rights, and moral autonomy to citizens (Polanyi 1944; Goldberg 1992; Tétreault 1998). Called "the double movement" by Karl Polanyi (1944) in his analysis of reactions to globalization in nineteenth- and early twentieth-century Europe, today's conflicts over the highly unequal results of globalization are occurring along similar lines of cleavage (see also Juergensmeyer 1993; James 2001). Once again, opposition focuses on the state as the dominant power-holder. In today's civil society battles, however, both religious and entrepreneurial contenders fight for access to state-conferred power and wealth rather than asserting independence from the state. Also, in spite of their populist and/or libertarian rhetoric, both camps engage in significantly undemocratic and even anti-democratic practices. Secularist democrats also are visible, generally as a smaller "third force" in this conflict among leviathans, and find themselves pulled toward one or the other in an attempt to effect the changes they seek (e.g. Tétreault 2003). Even so, their efforts show that democratic mobilization against the excesses of globalization has plenty of space in which to make normative, structural, and practical claims (Colás; Uvin, this volume; also O'Brien *et al.* 2000).

Widespread concern that the impact of globalization on individuals and societies has been more harmful than not are supported by statistics showing that both the rate of globalization and measures of inequality have increased enormously since the fall of the Berlin Wall in 1989, the conventional dividing line between the Cold War and the new Age of Globalization. In his BBC Reith Lectures, Anthony Giddens (1999) notes that even more than rising levels of trade, exponentially increasing financial transactions are creating a world economy whose size and velocity have "no parallels in earlier times" (ibid.: 27; also Mittelman 1996; Soros 2002; Stiglitz 2002; Peterson, Chapter 2 this volume). The extent of global inequality is equally unprecedented. Between 1989 and 1998, "the share of the poorest fifth of the world's population in global income has dropped" from 2.3 to 1.4 percent (Giddens 1999: 33). Twenty nations of sub-Saharan Africa have lower per capita incomes today than they had in the late 1970s (ibid.: 34), a time, not coincidentally, when most commodity price cycles were at close-to-historic highs and OPEC was basking in its apparent ability to set crude oil prices at whatever level its members pleased.

Reagan-era pressures supporting capital-led, top-down globalization were visible rhetorically and financially well before 1989, however, as a number of studies in a volume I coedited in the mid-1980s showed clearly (Tétreault and Abel, ed. 1986). But absent from these pressures and from elite responses to them was any effort to construct effective regimes willing and able to enforce regulatory standards on the growing volume and range of international transactions (Murphy 1994). The partial successes of sectorally and/or geographically limited institutions such as OPEC-member national oil companies (e.g. Tétreault 1995) and regimes such as the European Union's regulations on automobile plant location (e.g. Thomas 1997) hint at what might have been achieved had there been visionary leadership and a commitment to global governance among elites in the developed world. Instead, the modest fire walls separating national economies from "the market," already crumbling in the early 1970s, continue to disintegrate in big bangs and spectacular crashes, exposing us to stormy seas whose shoals few are equipped to navigate. In this volume, Alex Colás calls us to make equality the cornerstone of new, ethically informed theories of global political economy; Peter Uvin shows us what happens when such calls are ignored.

Among the most crushing realities dashing the dreams of hopeful bottom-up globalizers are debt, devaluation, and restructuring. Nations throughout the world have experienced the devastation of these plagues, some repeatedly, and African nations suffering from the ravages of colonial and neocolonial exploitation have become the equivalents of poster children advertising the results. One is Rwanda, a country institutionally and normatively "racialized" by systems of colonial control whose effects persisted into the post-colonial era. In response to inexorable external pressures on the Hutu government to restructure, democratize, and seek accommodation with the Tutsi minority, Hutu clients of the political leadership orchestrated a campaign of genocide against the Tutsi as a people, along with Hutu opponents of the regime (Gourevitch 1998; Uvin 1998; Melvern 2000). Large portions of the Hutu population answered the call with their machetes. The vulnerability of these people to appeals to "exterminate" a dehumanized

Other is hauntingly familiar to the vulnerability of Germans to nearly identical calls by Hitler to exterminate Jews (Goldhagen 1996; also Kershaw 1998; and for fin-de-siècle Austria, see Schorske 1980). These responses, Uvin argues here, are not merely the result of economic insecurity or the commands of state-backed authorities. They are the despairing reactions of people who feel personally humiliated by devastating forces they cannot control or even confront directly.

Similarities among pathological social responses to severe political and economic pressures on populations, responses that include in addition to fascist and nationalistic genocidal social movements, a resurgence of violent religious revivalism, invite new approaches to understanding the operation of the world system as such. Here we offer a conceptually rich and ethically grounded approach to re-envisioning world system analysis. Departing from the Eurocentric approach that presents "capitalism" and the rise of "the West" as producing a unique moment in world history, Barry Gills discusses the direction of his current work which attempts to integrate the political economy of the Western-dominated "modern world system" with antecedent trading systems centered on other regions, seeking to relocate human beings in complexes of connections in addition to those generated by capitalist relations of production. Gills disagrees with Polanyi (1944) and others who believe that "pre-modern" relations of production were replaced by market society. Rather, he sees capitalist relations of production articulated in ways that can enhance or destroy the capacity of individuals and societies to sustain themselves (see also Wolf 1982; Ayubi 1995). Thus, Gills's substantive and methodological concerns link those of Uvin, Colás, Elsenhans, Peterson, and Miller by integrating psychological, ethical, and ecological considerations with the macro social and macroeconomic models more conventionally applied at the world systems level of analysis.

Entrepreneurial cheerleaders

The most enthusiastic contemporary supporters of civil society and top-down globalization have been liberal governments, corporations, and wealthy individuals such as Bill Gates and George Soros (before his disenchantment), those whose ethical perspective is grounded in individualist values and negative liberty (Berlin 1969). Such "bourgeois" advocates of individual freedom from external constraints focus also on corporate bodies, especially firms and banks, and also voluntary organizations such as religious groups and other non-state and potentially anti-state institutions. In developed countries, their efforts tend toward delegitimating regulation and taxation in a strategy aimed at achieving "smaller government" and "greater efficiency." In former communist states, they provided lavish funding for social projects and NGOs intended to shelter nascent civil societies from surviving remnants of the old regime. Some achieved real victories in their efforts to extend individual freedom and human rights. Soros-supported NGOs in Central and Eastern Europe, for example, contributed significantly to protect dissidents and reconstruct social capacity destroyed under communism (e.g. Tétreault and Teske 1997).

Their international and transnational efforts were augmented by local action, particularly by religious groups and churches, unions, human rights and environmental groups, and political parties (ibid.). However, the material results of these efforts have proven to be both unstable and highly deficient, threatening the still wobbly democratic edifices they helped to erect. Extreme inequality, widespread poverty, unemployment, homelessness, addiction, official corruption, rising rates of sexually transmitted disease and organized crime (both of the latter connected to rising dependence on prostitution and trafficking in human beings for income and foreign exchange), are only some of the social pathologies that have gone hand-in-hand with economic and political liberalization. All are reducing life expectancies and some are erasing social capital almost as quickly as it is generated (e.g. Wedel 1998; Hall 2000; Jeffries 2000; also Peterson; Uvin, this volume). At the same time, foreign pressures to privatize national economies and open borders to trade and capital movements are far more intense than support for democratization, accountability, and economic assistance needed to ease the impact of transition on populations (e.g. Juris 1995; Kornai 1996; Wedel 1998; Bystydzienski and Sekhon 1999). They are matched by domestic pressures from state and non-state elites in the actual (states) and virtual (international organizations and financial institutions) locations where globalization is generated. In this volume, Barbara Jenkins and Jonathan Nitzan trace the patterns of these elite pressures and report some of their effects on the exacerbation of inequality.

The relationship between social capital and state capacity is complex. Repressive regimes erase social capital as a matter of policy, and states with high capacity are more effective erasers than those without. Yet such "authoritarian high modernist" states often trip over their own self-images of invincibility,[3] and also are exquisitely vulnerable to popular resistance and evasion (Gibson 1986; Scott 1998). Defects in state capacity open spaces for dissidents and grassroots civil society structures that support the delegitimation and possibly the demise of oppressive states by offering an alternative vision of sovereignty (e.g. Havel 1989; 1990). The result is "multiple sovereignty," under which "contenders or coalitions of contenders [advance] ... alternative claims to control over the government" and seek a "commitment to those claims by a significant segment of the subject population" (Tilly 1986: 53). In many countries today, the most prominent contenders and oppositional coalitions can be found in religious social movements (e.g. Juergensmeyer 1993; Marty and Appleby, ed. 1993; Tétreault and Denemark, forthcoming).

Curses from saints

Contemporary religious social movements worldwide are seen as only superficially analogous to the anti-modern, Protestant movements that sprang up in the 1920s in the United States where the term "fundamentalist" originates (Wills 1990; Marty and Appleby, ed. 1993). The earlier groups were primarily spiritual, nonviolent, and localized. Today's religious social movements are fully imbricated in globalization. They are self-consciously political, socially complex, and many are transnationally organized. Some of their leaders are educated and wealthy, men who themselves are socially disembedded and deracinated products of globalization (Roy 2001a,b). Their activities are financed not only by contributions from the religious masses but also from the coffers of high rollers, both those like the American Protestant Pat Robertson who shelters a complex of business and political interests under constitutionally protected subsidy, tax, and regulatory dispensations, and the Saudi Muslim Usama bin Laden, whose money comes from the investments of his very wealthy family. Their lavish resources enable such movements both to purchase weapons and to supply social welfare benefits that economically and ethically impoverished states and localities cannot afford. Their outward idealism allows them to proselytize effectively and mobilize political support, especially among those who share their cultural orientations. Rank-and-file members of saint-led movements tend to be young men with few social or economic resources whose ethical sensibilities are offended by political corruption and the various excesses of those profiting from the status quo (e.g. Roy 1994; Sells 1996; Tétreault forthcoming). Their constituents also include millions of religiously observant and/or culturally conservative persons who never would march in the streets or throw bombs but are deeply repelled and even frightened by unemployment, political corruption, state collapse, and the dissolving family and community ties that accompany rapid social change, itself seen as evidence of moral decline (e.g. Iannaccone 1993; Mayer 1993).

Unlike entrepreneurs who seek to shrink state capacity as a means to escape constraints on their negative liberty, saints wish to extend the state to enforce measures supporting positive liberty (Berlin 1968). Among the most radical of the positive liberties asserted by saints is their right to engage politically and even to overthrow the secular state and take over its machinery to impose religious norms and law on national populations (Juergensmeyer, 1994; Tétreault and Denemark, ed. forthcoming). Most saint-led movements are anti-minority (Mernissi 1992; see also the many post-11 September 2001 public statements of Christianist leaders such as Jerry Falwell and Pat Robertson in the United States). They advocate female subordination (Hawley, ed. 1994) even when they incorporate feminist dissidents (e.g. al-Mughni 2000; Gallaher forthcoming). Many also practice scapegoating: of women, homosexuals, foreigners, and religious and/or ethnic minorities (Bruce 1993; Hawley, ed. 1994). Some religious revivalists are associated with nationalist movements, raising the level of violence so often accompanying them (Girard 1979; Bruce 1993; Juergensmeyer 1994; Sells 1996). These characteristics make saints as much or more subversive of the liberty of "non-saints" as the entrepreneurs are of structurally disadvantaged persons and groups.

Third forces

Scientists also are active observers and even advocates of globalization. Their similarities to and differences from saints and entrepreneurs are instructive. All three groups see a kind of inevitability in the process, but what it means and how to deal with it are different for each. Like saints, scientists see danger in global integration, not because it is evil but because the earth is a single ecological system within which people and their activities contribute substantially to expanding contacts among its constituent parts. In consequence, the entire planet is becoming increasingly vulnerable to the negative results of both thoughtless and malevolent behavior. Clark Miller shows, in Chapter 10 this volume, how the popularization of the vision of spaceship earth strengthens pressures from scientists for a unified planetary approach to the amelioration of global climate change. Even so, upon whom the benefits of global integration and the costs of adjustment respectively shall lie is so much a focal point of international and interindustry conflict that prospects for successful amelioration are uncertain (see also Stevis and Assetto, ed. 2001).

Scientists' visions of globalization seem to reflect not only a high modernist conception of science but also, as Jenkins argues here, elements of a global culture expressed in myriad social products in addition to science and technology. The impact of globalization and its associated culture on the least powerful citizens of this globalized world are examined in this volume by Peterson and by Uvin. Nitzan and Elsenhans concentrate on the motives and the methods of the most powerful and, with Gills, look at its effects on macro-social and economic system. Elsenhans argues passionately for combating ideologically driven micro-level theory with macro-level analyses, and for a Keynesian approach to raising living standards for labor as necessary for a vital capitalist system. His normative approach coincides substantially with that of Peter Taylor and, ironically, with the attempt of Alex Colás who, from a very different perspective, seeks to mobilize an ethical consensus for making the reduction of inequality a priority of social-movement activism. Gills speaks on these ethical and theoretical concerns, arguing for an analysis of trends in the global political economy that concentrates on links between the macro-economy and ethical concerns for human dignity, cultural diversity, and environmental protection.

Cosmopolitania, nova imperia, or back to the future?

The chapters in this volume focus attention on sites where intervention in political-economic structures and practices are occurring – and should occur differently. They are countered by politicians and scholars whose ideals are different and argue for different kinds of change. After the terrorist attacks on the World Trade Center and the Pentagon in September 2001, for example, US president George W. Bush repeatedly asserted that these events were motivated by a hatred of American values and must be countered by force. The same sentiment, if not quite the same recommended response, is echoed in a significant thread in the academic literature on globalization, perhaps best exemplified by the work of Harold James. James argues that globalization is threatened by "reactionary resentment" against "a new and unfamiliar international or cosmopolitan world" (2001: 1), and his detailed comparisons between today's reactions and the politics of the era of the Great Depression are instructive. Unlike those who see globalization primarily as economic integration, and resistance to marketization as a reasonable demand for protection from its worst effects – Polanyi's "double movement" (1944) – James stresses psychological factors, chiefly envy, as the source of political pressure to halt globalization.

Others too emphasize psychological factors, but in more complex ways. For example, Mark Juergensmeyer (1993), agrees that cosmopolitan values and lifeways are triggers of communal reactions to the spread of western culture. However, he interprets these reactions as a revulsion against secularization and the suppression of local lifeways rather than as the result of simple envy. Peter Uvin (Chapter 7 this volume) carries this analysis further. He distinguishes between cosmopolitanism as a set of values and lifeways, and those who monopolize the benefits they generate. Reactions are aimed primarily at the latter, or at scapegoats. This vision is reflected in the literature of fiction as well as in the literature of fact (Ash 2002: 60).

In Abdel Rahman al-Munif's novel *Cities of Salt*, resentment among Arab villagers against foreign oil company workers is nourished by revulsion against the strangers' incompatible codes of behavior – how they laugh, talk, and dress, the kinds of machines they use, and how little they seem to respect local lifeways. The sense that the strangers and their desires have superceded the local population and its needs – indeed, that the strangers have gulled the rulers themselves, whose own best interests are being undermined by their credulous cooperation – infuses Munif's novel. The absence of mitigation of the economic upheaval the strangers create by bulldozing trees and houses and replacing them with a large industrial operation requiring that the residents abandon their homes and move elsewhere serves to create a smoldering resentment aimed at a wide array of targets (1989). A similarly textured and highly nuanced picture is drawn in Uvin's *Aiding Violence* (1998) which describes the contribution of the "foreign aid enterprise" to the Rwanda genocide. Once again, an alien yet exciting set of lifeways appears in a community together with people and practices that contravene local values and customs. Poor Hutu farmers resent the natty outfits, boom boxes, and Land Rovers of foreign aid workers, their disdain for local lifeways, and their arrogant dismissal of local knowledge that contributes directly to the economic immiseration of rural residents. Adding to the Hutu sense of injustice is the favoritism that the foreigners appear to show to the Tutsi minority, whose very marginality contributes to their adaptability and thereby their desirability as employees of the foreigners, who pay very high wages. As in Munif's story of the coming of oil to Saudi Arabia, political entrepreneurs were able to mobilize that popular resentment and use it as a weapon against their rivals.

In academic – and political – arguments against globalization's critics, cosmopolitanism is presented as though it were some kind of universal culture (e.g. James 2001). Indeed, as it is used in these contexts, cosmopolitanism is pictured as culture-free. Even if we grant that this is so, it is not value-free. Cosmopolitan values are "worldly," putting us at the very least in a materialist framework. In the examples I sketched above, the oil company and the foreign aid enterprise both sought the successful incorporation of subsistence communities into global systems of investment and trade. This implies "universality," a universal culture, in this case, capitalism. The commodification of land and its products, of human skills and talents, introduces market values into every society as it changes modalities of interpersonal and intergroup competition. Some people thrive under this new regime but to others it brings personal and collective insecurity. As both books show, such persons can be found in virtually every stratum of traditionally dominant social groups. Their now-uncompetitive members find that their former complaisance prevented them from learning the kind of cooperative behavior that, perhaps ironically, is so necessary if one is to be competitive. In the same (but opposite) way, marginality contributes to the competitiveness of minority group members whose survival attests to their capacity for flexibility and anticipatory adjustment.[4]

Worldliness is compatible with pre-capitalist and capitalist social formations. But cosmopolitanism also implies something less compatible with capitalism or with any other "ism" it is likely to encounter in the modern world. This is tolerance of difference. In consequence, although I can accept the idea that resentment and envy underlie some contemporary opposition to globalization, I do not accept the assumption that these are reactions against cosmopolitanism. To have a cosmopolitan society, tolerance must not only be widely shared but also, and even more importantly, institutionalized in a rule-governed regime, something that I would argue is at a very early stage of development in the contemporary world, and under attack almost everywhere. Here I want particularly to emphasize two things. One is the importance of rules and institutions of protection for the operation of a cosmopolitan regime of toleration. In their absence, the dominant will dominate and domineer, and thereby shrink or eliminate the social space available for dissent and innovation. The other is to distinguish between toleration and what passes for multiculturalism under capitalism: that is, homogenization. Toleration is similar to what Nira Yuval-Davis (1997) calls "transversalist politics," a coalition politics in which participants respect and celebrate rather than bury their differences in the process of achieving common goals. The aim is to achieve a practical accommodation that does not efface the identity or values of either partner. Thus, a regime of toleration resembles what María Rosa Menocal (2002) calls the "culture of tolerance" which she says governed relations among Jews, Christians, and Muslims in much of Spain during the medieval period. Here different cultures as expressions of the values and histories of ethnoreligious groups were protected as self-defined collectivities. These are not universalist cultures. What is universal in such communities is a commitment to toleration as a primary value, one that assumes that other, different values will shape the beliefs and practices of different segments of their component populations. Toleration stands in sharp contrast to the homogeneous universalism which constitutes the basic value of monocultural hegemonies from "universal" religions and nationalisms to authoritarian high modernism as a state ideology (Scott 1998). I would argue that all of these monocultural regimes are anti-cosmopolitan precisely because they either erase or privatize difference rather than protecting and incorporating it into public life.

Different views of cosmopolitanism underpin different contemporary visions of empire. Michael Hardt and Antonio Negri (2000) argue that the "Empire" that is taking shape from the shards and detritus of the short – and violent – twentieth century is a novel structure. In the past, precapitalist modes of production, a lack of state capacity, and an appreciation of diversity as "ornament" (also Menocal 2002) maintained and even cultivated difference. Difference was a resource for constructing systems of divide-and-rule that operated by fostering competition among the ruled and thus their dependence on the ruler. Consequently, the construction and maintenance of boundaries was a primary task of traditional imperial powers (e.g. Mernissi 1992: 6–7). Hardt and Negri see contemporary Empire differently. Like Michel Foucault (1995), they suggest that discipline is superior to punishment as a form of social control and, like Marx, they argue that state capacity is attenuated by capitalism which is the fountainhead of discipline in a globalizing world. In their analysis of Empire, Hardt and Negri move beyond discipline, however, arguing that in addition to intensified and generalized "normalizing apparatuses of disciplinarity that internally animate our common and daily practices ... this control extends well outside the structure sites of social institutions through flexible and fluctuating networks" (2000: 23). The distinction between the old system controlled by discipline and what Hardt and Negri see as a qualitatively new Empire controlled by "biopower," a "techie" version of the Gaia hypothesis (Lovelock 1979), is its comprehensiveness. Discipline in Foucault requires an outside and an inside, and thus carries a sense of an agent shaping an object. In contrast, biopower is both more "democratic" and more totalizing in that everything, including the brains and bodies of persons connected through machines and systems, is inside. Thus "[b]iopower is a form of power that regulates social life from its interior" (ibid.).

The totality of biopower means that the power structure of Empire subsumes its own resistance, a situation that Hardt and Negri view optimistically – as the democratization of power through local assertions of autonomy. Here, following Homi Babha, they imagine the spontaneous formation of utopian communities through which they understand locality as a network concept describing affinity groups that are "hybrids" of persons and communities that can be and likely are widely dispersed geographically.

> The utopia Babha points toward after the binary and totalizing structures of power have been fractured and displaced is not an isolated and fragmentary existence but a new form of community, a community of the "unhomely," a new internationalism, a gathering of people in the diaspora. ... "To live in the unhomely world, to find its ambivalences and ambiguities enacted in the house of fiction, or its sundering and splitting performed in the work of art, is also to affirm a profound desire for social solidarity." The seeds of the alternative community ... arise out of close attention to the locality of culture, its hybridity, and its resistance to the binary structuring of social hierarchy. ... Hybridity itself is a realized politics of difference, setting differences to play

across boundaries ... so that the mere fact of hybridity has the power to destroy hierarchy *tout court*.

(Hardt and Negri 2000: 145; quote from
Babha 1994: 18)

Hardt and Negri project a benign picture of a "multitude" that comes together to "[configure] its own constitution" and exercise its right to reappropriate the means of production through its acquisition of "free access to and control over knowledge, information, communication, and affects. ... The right to reappropriation is really the multitude's right to self-control and autonomous self-production" (406–7). They adopt the term "posse" to denote "the multitude in its political autonomy" and although they note in passing the use of this term in rap music and in "American fantas[ies] of vigilantes and outlaws" (407–8), they dismiss such images of skinheads and casual communal violence, replacing them with "singular subjectivity. ... [l]ike the Renaissance 'posse,' which was traversed by knowledge and resided at the metaphysical root of being" (408). In this, they forget Lord Acton and what he learned in his conflict with Pio Nono over the declaration of Papal infallibility: that absolute power is a recipe for totalitarian corruption (Wills 2000).

The practical difficulty of separating "good" biopower from "bad" constitutes much of the message in the burgeoning literature on terrorist networks. There, the proliferation of terrorist activities employing biopower suggests that dystopia is as likely to describe the communities of the globalized world as eutopia. Indeed, analysts of terrorist organizations employ the same concepts as Homi Babha, although not in the same way, to describe the manufacture of terrorists and their deployment in networks of violent resistance to Empire. Olivier Roy (2001a,b) talks about the "deracination" of members of terrorist organizations, the attenuation of ties that occurs when idealists leave home for distant and dangerous parts in search of a community united by an idealism that is simultaneously exhilarating and terrifying. Perhaps the best contemporary examples are the so-called Arab Afghans, young men from Algeria, Egypt, and the Persian Gulf states who went not only to Afghanistan but also to Bosnia and Chechnya to become soldiers of God. Gathering in places removed from the disciplining hierarchies of locality and family, these now-deterritoralized activists acquired hybrid identities constructed around charismatic and often authoritarian leaders who tapped into their religious idealism to transform them into "holy warriors." Their biopower was concentrated through military training reaffirming their social solidarity in a fight against a satanic adversary. Combat experience reinforced group loyalty, not only because of the transformative power of collective violence but also because combat creates dead and wounded comrades in whose memory survivors must redouble their efforts (e.g. Shay 1994).

Where is toleration in biopower resistance? Like the contrast between the homogeneous capitalist cosmopolitanism of globalization and the transversalist cosmopolitanism of particular communities negotiating their differences, the distinction lies in nonviolence – which, after all, has long been the primary objective of toleration: a *modus vivendi* removing first the threat of annihilation and then of group discrimination (Stone 1979: 152–3; Ashcraft 1996; Taylor 1998; also Menocal 2002). Yet, the homogeneity of Empire and the subsumption of all its parts into the universal whole seems in practice to trump its authors' hopes for democratic resistance, especially one based on what they say would be a communist expression of the heroic militancy of St Francis of Assisi (Hardt and Negri 2000: 413). This is a saint I remember well from my Catholic childhood as a person so gentle and tolerant of all other life forms that he removed worms from his path so he would not tread on them. Francis might be the patron saint of cosmopolitanism based on regimes of toleration, but he seems ill-suited to Empire from any perspective.

It might be, of course, that the shape of the world really isn't changing all that much, either toward universal capitalist high modernism or an Empire of biopower engaged in netwar. Niall Ferguson (2001) envisions a future very much like the past in *The Cash Nexus: Money and Power in the Modern World, 1700–2000*, a work in which he seeks to refute the claims of Paul Kennedy (1989) and other realist writers about the nature of power and money. Like Nitzan, Ferguson understands differential accumulation as a crystallization of power, although from the perspective of the state rather than the firm. Like Nitzan, he criticizes standard definitions based on variations of fixed capital to imagine the state as an entity controlling financial assets, not merely purchasing power but entitlements to income streams and the capacity to deploy them more effectively than its rivals: "We ... need to take into account a state's financial sophistication: its ability to appropriate resources from taxpayers and to borrow from investors. ... [This depends on] four institutions as the bases of financial strength: a tax-collecting bureaucracy; a representative parliament; a national debt; and a central bank" (Ferguson 2001: 420). It also depends on an open global system which Ferguson equates with economic liberalization rather than democracy, although he sees democratization of possible rivals as a strategy for extending the authority of a global hegemon (the winner in the differential accumulation sweepstakes among major states). Ferguson takes issue with Kennedy's definitions and measures of imperial "overstretch," spending too much on the projection of state power by a global hegemon, and argues that "understretch" is the ultimate cause of hegemonic decline. "It was not the excessive cost of empire that undermined British power; but failure to prepare adequately for the defence of that empire" (ibid.: 411–23, quotes from 423).

Most important for those who wish to apply critical theory to make the world more egalitarian, Ferguson argues straightforwardly for the United States to take on the traditional trappings and responsibilities of a global hegemon:

> Far from retreating like some giant snail behind an electronic shell, the United States should be devoting a larger percentage of its vast resources to making the world safe for capitalism and democracy. ...[L]ike free trade, these are not naturally occurring, but require strong institutional foundations of law and order. The proper role of an imperial America is to establish these institutions where they are lacking, if necessary – as in Germany and Japan

in 1945 – by military force. ... Even if the Kennedy thesis is right, imposing democracy on the world's rogue states would not push the US defence budget much above 5 percent of GDP. ... There is ... an economic argument for doing so, as establishing the rule of law in countries like Iraq would pay a long-run dividend as their trade revived and expanded.

(Ibid.: 418)

Ferguson believed when his book went to press that the United States would not defend its own primacy and the global capitalist order on which it is based because of "ideological embarrassment," an exaggerated concern about possible Russian and Chinese responses, and "a pusillanimous fear of military casualties" (ibid.). On September 20, 2002, a year after the terrorist attacks on Washington and New York, the United States announced a new strategic doctrine that reflects almost exactly Ferguson's recommendations.

Conclusions

The rapidly reorganizing global political economy calls for innovative measures from those who wish to enhance the life prospects and chances of human beings today and in the future. In place of reconstitutions of hegemony and empire, and the generation of new totalizing visions of various kinds of authoritarian high modernism, the chapters in this volume emphasize the importance of individual human lives. They argue for the mitigation of the agonies of adjustment, not only by raising aggregate measures of well being but also by paying close attention to the autonomy and dignity of persons and groups. Like social activists, the writers of these essays emphasize that globalization is driven both by economic impera-tives and by political decisions that favor the economic interests of some persons and groups over others. At the same time, they recognize that economically dom-inant elements of "global civil society" have weakened or blocked state capacity to respond to demands for protection from citizens injured by the rapid spread and intensification of capitalist relations. Indeed, some note that the successes of the globalizers include having persuaded not only their fellow citizens but also governments of their own and other countries that effective intervention by the state to promote equity and a fairer distribution of the material benefits from globalization is impossible. The failures of globalization are therefore products of a cavalier dismissal of the negative social, cultural, and environmental conse-quences everywhere in the world, and an equally cavalier rejection of demands for ethical intervention to ameliorate these effects. Both promise a future full of conflict.

Perhaps the most disquieting implication to be drawn from these pages is the existence of multiple, diverse oppositions to the conventional wisdom on the subject of globalization. This is because these essays taken together reveal a fatal flaw in critical theory. As Alex Colás argues, the critics of the status quo lack a unifying goal much less a single worldview that could serve as the basis for a successful challenge to the powerful dominant ideology and institutions that drive globalization in its current mode. The ecology of contemporary critical theory demonstrates the inherent vulnerability of plurality, with its diverse ideals and outlooks and its democratic organization of power, to the hierarchical organization and mono-cultural ideologies characteristic of domination in its various guises throughout recorded history. The dilemmas reflected most starkly in this volume in chapters by Clark Miller and Peter Uvin require a different kind of politics to manage what writers as diverse as Janet Abu-Lughod (1989) and John Dominic Crossan (1998) see as the same kind of world economy human beings have been creating for millennia. As I suggest here, a basic requirement of this politics is a regime of toleration that would protect not only individuals but also human collectivities and their social expression from absorption or annihilation. The remaining chapters offer multiple starting points for the imagination and articulation of plural visions of the general interest, simultaneously vulnerable and yet necessary to address these dilemmas ethically and effectively.

Notes

1 George Carlin, "Place for my Stuff," Wea/Atlantic; ASIN: B00005A8MZ.
2 "Europe" includes former European settler colonies outside of Europe proper.
3 Individual-level analogues are discussed in Bar-On (1999).
4 I have analyzed this at some length in my work on gender. See, for examples, Tétreault 2000, 2003a.

Part II
Aids to navigation

2 Analytical advances to address new dynamics

V. Spike Peterson

> We need a revamped materialism that will allow us to see the virtual realities of the globe.
>
> (Eisenstein 1998, 11)

It is now a commonplace that the meaning, constitution, and effects of borders – conceptual and territorial – are being radically transformed by globalization dynamics. To address the challenges posed by the speed, scale, and complexity of these changes, we require new theories of international political economy or, more appropriately, global political economy (GPE). This chapter takes as a starting point that the disciplines of economics and IR that produce the prevailing accounts of GPE remain dominated by productivist, masculinist, and modernist commitments that are analytically inadequate and politically problematic. In particular, prevailing accounts neglect significant aspects of globalization (increasing informal sector activities, feminization of flexibilization, crises of welfare delivery, diasporic identities and migration flows, shifting sexual politics and family forms) and pay little attention to how these are shaped by geopolitics, gender, and race/ethnicity. Moreover, political economists are just beginning to analyze the singular importance of financial (as distinct from monetary) institutions on a global scale, and only a few are epistemologically prepared for (or interested in) grappling with a virtual economy of *signs* rather than goods.

As a contribution to addressing these new dynamics, I begin this chapter by introducing an alternative analytics – an "RPV framing" – that rewrites GPE as "reproductive, productive, and virtual (Foucauldian) economies." Under the rubric of overlapping systemic "shifts" – of scale, production, and finance – I then discuss globalization as it shapes our lives today, and with uneven effects. Throughout this discussion, I implicitly and explicitly argue that new dynamics are more readily acknowledged and more productively addressed by adopting an alternative analytical framing that affords transdisciplinary, multilevel, and multicausal understanding. The need is for analytical advances that not only accommodate new developments but also cultivate the identification of *relationships* among disparate features of globalization, including the links among discourse, identity, culture, economy, and "the virtual." The RPV framing is an important dimension of this larger project.[1]

An alternative analytic: the RPV framing

> The complicity between cultural and economic value systems is acted out in almost every decision we make.
>
> (Spivak 1987, 166)

The RPV framing recasts GPE as the interaction of reproductive, productive, and virtual economies, the latter understood not in the conventional but in a Foucauldian sense of mutually constituted (therefore coexisting and interactive) systemic sites through and across which power operates. In Patrick Hutton's words, economy in Foucault's conception signifies the "production of linguistic and institutional forms through which human beings define their relationships" (Hutton 1988: 127, citing Foucault in *Power/Knowledge*, pp. 88–92, 158–65). This involves normalization processes of subjectivation and subjectification that are key to personal and collective identifications and their political effects. In short, the reproductive, productive, and virtual economies expand the terrain of inquiry beyond conventional economic phenomena. As systemic sites of power, involving meaning systems, normalization and institutions, they enable us to map identities and culture *in relation to* conventional social structures.

My elaboration of three interacting, overlapping, and coexisting economies is offered as a more nuanced and indeed "realistic" framework for the study of political economy. The RPV framing specifically rejects the separation of culture from economy, economics from politics, agent from structure, or domestic from international politics. Although analytically distinguishable, the three economies must be understood as not only overlapping but also mutually constituted and always dynamic. Hence, the framing is transdisciplinary, multi-institutional, multilevel, and "multicausal." Less a theoretical elaboration than a mapping technique, the framing directs our attention to more features of globalization and illuminates linkages and relationships across an expanded terrain.

In effect, the framing brings the identities, ideologies, and practices of "social reproduction," welfare, non-wage labor and informal sector activities *into relation with* the familiar "productive economy" of commodity exchange, as well as with the less familiar but increasingly consequential "virtual economy" of financial markets, cyberspace, and the exchange less of goods than of signs. The point is to move beyond the masculinist, modernist, and materialist preoccupations of prevailing accounts without abandoning their insights and while addressing significant features of today's GPE. Specifying and retaining the productive economy permits continuity with conventional economic analyses. At the same time, the productive economy proposed here is expanded both by including more features and by being inextricably linked to other economies. Specifying and including the reproductive economy invites attention to otherwise neglected agents and activities, and acknowledges the importance of gender- and race-sensitive research and analysis. For example, it renders visible the densely gendered increase in both licit and illicit informal sector activities, the feminization of flexibilization, the gendered and racialized nature and implications of welfare crises and citizenship claims, and the heterosexist politics of "the family" and its divisions of labor and resources. Specifying and including the virtual economy extends our analysis of dematerialization and how symbols and expectations mediate our constructions of "economic" value. It insists on the political significance of financial globalization, takes seriously the accelerating pace of technological change and time–space compression, and enables us to address an economy of signs.

The fluidity and flexibility of the framing pay the price of nonspecificity, but mapping is not designed for, nor capable of, generating causal predictions. Rather, it facilitates shifts in how we *see* the terrain and hence how we understand and might respond to it. In particular, the framing proposed here insists we recognize that social reproduction is constitutive of social relations, that identities, culture, and structures are mutually constituted, and that the virtual economy shapes and is shaped by everyday practice and uneven resource distribution. The framing attempts to acknowledge complexity while making sense of it, and to politicize globalization by exposing the sense that it makes. This involves three overlapping objectives: to demystify the operating codes of capitalism – the pursuit of profit as a social logic – and expose profit-seeking's domination dynamics, a project of particular difficulty yet urgency in today's world; to expose how gender/hetero-sexist coding permeates symbols, selves, and systems, and fuels denigration of all who are "othered" as feminine[2]; and to analyze, in a Foucauldian sense, the specificity of mechanisms of power – especially those most taken for granted – to build strategic knowledge.

Reproductive economy

Preoccupied with waged/commodified labor and market exchange ("productive" activities), neoclassical and most Marxist theories ignore the reproductive economy.[3] Preoccupied with what they cast as "politics" and "economics," liberal theories ignore sex/affective relations and social reproduction. In contrast, the reproductive economy in my account is central – even fundamental – to social theory, being extensively and inextricably linked to culture, politics, and economics. Because it is so neglected, I briefly suggest five ways in which the reproductive economy is key.

First, *intergenerational reproduction*: The reproductive economy involves negotiations regarding the conditions under which social members will be biologically reproduced. This involves cultural norms, demographic dynamics, reproductive technologies, and disciplinary regimes in regard to sex/affective relations. It also includes the meaning and valorization of erotic desires and sexual expressions (e.g. globalized media representations, sex tourism), agency and identities in relation to biological reproduction (e.g. "bride markets," international adoptions), conditions of health, choice, and technologies of reproduction (e.g. expensive fertilization clinics for some, forced sterilization for "others"), and the spatial and temporal constitution of social relations ("families," support groups, communities) that enable parenting/intergenerational reproduction. And of course, the capitalist–patriarchal dynamics of family property and patterns of inheritance are crucial for reproducing hierarchies structured by class and gender.

Second, *social/cultural/institutional reproduction*: We shift here to the social relations within which biological reproduction is embedded. These include ideological reproduction of beliefs about sex/gender, race/ethnicity, age, class, religion, and other axes of "difference." Stated simply, social reproduction involves not only parenting practices and institutions but also linguistic, cultural, educational, religious, economic, political and legal institutions. Subject formation is about socialization into – and selectively retaining – the norms and orderings of one's culture. While early childhood is psychosocially formative (not least because dependency fosters "passionate attachment" that is nondiscriminating [Butler 1997]), selective socialization is a lifelong process and especially shaped today by global media.

Third, *continuity and change*: Whatever its institutional forms, processes of parenting are embedded in and reinscribe power relations because infants are helpless and children are variously dependent. The "ordering" (language, cultural rules) we uncritically imbibe at an early age is especially resistant to transformation, both in a psychoanalytic sense of "split selves" to which we lack complete access and/or control and in the sense of deeply internalized identity (especially gender) commitments, the disturbance of which feels threatening. At a minimum, we must recognize how psychic investments and early socialization shape both the direction of and the willingness to change (recognizing that subject formation is not simply "contained" in infant life or family dynamics). A further point is the need to take seriously how symbolic and psychic ordering mediate material manifestations that we may wish to transform. At the same time, the private space of familial relations may be a key site of social resistance and transformation, as recently evidenced in the transformation of centralized state regimes in eastern Europe.

Fourth, *consumption*: Until recently, economists' concern with production was at the expense of taking consumption seriously. The latter was gendered as feminine and associated with the private/household sphere as a passive activity (De Grazia and Furlough 1996; Firat 1994). Today however, expanded marketing activities create and fuel desire for constantly changing consumer goods and render consumption a focal point of production and investment strategies. Here I note simply that the family/household constitutes both the traditional site of savings and consumption (linking reproductive, productive, and virtual economies) and a structural link between "first world" consumption patterns and "third world" production options, as producers conform to first world desires increasingly shaped by marketing forces rather than (sustainable) subsistence needs. The politics of consumption also include and link: gender-differentiated contributions to and control over household resources and decision-making regarding purchases, savings, and investments; identity issues insofar as "you are what you buy" and the creation of one's self is postmodernity's big business; and political-economy issues as consumer rights movements favor "voting with dollars" (as in consumer boycotts) and neoliberalism favors private sector goods and services over public sector regulation, accountability and provisioning.

Fifth, *non-waged labor/informal sector activities*: The significance of these activities is increasing and is increasingly acknowledged in mainstream accounts, but several points warrant emphasis. First, non-waged labor is a condition of – not coincidental to – the so-called productive economy and their interaction must be acknowledged. Second, the reproductive and productive economies overlap, especially as informalization accelerates and merges with flexibilization. (Racialized) gender as signifying system and division of labor is deployed throughout, both to structure and depoliticize hierarchical arrangements. Third, the value of any one of the resources pooled within households cannot be interpreted independently of its relation to the entire pool, and the value of wages derived from the formal economy cannot be interpreted independently of resources pooled in the informal/reproductive economy. At issue here is the extent to which households, rather than capital, pay the costs of socially necessary labor, and how this is related to global accumulation.[4] Fourth, these linkages and their gendered structuring are particularly visible in relation to public welfare provisioning, which is decreased with economic restructuring that favors capital mobility and the "competition state" (Cerny 1990). The "leaner and meaner" practices of neoliberalism have particularly devastating (though not homogeneous) effects on women as the (structurally) most vulnerable and also as the caretakers of society's dependent members.

Links to the virtual economy

The reproductive economy is key to identities, socialization, and ideological reproduction that sustain (or may disturb) the "taken-for-grantedness" of capitalist social relations and accumulation processes centered in the virtual economy. In more conventional economic terms, the reproductive economy is structurally linked to the virtual economy insofar as household savings and investment strategies are influenced by monetary policies that establish interest rates, but household strategies also affect – through savings, consumption, and investment practices and political activities – the economic decision-making that determines monetary policy. As Castells and Portes (1989: 6) put it, "research on [reproductive and informal] activities thus affords a unique glimpse into the ways in which individual strategies connect with the broader accumulation process and the superstructures that rely on it." Others argue that women's work has always been "an important source for the primary accumulation of capital" (Broad 2000: 34; also Mies 1998). Moreover, women's reproductive labor has historically been the primary source of human capital: "the knowledge, skills and other attributes relevant to working capabilities" (Gardiner 2000: 4; also Cloud and Garrett 1997). As an investment made in the family/household sector and a decisive component of labor and formal production processes that generate profits, human capital links all of the economies.

Productive economy

For the most part, this is the economy of conventional narratives, revolving around the identities and activities of production and consumption. It presupposes specialized (also gendered and racialized) divisions of labor and the production of goods and services for market exchange. Conventionally, its primary sites are workplaces, firms, corporations, transportation networks, and markets – but reproductive and virtual economies are not separable from these sites. The state shapes the rules, disciplines participants, and provides infrastructure. The global assembly line and decentralized networking have altered the geography of production (see Taylor, Chapter 3 this volume) and flexibilization has transformed the process of production. Transnational corporations and intergovernmental agencies (the IMF, World Bank) increasingly shape the context and range of governmental decision-making. Shifts in production are better accommodated in the RPV framing, as polarization, degraded manufacturing, flexibilization, and informalization can be analyzed in context and in relation to reproductive and virtual economies. For example, movement of people – for pleasure, work or political freedom – can be seen as embedded processes; the importance of investing in human resources becomes visible; and gentrification can be linked to urban housing issues and the international "maid trade." Perhaps most productive is illumination of links among the economies: how technologies shape reproductive choices, flexibilization practices, and innovations in financial instruments; how racial stereotypes shape whose reproduction is encouraged, how jobs and incarcerations are distributed, where tourists go and what they do, and how elite networks repeat historical exclusions.

Virtual economy

Specifying this economy extends our analysis of symbols and how they mediate our constructions of "economic" value. It enables us to address two of the most enigmatic aspects of globalization. The first is the explosive growth in financial transactions manifesting varying linkages to – and even delinked from – the real economy. We need new models for thinking about the meaning and value of abstractions in the sense of being *nonmaterial* (intangibles, information, services, "symbolic money"). We need to be able to link what are apparently disembedded but nonetheless *socially constructed* symbols – such as "credit money" (Thrift 1996) – to expectations, identities and practices of related economies. The second "enigma" is the exchange of abstractions – pure data – in the sense of virtual realities (cyberspace, computer-enabled communications, and time–space compression). Here we confront both the speed of circulation and the "emptying out" of meaning, "in which things and people become 'disembedded' from concrete space and time" (Lash and Urry 1994: 13), and we engage complex issues regarding the real and the virtual, responses to postmodernity, and questions of agency in the face of dematerialization read as deconstruction.

Specifying the virtual economy does not produce answers but does permit us to situate these developments in relation to financial transactions, dematerialized production, and symbolic ordering born of reproductive economies. We can, for example, explore information and communication structures as networked flows in relation to cognitive reflexivity (Lash and Urry 1994: 6–7). Or we can rethink Baudrillard's claims about advertising and representation in relation to marketing as a question of circulation in the productive economy (Sawchuck 1994). And explorations of desire in this framing can be linked to psychoanalytic discourses and the reproduction of heterosexist identities in service to consumer capitalism.

In sum, insofar as prevailing accounts of the GPE are dominated by productivist, masculinist, and modernist commitments, they in fact impede adequate under-standing of and critical practice in regard to the new dynamics of globalization. The RPV framing offers an alternative analytic for making sense of and responding to these dynamics. To better appreciate the need for analytical advances, the next three sections consider three interlinked and overlapping substantive shifts: of scale, production, and finance. These are simply an organizational device to further specify globalization dynamics and to illustrate the value of alternative analytics.

Shifts in scale, space, and time[5]

> We are confronted not by one social space but by many – indeed by an unlimited multiplicity or uncountable set of social spaces which we refer to generically as "social space." No space disappears in the course of growth and development: the worldwide does not abolish the local.
>
> (Lefebvre 1991: 86 emphasis in original)

In terms of space, the most obvious shift is from the social space of the territorial nation-state to supraterritorial "global" space "above," beyond, and encompassing all particular states. This resonates with references to the world as a "single place": "...an awareness reinforced by everyday experiences of diet, music and dress, as well as by photographs from outer space showing planet Earth as one location" (Scholte 1996: 46). The image of a global village or a seamless biosphere may heighten consciousness of our interdependence as global citizens and/or our bio-environmental dependence on a fragile ecosystem. But it may also fuel totalizing narratives and/or a "whole earth" naturalism that disembeds environ-mental devastation from its social context – with the effect of privileging a feminized nature over actual women.[6]

Regional blocs – agglomerations of nation-states – are another social space of increasing salience. Critics of "globalization" argue cogently that prominent scalar shifts are more a matter of *regionalism* than globalism.[7] They point to the significance of formal economic arrangements constituting the European Union and the North American Free Trade Agreement. And the statistics on economic activity among what Tooze (Tooze 1997a: 223) calls the Triad – the three most developed regions: North America, Western Europe, and Japan/SE Asia – confirm that flows of capital, trade, and knowledge are heavily concentrated within and among these three, effectively marginalizing countries outside the Triad.

Specifically, triad countries (with approximately 15 percent of the world's population) accounted for 65 percent of total world exports in 1990 and 66 percent in 1999; 68 percent of all imports of manufactured goods in 1990, and 69.5 percent in 1999 (United Nations 2001: 260–4). In effect, more than half of all developing countries are marginalized from the benefits – credit, infrastructural development, technology transfer – of foreign direct investment (FDI). Moreover, due to the world economic downturn, FDI flows declined dramatically in 2001, with little expectation of recouping this decline in 2002 (United Nations 2002: 14).

One effect of new regional concentrations is that previous regions, solidarities, and identities are reconstituted. For example, Smith argues that the "third world" has been "restructured out of existence" (Smith 1997: 174). Whereas more prosperous "newly industrialized countries" (Taiwan, Singapore, etc.) have moved out of third world status, sub-Saharan Africa has been "redlined" in global capital markets, effectively relegated to "fourth world" status "as an object of poor relief and riot control" (Cox 1991: 337).

The national to global shift is rendered visible and materialized by reference to the "global assembly line." This image reminds us that commodities are less frequently produced at a single site (as in the Fordist factory) but in dispersed locations, with diverse workers performing specialized tasks. This fragmenting of production displaces older identities – of factory floor unionists or proud "Made in America" automobile boasts – even as new identities are created in merchant banking (McDowell and Court 1994), offshore production sites, and border maquiladoras. In Chandra Mohanty's words: "An international division of labor is central to the establishment, consolidation, and maintenance of the current world order: global assembly lines are as much about the production of people as they are about 'providing jobs' or making profit" (Mohanty 1997: 5; also Pyke 1996). New identities may emerge from or destabilize conventional socialization into economic roles and division of labor expectations.

The geographical unevenness of production sites – and their employment opportunities – engenders internal and external labor migrations: to urban areas, export processing zones, seasonal agricultural sites, tourism locales, and global cities as hubs of the financial sector. Some migration is of skilled workers (linked to transnational corporatist opportunities, or the "brain-drain" from poor or repressive source countries[8]), but most of the growth in migration involves semiskilled or unskilled workers[9] who are rendered most vulnerable by current restructuring. Flexibilization (centered in the productive economy) and informalization (centered in the reproductive economy) are key to 'seeing' and analyzing these movements. Consistent with structural vulnerabilities and the nature of the jobs available (cleaning, harvesting, domestic service), it is no surprise that migrant worker populations are especially marked by race/ethnicity and gender (Sassen 1998).

These shifts in scale and the compression of time and space are materially possible because of the "revolution" in information and communication technologies. The rapid expansion of computer technologies and satellite communication have profoundly altered social life and our "sense" of time and space. Today's transportation and communication media permit rapid and frequent physical contact across territorial space as well as virtually instantaneous cyberspace "contact" that dissolves distance. The explosive growth in financial markets and esoteric instruments for hedging risks especially depend on advanced technologies. This is not to argue that technologies are determinative, that place, time, and distance no longer matter, or that the "global" effects of these technologies are homogeneous.[10] It is to insist that large-scale transnational processes, enabled by information technologies and normalized by neoliberal discourse, are deeply restructuring social relations. In addition to shifts already indicated, the development and selective application of these technologies has reconfigured production processes and products, the meaning and role of money, and the lives of workers – and nonworkers – worldwide.

Shifts in production and consumption[11]

> The logic of unfettered market forces, after all, is to increase global inequality and to produce a Benthamite world where ... the greatest happiness of the greatest number of consumers (perhaps 800 million people in the wealthiest urban regions of the world) is matched by a similar number who barely survive and a further 800 million who are on the point of starvation.
>
> (Gill 1994: 85)

From material-based to information-based production

The shift from Fordism to post-Fordism was registered internationally by an unexpected decline in the prices of and demand for (non-oil) primary products and raw materials. Once again, technologies play a key role. On the one hand, food production and productivity in the 1970s and 1980s were dramatically enhanced by "green revolution" technologies and policies designed to increase output. On the other hand, the decline in demand for raw materials is due to a switch away from material-intensive products to high-technology and knowledge-intensive (non- and dematerialized) industries.[12] These shifts have implications for all food and raw material exporting countries, but are especially damaging to least-industrialized countries. Development strategies in the latter have historically assumed that the costs of importing foreign capital goods would be paid for in part by raw materials exports to developed economies, where industrialized production would ensure increasing demand. Instead, declining ("a cumulative 50 percent over the last 25 years" [UNDP 1997: 9]) terms of trade hurt developing economies by exacerbating unemployment and inability to attract foreign investment. This puts further pressure on these countries to view (unregulated, informalized) labor as their most competitive resource. It also exacerbates out-migration in search of work.

As a corollary to the shift from material- to knowledge-based manufacturing there has been (in industrialized countries) both a downgrading of manufacturing (dramatic growth in low wage, semi- and unskilled jobs[13]) and a decoupling of manufacturing production from manufacturing employment. In the latter case,

industrial production remains important and may even increase, but – like agriculture before it – it involves fewer jobs in that historically higher-wage sector.

Growth in services

In tandem with these developments, and a significant source of new low-wage
(and some high-wage) jobs, is the phenomenal growth in the service economy.
This is most pronounced in industrialized countries – where service employment
constitutes 50–70 percent of the workforce – but is an emerging pattern in developing countries as well. Global trade in services has increased by 25 percent
between 1994 and 1997 alone (World Bank 2000: 6). Income polarization is a
distinguishing feature of this growth in services. In contrast to middle-income jobs
associated with Fordist material-based manufacturing, service jobs tend to be
polarized: either skilled and high-waged (professional-managerial jobs in health,
education, financial, and legal services) or semi-, unskilled and poorly paid
(in cleaning, food, retail, and telemarketing services). As one consequence, we
observe a pattern of income polarization both within countries – as job growth is
increasingly low-wage – and between countries – as the gap between developed
and developing countries widens.

This has long-term implications, not least in regard to public investment in
human resources necessary for knowledge-based industries and competitive labor
markets.

Growth in services is due in part to post-Fordist shifts away from material-based
production and in part to new demands for service inputs in support of upper-
income lifestyles. But we must also consider the context of global restructuring,
the explosive growth in financial transactions (the virtual economy), and shifts in
FDI, especially as these affect developing countries. The key points here relate
first to FDI shifts toward services (accounting for approximately two-thirds of
global FDI [World Bank 2000: 72]), and second to the heavy concentration of
FDI in developed countries.

Flexibilization

We can observe how various dimensions of these developments interact by
considering a key theme of restructuring: flexibilization. This refers to shifts in
production processes away from large, integrated factory work sites, unionized
workers, and mass production of standardized consumer goods to spatially dispersed (global) production networks, increasingly casualized and informalized
workers, and small batch, "just in time" production for segmented consumer
markets. At the core of flexibilization are efforts to deregulate production
processes and labor markets – increasing freedom for management – ostensibly to
eliminate inefficient "rigidities." As Standing notes, deregulation has been both
explicit ("whereby formal regulations have been eroded or abandoned by legislative
means") and implicit ("whereby remaining regulations have been made less
effective through inadequate implementation or systematic bypassing") (Standing

1989: 1077). Deregulation of production activities is linked to deregulation of capital movements and the explosion of financial transactions that shift investment from the "real economy" to ostensibly higher profits in the "virtual economy."

Flexibilization has been made possible by technologies that reduce the costs of spatially dispersed activities even as they enable centralized monitoring and coordination of decentralized production processes (Sassen 1998; Gill 1997). Electronic technologies and cyberspace are integral to flexible production because they determine not only what commodities (VCRs, auto subcomponents) are produced and transported, but also how quickly and effectively information can be circulated in support of far-flung, decentralized networks and specialized, "just in time" production. To cut production costs, flexibilization involves more subcontracting, "out-sourcing," indirect forms of employment, smaller enterprises (often linked to centralized networks), part-time and temporary employment, and avoidance of organized labor. Flexibilization of production then merges with informalization as firms avoid regularized and regulated work relations, un- and underemployment increase, "real" wages decline, and strapped families/house-holds turn to informal activities as a survival strategy.

Flexibilization is thus about cutting costs by globally seeking the cheapest components and cheapest labor, shortening product cycles and turn-over time, and responding quickly to changing market conditions. Hence, different styles of management, more surveillance, and corresponding identities are also required: "leaner and meaner," more innovative, entrepreneurial and risk-taking, more flexible across tasks, and less loyal. In important senses, these are as much identity issues as they are workforce practices.

In effect, flexibilization feminizes the workforce insofar as a growing number of jobs require few skills and the most desirable workers are unorganized (undemand-ing), understood to be docile but reliable, available for part-time and temporary work, and willing to accept low-wages.[14] Women continue to earn 30–50 percent less than men worldwide (DAW 1999), which reproduces the expectation and reality that women can be paid less for similar work. Women are preferred for the low-wage jobs associated with export-led industrialization, downgraded manu-facturing, and "unskilled" service jobs. In this framing, feminization of labor refers to women's increasing participation in the labor force, and/or women assuming jobs traditionally held by men. But an expanded sense of "feminization" draws our attention to other aspects of flexibilization – and informalization – that are deeply gendered.

Informal sector activities

Flexibilization increases economic activities that are "outside" of regulated and regularized production processes. It thus increases informal sector activities – hence linking the reproductive and productive (and ultimately the virtual) economies – and does so in at least three ways. First, flexibilization avoids the "rigidities" of regulated practices and centralized work sites in favor of more adaptable outsourcing, subcontracting, and casualization of labor (optimal for short-term, "just in time" production) that epitomize informal work or informalization processes. That is, informal work merges with flexibilized work/production insofar as less formal, regularized, and regulated work conditions become the norm.

Second, insofar as flexibilization erodes labor's organizing power, protection of workers' rights, and wage expectations, it exacerbates the decline in family income that "pushes" more people to generate income in whatever way they can; they often do so by engaging in a variety of informal sector activities, thus contributing to informalization. Third, insofar as flexibilization's avoidance of regulation translates into avoidance of taxes, it exacerbates the declining resources devoted to public welfare provisioning and spurs participation in informal activities – hence informalization – to compensate in part for this loss. In sum, flexibilization understood in terms of the productive economy (as encompassing but not exhausted by reference to "formal" economic activities) is continuous with and inextricable from informalization in terms of the reproductive economy (understood as encompassing but not exhausted by reference to informal activities).

Under diverse labels – the secondary, submerged, underground, or shadow economy – references to the informal economy carry a variety of meanings, all with political implications. In particular, defining the informal economy is politically significant for feminists because the boundary of public–private – and all that that entails – is implicated. At issue is no less than what range of activities are to "count" as "work"[15]: social reproduction, housework, dependent care, subsistence production, petty commodities, homework, legal but unrecorded payments, gambling, black market transactions, the drug trade, money laundering, clandestine enterprises and so on.

The conventional distinction is that – in contrast to formal sector activities – the informal economy refers to income generating activities that are "free" of regulations that discipline formal work arrangements. Even with this conventional definition, estimating the size and value of these activities is contentious, as they are both difficult to measure and exist outside of standard accounting procedures. But most commentators agree on two points. The first is that informal sector activities constitute a significant, even staggering, portion of "economic" activity (e.g. Fleming et al. 2000). The second is that informal sector activities are dramatically *increasing* worldwide as global restructuring involves a decrease in contractual, formal sector opportunities (e.g. Tabak and Crichlow 2000). Consistent with the sense of being "outside" of regulated activities, the informal economy is typically characterized as attempts to evade either taxation or prosecution.

In regard to the scale of these activities the following data are illuminating. Defined as proceeds from illicit earnings (e.g. drug-dealing, prostitution) and unrecorded but legal income (e.g. builders paid in cash), the shadow or underground economy in 1998 was estimated as a substantial $9 trillion, which is the equivalent of approximately one-fourth of the world's gross domestic product for that year (*The Economist* 1999: 59). And these figures do not even begin to account for household maintenance, dependent care or social reproduction more generally.

When we include this socially necessary labor – that is primarily assigned to women – the figures further unsettle conventional measures of "economic production." For example, Ruth Sivard notes that the value of women's work in the household alone would add between one-fourth and one-third to the world's GNP (Sivard 1995: 11). The United Nations Development Program (UNDP) Report argued that the monetization of nonmarket work would "yield gigantically large monetary valuations. A rough order of magnitude comes to a staggering $16 trillion... [of which] $11 trillion is the non-monetized, invisible contribution of women" (UNDP 1995: 6).

The informal sector is beginning to receive more mainstream attention because of its increasing volume, the nature of its activities, and the implications of its unregulated status.[16] But aside from feminist economists, most accounts neglect not only how informal activities are gendered and racialized, but also how social reproduction is crucial to, and inextricable from, activities in both informal and formal sectors.

Shifts in money, a.k.a. the international financial system

> The liveliness of this debate over globalization in international finance at the very least suggests that it is indeed an issue of some importance. My personal conviction ... is that it is the prime issue of international politics and economics.
>
> (Strange 1998: 18)

The most quantifiable shift in scale is the phenomenal growth in global financial transactions. In 1973 daily foreign-exchange turnover was $15 billion, in 1995 it grew to $1.2 trillion (*The Economist* 1997: 80), and in 1998 to $1.5 trillion daily – "an amount equal to around one-sixth of the annual output of the U.S. economy" (World Bank 2000: 71). The sheer size and volume of these transactions make it difficult to grasp their meaning. But do so we must, because these flows, through the setting of prices, link together "all of the other economic processes in the global marketplace" (Cerny 1994: 332). In short, what transpires in global financial markets shapes the direction of investments (e.g. short-term, long-term; in trade, financial instruments, human resources), the production of goods and services (e.g. material-based, knowledge-based; labor-intensive, capital and technology-intensive) and the structure of labor markets (e.g. what types of labor, located where, at what compensation, under what conditions). Stated differently, exchange rates and interest rates – which are key to business decision-making, public policy-making, and hence, our everyday lives – are increasingly determined by *financial* trading on world markets (Cerny 1996: 130).

What explains this phenomenal growth in the international financial system? The answer, of course, is complex, but we can gain some sense of the larger picture if we locate the dynamism of global money in relation to the history of deregulation, shifts in the scale and substance of specifically financial transactions, and the dematerialization afforded by electronic technologies.[17]

"Freeing" money from regulation

Financial deregulation is key, marked by the early 1970s shift from fixed to floating exchange rates. By the end of the 1970s many countries had reduced or abolished exchange (capital) controls, thus permitting the unregulated export of their currencies. At the same time, the circulation of petrodollar surpluses increased international banking transactions that profited from lending to developing countries. Offshore (deregulated) transactions expanded, especially the Eurodollar market in London, to accommodate the flow of dollars and evade existing banking controls. The 1980s saw further deregulation, competition, expansion, and volatility. London's "Big Bang" in 1986 opened stock markets to foreign investors, thus reducing obstacles to ownership and trading of shares by externally based banks, brokers, and fund managers (Scholte 1997: 434). In part to hedge their bets in currency markets, investors developed an array of financial instruments (e.g. derivatives, futures contracts) designed to offset risks. These instruments not only increase the volume and complexity of market transactions but also exacerbate instability by encouraging short-term, high risk, and speculative investments.[18]

Financial scale and flexibilization

Securitization, associated with desegmentation or disintermediation, accompanies and fuels these changes. The reference here is to blurring the traditional (and in the United States, heavily regulated) distinction between commercial banks (focused on "intermediated" financing, that is, lending money on the basis of personal knowledge of the borrower) and investment banks (focused on selling negotiable securities, which do not involve "personal" assessment, and which can subsequently be traded on secondary markets, the most attractive being international markets). In a broader sense, securitization refers to a shift from traditional lending activities to securities trading and financial innovation in securities markets, the advantage being increased flexibility and price sensitivity as previously distinct sectors are integrated (Cerny 1994: 336, 339).

One effect of these changes and the technologies that enable them is a shift in profit patterns. Increasing price sensitivity and speed of transactions tends to enhance competition and reduce the profit margins of the former slower and less sensitive system. Now trading in *volume* becomes one key to profits, and favors bigger investors. As a corollary, securitization is closely linked to the rise of institutional investors – insurance funds, pension funds, unit trusts – with their massive investment potential (Lash and Urry 1994: 18–20). The extraordinary expansion and transformation of global financial transactions involves an "enormous mass of 'world money' ... [that] has no existence outside the global economy and its main money markets. It is not being created by economic activity like investment, production, consumption, or trade. It is created primarily by currency trading... It is virtual rather than real money" (Drucker 1997: 162).

Hence as the deepening of international financial markets delinks them from the "real economy" the "real value" of money becomes less clear: it does not function in conventional terms (standard of measurement, store of value, or medium of exchange). Rather, it functions increasingly as a "standard of deferred payment": credit money displaces commodity money (Thrift 1996: 215) and "financial markets are now defined by a set of credit relationships with different time structures, etched in computer memories" (Corbridge and Thrift 1994: 11). In other words, money is becoming increasingly abstract as trade in virtual money, the mass of "symbolic" global capital, is dwarfing trade in goods and services – the real economy associated with commodity money. The argument is not that delinking insulates the real economy from global finance, because prices "set" in the virtual economy have decisive effects throughout the economic system: directing investments more generally and affecting production processes (flexibilization, informalization) that shape everyday lives worldwide. Rather, the argument is that credit money is both an enormous mass of symbolic capital less traditionally linked to the real economy and differently constituted than commodity money. This mass of credit money is key to the new economic and financial architecture and requires new thinking about the value of money and how this is determined, and with what effects.

In the context of deregulated financial markets, capital assumes a life of its own as its value is relatively independent of the circulation of commodities familiar in traditional economics. It is not that trade in goods does not matter – it too continues to grow – but that it is dwarfed by trade in capital movements whose link to the "real" economy is tenuous. Consider that: "In one day as much of this virtual money may be traded as the entire world needs to finance trade and investment [in goods and services] for a year" (Drucker 1997: 162). As a corollary, the scale and integration of financial markets makes the danger of contagion and chain-reaction disruptions all too real.

Virtual money and financial market power

The new scale of virtual money and the power of financial markets have multiple effects. Within firms and organizations, an increasing urgency in regard to "managing money" shifts attention, jobs, and status to the financial officers or departments of corporation and organizations. Within the state, power shifts from legislative to executive branches and departments or ministries that oversee financial planning. Within domestic economies, labor markets are reshuffled to accommodate shifting production and investment strategies, and the provision of welfare is ideologically constructed as a luxury that viable national economies cannot afford. In actuality, welfare cutbacks are selective. Corporate welfare, "welfare for the rich," is rarely diminished and may be enhanced, all in the name of sustaining a viable economy and competitive global market position.

At the same time, the contraction of welfare provisioning also *politicizes* citizenship, immigration, and democratization, as citizens and "others" confront who is inside (and outside) of what protection and welfare the state provides. Provision of public goods is increasingly determined by privatization practices and decisionmakers that are not accountable to citizens (e.g. Gill 1997). Conventional understandings of "democracy" are deeply challenged when decisions affecting public welfare are made less often by governments – with at least some sense of accountability to citizens – and more often by markets that are "free" from such demands or accountability.

More generally, investment in manufacturing suffers in favor of apparently quicker and higher profits in financial markets. Whereas profit can only be made once when selling a commodity, it can be made repeatedly when selling money, and flexibility is a given. In financial markets, exchanges can be handled – rapidly and in extraordinary volume – via computer blips on a screen. No need to build a plant or worry about suppliers, safety hazards, or vocal workers. In financial markets, there are considerable risks, but they are different and attempts to hedge against them present their own seductive activities. Unfortunately, the pursuit of ever more innovative instruments for investment present ever more complex challenges to understanding – to say nothing of effectively regulating – these markets (Underhill 1997).

In addition, the apparent speed and ease of profit-making in the financial sector puts additional pressure on the manufacturing sector. That is, as quicker and higher profits become the general *expectation*, management can use that expectation to justify further cuts in wages and worker benefits. Given these conditions, and the misleading but seductive ideologies that accompany them, it is not surprising that trade in virtual money dwarfs trade in products. Hence, the wildfire growth in financial markets (the virtual economy) is structurally linked to the shift from manufacturing jobs and Fordist practices to an increase in service jobs, flexible production, and informal, nonunionized, low-waged, and insecure labor forms (the productive and reproductive economies).

Finally, growth in financial markets that are increasingly difficult to regulate makes money-laundering easier and exacerbates the effects of large-scale organized crime.[19] The latter involves not only illicit drugs but also arms deals, and traffic in women, illegal immigrants, and even nuclear materials (Strange 1998). These activities are important not only for the social relations they engender and the violence they involve, but also for the costs they impose in unrealized state revenues of potentially greater "public" benefit.

Deterritorialization and dematerialization

Deterritorialization and dematerialization refer to the ease and intensity of trans-border flows, as electronically mediated transactions are increasingly disembedded from territorial, material space and their cultural attachments. Looking specifically at technologies brings the scale, speed, and implications of these changes into clearer focus. More than in any other sector of the economy, information technology has revolutionized financial services. This is due in part to the role of time–space compression in money markets (where mere seconds can determine the profit – or loss – of vast sums) and in part due to the abstract, symbolic, and informational nature of money (so readily accommodated by electronic transmission of "pure information").

First and most obviously, the electronic information revolution has transformed the speed, volume, scale, and scope of information exchange. Increasing speed and volume have dramatically reduced the costs of transmissions, and hence who undertakes them, and for what purposes. The scope of exchanges is the *global* in global financial markets, as the exchange of information that constitutes global finance crosses previously less permeable borders that structured social relations. Not only spatial distance but also conceptual and organizational boundaries (the meaning of money, banking, security/ies, work and leisure, public and private, global cities and territorial states, "real" and virtual economies) are collapsed or reconstituted. And not only ownership of market shares but also control over public planning and everyday life is implicated, given the direct and indirect effects of global finance on all other sectors of the economy and social relations.

This dependence on telecommunications and networked computers has various implications. In some senses it favors the bigger players who can afford the investment in data systems and innovations and whose capacity can realize profits off even very thin profit margins. But the decentralization of online access permits more players to participate, with less predictable effects. The rapid development of innovations – in financial instruments, payment processes, credit creation, diversifying, and assessing risk – provides great flexibility and very dynamic markets, but the velocity alone stymies the state's ability to monitor or regulate increasingly "invisible" transactions. Velocity is also related to "short-termism," as the current structure of the market privileges short-term gains over more carefully thought out (and potentially more socially responsible) long-term investments. Finally (but not exhaustively), the dense integration of these systems poses its own scale of risks. There are the now-familiar concerns about computer breakdowns with system-wide, potentially devastating effects. And it is not clear whether or how a collapse due to crisis in one area can be contained, not only because of contagion but also because of the complexity and non-transparency of the data involved on this integrated scale.

Centralization and decentralization

From a different perspective, communication technologies have made decentralization on a global scale possible even as centralized decision-making remains the norm and reproduces hierarchical relations. For many industries, distance is no longer an issue, because workers can be monitored (telemarketing, data entry), assembled parts can be cheaply transported (microchip industries), or the product itself is information (reading laboratory slides, airline reservations). Low-wage work sites may be globally dispersed (or out in the suburbs) and simply linked to the center via communications technologies. But in Sassen's words, "the territorial dispersal of current economic activity creates a need for expanded central control and management" (Sassen 1991: 4). In a similar vein, Thrift argues that while the number of international centers that "count" is understood to have decreased since the 1980s, those "that are left in contention have become more important. In other words, the interdependent connectedness of disembedded electronic networks promotes dependence on a just a few places like London, New York and Tokyo where representations can be mutually constructed, negotiated, accepted and acted upon" (Thrift 1996: 232).

These global or world cities are centers of not only financial activity but also an array of production and service activities upon which they depend and which they foster. Of particular relevance are the ways that global cities concentrate high-wage knowledge-based and low-wage service and downgraded manufacturing jobs, the latter filled predominantly by women and immigrants. Here the polarization described earlier is especially visible, both in income distribution and occupational distribution. Sassen (1991: 9–10) identifies two additional developments exacerbating polarization in such cities. One is the availability of low-wage jobs that enable and sustain high-income gentrification (expensive restaurants, luxury housing and hotels, gourmet shops, boutiques, etc.). The other is the effects of downgraded manufacturing, where "the share of unionized shops declines and wages deteriorate while sweatshops and industrial homework proliferate" (Sassen 1991: 9). Here again, the effects of globalization are uneven: some cities and regions gain prominence while others become marginalized; rural areas tend to lose both jobs and people to urbanization; overvalorized sectors (knowledge-based management, finance, professional jobs) enjoy high-quality benefits while devalorized sectors (manufacturing, low-wage services) suffer reduced wage packets and benefits; and women and immigrants participate in the labor force but typically under low-wage "dead-end" conditions.

Cyberspace and the economics of intangibles

Finally, I return to a consideration of technology in relation to the abstract and symbolic nature of money, especially in the context of today's virtual (world) money and global financial markets. Of course, money has always involved abstraction: as a means of exchange, store of wealth, or standard of value. But today's virtual money does not conform to these traditional definitions. In one sense, because it "serves no economic function and finances nothing, this money also does not follow economic logic or rationality" (Drucker 1997: 162). Recast in Strange's useful betting analogy, "it is the *opinions* [of participating bettors] not the objective prowess of the horse that moves the prices" (Strange 1997: 111, my emphasis). This is not entirely new, insofar as capitalism has always depended on constructing desire—for commodities, for symbols of power and success. But today's dematerialized economy takes this to a new "level" of abstraction. It is not only the quantity – which has increased so dramatically – but the elusive (because dematerialized and even irrational) and dynamic character of financial market exchanges that renders them simultaneously so potent yet so opaque.

For Nitzan (also in this volume), capital is disembedded from the material and must be understood as a "crystallization of power" to be measured only in differential not absolute terms. He writes: "Modern capitalists have become investors of 'funds,' absentee owners of pecuniary wealth with no industrial dealings; their investment is a business transaction in which they acquire a claim over a future stream of money income; and, accumulation no longer involves the augmentation of physical means of production, but of financial values. Under absentee owner-ship, capital is stripped of any physical characteristic, assuming the universal face of money value… What is being capitalized is not the *ability to produce*, but the *power to appropriate*" (Nitzan 1998: 182–3, emphasis in original).

Nitzan's rewriting of "capital" insists that the materialist/economistic bias informing both neoclassical and marxist accounts has prevented us from appreci-ating how completely the *value* of capital is embedded in – constituted by – *social* relations. Whereas the real economy and financial transactions were previously interwoven, they are delinked as investors of "funds" have no industrial dealings and capital is not based on material measures. Rather, capital must be understood exclusively as a "pecuniary magnitude"; it represents an abstract distributional claim – a claim on anticipated future profits, the realization of which depends less on material production than constructed desires, perceptions, and trust. The vendibility of capital (making money off of money) renders it apparently boundless; and its abstract, virtual nature renders it universal. Hence, it constitutes a uniquely *flexible* power – and must be understood in new terms (Nitzan 1998).

In a related sense, virtual money exists in the cyber-space of what some call an economy (or even an empire) of signs. The point here is that objects seen or heard in cyberspace "are neither physical nor, necessarily, presentations of physical objects, but are rather – in form, character, and action – made up of data, of pure information" (Benedikt, quoted in Der Derian 1992: 200). Their meaning, and in this case, value depend not on any materialized "ground" but entirely on their location in relation to other representations. In this, they resemble Nitzan's claims that capital today is a measure of *differential* rather than absolute value. By refer-ence to analytical framing, virtual money is more a matter of textual, cultural, and symbolic meaning than the material measures taken as given in "economic" accounts. In an ironic twist, it is the GPE that discloses the constitutive salience of the symbolic. That is, the development and globalization of computer technologies has enabled a political economy of virtual money and disembodied signs that starkly exposes the centrality – the constitutiveness – of symbolization.

Conclusion

My intention has been to facilitate analytical advances through introducing the RPV framing and surveying new globalization dynamics cast as three overlapping "shifts" with extremely uneven effects. First, shifts in scale, space, and time are discursively familiar (global–local, regionalization, instantaneous broadcasts, a global audience) but often mask more complex intersections and exclusions. What certainly warrants greater attention is the unique dematerializing and deterritori-alizing effects of information technologies, which transgress familiar physical as well as conceptual boundaries worldwide. On the one hand, polarization is reflected here in an elite of those with access to and knowledge of sophisticated technologies and an expanding "bottom" of those without access to technological infrastructure or valorized technical skills; these patterns are exemplified in flexibilization (the productive economy) and informalization (the reproductive economy). On the other hand, polarization is reflected as well in an elite of those benefiting from dematerialized financial markets and the "rest of us" who must "adjust" to the vagaries of these markets and are the biggest losers when financial crises ensue; these patterns are exemplified in the effects of the virtual economy.

Second, shifts in production are marked by declining terms of trade for primary products exporters, degraded manufacturing, and "emptying out" of middle-income jobs as "the skills have been taken into the machines, leaving it to the unskilled to operate them and the highly skilled to program them" (Sivanandan 1989: 1). Low-wage service jobs increase as an effect of information-based technologies, growth in tourist industries, and meeting the lifestyle "needs" of elites, especially in urban areas. Flexibilization as the dominant production process increases low-wage, semi-skilled, subcontracted, nonunionized, temporary, part-time, and often dangerous work options. In the face of declining formal sector opportunities, informal activities assume tremendous economic significance – but are neither "counted" nor taxed, with negative effects on the visibility of this work and the delivery of welfare from public revenues. In these shifts, global unevenness is captured by reference to "polarization": the growing gap in skills, employment, and income between haves and have-nots both within and between countries. This "economic" unevenness is deeply marked by gender and race/ethnicity.

Third, shifts in money-making are dramatic and power-laden. With deregulation of financial markets, national boundaries – marking currency values and planning opportunities – are eroded in favor of global markets and their "non-public" priorities. The speed and scale of financial transactions are themselves transformative, but innovations in instruments and processes intensify the flexibility and volatility of these markets. The lure of quick and "easy" profits exacerbates volatility and discourages investments in manufacturing and longer-term, more public-oriented projects. Most striking is the phenomenal growth in virtual money that is delinked from the real economy of goods and services and mirrors the "economy of desire" and "empire of signs" more familiar in postmodern accounts. Here, the exchange of pure data takes on a life of its own, producing an elite of "high-rollers," playing what Strange (1997) calls "casino capitalism," with little accountability when collapse and crisis occur. As Underhill (1997: 3) puts it: "While the confidence of market authorities may be shaken and government policies called into question, the screen-driven markets continue their journey through cyber-space, carrying our savings, insurance schemes and future with them."

The trade-off for a coherent picture of globalization is neglect of inconsistencies and resistances. These are vital aspects of mapping power, but remain undeveloped in this abbreviated account. I have focused instead on presenting an analytical alternative because reigning models are simply inadequate for addressing new dynamics. They are inadequate from the more familar (if marginalized) vantage points of feminists seeking attention to social reproduction and non-waged labor and marxists seeking attention to uneven development and relentless exploitation. They are also and particularly inadequate from the less familiar vantage point of postmodernists seeking attention to signs, representations, culture, and "the virtual." As an alternative "analytical advance," the RPV framing links reproductive, productive, and virtual economies. It offers more relational and more critical understanding, in the hope of encouraging more effective resistance to current and emerging asymmetries of power.

Acknowledgments

The work presented in this chapter has benefited from the support of numerous individuals and institutions. I am especially indebted to Erik Andersson, Paula England, Kathleen Fernicula, Virginia Haufler, Gregory Knehans, Lily Ling, Cecilia Lynch, Nick Onuf, Jindy Pettman, and Dereka Rushbrook for feedback on parts of this and related chapters, and to the Department of Gender Studies at Göteborg University for a Research Fellowship during 2000.

Notes

1 See Peterson 2003.
2 Briefly here, I understand feminism not only as a movement to empower women but as a systemic, transformative critique of structural hierarchies that are linked and ideologically "naturalized" by denigration of the feminine (i.e. casting the subordinated as feminine – lacking agency, control, reason, skills, or culture – even if they are not women but racially, culturally, or economically marginalized men). In this crucial sense, feminist critiques are neither simply about male–female relations nor limited to promoting the status of "women." Their transformative potential lies in subverting all hierarchies that rely on denigration of "the feminine" to naturalize domination. By politicizing the historical, material, and ideological production of patriarchy (women's oppression), feminists document how devalorization of "the feminine" has become common sense and is invoked to depoliticize multiple hierarchies. This common sense is culturally and collectively internalized, so that we are all variously complicit in its reproduction. And it is also implicitly and explicitly manipulated to reproduce inequalities as if this were natural and inevitable, thus undercutting critique and resistance. In short, devalorizing the feminine *produces even as it obscures* vast inequalities of power, authority, and resource distribution. Exposing how this power operates must be one objective of a critical political agenda.
3 The *relationship* between reproduction and production has long been debated, but marxists evidence little movement beyond subsuming women's liberation within class liberation. For more on feminist and marxist/socialist economics see, for example Hartmann 1981; Beechey 1987; Matthaei 1992; Davis 1997; Mies 1998.
4 More specifically, today's firms increase profits not only by increasing productivity/accumulation at a given level of subsistence/wage expectations (the postwar growth model), but also by relocating where economies are less marketized (labor less commodified), households meet more of the costs of social reproduction, and the firm's profits are sustained through significantly lower wage costs. Hence, the value of various forms of informal income that are pooled – as well as wages, currencies, prices, and profits – are *interdependent* elements in a system of value determination.
5 On supraterritorial space see Scholte 1997; Robertson 1992 is credited with the "single place" trope; in addition to those cited, other sources for this section include Helleiner 1994; Pellerin 1996; Sassen 1998.

6 By taking difference seriously, feminists have generated some of the most incisive critiques of totalizing theory/practice. For critical analysis of the "whole earth" metaphor see Runyan 1992; and of "Spaceship Earth" as invoking both environmental awareness and celebrations of global corporate integration see Cosgrove 1994.

7 But see Castells' (2000: 110–16) critique of the regionalizing thesis.

8 Consider the alarming statistic that "some countries in sub-Saharan Africa, the Caribbean, Central America, and South Asia have, in fact, lost one-third of their skilled workers" (World Bank 2000: 39, citing Carrington and Detragiache 1998, no page number).

9 But see Beechey 1988 for a feminist critique of how skill is characterized.

10 While the growth in electronic technologies and their distribution worldwide is well documented, they are particularly marked by unevenness in access and effects. See, for example, Eisenstein's critique and empirical data (1998); *The Economist* (1998), *Pocket World in Figures* 1999: 82–3; and UNDP 2001.

11 Points and arguments in this section are drawn from works cited, as well as Sassen 1991, 1993, 1998; Drucker 1986, 1997; Myles 1991; Lash and Urry 1994.

12 Consider that the "raw materials in a semi-conductor microchip account for one to three percent of total production cost... Fifty to 100 pounds of fibreglass cable transmit as many telephone messages as does one ton of copper wire... [And to produce that amount of fiberglass cable] requires no more than five percent of the energy needed to produce one ton of copper wire" (Drucker 1986: 773). As Drucker notes, it is not that food supplies and manufacturing production have become less important, but that they are produced with fewer and different inputs. These points link to Taylor's depiction (this volume) of "single commodity" countries: Argentina exporting beef, Brazil coffee, Malaya rubber, etc.

13 Sassen (1998: 47) identifies three converging trends to explain this downgrading: the reorganization of the work process (subcontracting, sweatshops, home-based work) in ways that isolate workers and prevent collective organizing; technological transformations that downgrade skill levels through expanded use of machines and computers; and growth of high-technology industries employing low-wage workers.

14 Flexibilization reflects post-1970s restructuring that is conducive to women as workers, but generally in less desirable economic conditions. Women are both "pulled" into the labor force as low-wage, unskilled employment opportunities increase, and "pushed" into income generation when declining family incomes force more members to seek income by whatever means available. From their analysis of cross-country data and long-term processes of economic development, Çağatay and Ozler (1995) conclude that women's labor force participation rate is in fact U-shaped: decreasing during initial stages of capitalist development and increasing in advanced stages. Men's labor force participation rate is observed to fall slowly as development proceeds.

15 For more on including women's work in national and international accounts, see Waring 1988; Sivard 1995; United Nations Women 1995, 2000; Cloud and Garrett 1997.

16 Regarding the scale of the underground economy, Walker (1997: vii–xiii) notes that "in the most careful analysis ever conducted of this issue, Feige concludes that the amount of U.S. currency held abroad indicates that there is an underground economy equal to the size of the U.S. economy hidden amongst the reported economic activities in the world's countries."

17 The following discussion of financial markets is indebted to Gill 1997; Strange 1997, 1998; Cerny 1994, 1995, 1996; Thrift 1996; Underhill 1997. Other important studies of financial globalization include Cerny 1993; Helleiner 1994; Kapstein 1994; Sobel 1994; Corbridge and Thrift 1994; Eichengreen 1996; Pauly 1997; Cohen 1998.

18 Growth here is "truly phenomenal," prompting the IMF, the Bank of International Settlements and the United Nations Conference on Trade and Development (UNCTAD) to agree that trading in derivatives is "the most important innovative change in the

international financial system since the mid-1980s" (Strange 1998: 29). Gill 1997 considers how financial innovations affect everyday life, for example, in purchasing cars, securing fixed rate mortgages, and anticipating retirement funds. Cerny (1996: 129–30) considers how global finance has become the exemplar of flexibilization, with rapid development of variable financial instruments, creative process innovation, and segmenting market demand.

19 "Between $500 billion and 1.5 trillion (or 5 percent of gross world product) may be laundered every year" (*The Economist* 1999: 17).

3 Metageographical moments

A geohistorical interpretation of embedded statism and globalization

Peter J. Taylor

At times it seems that there are as many opinions about globalization as there are authors who write about it. This is partly a feature of the peculiarly diffuse nature of the literature on this phenomenon: business gurus, populist journalists, and social theorists are all well represented. Furthermore, globalization has entered the political arena, often bringing out the worst in politicians ranging from the specific and reactive, anti-foreign xenophobia, to the more general and proactive, anti-social neo-liberalism. In fact globalization is a very modern concept, reflecting as it does the ambiguities of living in a world of massive and continuous social change. My purpose here is not to try and "tame" the concept by offering my own narrow definition – that would destroy its authenticity. Rather I seek to provide basic coordinates, both spatial and temporal, through which to interpret contemporary social predicaments.

Globalization is inherently geographical. Hence, there has been much discussion of its spatial coordinates. Two particular perspectives are prominent. Most obviously, globalization implies a changing scale of human activity: processes previously operating at the level of the state have been relocated "upwards" to larger, including worldwide, patterns of operation. A more subtle argument is that globalization is associated with a fundamental change in the nature of social space: from an old "space of places" to a new "space of flows." There is no need for these two geographical perspectives to be contradictory but in most studies one or the other of them tends to dominate the discussion. This is visible in their associated temporal coordinates. Treating globalization as a shift in scale allows for a "comparative globalization" approach wherein historical "trans-continental" societies are compared to contemporary globalization. In contrast, treating globalization as a new form of space means that there are no precedents: globalization is historically unique.

I take neither position here. Both can be criticized for their inability to develop an adequate geohistorical interpretation of globalization. Such an approach requires an integrated framework of time and space. This is impossible with the two perspectives described above: the comparative method elides continuities and connections, while the tradition of seeing the present as unique erases continuities and connections. There is, of course, a very common geohistorical interpretation of globalization, which describes a "shrinking world." The argument is that improving transport and communication technologies have progressively lessened the "friction of distance" culminating with the contemporary "end of geography" in the instantaneous organization of international financial markets. This "space–time compression" combines elements of both the scale and flow positions – faster flows allow for larger organization – and provides important insights into contemporary social change but it is quite limited as an argument for identifying the spatial and temporal coordinates of globalization. Instead of this "whiggish" geohistory, I will develop a new argument based upon my treatment of modernities within world-systems analysis (Taylor 1999) using the concept of metageography.

Metageography is the term coined by Lewis and Wigen (1997) to describe the geographical structures through which people order their knowledge of the world. It is part of a society's taken-for-granted world. Rarely questioned as to its veracity or utility, a metageography constitutes an unexamined spatial discourse that provides the framework for thinking about the world across the whole gamut of human activities and interests.[1] Lewis and Wigen (1997) call their book *The Myth of Continents* because the latter constitute classic examples of unexamined spatial categories. If we take the larger of the two land masses stretching southwards from the Artic Ocean, usually referred to as "Eurasia," it has six main peninsular regions. These are from east to west: Siberia (northwest Asia), China (east Asia), "Indo-China" (southeast Asia), India (south Asia), Arabia (southwest Asia), and Europe (west or northwest Asia?). Only the latter peninsular region "qualifies" as a continent: this is the metageographical starting point of the Eurocentrism that Gills critiques (Chapter 8).

But a metageography is not eternal. I historicize the concept through adding the idea of a moment as a critical time of transition between metageographies. This enables me to ask, does contemporary globalization constitute a meta-geographical moment? My route to answering this question takes in three arguments. First, I outline a geohistorical interpretation of the modern world-system in terms of metageographies. This identifies an embedded statism at the heart of our contemporary metageography. Second, I consider the nature of this meta-geography as an unexamined spatial discourse that has seriously distorted our contemporary understanding of the modern world-system. This identifies social science as an important victim which, for instance, has always left "international relations" out on a limb. Third, I consider the evidence for the erosion of the current metageography under conditions of contemporary globalization with particular reference to world cities. I conclude that globalization can indeed be interpreted as a metageographical moment; rather than representing an erosion of the state, globalization is best viewed as an erosion of embedded statism.

Metageographies of the modern world-system

As collective geographical imaginations, all societies have distinctive metageo-graphies. Well-known examples are the traditional Chinese view of the world centered on the "middle kingdom," the Moslem division of the world into the

"House of Islam" and the "House of War," the medieval Christian "T and O" map with Jerusalem at the center, and today's world political map of "nation-states." These "world maps" constitute anchors which tie each society to both physical and metaphysical worlds; they provide the spatial context which makes sense of human social activities and ideals. As such they are as much about cosmology as geography, at least in the way we interpret the latter today.

The thesis developed here is that in the modern world-system, the balance between the physical and the metaphysical has altered to the detriment of the latter. From the European discovery of the Americas, through the scientific revolution and the secularization of the state, to contemporary globalization, traditional cosmologies have been in retreat from an ongoing "modernization" of knowledge. Following Berman (1988) I interpret modernity as indicating a state of perpetual social change which means that people living in modern society are in dire need of "anchors," such as a metageography, to help stabilize their experiences. Since the modern world-system is the capitalist world-economy (Wallerstein 1979), it is the material basis of geography that becomes central to how the world is viewed. But it is precisely this material basis that is the motor of the incessant change. Thus it cannot be expected that a single metageography can survive through the unfolding of the capitalist world-economy. Hence the representative of the modern world in the list of examples of metageographies above – the map of nation-states – is not the metageography of the whole of the history of the modern world-system. In the modern world there has been more than one metageography.

Modernity has taken many forms over time and space since the emergence of the modern world-system in the "long sixteenth century" (*c.*1450–1650). I have argued elsewhere (Taylor 1999) that there have been three prime modernities in the history of the modern world-system. These modern constructions with their critical systemic repercussions are associated with the world-system's hegemonic cycles. The first hegemon, the United Provinces, was largely instrumental in creating a new mercantile modernity in the seventeenth century with navigation as the key practical knowledge. The second hegemon, the United Kingdom, was largely instrumental in creating an industrial modernity in the late eighteenth and nineteenth centuries with engineering as the key practical knowledge. The third hegemon, the United States, was largely instrumental in creating a consumer modernity with media/advertising as the key practical knowledge. I argue here that each of these modernities is associated with a distinctive metageography.

As spatial frameworks, modern metageographies are best identified by their geometries. The geographical metageography of mercantile modernity is a topological metageography of trade routes extending from the Philippines in the "far west" to the Moluccas (the Spice Islands) in the "far east." For industrial modernity there is a centripetal metageography with the world seen as a single functional region serving a north Atlantic core. With consumer modernity there is a mosaic metageography of nation-states, national markets in which to ply wares. In each case, there is a metageographical moment when the old is eroded leaving a geographical opportunity for a new picture of the world to emerge. Like all geographies, metageographies have three aspects: pattern, content, and meaning.

Hence, after considering their metageographical moment I will briefly consider each metageography in turn in these terms.

The topological metageography of mercantile modernity

The metageographical moment, which opened up the way to the first modern metageography, is the archetypal example of the process. The traditional Christian cosmology simply could not contend with the European discovery of the Americas: adding a fourth continent made an imagination limited to three continents redundant (Zerubavel 1992). Of course, this "discovery" also began the process that led to the famous "triangular" Atlantic trade. At the same time, Europeans were developing routes through the Indian Ocean to the Pacific, avoiding Islam and Muslim control of Eurasian overland routes. The end result was that by the seventeenth century, for "modern Europeans," the oceans represented a set of pathways linking together ports, plantations, forts, mines, and waystations into a single trading system.

The topology of this metageography is shown in Figure 3.1. There are five main European players with the original Spanish and Portuguese trading being joined by French, English, and Dutch merchants by the end of the sixteenth century. By the mid-seventeenth century it is the Dutch who dominate the overall pattern. Their success was built initially in Europe: first, the longer-term control of the Baltic trade by the Low Countries and second, their successful strategy of blocking off Antwerp from the sea to give them access to the Rhineland heart of western Europe. Beyond Europe, the pattern consists of a north Atlantic triangular trading core with further linkages east and west where Spain and Portugal retain some influence. At the core of the system lay Amsterdam, the "world's entrepot," whose commercial calendar was organized around the return of the four great fleets from the Baltic, the Levant, the West Indies, and the East Indies

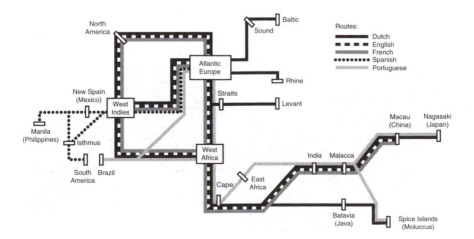

Figure 3.1 The topological metageography of mercantile modernity.

(Israel 1989: 257–8). As well as the commodities, information arrived with the fleets and from other parts of Europe to make Amsterdam Europe's first "world clearing house" for commercial information (Smith 1984).

With respect to the later metageographies, the meaning of the first modern case is particularly interesting. For these first modern Europeans, the rest of the world was viewed as a cornucopia, a land of plenty from which to win great wealth. Hence there was no assumption that these other regions of the world were inferior. This is in keeping with the reality: throughout mercantile modernity, Europe was not the leading world region as Frank (1998) has so clearly demonstrated. But it was not just the traditional European awe of the "fabulous east" which is to be found in contemporary minds; European reactions to African cities similarly show none of the later superiority complex: Benin, for instance, was compared favorably to Amsterdam (Oliver and Fage 1988: 89–90). The first modern European metageography was only topological precisely because, beyond the Atlantic, it consisted merely of feeder paths into established Asian trading networks.

The centripetal metageography of industrial modernity

The industrial revolution in north-west Europe changed the balance of power between world regions. As such it generated a metageographical moment. New production, armaments, and wealth meant that militarily and economically Europeans could take over and restructure the world to suit their own ends. In effect the Atlantic triangular pattern from the topological metageography was writ large to produce worldwide European control. The victory of the British over imperial China in the first Opium War is the symbolic event that confirms the overturning of the traditional world hierarchy of east over west. The world is no longer a cornucopia that exists to profit from; it is a place to be designed for industrial needs.

The resulting centripetal metageography is shown in Figure 3.2. The pattern is extremely simple: there are just two regions, an industrial core with the rest of the

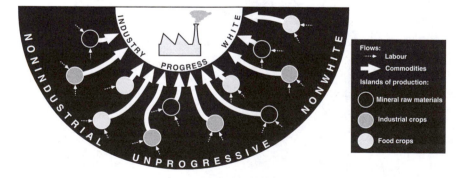

Figure 3.2 The centripetal metageography of industrial modernity.

world supplying its needs. The initial development of industrialization in Europe was based upon local access to coal and iron ores but, beyond these basics, raw materials farther afield were soon needed. This required the creation of new production zones which came in three forms: first, minerals for the engineers (beyond traditional gold and silver to copper, diamonds, nickel, tin, zinc, and later petroleum for fuel and plastics); second, industrial crops for the factories (beyond tobacco to cotton, jute, oil seed, rubber, wool); and third, food crops (beyond sugar to grains, meat, fruits, drinks). Of course, these developments took little heed of existing settlement patterns so that large-scale migrant labor became the norm. Typically, each individual "island of production" existed in a "sea of cheap labor": it was a case of labor in from the outer periphery and commodities out to the industrial core. In this way different parts of the world became specialized in single commodities, so much so that countries came to be commonly associated with particular commodities. Well-known examples are: Argentina and beef, Australia and wool, Brazil and coffee, Bengal and jute, Ceylon and tea, Malaya and rubber, New Zealand and lamb, Northern Rhodesia (Zambia) and copper, South Africa and diamonds, Sudan and cotton, and later, the classic case of the Middle East and oil.

The meaning of this metageography is straightforward: a simple human hierarchy has been constructed defining Europeans as superior to peoples from other parts of the world. Combined with a temporal metahistory of progress, as typified by the Whig theory of history (Taylor 1996a: 133–6), legitimation was provided for both pro-white, scientific racism, often integrated with a pro-temperate climate, scientific environmentalism, and a virulent political imperialism with whites ruling nonwhites. In becoming custodians of the unfortunate non-progressives, imperialists did attempt to make the colonies "pay for themselves," of course, by ensuring that each colony included a specialized island of production. One outcome was the celebrated world map of the British Empire showing pink areas everywhere (Cook 1984). Appearing on the walls of classrooms in all continents, this was the most well-known expression of the centripetal metageography.

The mosaic metageography of consumer modernity

Today the world map found on classroom walls is more universal: it shows the boundaries of all states across the world.[2] With independent states replacing empires the mosaic map is truly a postcolonial artifact. The metageographical moment from which it arose is decolonization. The first half of the twentieth century saw the gradual demise of Europe as the "natural" locus of world leadership. Even at the height of the new imperialism, the emergence of non-European world powers at the turn of the last century in the Pacific – USA and Japan – signaled a changing world hierarchy (Bartlett 1984). Japan, in particular, as the first "non-white/non-European" state to make an independent impact on modern world politics, was symbolically important. Although legitimation of European rule was increasingly challenged, political change was much slower as reflected in the outcome of the two world wars: after World War I the area of European imperium was actually increased whereas the end of World War II marked the critical beginning of its final demise.

The world political map that was formed after 1945 has been identified as fundamentally different from all previous international systems (Hinsley 1982). Under the auspices of the United Nations, the only legitimate wars became wars of defense. In other words boundaries became sacrosanct. Thus, decolonization resulted in new states within colonial boundaries. This boundary maintenance obsession has created a remarkable stability to the world political map: even the later breakup of communist states was kept to existing boundary lines by making new external sovereign boundaries out of old internal provincial boundaries. The result is a world political map which appears almost "natural," where political boundary lines (red) share a similar visual status to coastlines (black), rivers (blue), and mountain ranges (brown) on maps of the world. It is this status that creates the metageography.

Metageographies are not simple political creations: delegitimating war by the United Nations cannot of itself make a geographical imaginary. The mosaic metageography is a product of nationalism. The political boundaries do not just delimit the territories of states; they also define the homelands of nations. Combining the political institution of state with the cultural attributes of nation is a nineteenth-century European political invention that created nationalism as a global movement in the twentieth century. The basic nationalist claim is that nations are the natural divisions of humanity expressed through statehood (Smith 1982). Thus nations typically "find" primeval justification for their presence as nation-states and it is this constructed "timelessness" which promotes the illusion of naturalness. Hence the world political map is no ordinary map. It places every viewer, through her or his nationality, within a spatial framework of humanity.

The United States is, of course, the first postcolonial state. Pre-nationalist in its origins, it has developed a civic nationalism rather than an ethnic nationalism, with its territory deemed to be a sanctuary for "timeless values" (freedom and democracy) rather than for a timeless people. Hence, despite a minor foray into imperialism at the turn of the twentieth century, the United States has been able to portray itself as an anti-imperial champion. After 1945 it was able to harness the implicit democracy within nationalism to create a post-colonial "free world" open for American business. The subsequent "American invasion" was by "multi-national" corporations which viewed the world political map as an array of "national markets" for production and consumption of their goods.[3]

The meaning of this mosaic metageography is more subtle than its forebears. Of course, political independence did not eliminate the old centripetal pattern which lived on in concepts such as "underdevelopment," "Third World," or simply "South." But the mosaic metageography incorporates an inherent sense of equivalence between states that can be expressed as an international egalitarian discourse summed up in the slogan "development for all" (Taylor 1996a: 136–40). In the centripetal metageography the center experiences progress that is inherent in superior Europeans; all other civilizations are deemed to be "stagnant." Under

American hegemony, the concept of progress is replaced by development that is a matter of states, not civilizations. Hence, the promise of Americanization, the American dream as world dream, is promoted as a possibility for any country as long as it employs the correct development policies.[4] Originally this involved "iron and steel works all round" as "underdeveloped countries" attempted to replicate nineteenth-century European development. But Americanization gradually converted new political citizenship into an economic citizenship or "consumption-ship" in the famous "postwar boom" which was, of course, in line with the needs of US multinationals working in a mosaic of national markets.

Embedded statism: living with the last metageography

Living with a metageography is to be largely unconscious of its influence on our thinking and activities. Its spatial premises enter the realm of "common sense" where interrogation is deemed both unnecessary and quite uncalled-for. The mosaic metageography has fixed an embedded statism into our knowledge of the social world. This is as much true of the thinking of social scientists, who are supposed to be critically aware of their environs, as it is of society in general. Certainly there have been important recent statements warning us of the perils of unexamined territorial thinking – Ruggie (1993a) in international relations and Agnew (1993) in political geography are the most influential examples. However, it is my thesis here that these warnings, although valuable correctives, reveal that their authors have not fully understood the intellectual and social depth of the statism which they attack. Quite simply, statism is embedded in our society through the mosaic metageography.

The most common indicator of embedded statism is a collective loss of history producing intellectually lonely conceptualizations. With no past situations for company, the contemporary way of doing things comes to resemble the "natural order" of things. This profound lack of imagination produces a world of no legit-imate alternatives: nation-states are our present and our future. Such ahistorical "common sense" can be found in current controversies on the future of national currencies. In the next section I treat the idea of having a "national currency" as a classic case of embedded statism, revealed as such through recovering its very recent historical construction. This argument stands as a prelude to a more general exploration of the embedded statism at the heart of the idea of there being such a thing as "social science." This section that follows reveals social science as both a creation and creator of states. The very depth of insidious state invasion into the work of those who would understand our social world is the subject of the section "State-istics and analysis." That the facts used to understand states are produced by states – I call them "state-istics" – reveals the incestuous relations between social sciences and nation-states. If ever there was a situation where a "declaration of interest" was called for, then this is it. But there is no call. This arrangement is all "common sense" within the mosaic metageography.

Confusing natural with national: the case of territorial currencies[5]

Today we associate countries with currencies: Russia and its ruble, Britain and its pound sterling, the United States and its dollar, Japan and its yen, and so on.[6] Most people might not know that the currency of Thailand is the baht, but they would expect there to be a specifically Thai money, whatever their notes are called. States and currencies go together, an indicator of sovereignty and for the people a symbol of national identity. In the words of Helleiner (1999: 310) this all seems "quite natural." How else would you expect money to be arranged across the world? In fact, any basic geohistorical consideration of money would soon show that the association of state and currency is quite "unnatural." Money is about transaction, about flows between places; modern states are about territories, about bounding transactions and, truncating flows. Hence Helleiner terms contemporary currencies "territorial currencies," a new form of money. Although each particular currency may have a long pedigree, its specific role today as a national currency is unique to our times. National currencies are part of the process of nation-state building. Since nation-state building progressed at different rates in different places the system of national currencies did not emerge at the same time everywhere. National currencies as we know them today were constructed in the period between the mid-nineteenth century and the first half of the twentieth century. Thus national currencies grew with and reinforced the emergence of the mosaic metageography of which they are archetypal artifacts.

The creation of territorial currencies required two basic geographical shifts against monetary rivals. First, the removal of foreign currencies as legal tender was necessary. For instance, before national currencies, the Mexican dollar ("pieces of eight") operated as a sort of general currency across North America. This, and the use of all other foreign money, was only abolished by the US government in the 1850s. Second, curtailing the issuing of local bank notes, many with only a limited range of recognition, was necessary. Helleiner (1999: 320) reports over 7,000 different notes issued in the United States in the 1850s. After the civil war this was controlled through public licensing of the banks allowed to issue notes, but standardization did not come until the creation of the US Federal Reserve with its note monopoly in 1913. The latter allowed notes to represent a national currency through using propaganda in their design. But an even more important nationalization of money came with the provision of low-denomination coins for the poor. This confirmed "one nation, one money," as Helleiner (1999: 310) so aptly terms it.

There was nothing inevitable about this rise of national currencies. In 1867 the French called a conference to promote a universal currency with the aim of cutting out inefficient transaction costs for international trade. This was during the high water mark of European free trade but international liberalism was soon to be defeated by national protectionism and free trade's demise took with it any hopes of a universal currency – for then, not now. The rise of the eurodollar market in the 1960s marked a return of cosmopolitan currencies and the current establishment of the euro marks another blow to national, although not territorial, currencies. Of course, the fact of relatively recent creation does not make national currencies any less of a populist symbol to be used politically against international financial markets and imposition of transnational currencies. There is depth to this politics precisely because it is integral to the mosaic metageography: national currencies have been embedded in our geographical imaginations.

Social unitarianism, spatial congruence, and the social science trinity[7]

Although there is a long tradition of pondering the relations between people, peoples, and their environments, social science is a relatively recent invention. As an idea it is a product of the nineteenth century but it only came to full fruition as acceptable disciplinary knowledge in universities in the twentieth century. It was constructed on the frontier between the much more established knowledges of natural science and the humanities. Based on the simple premise that it was possible to use the methods of the former to study the subject matter of the latter, social science was developed initially under the pervasive influence of social progress and reform. Originally there was a flowering of new, separate, social knowledges in orthodox political economy, positivist "social science," and liberal political philosophy. This early social science directly reflected the centripetal metageography of its time. Its theories and models were only designed as applicable to "industrial society"; the rest of the world, being nonprogressive, was intellectually uninteresting and left largely to the curiosity of anthropologists, human geographers, Orientalists, and their ilk.

Subsequently political economy has transmuted into economics, positivist "social science" into sociology, and political philosophy into political science. Although building upon European antecedents, this "trinity" of contemporary social sciences was finally created and promoted through American academe in the mid-twentieth century. I use the word trinity here not just in the quantity sense, but also to indicate a collective mutuality. All three disciplines have maintained some of their forebears' broader knowledge claims but essentially they have become more specialized, concentrating on "economy," "civil society," and "politics" respectively. And this is where the mutuality comes in: between them they claim to study all social relations, leaving no intellectual space for other disciplines.

The social science trinity also captured all geographical space for themselves. As the centripetal metageography declined so the old "non-industrial" disciplines such as anthropology began to lose influence in the realms of academe. With the coming of the new mosaic metageography, the trinity was expected to provide knowledge of all countries equally; it obliged by simply transferring knowledge derived from "developed" countries to "underdeveloped" countries. The result was the creation of a variety of modernization and development theories for, but not of, "Third World" states. And, of course, this new social unitarianism extended to time. Taking a particularly narrow view of the science it was importing into the study of human activities, twentieth-century social science at its worst offered timeless and spaceless knowledge based upon universal theory.

But there was a hidden premise in this universal theory. Embedded statism contains the remarkable geographical assumption that all the important human social activities share exactly the same spaces. This spatial congruence can be stated simply: the "society" which sociologists study, the "economy" which economists study, and the "polity" which political scientists study all share a common geographical boundary, that of the state. However abstract the social theory, it is national societies which are described; however quantitative the economic models, it is national economies which are depicted; and however behavioral the political science, it is national governance that is at issue. From a geographical perspective the trinity provides "one scale" social knowledge as directed by the mosaic metageography.

This scale bias can be best shown in studies that deal with more than one state. The norm has been to cultivate comparative analyses rather than relational ones. In comparative sociology or comparative politics, for instance, the UK might be compared to France but with little concern for how the two countries actually relate to one another. For studying relations between states, there has emerged a special discipline of international relations (IR), which in its dominant "realist" manifestation claims to be beyond social science. Its international anarchy assumption proscribes finding relations other than war and preparation for war. Hence the realm of human social activities above the state are either ignored (as in most social science) or deemed to be asocial (as in most realist IR). There is one important exception, which is trade theory in economics. This was central in traditional political economy but it has been marginalized in the more specialist economics discipline where it plays the role of a timeless and placeless mantra for promoting free trade.

There are, of course, many good reasons for developing social knowledge at the scale of the state. The rise of the mosaic metageography is part of the rise of states as the prime actors in social affairs. No longer just remote vehicles for collecting taxes to fight wars, in the nineteenth and twentieth centuries states grew immensely in relating to their citizens, from "cradle to grave" as the saying goes. This is the nationalization of states previously discussed. For instance, national currencies led to central banks through which national governments could pursue macroeconomic policies of demand and/or supply management in the national economy. Clearly any meaningful social knowledge of these times must have the state as a prime subject. But if it is to be a critical social knowledge it must also appreciate that the nation-state is much more than a subject. The fact of embedded statism implies that the trinity has failed in this respect; the state is unexamined at the very heart of the project, that is, with respect to how the knowledge is organized.

State-istics and analysis[8]

With the demise of cosmologies, social knowledge has become fundamentally evidential. Hence the nature of the data is crucial: it helps define the organization of the knowledge. The common term for social data is "statistics," a term which derives directly from the word "state." This is, of course, no accident: large-scale data collection on human activities has its origins in state needs and continues to be dominated by states. Hence my portrayal of it as state-istics.

Like all scientists, social scientists collect data. However, within social science there is little or no "big science" where very large sums of money are committed to solving theoretical problems. "Big science" enables natural scientists to concentrate on developing measurements specifically designed for their theoretical purposes. In social science, most data that are collected relate to small-scale cumulative scientific activity. To get an evidential handle on big issues, researchers normally rely on the statistics that are available, that is to say, those already collected. Collection is carried out usually by a state agency for the particular needs of government policy, not, of course, for social science research. But the problem is much more than the possibility of having to use unsuitable data. Basing "big social science" on state-istics means that the state defines the basic dimensions of the leading-edge, "macro" social research and therefore the framework within which most social research is conducted. This is clearly demonstrated in the dominance of attribute measures over relational measures in social research.

Measurement can take one of two forms: attribute measures on objects or relational measures between objects. The needs of social science and the state diverge at this very starting point. All theory about human social activities is basically about relations between individuals, groups, and other human collectivities. Therefore the data need is for relational measures of flows, connections, linkages, and other less tangible relations. The prime concern of the state for data has always been accounting, finding out the numbers of phenomena within its territory or parts thereof. Thus, as any quick browse through a census volume will confirm, the vast majority of statistics are lists of attributes by place. But social scientists rely on these state-istics and they have used intelligent ways of getting round the attribute bias. For instance, a dynamic without relations is defined commonly in terms of changing attribute measures across a set of census dates. More sophisticated still, relations themselves are redefined as not between objects *per se* but as occurring between the attribute measures on the objects. The whole toolbox of mathematical statistics on covariation has been developed to cover this sleight of hand.

Finally it should be noted that through its association with the state the social science trinity has created another critical dominance, that of analysis over synthesis. There are many reasons for this ranging from the problem-solving reform origins of much social knowledge to simple emulation of supposed "scientific analysis." Certainly analysis became institutionalized through expectations of journal editors and peer referees, and consequently through the reward mechanisms within universities. Analysis also directly reflected the nature of the trinity in being a division of social knowledge eschewing traditional social synthesis. The more synthetic disciplines such as human geography, were those that declined with the centripetal metageography. In fact, in order for the minor disciplines to survive, synthesis had to be abandoned and analysis, in the form of the trinity, internalized into their disciplinary organizations. Thus the adjectives "social," "economic," and "political" have been added to anthropology, geography, and even history in the twentieth century to define new "subdisciplines" to guard against the danger of resurgent synthesis. The subdisciplines have become vehicles of analysis and, as such, contributed, albeit in a minor way, to constructing the unitarian modernization and development models thus betraying their disciplinary origins. Embedded statism works in mysterious ways, but it is not universal. Dependent on the mosaic metageography, the trinity's demise will be nigh with the next metageographical moment.

Contemporary globalization as a new metageographical moment

A metageographical moment defines a transition in our collective geographical imagination. It marks the disintegration of an existing metageography and provides opportunities to create a new metageography. It is not, of course, instantaneous, but there should be a clear-cut change in the way the world is viewed and interpreted. Thus, if we are considering the present as a metageographical moment, we should be searching for evidence of an erosion of embedded statism, of a serious decline in acceptance of the state as the "natural" locus of power across the gamut of human social activities. At even the most cursory level of consideration, globalization seems to fit the bill as a metageographical moment.

At its heart most of the debate about globalization has been concerned with the future of the state. For instance, David Held and his colleagues (1999: 2–10) align positions on globalization along a spectrum with the "hyperglobalists" at one end and the "skeptics" at the other. The former define a "global age" and the end of the state, the latter define an enhanced "internationalization" with states remaining as key actors within regional blocs. In between are the "transformationalists" who accept the unprecedented levels of global interconnectedness but view this as transforming state power not eliminating it. Part of the problem with this argument is that the debate was set by the hyperglobalists which has produced a "global versus state" agenda. The transformationalists try to free themselves from this simple opposition but in doing so they deal more with the transformation of the state than with global transformation itself (Taylor 2000). In contrast, my starting point is the question of the geographical scale at which human social activities take place.

Alternative spaces

There is one thing all positions in the debate are agreed upon: there have been changes in the pattern of geographical scales at which human social activities are organized. To be sure the degree of change is in dispute but even the skeptics challenge the simple one-scale pattern of human organization ensconced in the mosaic metageography. Recognizing new internationalization and the future importance of regional blocs is a long way from leaving the "international sphere" to the asocial study of international relations. This focus on supranational institutions, which is shared by the transformationalists, can be interpreted in two different ways. Either there is a new multi-scalar organization of human social activities where the state remains an important, perhaps even the most important, scale, or the new regional institutions, with perhaps the European Union leading the way, are producing a new, larger, regional scale of human social organization. The latter would create a new mosaic geography with a reduced number of "pieces," reversing the proliferation of states which characterized the twentieth century. Whichever position is taken, however, the thinking remains territorialist in nature with boundaries continuing to feature prominently. This is a continuation of the boundary obsession found at the heart of the mosaic metageography. Hence depicting globalization as supranational suggests a relatively moderate transition in a contemporary metageographical moment.

Instead of supranational institutions, I think it more efficacious to focus on the transnational processes within globalization. Boundaries are about truncating flows, and this is precisely where states are being challenged because new technologies have made policing borders more difficult than ever before. The worldwide web is, in old terminology, a "smuggler's charter." This is not to argue the hyperglobalist position of a "borderless world," but it does mean that transnational processes can undermine the mosaic metageography much more completely than supranational institutions.

The best conceptualization of this change comes from Castells (1996) in his identification of a contemporary "network society." He contrasts the "space of flows" which constitutes the latter with the "space of places" which proceeded it. According to Castells, before the 1970s society was organized territorially, as reflected in the mosaic metageography, with agriculture, industry, and services based in local and national economies. All this changes with the coming of the "informational age" where new enabling technologies combining communications and computers provide the potential for new transnational projections of power. This was first recognized in the early 1970s as multinational corporations were found to have "global reach" and economic clout greater than many individual countries (Barnet and Muller 1974). At about the same time the international financial market "took off" so that by the 1980s it dwarfed all national finances (see the discussion by Peterson, this volume). Government control of finances sealed by the institution of central banks was put back into doubt. The end result is a global space of flows in an economy where success is based on access to information. This interpretation of globalization is self-evidently an extremely radical challenge to the material basis of the mosaic metageography.

While using Castells's argument to categorize contemporary globalization we do not have to share his geohistory. As Arrighi (1994) has clearly shown, international financial flows transcending states have been cyclical phenomena in the capitalist world-economy. Hence critical systemic "spaces of flows" precede the 1970s. Interestingly, Arrighi suggests that Castells misses earlier spaces of flows because he is a victim of embedded statism in his treatment of pre-1970 spaces.[9] For Arrighi, spaces of places and spaces of flows have developed simultaneously in the modern world-system although they vary in relative importance at different times. This is, of course, what the sequence of metageographies I described previously suggests. The initial topological metageography clearly represents a space of flows; the centripetal metageography describes a mixture of the two types of space; and the mosaic metageography is a space of places. Returning to Castells, it would seem that globalization has reversed this metageographical trend from a more territorial geographical imaginary back to a space of flows.

World cities in a network metageography?

For Castells (1996: 415) world cities constitute the "most direct illustration" of the nodes and hubs in his global space of flows. Of course, it has always been the nature of cities to be the nodes in networks of flows. Hence, we have to ask again whether Castells's identification of a unique present, with world cities operating in a "global network" of cities (380), is indeed singular. Certainly there have been large-scale networks of ports which long predate the modern world-system and which form the spatial organization of the capitalism that Gills identifies (this volume). The emergence of the modern world-system produced its own port network as depicted in the topological metageography. "Atlantic Europe" in Figure 3.1, for instance, is constituted of the great port cities of Amsterdam, London, Bordeaux, Lisbon, Seville, Bristol, Rotterdam, Le Havre, and so on. Furthermore, there have been great international financial centers in the modern world-system – Arrighi (1994) lists Genoa, Antwerp, Amsterdam, London, and New York in chronological order. For Braudel (1984) these were "world-cities" in the sense of being the leading city of their respective eras with system-wide influences. Today, following the work of Sassen (1991), it is usual to identify three "global cities" – London, New York, and Tokyo – as leading world cities. Castells places them at the top of his hierarchy (380) for example. This putative "shared leadership" is not necessarily unusual since singular world-city leadership historically declines in line with hegemonic cycles. But the global spread of leading cities, straddling the world's time zones in a financial market that never closes, does represent a new scale of financial activity. But does this globalization represent a genuinely new urban geography.

I am going to answer this question positively because the economic restructuring associated with globalization has enhanced the role of cities to an extraordinary degree. The informational age has favored the growth of economic sectors where knowledge (i.e. how you use information) is a key component of production (see discussion of the rise of services by Peterson, Chapter 2 this volume). In advanced service sectors, of course, knowledge is the product. Hence the traditional role of cities as "service centers" has meant that the major cities that provide corporate services have prospered outstandingly with globalization. These advanced producer services (such as accountancy, advertising, banking/finance, insurance, management consultancy, law, etc.) have "gone global." Initially, this locational expansion was necessary to serve multinational corporation customers. Subsequently, service firms developed their own global strategies. Making full use of the enabling communication technologies, advanced producer service firms themselves created a cutting-edge global industry. Hence, service firms, traditionally associated with a client base in a single city, have become global corporations. But to stay at the cutting edge, they have to be located where large quantities of the most up-to-date information intersect with clusters of advanced "professional/creative" expertise to make new customized knowledge products (Sassen 1991). This means that to be a successful player in the field, a global service firm has to have an array of offices in world cities across the globe.

Collectively, the many global firms with multi-city networks of offices have produced the contemporary world city network (Taylor 2001). The Globalization and World Cities (GaWC) research team at Loughborough University has been experimenting with first, how to identify world cities and second, how to locate them in a world city network. Identification was carried out using data on seventy-one service firms that created an inventory of fifty-five world cities at three levels of service provision; ten alpha world cities (including Sassen's three "global cities"), ten beta world cities, and thirty-five gamma world cities (Beaverstock *et al.* 1999). The distribution of these cities shows three distinct clusters centered on northern America, western Europe, and Pacific Asia: globalization is certainly not an even geographical process. Rather than simple location, however, emphasis in a network society should be on the connections between cities. In Figure 3.3 a "global corporate service space" has been constructed by computing the connections between cities among forty-six major service firms with offices in more

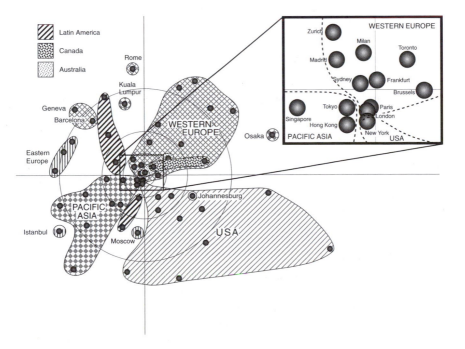

Figure 3.3 A putative future network metageography of cities.

than fifteen cities. Inverting similarities in profiles of firms between pairs of cities to produce "functional distances" (i.e. the more similar two cities are, the smaller the "corporate service distance" between them), enables us to use multidimensional scaling to define the new space (Taylor *et al.* 2001). As Figure 3.3 shows, the space is highly centric in nature with the major alpha cities at the center and lesser world cities relegated to a periphery. However, there is also a distinctive regional pattern in which the three main globalization arenas are easily discernable. This new world map represents a unique "visualization" of the modern world-system as a network of cities linked together in a mixture of hierarchy and regionality.

We come now to the question posed in the title of this section: can/will the world city network constitute a new metageography in keeping with contemporary globalization? The answer to "can" is obviously yes. With the disintegration of the mosaic metageography as described earlier, the opportunity exists for the making of an alternative collective geographical imagination. But this is not a simple and quick switch. In answer to "will" our confidence must be highly circumscribed. As things stand at the moment, cities appear to be the most likely candidates to threaten the primacy of states as the building blocks of a spatial framework of the world. As well as the economic trends described above, political developments are enhancing the status of cities. Most notable is the widespread promotion and adoption of "strong mayor" forms of city government. Election to such posts may be instrumental in the disintegration of national party systems. But there is, as yet, little or no evidence of a transfer of primary allegiance or identity from state to city. Figure 3.3 is presented as merely indicative of the possibility of a new network metageography.

Transdisciplinary social science

Networks and boundaries are uneasy bedfellows and therefore we can expect the scope of great cities to be truncated by the world of boundaries created by nation-states. But the mosaic metageography has created an additional penalty: cities have been major victims of embedded statism. In urban studies, relations between cities are usually conceptualized as "national city systems" or "national urban hierarchies." In other words, relations are modeled as stopping at the state border: for instance New York is conceived as an American city and not a world-city. Of course, given the nature of state-istics, even these truncated intercity relations usually remain at the conceptual level only; measures of flows, connections, or linkages are conspicuously missing. Studies of cities are usually comparative and focus on demographics because that is what census data provide: this is what states need to know in their accounting.

Focusing on the population sizes of cities has generated a tradition of research on "urbanization" which is patently anticity in perspective. Cities are portrayed as problems for their geographical neighbors rather than as the economic and cultural opportunities that they are in reality. At the global level this has led to a focus on large megacities and the problems they pose. Of course, "big cities" are easily identified. All that is needed is a population threshold and census figures from the appropriate countries (actually the data are brought together in UN publications). In contrast, just try to find meaningful data on relations between London and New York, the two leading world cities. There are no, and I would go as far as to say there *can* be no, state-istics on such important information; the GaWC work described above is largely about trying to construct such intercity measures. Official data never enter the equation.

This brief indictment of the treatment of cities through embedded statism means that we cannot expect the trinity of social sciences to have made much contribution to the idea of cities as the crossroads of society. Within the social sciences, cities mainly constitute problems, with much use made of attribute measures in the "census tract" research tradition. But there is a positive side to urban studies. As an alternative way of organizing social knowledge, this type of area study shows potential for a more synthetic approach – seeing the city as a whole (albeit shorn of its external relations). A similar effect is visible in regional area studies where, for instance, an Africanist cannot be narrowly political or economic or social. However, in practice, these fields of study never achieved the prominence or status of the trinity disciplines. Throughout the life of the mosaic metageography, the domination of the trinity in social knowledge was not in doubt: the spatial entity was the nation-state and the methods were analytical. But how far is the trinity dependent on embedded statism? How will it fare as the latter is eroded?

The trinity has not been able to handle globalization very well (Taylor 1996b). But globalization has hardly been neglected in social research. What has happened is that there has been a flowering of transdisciplinary studies that have coped quite well in the new circumstances. The field of cultural studies is a typical example. With its roots in traditional anthropology, it has developed on the interface between the humanities and social sciences to become one of the most vibrant sources of ideas about globalization. Notice that I have referred to it as a "field" rather than as a discipline. In studying globalization, narrow specialization, especially with theory embedded in statism, is a disadvantage for understanding the new processes. Another field is business studies. While the discipline of economics continues to tell us about national economies (or "the economy" as they would refer to it), business schools across all continents have emerged from their "management" origins to provide eclectic research agendas on the world economy and globalization.

The emergence of IPE (international political economy) out of IR is particularly instructive in this context. Led by Susan Strange (1988) and her campaign against narrow disciplinary approaches,[10] it became clear to a new school of researchers that international politics and international business could not sensibly be studied in isolation from each other. Obviously boosted by the end of the Cold War and the more transparent nature of international economic competition in the 1990s, nevertheless the pioneers of this school predate this change with their initial "states and markets" approach. Although keeping the term "international" in its title, IPE has become a very heterodox body of knowledge. As well as the original school largely derived from IR, there has been a revival of pre-embedded statism knowledge such as institutional economics (e.g. on the social constitution of markets) and the creation of new knowledges such as world-systems analysis (e.g. on global commodity chain analysis and world cities) which all can find a place under this intellectual umbrella. There is a new common sense: heterodoxy and eclectism are necessary in new circumstances where no discipline can claim a monopoly of social knowledge. As both Peterson and Gills (this volume) affirm from very different starting points, transdisciplinary knowledge is required to study transnational processes.

Notes

1 My favorite example of the overpowering influence of a metageography comes in nature books where animals and plants are "nationalized" as in "British Trees" or "British Insects." This represents the power of what I call below a mosaic metageography based upon nation-states. There are even books on "British Birds" although many are migratory and spend much of the year either far north or far south of Britain.
2 Since this is the metageography with which all readers will have grown up, and continue to carry around in their heads, unlike the previous cases I have no need to use a figure to show this geographical imaginary.
3 For elaborations on this, see Slater and Taylor (1999).
4 This is, of course, the message of Rostow's (1960) most famous development ladder in a "non-communist manifesto."
5 This section draws heavily on the argument in Helleiner (1999).
6 Of course, this situation has been recently highlighted by the creation of the euro replacing national currencies in most of the EU. In the resistance to this move, critics have betrayed a remarkable statism in their argument that their territory (e.g. the UK) needs flexibility in its fiscal management while omitting to notice its own fiscal penalties imposed on subregions (e.g. the north of England where extra unemployment is deemed necessary to dampen inflation in the south of England).
7 This section draws from and builds upon Taylor (1996b, 2000).
8 This section draws from and builds upon Taylor (1997b).
9 Arrighi does not use the phrase "embedded statism" but identifies it clearly as "the bias of our conceptual equipment in favour of space-of-places that defines the process of state formation" (1994: 84).
10 She attempts to subvert "the exclusivity of the 'disciplines' and sub-disciplines of social science .... [because] ... our times no longer allow us the comfort of separatist specialisation in the social sciences, and ... the attempt has to be made at synthesis and blending ..." (Strange 1996: xv–xvi).

4 Creating global hegemony
Culture and the market

Barbara Jenkins

Introduction

The deconstruction of realist notions of power in the international relations literature led to alternative considerations of how global power is established and spread. Amongst these critical approaches, theories based on Gramsci's notion of hegemony are particularly persuasive in their explanations of how global capitalism became dominant and naturalized as a system of power (Cox 1987; Gill 1993; Mittelman 1996). According to these accounts, global politics take place in the context of a world order that is in part constructed and naturalized by ideas and ideologies. The current world order, characterized by Robert Cox as Pax Americana, is constituted on the basis of a hegemonic liberal economic discourse that privileges the free movement of goods, money, and investment across borders. Although couched in terms of openness, free trade, and deregulation, this ideology in fact benefits the United States disproportionately because of the predominance of US multinationals and banks in the global economy. In addition to the US government, various international institutions such as the International Monetary Fund (IMF), the World Bank, and the World Trade Organization (WTO) also reinforce neoliberal economic ideology. OECD countries, with the United States exerting hegemonic dominance, finance and control these ostensibly "international" organizations.

Stephen Gill (1988) amplifies Cox's ideas by positing the formation of a transnational bourgeoisie, exemplified by the Trilateral Commission, which orchestrates and reinforces the spread of Pax Americana. Both Gill's and Cox's accounts describe a class-based, capitalist world order structured by the mode of production. Specific actors may construct world orders in highly ideological terms, but such orders are ultimately forged on the basis of a particular mode of production, in the case of Pax Americana, one based on the internationalization of production processes.

Although these approaches provide essential insights into the formation of a kind of transnational rule outside the realm of raw power politics, they lack a cultural dimension. Despite their heavy reliance on the work of Antonio Gramsci, who placed particular emphasis on the role of cultural institutions in embedding capitalism in social practices, none of these interpretations makes reference to cultural explanations of power. Without denying the important role that exchange relations and class relations play as regulators of economic activity, however, I would like to underscore Pierre Bourdieu's point that while power in a capitalist society may ultimately be economic, the form it takes, or the way it is lived, is cultural.[1] Thus, I accept the importance of these critical studies, but would like to expand their insights by looking at how culture perpetuates, reinforces, and legitimates global capitalism. What is the culture of this world order? How is it lived on a day-to-day basis? Without going so far as to argue that there is a global culture, I will look at various approaches from the Cultural Studies literature that provide key insights into a provisional answer to these questions. What follows is not a theory of global culture but rather an eclectic sampling of some of the arguments Cultural Studies has to offer the study of International Political Economy (IPE). I hope that this survey will spark more work on the role of culture in constructing world order and more detailed studies of some of the specific subjects discussed below.

I divide the chapter into three parts with discrete but interrelated themes. The first section takes a decentered look at the way culture reinforces and perpetuates power by focusing on the role of culture in constructing and maintaining relations of inequality. The next section borrows from discussions of the impact of capitalist commodification on culture and society in a preliminary examination of how market culture shapes global consumption and the acceptance of global capitalism. Finally, in an attempt to reassert the importance of human agency, the last section looks at the role of culture in resisting hegemonic discourses. I hope this essay illustrates some of the many ways to include culture in considerations of world order.

Culture and inequality

Capitalism and difference

The smooth functioning of global capitalism relies on relations of inequality and difference. For example, the devaluation of women's work and the fact that, on average, women are paid considerably less than men is based on the idea that a woman's place is in the home looking after her family, and that this does not constitute productive "work" (so she does not have to be paid). Yet women's contributions to the everyday coherence of the home and family are essential to an economic system that requires people to go out and sell their labor and thus constitute a labor force. Whether or not she is employed outside the home, it is the woman's job to organize domestic work, child-rearing, childcare arrangements, and family consumption. This not only allows for social stability, but also performs a key role in stabilizing the supply of labor and demand for consumer goods (Rose 1996: 37). Of course, many women do work outside the home, but the assumption that women should remain in the private realm of the home and not operate in the public realm of "work" allows for an essential twist of logic once a woman does enter the workforce. Since women belong in the home, their entry into the workforce means they are secondary wage earners and therefore need not be paid at the same rate as men. In an age of supposed sexual equality, this translates into a generalized practice where society frequently devalues jobs performed by women because, after all, women are not supposed to be in the workforce to begin with so what they are doing cannot be important. For women, the economic cost of these ideas is enormous. North American women are paid about 70 percent of the average male salary.

This twist of logic is also the economic basis of a considerable proportion of global production. Women are frequently the primary employees in export processing zones in industrializing countries, for example. The consumer electronics industry, microelectronics, and textile and clothing firms all depend on cheap female labor in industrializing countries for their profitable functioning (Elson and Pearson 1981). In industrialized countries, the importance of maintaining global competitiveness through lower wages, benefits, and social overhead particularly affects women as they are pushed into part-time employment and low paying support jobs in the rapidly growing service industries that are considered women's work.

Global capitalism also depends on differences based on race. The most obvious example is the process of colonialism; clearly, it was necessary for Europeans to believe that they were superior to the nonwhites they were colonizing in order to legitimate their domination. In many countries, such as Jamaica or Argentina, colonizers wiped out most of the indigenous population, evidence of the disregard colonizing societies held for nonwhite life. Even die-hard liberals such as John Stuart Mill believed that most nonwhite nations were uncivilized and therefore incapable of self-government. Mill argued "The sacred duties which civilized nations owe to the independence and nationality of each other are not binding towards those to whom nationality and independence are a certain evil, or at best a questionable goal" (quoted in Said 1993: 96). These ideas continue in a more subtle manner under neocolonialism. Multinationals base their labor-intensive operations offshore ostensibly because wages are low, but the often horrific working conditions in these factories also lower costs. How can the employment of children or disregard for employee safety and health be justified in offshore operations when these practices are not tolerated in the industrialized west? This double standard in working conditions reflects a lack of concern for the lives of the people who work in these offshore factories.

Inequality on the basis of gender and race overlaps with inequality based on class. Clearly, for capitalism to run smoothly there must be widespread acceptance of the "fact" that economic inequalities are somehow natural, that social and political inequalities between rich and poor are an inevitable and normal aspect of our way of living. The fact that the poor in global capitalism are disproportionately women and/or nonwhite indicates that these relationships reinforce one another and interact in complex ways. Obviously, not all women or nonwhites are poor and oppressed and not all white men are oppressors. As systems of inequality overlap, various permutations occur which obfuscate clear delineations between the racial, gender, and class differences I emphasize. Nonetheless, as I show in the examples to follow, conditions persistently reinforce differences on a daily basis in our everyday lives. And on a daily basis, businesses profit from these inequalities because they lower the costs of production.

Since global capitalism thrives on and requires these inequalities, examining how and why inequalities become accepted is integral to understanding how world order is constructed. Obviously, someone is exerting noncoercive power – no one holds bombs and rockets over anyone's head, and there is no global police force patrolling to catch the noncompliant. People, including those who are oppressed, accept the inequities at the core of the world capitalist system because such inequalities seem normal, natural, and in Gramsci's words, "common sense." Gramsci addressed precisely these factors in his study of how Italian capitalism remained hegemonic. He examined the manner in which schools, churches, and other organizations of civil society reinforced and organized class inequities. His key contribution was to realize that a true socialist revolution had to be fought through making changes in civil society and not solely on the basis of armed conflict.

One can expand Gramsci's analysis of power by examining Michel Foucault's (1991) notion of *governmentality*. Foucault argued that rather than relying on the exertion of power from a central organization such as the state, the replication of power happens in a more decentered, yet equally potent way. Everyday encounters enforce various "codes of conduct" that promote the smooth functioning of capitalism. I noted above that the family is one social form that enforces social order outside the direct influence of the state, but numerous other examples exist. In terms of economic governance, for example, the establishment of various accounting rules and practices and forms of financial regulation are key to establishing order in the apparently disorganized realm of competitive capitalism. On the international level, Sinclair (1994) examines how credit-rating agencies restrict and shape state economic policies to conform to the dictates of neoliberal economic principles.

As Rose (1996: 37–8) argues, "The strategies of regulation that have made up our modern experience of 'power' are assembled into complexes that connect up forces and institutions deemed 'political' with apparatuses that shape and manage individual and collective conduct in relation to norms and objectives but yet are constituted as 'non-political'." Many other examples of the role of decentered organization in the exertion of power internationally await to be discovered. It is in this sense that culture becomes an essential consideration as a form of decentered political regulation.

Sinclair (1994) illuminates how such decentered forms of regulation operate on the international level. He examines how credit-rating agencies restrict and shape state economic policies to conform to the dictates of neoliberal economic principles. Many other examples of the role of decentered organization in the exertion of power internationally await to be discovered. It is in this sense that culture becomes an essential consideration as a form of decentered political regulation.

Producing art, reproducing domination

Integrating culture into arguments based on Gramscian hegemony or Foucault's notion of governmentality broadens and deepens explanations of the spread and acceptance of global power. Cultural production strongly reinforces the inequities that support global capitalism and contributes to common sense understandings of the "natural" order of the world. In what follows, I give numerous examples of how this occurs in an attempt to provide a range of cases from various forms of cultural production. The result is only a cursory survey of the relationship between culture and inequality – most of the examples are drawn from book-length studies and all deserve further study and investigation. My intent is to point to some of the ways in which culture contributes to world order.

Beginning with the world of popular culture, musicologist Timothy Taylor argues that the growing popularity of "World Beat Music" contributes to politically constructed conceptions of the "First" and "Third" worlds, thereby naturalizing them and reinforcing common sense understandings of global hierarchies. In the 1980s, it became a trend for well-known pop artists such as Peter Gabriel and Paul Simon to integrate music from Africa and South America into their work. Albums such as Simon's *Rhythm of the Saints* and *Graceland* or Gabriel's *Us* included collaborations with non-Western musical artists such as Youssou N'Dour and Ladysmith Black Mambazo. These albums were instant commercial successes that brought attention and recording contracts to the non-Western artists involved. Despite this success, critics took both Simon and Gabriel to task for using these musicians to forward their own musical careers and for appropriating the cultural expressions of people who use music as an antidote to racism or poverty or to assert their own identity.

The Western musicians, taken aback by these criticisms, denied any wrongdoing or attempt to appropriate. In Simon's words, "Culture flows like water. It isn't something that can just be cut off" (Taylor 1997: 22). Despite Simon's efforts to publicize non-Western music, his claims are highly political and distinctly cultural. While the music of the South African musicians that he is referring to seems to "flow like water," Simon's does not because it is protected by copyright and the full force of the law and no one is allowed to borrow it without a license. This in turn reflects more generalized Western conceptions of non-Western music: while Western music is perceived as a conscious cultural construction involving high technology and the deliberate integration of the fragments of modern global society, non-Western music is conceived as "natural," primitive, and "authentic." Indeed, the exotic, primitive, and implicitly sexual rhythms of non-Western music constitute its basic appeal in the West. It is an antidote to the highly technical, constructed rhythms of rock. This nature/culture dichotomy is also a familiar element in feminist analysis because it is a distinction that is integral to the creation and distinction of gender roles. Implicit in this dichotomy are the rights, superiority, and willfulness associated with "rational" cultural activity as opposed to the beauty, mystery, and passiveness of the "natural."

Another pervasive but relatively unnoticed example of how culture perpetuates common sense acceptance of inequality is the "built environment" and the way architecture and urban planning subtly reinforce hegemonic relations of domination. As I have argued elsewhere, architecture was a key element of the colonial programs of the British and the French both to assert power and attempt to assuage the resentment of those who were colonized by incorporating local motifs and designs into new buildings (Jenkins 1999). Gwendolyn Wright, for example, describes attempts by French colonial governments in Algeria and Vietnam to counterpose a rational, technical, "civilized" West with a primitive, ornate, mysterious non-West. Thus, newly built sections of colonial towns hosted modern buildings and straight, tree-lined streets intended to illustrate the superior culture of the colonizers (Wright 1991). Architects often decorated colonial buildings with local symbols and motifs in order to appeal to the tastes of the colonized and make the buildings appear to serve their interests. Similarly, Thomas Metcalf argues in his analysis of the British Raj in India that in order to rule it was necessary to "know" the Other. Labeling Indian architectural styles was an integral element of the more general classification of Indian culture by British academics. British historians assigned architectural classifications according to religious lines as "Hindoo" or "Saracenic," then later developed a distinctive "Indo-Saracenic" classification combining elements from each. Drawing the outlines of Indian architectural heritage as if choosing colors from a palette, the British became "the self-proclaimed master[s] of Indian culture" (Metcalf 1989).

In North America, municipal zoning laws and building codes shape architecture and urban planning to divide classes geographically and keep "undesirables" out. Mike Davis (1992), for example, describes a spatial apartheid in Los Angeles created by restricting building in the financial district to upper- and middle-class housing and commercial uses and dividing this area from the downtown core by a highway. Generally, one need think only of the organization of any North American town: there are "good" neighborhoods and "bad" neighborhoods designating class and/or racial divisions, flashy skyscrapers or prominent commercial buildings indicating corporate power, and a town hall in the center of town demarcating local political power.

Spatial relations also reinforce gender differences. As urban areas divided into a business core and residential suburbs, the roles of women within the private realm of the home became spatially confined. Elizabeth Wilson (1991) goes so far as to argue that much urban planning since the nineteenth century sought to control and subvert female sexuality by keeping "good" women safe and super-vised in suburban homes while "wicked" women such as prostitutes inhabited the city core. In Victorian times, this confinement reached extremes, as nineteenth-century morality prohibited women from leaving their homes alone and praised the respected "angel of the house" who eschewed worldly interests and devoted her life to looking after home, husband, and children. In the acceptable Victorian bourgeois household, it was the husband's duty to support the family. Women in the household played only a "service" function, as opposed to a "productive" one (Roberts 1990). The legacy of this attitude continues today as women leave the home to enter the outside workforce. They tend to take on the lower paying service jobs that are largely similar to the work women provide in the home. Indeed as I noted earlier, the assumption that women's labor is worth less derives largely from the assumption that a woman's place is in the home and her role in the workforce is only as a secondary wage earner.

Another example of the influence of culture on gender differences is the portrayal of women as objectified, passive recipients of male attention in oil paintings, a centuries-old practice most clearly evident in the painting of "nudes." As John Berger (1972) points out, the many thousands of oil paintings of nudes that exist are almost exclusively of women; with few exceptions, they portray women as aware of being viewed by a male spectator, and often conniving in their own treatment as objects. Similarly, Carol Duncan notes how so-called "protest art" such as Cubism and Abstract Expressionism in painting, or Modernism and Deconstructivism in architecture, expresses the singularly male, often macho mystique of the avant-garde. Duncan (1993) remarks that a display at the Museum of Modern Art (MoMA) in New York, dedicated to illustrating the revolutionary styles and statements of twentieth-century artists, features two paintings notable for their misogynist and pornographic content. "Les Demoiselles d'Avignon" by Picasso and "Woman I" by Willem de Kooning are the first two paintings in the exhibit, chosen because they exemplify revolutionary contributions to modern style. Both paintings, however, portray women as gorgons and whores, exposing their genitalia to reveal their "primitive sexuality" to an implicit male viewer. Duncan argues that art critics review these paintings as examples of advances in technique while remaining silent about the misogynist portrayals of women so common in avant-garde works. The result is a body of art that assumes male audience, while relegating women in the museum to the "visitor's gallery." Duncan's description of MoMA's art displays led her to a broader questioning of the role of the museum in reproducing power. Specifically, she was concerned with the way that art museums "offer up values and beliefs – about social, sexual, and political identity – in the form of vivid and direct experience" (Duncan 1995: 2). Her description of gender values is part of a broader analysis of the political and ideological role of the art museum. In this regard, her work was preceded by Bourdieu and Alain Darbel, who argued more narrowly that art museums were integral to class identity, giving upper-class visitors a sense of superiority and of rightfully belonging in that atmosphere because they "understood" the art. Conversely, working-class visitors felt intimidated, as if they were visiting a sacred site or church (Bourdieu and Darbel 1969). Moving beyond class, Daniel Sherman and Irit Rogoff (1994) further argued that the classification integral to museum displays conveys meanings for objects and puts them in a context, often in some constructed discursive field such as "the nation" or "the community" or "the primitive." Obviously, this classification and contextualization, and their consumption by a public audience, constitute a discourse in itself. This process takes on global political significance when one considers the role of anthropological museums describing "primitive" peoples or societies, such as the legitimation of colonialism implicit when the British Museum displays the Elgin marbles "rescued" from unappreciative natives. In sum, although ostensibly merely displaying art or artifacts, the museum organizes viewing in a highly constructed way, providing the viewer with political messages portrayed as apolitical "art."

Duncan's analysis of the museum dovetails with Nikolas Rose's argument about governmentality mentioned above. It is easy to take for granted the various ways in which institutions such as museums embody what Rose (1996: 42) refers to as "particular conceptions of the objects to be governed – nation, population, economy, society, community – and the subjects to be governed – citizens, subjects, individuals." Along these lines, Duncan argues that museums were key to building a sense of who was a citizen as well as sensibilities about class differences that quickly developed a transnational appeal.

In her analysis of the Louvre, Duncan (1995) argued that the art museum prompted visitors to assume a new ritual identity and perform a new ritual role. By the nineteenth century the Louvre, which French rulers converted from a royal palace to a public museum after the revolution, confirmed to its bourgeois visitors their enlightenment in being able to enjoy such "civilized" pleasures. The museum signified a kind of social distinction because the art it contained was a symbol and source of both moral and spiritual superiority. Furthermore, because the museum featured national works of "genius," which in turn were sponsored by the state, the bourgeois (male) citizen found a common culture that united him with other French male citizens. At the time, the Louvre organized works of art chronologically and nationally to illustrate the course of "genius" in individuals and nations, allowing the visitor to reenact that history and thereby "know him-self as a citizen of history's most civilized and advanced nation-state" (Duncan 1995: 27). The museum itself embodied the idea of citizenship and the state and represented the evolved and civilized culture of national citizens in a rationally organized and clearly labeled manner, enabling the citizen–state relationship to appear in material form before the viewer's eyes (Duncan 1995: 26).

The Louvre in turn served as a model for other national galleries and museums, and a series of them sprang up across Europe and the United States. By 1825, almost every Western capital had one, prompting Duncan(1995) to argue that although shaped by national historical conditions, these museums belong to a larger, international history of bourgeois culture. Such museums appeared just at the moment when the bourgeois state was redefining public space, reflecting the similar ideological benefits such spaces provided to various Western bourgeoisies (Duncan 1995: 21–47). Drawing from Gill's (1988) argument mentioned above one can point out that the rapid spread of art museums from France to Germany to London then to Chicago and New York indicates the development of a transnational bourgeois "taste" which reinforced common bonds and superiorities across borders. In a cultural sense, it is the beginning of a process equivalent to what both Cox (1987) and Gill (1993) describe in economic terms: the growth of a transnational bourgeoisie which is essential to the spread and hegemonic dominance of contemporary global capitalism.

In a more technical sense, claims about transnational bourgeois taste parallel arguments about governmentality. For hundreds of years, elites have considered the concept of taste, particularly as it relates to "good design," as an important form of governing individual behavior. The idea that there is a connection between good design and good society dates back to ancient times, but it is particularly important in the work of David Hume, Joseph Addison, Adam Smith, John Ruskin, and William Morris. In the twentieth century, designers such as Nikolaus Pevsner (Britain), Adolf Loos (Austria), and Le Corbusier (France) argued that good modern design was of vital concern to the state because it contributed to personal and social hygiene and "stimulated the intellectual and spiritual faculties while keeping at bay all the escapist, narcotic and sensationalist tendencies of modern life which discouraged a serious-minded approach to citizenship" (Lubbock 1995: 322). Jules Lubbock shows how designers in post-World War II Britain exerted exceptional influence by actually converting modernist ideas about good design into policy. Government-built housing in the post-war period displayed all the contemporary ideas of "good design": designs intended to banish the disorder and bad taste of working-class people and replace them with clean, orderly furniture and rationally designed housing. Whether it was successful or not, this policy linking good design and good behavior was a concerted attempt to govern people through supposedly technical and apolitical means.

Summary

This somewhat eclectic selection of examples of decentered cultural power may not appear to constitute a fundamental source of power individually. Piled on top of one another, bombarding the individual on a daily basis, however, these more localized constructions of power are critical to maintaining global capitalism because they reinforce socially constructed notions of gender, class, and race that are critical to the smooth functioning of capitalist markets. Without the wide-spread attitude supporting the convention that women should be paid less than men because they are merely provisional members of the labor force, for example, it would be difficult for export-processing zones to reap the massive profits which have spread their popularity, or for much of the service industry in advanced industrial states to thrive. Similarly, without some notion of racial inferiority or superiority, or an understanding of the difference between the "First" and "Third" Worlds, how could those in the West accept reports of Western multi-national corporations (MNCs) blithely ignoring safety and environmental standards that result in massive death tolls such as at Bhopal, India, or relying on substandard working conditions in offshore factories? These standard operating procedures create cost-savings critical to the profitability of the MNCs that make globalization tick. Cultural production contributes to the smooth functioning of the market by reinforcing socially constructed notions of gender, global postcolonial relationships, class, and race.

Before moving on to a more general discussion of the relationship between cultural power and markets, I think it is important to consider briefly a slightly different question: how might hierarchies in the international political economy affect local culture? Stuart Hall (1997) argues, for example, that there is a strong correlation between distinct national cultures and a state's position in the inter-national political economy. The quality of "Englishness" when Britain was at its peak of commercial and military power, for example, was that of a strongly centered, highly exclusivist, and exclusionary identity. Other countries, whether France, Russia, or colonized India, were firmly placed and represented by the

"English eye" – a male eye, that is – firmly grounded in the masculine concept of the English gentleman. Edward Said (1993) argues that this sense of being the center of the universe and of the natural position of Britain as master and the colonies as its tributaries, was implicit in portrayals of Britain and the colonies evident in British literature. But just as Britain's global superiority wavered over time, so did its identity (Hall 1997). British identity became relatively decentered and unsure, and was manufactured only with great ideological effort characterized more by a defensive exclusivism than a positive assertion of identity. The period of American hegemony, by contrast, has always been more decentered and multinational than the British one and far less absorptive. Rather than trying to acquire new territories, the United States seeks to control them, as in the United States's relationships with Latin America (Hall 1997).

One of the reasons that the Pax Americana is so decentered is not only that its powerful allies, such as OECD governments, share a stake in the system and help foster American rule, but also that the *mentality* of the market so imbues the hearts and minds of a large percentage of the world's population that direct acquisition of territory is not necessary. To understand how this happened, a further discussion of the cultural changes associated with expanding capitalist markets is necessary.

Building a market culture

Although decentered explanations of cultural power are key to understanding how actors and conditions replicate domination, such explanations ignore broad areas of cultural influence. Aside from accepting the relations of inequality upon which global capitalism rests, one also has to question why people eagerly participate in their roles as consumers and in the creation of demand. Relations of inequality are essential to the profitable functioning of capitalist production and to the development of the national and transnational class structures upon which production is based. But one also has to consider the cultural impact that capitalist production in turn has on societies around the world and how it creates the demand that allows profits to be realized. Thus, as a complement to the preceding section I now emphasize demand as opposed to production. Is there a "culture of the market"? If so, what role does this culture play in the replication of world order? There are many approaches to answering this question, several of which I will consider next.

Culture industry and the media elite

The Frankfurt School, in particular the work of Theodor Adorno, provides one of the best-known theories of the relationship between culture and capitalism. Adorno (1972: 133–4) argues that a monopolized culture industry uses the technology of mass production to acquire power over society by imposing a model of culture that serves its economic interests. According to Adorno, the standardization of mass production of art, film, and music erased the distinction between art and society; the market absorbed the needs of both. The standardized plots of mass produced films, for example, taught consumers conformity and captivated them with the myth of success until, "Immovably, they insist on the very ideology which enslaves them" (Adorno 1972: 133–4). Although not part of the Frankfurt School, Richard Hoggart (1957) made a similar argument in his examination of changes in traditional working-class culture in twentieth-century Britain. He argued that American popular culture and the influence of a media elite were changing working-class attitudes toward being "part of the herd," and celebrating the lowest common denominator, which culminated in "a passive visual taking-on of bad mass-art geared to a very low mental age" (Hoggart 1957: 167).

There are valid objections to this sort of "instrumentalist" argument. First, the implied passivity of working-class people seems to deny agency, exemplified by Adorno's (1972: 144–5) argument that even when people try to rebel, all they can muster is a "feeble resistance" that in turn is produced and controlled by the media. Second, the "top-down" flow of power inherent in this approach has been criticized by those who are wary of explanations grounded on class-based conspiracies and seek more decentered explanations of the mechanisms of domination (e.g. Bennett 1999). Intuitively, however, I think there is considerable validity to Adorno's and Hoggart's argument. Everyone knows what a best-selling Hollywood film looks like, what the plot is, how it will end, and who will star in it. And Hollywood in turn plays to demand; producers know what people want to see and most Hollywood films reflect these guidelines. It seems plausible that viewers' demand, conditioned by years of mindless drivel pitched at the lowest common denominator, also shapes supply.

I think it is also obvious that television, film, and other media condition our wants, needs, and expectations on numerous levels. Consider Sherif Hetata's anecdote below about the mechanisms of this process in India. He is discussing a friend who is a peasant and lives in a mud hut along with his animals and large family. He wears traditional clothes and eats traditional food:

> But when he married, he rode around the village in a hired Peugeot car with his bride. She wore a white wedding dress, her face was made up like a film star, her hair curled at the hairdresser's of the provincial town, her finger and toe nails manicured and polished, and her body bathed with special soap and perfumed. At the marriage ceremony, they had a wedding cake, which she cut with her husband's hand over hers. Very different from the customary rural marriage ceremony of his father. And all this change in the notion of beauty, of femininity, of celebration, of happiness, of prestige, of progress happened to my peasant friend and his bride in one generation. The culprit, or the benevolent agent, depending on how you see it, was television.
>
> (Hetata 1999:178)

Further testimony to this instrumentalist argument is the high level of concentration in the global culture industry, which means that a very small number of international firms really do have a lot to say about what is consumed culturally. Although small local competitors exist, the global popular culture industry comprising music, television, and film is dominated by twenty or thirty large multinational companies, all based in Organization for Economic Cooperation and Development (OECD) countries.[2] With a cookie-cutter formula for what constitutes a gripping plot or a popular song, these companies churn out cultural commodities that are not just a response to demand, but also *create* demand through the marketing of stars and myths of success and happiness. To cite another Indian example, Arundhati Roy's poignant novel, *The God of Small Things*, highlights this process through the description of her heroine's enraptured consumption of the film *The Sound of Music*. Even after dozens of viewings, the girl's worship of Julie Andrews, her love of the Western music, and her absorption in the romance of the story never subsides.

How can there not be political consequences from the consumption of Western culture, as Hetata and Roy describe? Such changes in "taste" strengthen the sales of global culture-producing companies, creating vast new markets and reinforcing the economic strength of these firms. Growing demand for their products translates into political power. International culture companies use their political clout to influence trade negotiations at the international level via the WTO, or regionally through agreements such as the North American Free Trade Agreement (NAFTA) or the European Union. This guarantees them even more market access (the US film industry is the most prominent example of this). These demands for market access are couched in the discourse of free trade, and it is here that Cox's and Gill's emphasis on the importance of international institutions in regulating world order seems so incisive. Embedded in the broader context of the "there is no alternative" mentality of global neoliberalism reinforced by the IMF, World Bank, and OECD, the demands of the culture companies and the US Trade Representative appear natural, reasonable, and rational. It seems only fair that US firms should have equal access to markets, especially when they know there is demand for their products. Open market access appears to be cosmopolitan and rational as compared to emotional, irrational nationalism.

The campaign led by France and Canada to exempt cultural industries from the rules of the WTO exemplifies the high stakes of this battle. Certainly, one must regard Canada's and France's insistence on the exemption of cultural products from free trade regulations, expressed in terms of protecting national identity, as an attempt in part to protect the market share of domestic cultural producers. There is no question that in the face of competition from the sleek Hollywood machine, many of these smaller producers could not survive. This is true not only for the film industry, but also for the publishing industry. But because of this, culture is one case where the laws of neoclassical trade theory regarding the mutual benefits of free trade do not apply. As Frederic Jameson (1999) notes, acquisition of free access to foreign markets for Hollywood coupled with the denial of subsidies for local cultural producers means the obliteration of local culture industries. Hollywood wins at everyone else's expense. In light of this reality, protecting market share and national identity become inextricably intertwined. Since most of these companies produce films or publish books created by national artists, their demise would undoubtedly have an impact on national culture and identity, which in turn is central to the raison d'être of the state. Yet, the seemingly inexorable global spread of culture industries, fueled by consumer demand, is likely to prevail, heralded by WTO moves to overrule attempts such as Canada's ban on split-run magazines under extreme US pressure and threats of trade retaliation.[3]

Without diminishing the importance of international institutions, we must remember that this political process would be useless to the MNCs if they doubted that there would be eager demand for their products once they should receive free access to markets. The changes in taste that I outlined above alter people's mentalities, their ideas about modernity, and the desirability of traditional cultures and practices, and even local political practices. Obviously, the process is not unidirectional, as those who focus on the relationship between the global and the local understand. Negative cultural and political reactions to Western influence or, in the case of the West, nationalist backlashes or religious reactions to the dubious morality of the culture industry are as likely to happen. The point is, however, that these cultural changes have political implications both globally and locally that we cannot ignore. Understanding how cultural forces and institutions create the "global consumer" is integral to understanding how individuals accept and spread global capitalism.

Having said this, Adorno's instrumentalist approach with its focus on the global culture industry does not provide a complete explanation of the development of global consumption. The impact of living in a capitalist market economy, of being immersed in the commodified culture of the market, is also an important consideration.

Cultural commodification

International Political Economy theorists widely discuss the political implications of the spread of global capitalism, especially its market-driven restrictions on national political autonomy. The cultural commodification that accompanies the spread of capitalist markets is integral to understanding the national political abdication often associated with global capitalism. Writing at the end of the nineteenth century as a witness to the squalor of late-industrial revolution England, William Morris (1885/1980) wrote passionately about the perverse effect capitalism had on culture. Although he more often used the term "commercial society" as opposed to capitalism, his words are relevant to the kind of cultural experience I am referring to. From where, Morris asked, does art spring? "Art," he answered himself, "is man's embodied expression of interest in the life of man; it springs from man's pleasure in his life … it is especially the expression of man's pleasure in the deeds of the present; in his work" (Morris 1980: 140). However, in late-industrial-revolution England, work provided few pleasures and much bitterness. Sordid and hideous towns, ugliness, and misery prevailed. Such conditions affected more than the working classes, he argued. A convinced socialist, Morris maintained that when rebellion against a corrupt society is the only worthwhile activity and when lives are wasted in a ceaseless struggle against fellow men, everyone suffers:

> High and low, therefore, slaveholders and slaves, we lack beauty in our lives, or, in other words, man-like pleasure. This absence of pleasure is the second

gift to the world which the development of commercialism added to its first gift of a propertyless proletariat. Nothing else but the grinding of this iron system could have reduced the civilized world to vulgarity ... when art is fairly in the clutch of profit-grinding she dies, and leaves behind her but her phantom of *sham* art as the futile slave of the capitalist.

(Morris 1885/1980: 142)

Morris's words will resonate in the discussion of cultural resistance in the last section, for many consider pleasure to be a fundamental source of rebellion and resistance. Absence of pleasure, therefore, is a serious, hopeless situation. Of course, Morris's propagandistic discussion of slaves and slaveholders is hyperbolic, and his description of the "grinding iron system" perhaps more appropriate to the time he was writing. His argument regarding the cultural impact of "commercial society," however, echoes contemporary discussions of the commodification and absorption of culture into capitalist markets. Consider Jameson's (1995: 4) notion that in contemporary times, the cultural has become economic and the economic cultural, with aesthetic production integrated into commodity production generally as part of the "frantic economic urgency of producing fresh waves of ever more novel-seeming goods." Meaning and culture become commodified, numbing their potential for political resistance. The consequence, he argues, is evident in much postmodern cultural production – a kind of depthless ahistoricism denying any meaning beyond the portrayed object. Rather than the conversion process that Adorno and Hoggart believe accompanies the commodification of culture, to Jameson it is more that one cynically, or resignedly, converts to the system.

From where does this resignation come? In part, I believe, it comes from a tacit recognition of the inexorable nature of capitalist markets. Resisting commodification or denying the rigors of market logic brings fruitless pain since the market crushes resistance. Claus Offe (1973) and Charles Lindblom (1977) describe capitalist markets as highly efficient institutions that automatically expel transgressions of market "rules." Lindblom describes the market as a kind of prison that closes down automatically to punish anything that tries to escape its implacable logic (Lindblom 1977; Offe 1973). Once we add the global nature of capitalism to the equation, things become even more automatic and beyond control. The MNCs seem to have an insuperable advantage, especially when new technologies provide forms of communication that allow for instantaneous information and rapid flows of money, commodities, and inventories anywhere in the world (Diebert 1997).[4] What is the point of resisting the global capitalist, technology machine? A sense of alienation and loss of control ensues – the corollary of "There is no alternative" is, "So why bother doing anything about it?" The result is an overwhelming desire to throw up one's hands and abdicate responsibility for something that seems totally beyond anyone's capacity to change.

A look at the demise of social democracy in Sweden is illustrative. The common political economy explanations for the demise of Sweden's unique welfare state, such as the internationalization of Swedish industry and finance, and the resulting inability of the Swedish state to control fiscal and macroeconomic policy are central to what Tom Notermans (1993) calls the Swedish state's abdication from national policy autonomy. In the face of immense international economic pressures arising from the global deregulation of financial industries and the internationalization of production, he argues, the Swedish government gave up and deregulated (Pontusson 1992; Notermans 1993).

Swedish cultural producers sound similar themes. In a discussion of architectural trends and their relationship to the death of Sweden's welfare state, one architect lamented, "The way the system is built, every kind of responsibility sort of sinks into a mud which makes things very difficult" (Åman 1996). The "system" the architect is referring to is the market. The architects talk of their frustration at losing their autonomy to developers and contractors who use mass produced, ready-made components in construction and take shortcuts to ensure that their buildings are profitable. The result, they claim, is the loss of individual styles and new aesthetics, of any attempt to assert a new dimension of meaning to space. The political economists talk of the pressures to conform to the dictates of international finance and the problems with implementing an industrial policy when national firms are increasingly locating production beyond national boundaries. In the end, both the architects and the economists conclude that decisions are the product both of politics and a sense of resignation in the face of overwhelming power: the market exists and the reality of its confines must be acknowledged. There is an enormous pressure to hand over responsibility to anonymous international capitalist markets, under the rationale of "market imperatives."

An analysis of the cultural dynamics of capitalist markets is key to understanding the powerlessness and lack of responsibility both architects and national policy makers experience, as well as the indifferent consumer tastes of Adorno's "duped masses." What is this abdication and indifference a reaction to? From where does the feeling of powerlessness come? One way to answer these questions is to focus on the process of commodification inherent in capitalist markets. In order to be bought and sold, goods and non-goods must be commodified. Money, buildings, works of art, films, all must be turned into commodities in order to be integrated into the market nexus. Producers of these commodities must obey certain rules in order to survive: they must acknowledge the realities of the market. They must produce goods for which there is a demand, according to rules that will not alienate buyers or investors, and they must produce efficiently in order to compete with other producers. Participating in this market may involve sacrifices in individual values or tastes, but it also can bring material rewards and prosperity.

Both psychologically and politically, however, the implications of this prosperity can be debilitating: feelings of powerlessness, a sense of alienation and anomie (both individual and national) and a loss of individuality and the power to act. A related factor is the erosion of distinctive identities: Who am I? Who are we? Where do I/we belong? In other words, the transition from individual to mass consumer is due not only to the actions of large MNCs but also to the dynamic of the capitalist market itself, which reinforces a sense of cultural uniformity, conformity, and the uselessness of cultural and/or political resistance or protest.

Some argue that the economic logic of the market and its emphasis on contractual relationships also enhances the trend toward the abdication of moral responsibility. For example, Paul Du Gay (1996) describes the dismay of the Public Accounts Committee of the House of Commons in the UK over a series of incidents revealing a marked disregard for the "proper conduct of business" within government bureaucracies. The committee bemoaned the improper spending and decline in standards of conduct that had accompanied the introduction of market-oriented and entrepreneurial systems of organization into the bureaucracy. These were part of an overall process of reform instigated in the 1980s. However, the committee did not target the reforms as the source of wrongdoing.

The committee had implemented the reforms to create greater flexibility in light of globalization, and also to improve the traditional ethos of the bureaucracy. What the committee did not foresee was the likely impact of the introduction of entrepreneurial values to all forms of conduct and the application of contractual relations to human interactions. What occurred in the process was the "re-imagination of the social form as economic" (du Gay 1996: 156). The emphasis on treating individuals as "entrepreneurs" rather than "bureaucrats" encouraged the pursuit of individual interests in management, eroding the ethos of responsibility characteristic of traditional bureaucracy and allowing individuals to sidestep public moral responsibility.

As will become clear below, I do not fully accept that the market is a "prison" or that moral irresponsibility in market culture is inevitable. Important instances of cultural resistance and cultural change belie the underlying force of this argument. I do think, however, that the psychological, social, and cultural implications of the expansion of markets are important aspects of understanding global capitalism. There is nothing particularly new or novel in this idea; in addition to the authors listed above, it resounds through the nineteenth-century work of John Ruskin (Williams 1958: 136–142) and his abhorrence of the artistic consequences of industrialization, to the writing of Karl Polanyi (1944) and his analysis of the "false commodification" inherent in capitalist markets. Culture, politics, and economics conform to the market regime, creating a seemingly closed system that appears to reproduce itself endlessly, thwarting change.

Of course, none of the authors mentioned above, despite their pessimism about the broader impact of capitalist markets, believed that there was no way out of this "system." In fact, a major purpose of the writing of Morris and Ruskin was to attempt to change capitalism or commerce so that life could become fuller for everyone. For the socialist Morris, changes in class relations and the nature of work had to precede cultural changes; one needed leisure time and fulfillment in one's work in order to engage in the pleasure of artistic activity. The more conservative Ruskin thought that improving access to culture for working-class people was enough to improve the quality of their lives. Contemporary theory, even on the left, leans more to Ruskin's approach. That we live in a capitalist world is given – what is important is how we live in that world and how we interpret it as individuals and as communities. Both the production and the consumption of culture are key to resistant interpretations of identity and to merely "living" in a capitalist market society.

Culture, domination, and resistance in the global political economy

In summary, what does this global capitalist world look like? So far, I have painted a picture of a decentered but omnipresent hegemony disciplined by the market, patrolled by the United States and its allies, and operationalized by huge multi-national companies from OECD countries. On an institutional level, it is governed by meticulously negotiated regulations set out in the rulebooks of the WTO, NAFTA, and other regional trade arrangements, and it is financed by the IMF, the World Bank, and various private institutions. These banks and multi-national firms are the primary political force behind both national and inter-national attempts to regulate the formation of global markets. They lobby the state and use direct and indirect influence to insure an ever expanding sea of con-sumers. The structural power of the market hangs like a threat over all of this: any derogation of market discipline will be sternly punished by capital flight or capital strike. Now add the cultural emollient, the day-to-day interactions by which one lives in the system, and the bombardment by messages about what it means to be a citizen of the twenty-first century – how one is to look and act; what one is to wear and buy; what is one's proper role in society; who is inferior and who is superior; who is "normal" and who is "other"; what is beautiful; what is in "good taste"; what is civilized. Reading the newspaper, watching films and television, and going to the museum constantly reinforce a sense of order and stimulate consumer behavior. To ensure the free flow of values now packaged as cultural commodities, the MNCs push forward to include even our thoughts and feelings in the rulebook of the WTO. Led by the United States, the culture industry urges that final step: the complete commodification of culture by its inclusion under global trade law. Drowning in anomie and indifference, sure their individual actions will make no difference, the average citizen mutters a protest but continues apace to consume global cultural commodities.

So there it is – an implacable, impenetrable juggernaut that will rule forever. Of course, one can exaggerate this vision of an omnipotent, unchangeable global structure. Recall Hall's (1997) point that this hegemony is a decentered, more multinational hegemony than the one in evidence during the Pax Britannia. The Pax Americana is more diffuse than the Roman empire, which used a common language and deliberately built theaters and amphitheaters in conquered lands to encourage the spread of Roman influence; or British hegemony, which used the English language, education, and infrastructure to integrate the empire (Hall 1997; Held 1999). As much as global capitalism depends on the creation of a mass of global consumers, it also, as Hall notes, thrives on difference. One need only think of the growing popularity of "exotic" foreign cuisines in Europe and North America or the burgeoning worldwide sales of "World Beat" or International music to acknowledge the growing cosmopolitan aspects of consumption. As much as Taylor (1997) emphasizes that global structures of domination are inherent in the Western packaging of non-Western music, he also sees that for Western consumers buying this music is evidence of their good "taste." Acquiring a taste for "exotic" music sets one apart as a cosmopolitan and "cultured" individual. It imparts status, if only on an individual psychological level. However hierarchical the production and sale of this music is, its actual consumption encourages the acceptance and celebration of someone else's culture. The same may be said of international cuisine, fashion, and literature. As cultural forms from diverse parts of the world become absorbed in global markets and are consumed, they become part of an individual's conception of entertainment and pleasure, resulting in openness and an acceptance of difference.

Michel de Certeau (1984) broadens this notion of consumption to include "ways of using" the constraining order. A North African living in a low-income housing development in France, for example, insinuates into this situation ways of "dwelling" particular to his native Kabylia. He superimposes and combines his own practices with those imposed upon him. Thus, "Without leaving the place where he has no choice but to live and which lays down its law for him, he establishes within it a degree of *plurality* and creativity. By an art of being in between, he draws unexpected results from his situation" (de Certeau 1984: 30). All of this occurs within the context of everyday life.

Mary McLeod (1996) makes a similar point with regard to architecture. McLeod argues that "transgression" or protest in architectural design seems to operate in an environment of machismo and avant-garde aggression as it is practiced by middle-aged men. Even philosophers have a singular role in urging social protest that seems to emphasize the "thrills of transgression and 'difference'" (McLeod 1996: 10). Foucault, for example, despite his focus on the "other" (autre) seems to have nothing but disdain for the places that the "other" (in the form of woman) inhabits. Everyday places such as the home, the public park, and the department store may sometimes be sources of oppression for woman, and may not exemplify post-structuralist claims of difference, but they are also sources of comfort, security, and even autonomy for women. McLeod further argues that post-structural architecture posits "a notion of 'other' that is solely a Western dismantling of Western conventions for a Western audience," with "other" confined to what is defined by a Western avant-garde. She calls for politically and aesthetically constructive positions with less emphasis on negation and more emphasis on everyday buildings that can be seen in terms of pleasure, comfort, humor, and emotion (McLeod 1996).

Postcolonial architectural critic Vikramaditya Prakash (1997) also warns of the dangers of relying purely on negation for resistance, particularly the negation of the West that is involved in attempts to develop a self-consciously anticolonial architecture. By focusing on their "regional" identities, she warns, non-Western architects run the risk of becoming representative tokens from the margins while being re-marginalized as exterior to global culture whose center is the West. How do you assert difference in an affirmative manner, she asks, that is not simply the reversal of the colonial? Her complex and somewhat elusive answer is that postcolonial architects must resist the temptation to "anchor" their identity. Instead, they should pick the debris left by global chaos and knit it into a veil according to a strategy for power, a veil that once suspended, reveals by concealing (Prakash 1997).

Global flows of people via migration can also diffuse the pressures of global markets. Although these streams of people are usually a response to war, violence, and repression, they are also a response to economic changes. An example of this is the flow of Mexicans northward into the United States, due in large part to the integration of North American markets, the growth of the maquiladora sector on the US/Mexican border, and the displacement of Mexican peasants and workers resulting from the stipulations of NAFTA. As economic pressures push Mexican migrants northward, they hit what is in places a literal steel wall (constructed of metal left over from the Gulf War) telling them who is "inside" or "outside" the mythical sovereignty of the United States (Walker 1993; Weber 1995). Yet these changing economic flows are in fact reinscribing the ancient Aztec land of "Aztlán" which was said to run from Mexico City to what is now the southwestern United States. This reaffirmation of Aztlán has become a source of cultural empowerment and resistance for Chicanos living in the southern United States and the subject of songs, poems, and performance art that constitute the "Border Art" phenomenon. The crushing pressures of continental economic integration are therefore mitigated by cultural resistance and the reaffirmation of a cross-border Chicano/Chicana identity (Aitken and Jenkins 2000).

Similarly, Diebert (1997) emphasizes that the technological flows so ideally suited for the global production networks and financial movements of the multinationals are also the source of cross-border alliances between grassroots movements concerned with the environment, feminist issues, and peace. Appadurai (1996: 7) tells how Muslims all over the world are reunited momentarily by the sound of a tape recording of a religious leader, and how women working in the home reconstruct their own lives by reading romances or watching soap operas. The juggernaut of globalization may continue apace, but inherent in it are cultural contradictions that lead to the celebration of difference, the reaffirmation of cultural identities, and resistance to the anomie and alienation that global uniformity can bring. Above all, the appreciation of such cultural forms brings pleasure, and with it a kind of hope that there is some meaning to life, the embodiment of Appadurai's (1996: 7) argument that where there is consumption there is pleasure, and where there is pleasure, there is agency.

Finally, I think that it is important to reconsider the liberal idea that the expansion of capitalist markets can have a liberating aspect as well. Critical approaches to international political economy often refuse to acknowledge the progressive aspects of globalization. The challenges to entrenched cultures and ideologies that accompany the spread of global capitalism, however, can be creative and enabling forces. Geeta Kapur (1998) argues that new links between India and global markets, for example, have brought "unbottled genii" and innovation, breaking down the constraints that even critical schools of thought such as post-colonial theory entailed:

> ... globalization allows for the first time a freedom from the national/collective/ communitarian straitjacket; freedom also from the heavily paternalistic patronage system of the state. It allows freedom from a rigid anti-imperialist position in which post-colonial artists find themselves locked; and the freedom

to include in post-colonial realities other discourses of opposition such as those of gender and the minorities – discourses that question the ethics of the nation-state itself.

(Kapur 1999: 204)

In sum, capitalist markets involve changes that are never final. Individuals and collectivities consume, interpret, and protest these changes in ways that cannot but help alter the nature of capitalism and even of protest itself. Obviously, cultural factors are not the only influences that bring change – technological, economic, and political changes are also important. But one cannot deny the importance and pervasiveness of cultural resistance and its role in changing global capitalism, and its structures of domination and constraint should not be neglected.

Conclusion

I intend the eclectic approach of this essay to probe and provoke new ways of thinking about world order and to encourage new investigations into the impact of culture on world politics. Culture is implicated in the construction of world order in innumerable ways. It reinforces the unequal relations based on gender, race, and class on which capitalist production thrives; it provides us with living examples of how one should or might think and behave; and it resigns us to living in a self-perpetuating system based on cold-blooded relations of exchange. On the other hand, culture is also a fundamental source of change, resistance, and renewal in a world where current "realities" seem written in stone. In short, examining culture provides us with a fuller sense of how global capitalism is lived, all the more reason for expanding the role of culture in explanations of world order. There is a need for further study of the role of specific forms of cultural production such as art, music, and architecture in constructing global capitalism. More attention also must be paid to the development of market culture and the impact of commodification and market regulation on our identities, morals, and senses of individual efficacy. Although often highly personal, these factors are central to the uncritical acceptance of capitalist markets so necessary for their expansion. Much work in these areas has already been carried out in the field of Cultural Studies and political economists need to break down the false barriers between disciplinary fiefdoms to borrow the wealth of ideas these studies offer. The effort will yield creative and innovative new projects destined to change the nature of political economy in a fundamentally positive way.

Notes

1 Of course, many scholars, including Marxists such as E.P. Thompson, have underlined Bourdieu's point. As Thompson noted in the 1960s, if class is mostly determined by the productive relations into which people are born, class-consciousness is "the way in which these [class] experiences are handled in cultural terms: embodied in traditions, value-systems, ideas and institutional forms" (Thompson, 1965: 9–10) Class, in Thompson's

view, had to be understood as both a social and cultural formation that needed to be studied over a long historical period as it was lived, in order to give a sense of agency to working-class people.

2 The top ten media conglomerates by sales turnover are Time-Warner, Disney, Bertelsmann, Viacom, News Corporation, Sony, Universal, TCI, Philips, Polygram, and NBC (Held 1999: 348).

3 The Canadian government had prohibited the practice by US magazines such as *Time* of "satellite printing" a second issue for the Canadian market that included advertising targeted at a Canadian audience. The government argued that without providing any significant Canadian content or coverage of Canadian events, US publications were siphoning off advertising revenues from smaller Canadian magazines, threatening the viability of the Canadian magazine industry. The WTO told Canada it must rescind this ruling.

4 Diebert (1997) argues that particular forms of communication, from parchment books to the printing press to computer technologies, favor different sectors of society and enhance their predominance. He argues that contemporary forms of computer communication and media communication are particularly suited to the interests of multinational corporations and thus increase their global power. He does not argue that the multinationals are the only ones to benefit from these technologies, however, and also sees new opportunities for communication between previously divided groups that may now communicate and cooperate globally. See in particular his chapters 6 and 7.

Part III
Sacking the city

5 Globalization as global history

Introducing a dialectical analysis

Barry K. Gills

History teaches us everything, even the future. World history is clearly multi-civilizational. The history of capital within world history is therefore also clearly multi-civilizational, not uni-civilizational, or uni-cultural. Is the future of world history, as well as of capital and even of globalization, also not multi-civilizational? I think so. Although capital operating on a world scale through commerce (involving both production and consumption) does have a historical tendency to reduce all economic forms to a unity (i.e. capital), it has never been accompanied by a true cultural uniformity all over the world. It always coexisted with cultural diversity. So how can a concept such as globalization, which seems so ultra-contemporary, be related to global history, which rests on a knowledge of the past that is not necessarily relevant to the present and future as (pre)configured by contemporary globalization processes? And why or how can I posit an identity between these two terms, using the connective word "as," as I do in my title: "Globalization *as* global history"?

I will introduce a set of hypotheses to make my reasoning clear.

1   Globalization is intimately about global history: past, present, and future, and there are no absolute dichotomies between past and present or between present and future. Rather, aspects of continuity unite these three into a single stream of world historical time and history.
2   By using a critical historical method or a historical mode of enquiry, that is, by *historicizing globalization*, we come to better understand the concept and its complexities and are less mystified by it, in both theory and praxis.
3   This critical historical method, when allied to a critical social theory, should focus on understanding both change and continuity in the (world) historical process, itself to be understood not as a strictly linear progression of developmental or evolutionary stages (as in modernization theory), or in a strictly cyclical manner in which there is a simple repetition in a law-like pattern (as in world-system theory), but rather in a *dialectical* manner, where forms and principles of regulation exist in a high state of historical tension.
4   We need a rectification of our common understanding of world or global history, and of globalization, from the current paradigm of *embedded Eurocentrism*, a construction of knowledge which systematically distorts world/global

history and obscures the fact that globalization has always been multi-civilizational and also multi-centric.

5   The processes of globalization are embodied in material and ideational or cultural exchange that brings greater *interconnectedness*. Global history may be defined as a set of processes leading to greater unification of the world and of humanity through these interconnections – even to "the-world-as-a-single-place." However, globalization has never brought total uniformity, homogeneity, or homogenization, but rather always coexists (as a historical tendency) with diversity, heterogeneity, heterogenization. There is a dialectic between these oppositional historical processes – between homogenization and hetero-genization, in the whole story of globalization as global history. This idea applies to these as both states of being and as historical processes, but the emphasis here is particularly on the latter.

6   However, many elements in globalization today can be seen essentially as continuity and indeed as *intensification* of long-established forms or historical patterns and tendencies in global history.

7   Finally, globalization understood in this historical dialectical manner, is met by counter-globalization, which is, in effect, an intrinsic part of the historical pattern that contains in itself a transformative potential. This is the *dialectic of global history*.

I would like to begin discussion of these hypotheses by referring to a text written by an analyst of these questions:

> [I]ntercourse with [this country] may have had … [great] influence … on the civilization of mankind. … [It] is of the greatest consequence to ascertain the channels through which, at various periods, it found its way, or into which it was conducted; and the whole course of history tends to prove that the countries which became the staples or the depots of this commerce, uniformly attained a high degree of opulence and refinement…. The result of this dispensation of Providence, (by which the parts of the earth most remote with respect to Europe have been enriched with the most costly and highly valued, though not the most necessary productions) has been, the mutual intercourse and civilization of nations; which, if they had continued uncon-nected, would have remained still in their infancy, as must be the case with all isolated nations…

Now the country in question is India (although China, if you had thought of it, would have been a good guess); the author is A.H.L. Heeren; the text is from a multi-volume study entitled *Historical Researches into the Politics, Intercourse, and Trade of the Principal Nations of Antiquity, Part I: Asiatic Nations*; the time of writing was two hundred years ago, *c*.1800, and the reference was to ancient world commerce.

What is most significant about this text is that it was written by a European world historian *before the advent of embedded Eurocentrism* and its distortion of world history and the respective roles of Europe and Asia in that history. It is clear that an eminent European historian, and therefore European scholarship, understood globalization processes in global history (though, of course, they did not use those terms at the time). Heeren also was aware of the intimate relationship between East and West, their long historical mutual influence, and the relationship between material or commercial *interconnectedness* and what Norbert Elias referred to as the "civilizing process." The only difference is that Heeren regarded India as the font and pivot of much of global history, and not Europe. This view, in fact, reflected (accurately) not only what he saw and knew in his own day and time, but also the typical historical relationship between Europe and Asia going back several millennia. If any place was the center of world commerce (and thus of world civilization itself) it was India and China, and they remained so for many centuries before the rise of the West in the past two centuries.

There are today three main schools of thought on the historical origin of globalization. There are those who argue that it begins at the year dot (i.e. with the origins of human culture or, for some, with the origins of civilization defined as the culture of living in cities); those who contend it begins with "1492" (i.e. with the singular and powerful historical event of the collision or fusion of two hitherto separated world historical social systems, namely the Afro-Eurasian world system and the world system of the Americas – the MesoAmerican and Andean – an event which did produce a truly global system for the first time in world history and remains an extraordinarily important event and turning point in global history); and third, those who argue that it began "yesterday," that is, in the 1980s and the 1990s with the advent especially of information and communications technologies and of a new type of global production and finance. My own view is somewhere between the first two but clearly in opposition to the last. This position is conditioned by my analytical framework of understanding world or global history, to which I now turn.

"The difference a hyphen makes": continuity versus discontinuity

I would like to discuss what I suggest are key concepts and methods by which we can and should study globalization as global history. This involves briefly outlining some aspects of world system theory. The goal of this historical analysis is to contribute to a *humanocentric* account of world/global history and to *cosmopolitan praxis* within it (Frank and Gills 1993/6).

In so far as there has been a "world system" in world economic history, it has always predominantly been "capitalist." However, the world system, in fact, is not a creation merely of trade (the production of commodities for exchange) but of "capital accumulation." The existence of capital accumulation on a world scale is one of several millennia, not several centuries. It is this central contention that is the basis of the "continuity thesis" in world or global history (Gills 1996) and my starting point for world system analysis of capital and power in the processes of world history (Gills 1995).

World system analysis differs from Wallersteinian world-system analysis (Wallerstein 1974b, 1980, 1989) in a number of very significant ways (Gills and Frank 1990, 1992; Wallerstein 1992, 1993, Frank and Gills 1993/6; 1995a; Gills 1995). However, the essential disagreement surrounds the contrasting interpretations given to the notion "ceaseless accumulation." For Wallerstein it is the *differentia specifica* of *modern* capitalism, while, in fact, it is a *constant* feature of the world system. This disagreement leads us to very different understandings and analyses of the historical origins and development of "capitalism" in world history, of the origins and development of the world system, and to a radically different sense of what a "transition to capitalism" might be in world historical terms and particularly of the role of Europe within it.

The most significant changes and discontinuities in global history are therefore understood differently if they are less focused on the notion of the singular and uniquely European "transition to capitalism" and more concerned to explicate the long global history of capital and the shifting locus of capital accumulation and power over space and time. Significant change over world historical time involves both continuity and discontinuity, with change occurring in the technological and social relations governing material life, the development of the "technics" of power organization, and the locus of capital accumulation and its hierarchical organization. I have suggested that the "hegemonic transition" (Frank and Gills 1993/6) may be more significant than the supposed linear transitions between one "mode of production" and another.

Both traditional Marxist and liberal understandings of world economic and social history emphasize a linear pattern of stages of development in which the "rise of the market" and of "capitalism" are slow and historically "late" developments. Capital accumulation is deemed to be important only in fairly recent history, at most for the past few centuries. The framework presented here, however, argues for a nonlinear perspective, which rejects the assumed dichotomy between "capitalist" and "pre-capitalist" stages in world economic history. Rather, it explores the thesis that capital accumulation has played a continuous role from the beginning of world history, and has influenced the ways states and societies have evolved and interacted.

The dialectic of forms

The *dialectic of forms*, the method of world historical analysis that I propose, attempts to understand the nature of the perpetual coexistence of contending economic forms (including capital) and the historical tensions among these contending forms throughout world history. Therefore, the governing processes of world history are to be viewed as being neither strictly linear nor cyclical, but rather as perennial and dialectical.

In terms of world economic history, we have tended to view the premodern as being rather too primitive, and the "modern" as being rather too modern.[1] The antidote to the linear approach is to emphasize the idea of a *dialectic* in world history. The dialectical method of reasoning can be traced to earliest recorded

Chinese thought, the Platonic discourses, and the historical method of the fourteenth century Islamic thinker Ibn Khaldun, among others. The most basic definition of dialectic, according to the *Oxford English Dictionary*, is "the existence or action of opposing forces or tendencies in society" and an understanding of history as "a series of contradictions and their solutions," though not necessarily a unity of opposites as in the Hegelian version of dialectics.

These historical tensions are the primary subject of my analysis.

Capital versus *oikos*

I identify the historical tension between capital and oikos (two perennial forms of economic organization) as a key element of global history. The antagonism between these two contending forms is based on their different uses of property and labor in pursuit of the production and extraction of surplus. Capitalism has an innate antagonism to any form of communal property, and to its social ethos, as capital is fundamentally based on private property, commodified exchange relations, and on the acquisitive spirit (the *appetitus divitiarum infinitus*). The antagonism of capital versus oikos generates not only conflict or tension between the forms themselves, but also class conflict. Interelite class conflict, between the capitalist class and the landed or "feudal" class, is a constant feature of world history. The state is a terrain of this contest and is pulled in both directions. Moreover, these conflicts spill over into, and involve, class conflict among the elite, propertied classes, and the common or laboring classes. The tension between these forms has also been implicated in the confrontation between "civilization" (here representing capital) and "barbarism" (here representing oikos) and the unrelenting expansionist tendency of the former. The "free" tribal areas of the world have, for millennia, been exorably "incorporated" into the ever-expanding purview of civilization, capital, and the world system. Trade, colonization, conversion, and conquest have forever been key levers in this long and bloody encounter between cultures based on radically different social ecologies and organizing principles.

Karl Rodbertus first developed the concept of the "oikos economy" and, more importantly, the idea that was widely accepted of its economic dominance throughout ancient economic history. This idea carried over into conventional understanding of the medieval era (in Europe) and the presumed ubiquity of the manor (and the guild) and paucity of capital. Karl Bucher regarded the oikos as one of the "stages" in historical development. Gordon Childe analyzed the role of the royal (or palace) and manorial (household) estates in Bronze Age Near Eastern economic history as a constraint upon economic development due to the concentration of the surplus among a narrow elite. For Weber (1978: 379, 381) the oikos is a variant of the development of the undifferentiated or unified household, which combines "household," "workshop," and "office." This may be the authoritarian household, and patriarchal household, of a prince, manorial lord, or patrician. Its dominant motive is not capitalistic acquisition but the lords want satisfaction in kind. For Weber, this could involve the lord in "any means, including large-scale trade" and even "market-oriented enterprises" which could be attached to the oikos unit (Weber 1978: 379, 381). Nevertheless, "the utilization of property" is decisive for the oikos lord, "not capital investment."

In my view a key characteristic of the oikos form is its tendency to make use of dependent, household-tied, or unfree labor, rather than "free" or commodified wage labor which can, however, be highly specialized and skilled. The oikos is therefore associated with interpersonal relations within family, kinship, household, and the state (or royal household). Therefore, normally, the transfers of value in the oikos sphere are analytically outside the category of capital. Types of transfer of value that may be treated under the category of the oikos may include, for example, taxes paid to the state (whether in kind, cash, or labor); tithes paid to the church (in kind, cash, or labor); rents or dues paid to a landlord or to the manorial lord of an estate (via cash, kind, or labor services); and "gifts" that are obligatory interpersonal exchanges, both public and private in nature. Thus, the general association of capital and oikos forms with contrasting types of labor and value transfer lead us to the second dialectical theme, that of the tension between "free versus unfree labor" in world economic history, discussed later. In my understanding of world history, at no point is either form, capital or oikos, entirely eliminated from economic and social history. However, any complete reversion to oikos forms would imply the end of capital and capital accumulation, an idea implicit in Marx's "eschatology" and communist ideology. In previous eras also, dissenting or "anti-hegemonic" social movements often advocated a return to oikos forms. The contemporary neoliberal idea of globalization implies a very different end of history, one in which the oikos form is (perhaps) eliminated and all economic life is organized via capital and the "free market."

In terms of long historical patterns of the "dialectic of forms" between capital and oikos (and, by association, between free and unfree labor) I emphasize the fluctuation or oscillation between periods marked by greater commercialization, commodification, and capitalization of the economy versus the opposite tendency. In this historical opposition, the rising prevalence of capital is associated with the elaboration of the division of labor accompanied by greater specialization and commodification of labor, while in the economy as a whole commercialization and financialization increase. These economic forces bear a direct relation to changes in state formation and the emergence and reproduction of sophisticated, centralized, and bureaucratic forms of state power. Oikos prevalence, by contrast, is associated more with reversion to de-commodified, de-commercialized, and de-capitalized economic processes, involving different modes of political and social organization, such as less centralized and bureaucratic state organization and de-centralized or fragmented political authority. When viewed as a positive alternative to the social relations of capital, the oikos forms represent a different value system and social ordering principles to that created by commodity exchange relations and the pursuit of capital accumulation. The cohesion of societal relations, including both interpersonal relations and community relations, are constructed on values that must rely on principles such as mutual obligation, love for fellow beings, social responsibility, ethical, religious, or spiritual norms emphasizing mutual aid and care, or a code of conduct stressing personal honor and service to the community, to social superiors, and to institutions representing these values, whether secular or sacred.

Free versus *unfree* labor

The opposition "free versus unfree labor" should not be understood as a clear linear progression in world history but rather as a perennial dialectical tension. This historical dialectic of free versus unfree labor is a central aspect of world economic and social history. Its patterns are closely aligned with changing configurations of power, and in particular with the historical dialectic of forms between "capital versus oikos" and to the "long cycles" of expansion/contraction, capitalization/de-capitalization, and entropy/organization in the world system. The definitions of "free" and "unfree" labor depend on the juridical, social relational, and institutional aspects governing the relations of the transfer of value. Such socio-legal concrete instances delineate the conditions of servitude, or obligation, on the one hand, and the legal provisions for protection of the person from (extreme) exploitation, on the other. The free category requires a definition whereby the person is separated, in law and in practice, from her/his labor power, which is why it can be associated with the "free wage" form. In the case of unfree labor, this requires that the person not be completely separated from her/his own labor power. Adams (1895) discussed how Roman law was deliberately crafted by the upper classes to favor the interests of (money) capital and very explicitly to convert (free) debtors into (unfree) slaves. Cusack (1868) contrasted this "cruel severity of the law of the insolvent debtors" characteristic of Roman practice, to the "milder and more equitable arrangements" of Celtic law and practices as embodied in the Brehon Code. Whereas the Roman law allowed the person of the debtor to be at the mercy of the creditor, who might sell him into slavery to redeem the debt, the Celtic law allowed only the seizure of goods, and even this was generally under conditions more favorable to the debtor than to the creditor. However, there are myriad and quite complex variants of labor forms in the ancient, medieval, and modern periods, and the basic forms are not always pure and separate, but often occur in complex combinations. However, the rule for capital is that choice of variant of labor form ultimately depends on what yields the highest returns to capital under prevailing economic conditions. According to Weber, labor's utilization in enterprises from ancient times onward has involved "all imaginable transitions from almost total mobility to complete regimentation in barracks" (Weber 1978: 383). Moreover, Weber also recognized that there was "capitalist utilization of unfree labor" and the use of unfree labor for production for the market, ranging from ancient Carthaginian estates to early modern Russian factories (using serf labor). According to Weber, therefore, given even the oikos form's proclivity to use market-oriented production, "there is a scale of imperceptible transitions between the two modes of economic orientation, and often also a more or less rapid transformation from one into the other" (Weber 1978: 381). Therefore, we must be wary of a straight-line progression in world history in regard to the form of labor and to its "emancipation." Since these matters, and also the trajectory of technology (which seems linear) are controlled or directed by power, there is no clear linear progression in moral terms.

Organization **versus** *entropy*

> (where entropy is understood as in Yeats's poem "The Second Coming" in the sense of "things fall apart, the centre cannot hold").

In the Western tradition, the foundational myth is one of a linear progressive history, moving through stages toward an eschatological climax. This can be traced to St Augustine's rejection, in *City of God*, of Plato's circular pattern of movement by emphasizing the Incarnation of Christ as a pivotal moment in historical time and thereafter judging all time relative to that event. The Christian linear eschatological understanding of time was secularized during the European Enlightenment by Hegel and by Marx, who each interpreted the "end" of history differently (as has Fukuyama more recently). However, this Western tradition of a linear myth of (world) history can be contrasted to the non-Western (and usually dialectical) understandings of historical time and movement, represented by Indian, Sinic, and Mayan cosmologies, among others. In these non-Western conceptions of world time and history there is no finality, no end state, but rather a continual variation between the building up of orderly structures and their eventual disintegration or destruction. My own model of historical time and movement consists of the pattern: entropy → organization → entropy. Therefore, it has more in common with the non-Western historical understandings and may represent a contemporary reconceptualization of the non-European historical imagination, with some resonance with recent scientific thinking surrounding chaos theory and hyper-complexity. By removing Eurocentric bias we are better enabled to confront the problem of entropy in the contemporary world. In terms of the problem of globalization, one can see that the concentration of capital effected by the logic of "global capital" and other aspects of neoliberal globalization are bringing about fragmentation in society, that is, intensification of entropy.[2] I discuss this problem in more detail in the final section of this chapter.

The relationships between these contending forms are analyzed as *world historical processes* and not merely as static comparisons (e.g. *à la* Weberian category concepts). That is, world system theory and "the dialectic of forms" as a method of historical analysis inheres in a critical nomothetic and diachronic analysis rather than in a static comparative ideographic and synchronic analysis. The nomothetic pertains to the study or discovery of general laws or patterns as opposed to the individual, single, or unique event or fact (the ideographic), whereas the diachronic refers to the historical development of a culture, a language, etc., as opposed to the synchronic, which pertains to the state of such at a particular moment of time and space, without regard to historical motion or development.

Long-term processes of social change can be studied as historically recurrent patterns (dialectical and dyadic) rather than singular linear progressions or sequential stages. For example: *capitalization* versus *de-capitalization*; *commercialization* versus *de-commercialization* (or perhaps *capitalization* versus *feudalization*); and *commodification* versus *de-commodification*. World system theory seeks to understand the relationship of these patterns in the overarching world power structure to others such as *hegemonic transitions* and *center shifts* in the world system and in relation to world systemic conditions of *organization versus entropy*, or *equilibrium versus dis-equilibrium*. Put differently, world system theory investigates the systemic conditions associated historically with periods of prosperity, economic expansion, and cosmopolitan intercourse, and those which are associated with crisis, contraction, and fragmentation. Such world-system cycles, each of several centuries duration, stretch back several millennia (Gills and Frank 1992).

"Capital," "capitalist class," and "historical capitalism(s)": disentangling definitions

From these premises, the central question that follows should be:

> What is the role of *capital* in world/global history?, i.e. how have "capitalist practices" and the process of capital accumulation influenced the course of world/global history?

This question implies a study of the global history of capital, the social power of the capitalist class, and the instances of "historical capitalism(s)." This is necessary to discover the *global history of capital* as opposed to accepting the premise that capital has only a Western origin. In my view there is much to be gained in terms of analytical precision and clarity by making a distinction among the concepts "capital," "capitalist class," and "capitalism." Adam Smith, like other early political economists, used the term "capital" to mean merely "stock" or the goods in inventory (Smith 1937). Marx used the term capital to denote not a thing but a social relation; that is, the (exploitative) power of the owner of the means of production to command labor power and extract surplus value from it (Bottomore 1991). Weber, apparently following Aristotle, defined capital as private acquisitive capital used to acquire profit in an exchange economy (*Erwerbskapital*).

I define capital as a social relation, rooted in private property, operating through the use of money and commodity production and exchange, in command of labor power, and seeking profit through a transfer of value. As a form of social power, capital does command the power of both free and unfree labor. As a social relation it involves an exploitative transfer of value from labor to the holder of capital. By seeking profit (and its realization in monetary form), it is inextricably connected not only to the exchange relations of a commodified economy but also to the *unceasing* quest for the increase of capital, its "accumulation." In effect, there can be no capital without capital accumulation, and this is "ceaseless." Economically it is a condition of capital accumulation that the producer be separated from the consumer and that values be expressed in the setting of relative prices.

It is central to my argument that capital and capital accumulation be recognized as having existed from quite early in world economic history and, thereafter, having played a continuous and important or even "governing" role (in terms of "logic") in the creation and development of the world economy and thus the world system. Therefore, long-distance commerce and capital's role in it has been crucial in shaping the world system for several millennia. This must be the case because "inter-regional or long-distance trade cannot by definition function without capital, money, and prices" (Chaudhuri 1985/97: 203). Thus, world system analysis starts from the position that many local economies, even in "the remote historical past," have had "an exchange economy based on division of labour and the implied condition of capital accumulation" (Chaudhuri 1985/97: 203). However, it is long-distance exchange, which separates producer and consumer over both geographical space and real time, that perhaps most encourages the development of "a more advanced circuit of capital" (Chaudhuri 1985/97: 203).

Even so, to argue as I do for the centrality of capital accumulation in world economic history is not to insist that it is all a history of constant unchanging or historically undifferentiated "capital*ism*." Also, in contrast to either conventional economic history or Wallersteinian world-system analysis, from a world-system perspective, capital accumulation in the ancient and medieval periods of both Occident and Orient (and the pre-Columbian Americas) should not be relegated to a residual category such as "proto-capitalism" or worse still, "pre-capitalism" or "pre-capitalist."

Moreover, the Oriental (as opposed to Occidental or Western) origins of capital, the state, and civilization (defined as the culture of living in cities) are understood as parallel historical developments. Therefore, the origins of civilization, the state, and capital in the first urban centers should not be understood as having occurred "first" in some pristine case, such as Sumeria, and subsequently diffused, but rather to have developed more or less in tandem from the late Neolithic onward (allowing for some unevenness) across a much larger economic nexus across Eurasia.[3] That is, in my view, the embryonic world system, conceived as long-distance exchange and the gradual development of the division of labor and settlement growth and differentiation, gave rise to the first fully developed cities and to capital and to the state as well.[4]

Therefore, the process of capital accumulation in world history is situated within a continuous *city-centered* nexus of trade and production,[5] which has never existed independently of an "international" or interstate framework and a multi-civilizational, multi-centric context. The separation of "International Relations" (IR) from "International Political Economy" (IPE) is as untenable historically as it is in the contemporary context. In this sense, world system theory is certainly a branch of IPE, pursuing a world historical analysis to its logical conclusions by pushing the categories of analysis back in world time.

The underlying material basis of capital, is, simply put, the storing of a surplus. Surplus only becomes capital, however, through a particular kind of conversion, one which requires a formal *value complex* in which not only certain goods but also human labor itself become measurable quantities subject to purchase. Capital is therefore Janus-faced, being both a means of wealth creation and of human exploitation.

The control of economic surplus is a fundamental form of social power in virtually all human societies. Marx rightly believed that all historical social systems could be studied and compared on the basis of how an economic surplus was produced, extracted, redistributed, and consumed. Capital is not, however, the only form that economic surplus takes historically. In Adam Smith's political economy lexicon, a man was "rich or poor depending on the amount of labour that he can command or afford to purchase" (Speigel 1991: 248). This command can take a variety of historical forms, not all of which are capital.

The emergence of capital is always historically associated with the "privatization" of control over surplus and command over labor power. Thus, capital occurs in tandem with certain types of class formation, which must include a private propertied class. Max Weber (1978) suggested a fundamental division between the "positively privileged property classes" (including holders of capital) and the "negatively privileged property classes" (e.g. laborers and debtors).

But whereas Marx ties capital to wage-labor, historically, capital is in fact not restricted to "free" wage-labor. Capital utilizes many forms of value, including both free and unfree labor. There is no necessary incompatibility of capital, or therefore of "capitalism," with even the most severe forms of slavery. Indeed, the history of so-called "primitive accumulation" in early modern global capitalist practices illustrates this point clearly, as slavery on a vast scale was inextricable to the rise of early modern capital(ism) in Europe and also on a world scale.

Now, once we accept the existence of capital and, with it, of a capitalist class, from very early in world economic history, our understanding of the origins and development of historical capital(ism)(s) changes as well. The historical origins of "capitalism" as opposed to "capital" is usually sought by trying to identify a point in national or world economic history when capitalist social relations become overwhelmingly dominant. For some, such as Braudel, this point comes as early as the thirteenth century in Europe; for others, like Wallerstein, it occurs in the "long sixteenth century"; still others reserve the transformation for the time of the great "industrial revolution" of the late eighteenth and the nineteenth centuries. This threshold of "historical capitalism" is understood in Wallersteinian world-system theory, as well as in standard liberal and modernization accounts of economic development, to be co-terminus with the origins of the world system which radiated outward from newly capitalist Europe. Here we have the origins of embedded Eurocentrism and its mono-cultural narrative of global history, which reflects the emergence of Europe as a global power center and its gradual subordination of other civilizations, cultures, economies, and their world-views to a single Western mentality and power.

Again, I certainly do not suggest that all of world economic history is simply (unchanging) "capitalism." Max Weber suggested that there were historical instances of "ancient capitalism," "medieval capitalism," and "modern capitalism," insisting that each instance has distinctive characteristics (Weber 1976). I can accept instances of "ancient capital," "medieval capital," and "modern capital," and possibly even "ancient globalization," "medieval globalization," and "modern globalization" (and possibly "postmodern globalization"), but only while recognizing that a focus on "capital" may not necessarily tell us everything or be the whole picture economically or socially in any historical period. By smashing the false dichotomy between capitalist and pre-capitalist "stages" of world economic history, we can also shatter conventional and Wallersteinian Eurocentric interpretations of "historical capitalism" which insist that Europe alone created capitalism and thus the world system also, a position from which it follows that this version or *historical variant of capitalist civilization* is the only valid one, past, present, and future.

Oriental historical capital(ism)?

Thus, the continuity thesis suggests that capital accumulation has played an important role in both Occidental and non-Occidental history from ancient times onward, including during the erroneously considered "feudal" medieval centuries of world history, which were feudal for Europe perhaps, but not characteristic of the entire world system. The prevalence of capitalist practices in the local, regional, and world commerce of the medieval Islamic world and the Hindu and Confucian zones of Asia is a historical reality that should be vigorously re-investigated, laying finally to rest the ghost of Marx's Asiatic mode of production (Abu-Lughod 1989; Chaudhuri 1990/94; Frank and Gills 1993/6; Goody 1996; Frank 1998). Rather than being backward and stagnant, the medieval economies of Asia were more often the "engine room"of Eurasia's world economic system, to which much of Europe (outside southern Iberia, Italy, and Flanders) was a mere peripheral and fairly backward appendage. Such a perspective is crucial to an overdue rectification of our understanding of the relative contributions of East and West (or Asia and Europe) to the global history of capital(ism) and to world/global history in general (Hodgson 1974, 1993; Lombard 1975; Frank 1998). As Tawney pithily concluded in 1936: "To draw from English conditions a picture of a whole world stagnating in economic squalor, or basking in economic innocence is as absurd as to reconstruct the economic life of Europe in the twentieth century from a study of the Shetland Islands or the Ukraine" (Tawney 1936: 16).

As I have suggested, where there is capital, there is also a capitalist class, whether in the ancient, medieval, or modern periods of world history. Conventional understandings of economic history, whether liberal or Marxist, have tended to consider "merchant classes" as pre-capitalist or even non-capitalist. Moreover, the ubiquitous "merchants" of world history are rarely referred to by scholars as "capitalists," though in many if not all cases that is *exactly* what they are. These so-called merchants typically operated in a network of interlocking spheres of capital, encompassing the production, commodity circulation, and credit spheres. If this is the common model of historical capitalist practice, which I believe it is, then the ancient and medieval "merchant classes," whether Oriental or Occidental, actually represent *the capitalist class* of those periods and places in world history.[6] Weber suggests: "All over the world, for several millennia, the characteristic forms of the capitalist employment of wealth have been state-provisioning, tax-farming, the financing of colonies, the establishment of great plantations, trade, and money lending" (Weber 1978: 614). The Assyriologist Mogens Larsen (1967) demonstrated that joint capital enterprises existed in the second millennium BCE in Assyria and Anatolia. The Sumerologist Samuel Noah

Kramer (1959) insisted that the third millennium BCE city-state of Lagash was a "mixed economy," "partly socialistic and state-controlled, and partly capitalistic and free."[7]

Even as late in world history as *c*.1800, that is, three centuries after "1492," Heeren (1833: 2–3) could write the following passage:

> Even when we trace the progress of the arts and sciences, notwithstanding the pains which the nations of the west have bestowed in cultivating such pursuits and conferring upon them, as it were, an impress of their own, we find ourselves uniformly recalled to the east as the place of their origin. ...Europe has no production which Asia has not; and most of those which she possesses in common with the latter are inferior.

Conventional wisdom tells us that "capitalism" as an economic system was entirely a modern invention of European origin, which was later diffused to non-Europeans by trade, investment, colonialism, and conquest. However, as I have already argued, capital itself was actually an ancient Eastern invention rather than a modern Western and European innovation. Even Max Weber, who in some readings or interpretations epitomizes the idea that the West was in possession of a unique and superior form of capitalist rationality that accounted for its historical advantages and rise, argued in discussing late medieval European capitalist practices relating to credit, that "the forms themselves have perhaps a common Oriental (probably Babylonian) origin, and their influence on the Occident was mediated through Hellenistic and Byzantine sources" (Weber 1978: 613).

Therefore, rather than interpreting world economic history as a case of Western capitalism versus Asian non-capitalism, it would be more correct to start from the assumption that there have been capitalist practices in both regions for a very long time indeed. However, the level of "capitalization" and "commercialization" in the economy has fluctuated in both regions over time, and this influences their power positions relative to each other. These fluctuations need to be investigated empirically in a way that understands the rhythms of both Europe and Asia within the *same* world systemic context, which includes the mutuality of influence among the two major regions of Eurasia (McNeill 1963; Curtin 1984; Abu-Lughod 1989; Bentley 1993; Hodgson 1993; Frank and Gills 1993/96; Goody 1996; Denemark *et al.* 2000). The old shibboleth, "east is east and west is west and never the twain shall meet" disguises (distorts) a very different reality – that the "separateness" of Asia and Europe has generally been exaggerated by historians and social theorists alike, and thus also their many presumed differences, perhaps especially in relation to capital and historical capitalism.[8] The critical importance of the role of the changing power hierarchy among states and civilizations in the world system is thus also obscured in this (false) debate over who "invented" capitalism first.

Even if "historical capitalism" may have more of an Asiatic than a European origin, or better, a world system origin, there are important differences between historical variants of capitalist practices between (teacher?) Orient and (pupil?) Occident. A key issue here is the nature of "the firm" and the variations of type among joint capital ventures, partnerships, and family enterprises, and their different institutional characters. Needless to say, we are still to this day debating the relative merits of different variations of the capitalist firm, its larger social and legal underpinnings and regulation, especially between Oriental and Occidental "models" of capitalism. In the recent so-called "Asian crisis," which was in fact a global crisis or a crisis of global capitalism as some called it, some tried to depict the situation as due to an "Asian disease," that is, a deviation or abnormality of the Asian variants of capitalist practices compared to those of the contemporary West. To Weber, and many who still follow him, it is these specific legal conventions that are the characteristic "*uniquely Occidental*" development (and the ultimate source of Western superiority).

However, rather than a false historical comparison between Western capitalist and Eastern non-capitalist practices, what emerges is a need for objective analysis of the important and enduring historical distinctions between Western and non-Western *institutional variants of capitalist practices*.[9] Such a comparison, while instructive, should not, however, be a substitute for a world systemic analysis of mutual influence and interconnectedness in the context of common rhythms and patterns of the world system.

Clearly, non-Western social systems and ideational forms are not necessarily, either historically or in the present era, incompatible with capitalist practices. On the contrary, capitalist relations have existed and even flourished under Islamic, Hindu, and Confucian frameworks, to name but a few. Weber and Tawney, in their famous studies of this general problem, were concerned to investigate the idea that certain types of religious attitudes, particularly North European Protestantism, might be *more* conducive to (particular types of) capitalist practices than others and have different types of consequences. In the context of comparisons of historical variants of capital(ism) and capitalist practices, such an ideational approach raises still valid and important questions.

Chaudhuri's (1985) work certainly attests to the vitality of capitalist practices in the Indian Ocean during the medieval and early modern centuries under both Muslim and Hindu religious frameworks. Rodinson's (1974) analysis of Islam and capitalism rejects the idea that Islam was incompatible with capitalism or was responsible for the relative backwardness of the Muslim world in the modern era. Rodinson found no incompatibility of the prescriptions in the *Qur'an* and the *Sunnah* that would constitute serious obstacles to capitalist development. Marshall Hodgson (1974, 1993) was of a similar view, finding that independent individual (i.e. rational) calculation was well established in Islam and freely made contracts were in accord with *Shari'ah* law. Money and profits have never been despised under Islam (despite the Qur'anic prohibitions on unearned interest, interpreted as usury or *riba* in Islamic finance, and on monopoly and certain forms of exploitation) and indeed the Prophet Mohammed commended productivity above prayer and piety. Jack Goody (1996) has argued that there were no deep impediments that were structural such as differences in rationality that prevented the oscillation of power between East and West, but rather only more contingent ones. David Landes (1998) on the other hand, has recently tried to revive "Orientalist" prejudices within this debate by arguing that both Islamic and

Chinese thought systems were generally inhospitable to modern (capitalist) development in contrast to the superiority of the Judaeo-Christian tradition. Blaut (1992: 366) considers the presumption of rationality as the cause of Western superiority to be the supreme example of Eurocentrism in historical thinking. Even Samir Amin (1988: 84) has argued that many religious or social-ideational frameworks, including Christianity, Islam, and Confucianism, may function as ideologies of capitalism.

Indeed, the spirit of acquisitiveness that animates capitalist practices was to be found widely dispersed in both the ancient and medieval world (as in the modern) across both Occident and Orient. Weber sums up the point as follows: "the ancient and medieval business temper...typical of all genuine traders, whether small businessmen or large-scale moneylenders, in Antiquity, the Far East, India, the Mediterranean littoral area, and the Occident of the Middle Ages: [is] the will and the wit to employ mercilessly every chance of profit, 'for the sake of profit to ride through Hell even if it singes the sails'" (Weber 1978: 614).

In conclusion, therefore, recognizing the common existence of capitalist practices in East and West for much of world history allows us to completely reassess the overarching dynamic of the world system and the capital accumulation process on a world scale. This is the intention of world system theory: to reveal the common rhythms, the competition and rivalry, and the mutual influence among all the zones of the world economy over a period of several millennia without prejudice as to cultural or religious orientation, but with an objective structural emphasis on the process of capital accumulation on a world scale and on the real patterns of this process, both in terms of the "long cycles" of world economic expansion and contraction, and the "center shifts" between rival economic and political power centers, which result in reconfigurations of the hierarchical power structure of the world along with their civilizational implications.

World historical patterns and globalization

We should be especially wary of the idea of a straight-line progression in world history in regard to the form of labor, that is, the idea of the gradual "liberation" or "emancipation" of labor, progressing from extremely unfree (slavery) in the ancient period, to somewhat less unfree (serfdom) in the medieval, to the final realization of universal "free" labor in the modern era of global capitalism. Actually, the institution of slavery has been a constant feature of world economic history from ancient through medieval and early modern and into our own times (Thomas 1998). We know that the expansion of capital is not exclusively associated with the expansion of free labor. In the case of the efflorescence of capitalist practices in the Occident in both the ancient Hellenistic/Roman period and during the "primitive accumulation" of the rise of early modern European capital (some 1500 years later), there was an unmistakable and close association between the expansion of capitalist practices and slavery. The pivotal role of the slave trade (Williams 1944; Thomas 1998) and slave labor in the origins of "modern capitalism" on a world scale tells us that no linear pattern of the emancipation of labor is associated with capital in world history. Slavery is once again on the increase in our contemporary world economy, in areas ranging from Eastern European and Southeast Asian sex trades to the bonded and child slave labor in India and elsewhere, including the cocoa plantations of West Africa and the mines of South America.

The fundamental reason that the expansion of capital and the emergence of "historical capitalism" is not associated exclusively with the emancipation of labor resides in the very nature of capital itself, which thrives on an increase in the rate of exploitation. This tendency to seek an increase in the rate of exploitation of labor is simply the underlying logic of capital as a social relation, that is, to extract surplus value and to accumulate a profit. This quest for an increase in the "rate of profit" affects all forms of labor, including industrial wage labor, whether via the immiseration of the proletariat, or more recently via the "flexibilization" of labor and the global mobility of capital in search of lower labor costs, the proliferation of slavery (Thomas 1997) and the drive to (re)establish (neo)colonial forms of subjugation.

Therefore, class struggles between labor (both free and unfree) and capital are an intrinsic element in the history of capital and its role in world economic history, whether we are speaking of ancient, medieval, or modern capital. The upshot of this analysis is to examine how changes in forms of labor are related to wider social, political, and systemic conditions in world economic history including "long cycles" or "pulsations" such as "capitalization versus de-capitalization" and "expansion versus contraction" in the world system as a whole. It may be most important when we consider the "transitions" to examine why the conditions of capital accumulation changed when and where they did, and not only due to technological conditions but also to socio-political conditions and struggles. Therefore, the real question is not about defining *capitalism* or seeking its origins, since *capital* and capitalist practices have been a consistent part of world economic and social history for millennia. The real significance of a thorough reexamination of the role of capital in world history is in reinterpreting and judging its larger systemic and social effects: economically, politically, ideologically, and culturally.

As Weber observed "Again and again we find that it is precisely in the periods of 'justice and order' equivalent of course to periods of economic stability that there occurred a swift decline of *capitalism*" (Weber 1976: 66). It is perhaps the greatest peculiarity of the West and its particular and modern variant of historical capitalism that it gave so much freedom to capital – not only freedom to exploit labor, but even to threaten the larger economic system with de-stabilization (or disequilibrium). In my view, world system or global history can be understood as a perpetual social contestation between the impetus to allow capital to expand unrestrained, whatever the social and other consequences (such as environmental degradation), and the impetus to constrain a predatory capital(ism) and protect labor, society, and nature from capital's depredations. I argue that the current debate over the relationship between globalization and global capital(ism) might benefit from such a world historical perspective. There is more than just "the business cycle" at issue here. The central historical question, posed throughout global history, is how to tame the beast of capital, how to allow its wealth-creating benefits to exist without allowing capital to exceed moral, social, and environmental limits set in defense of society's interests.

Current social contestations surrounding globalization, its causes and consequences, can be better historically grounded and understood through a dialectical global or world system history perspective. Are we in a period of expansion of world civilization via global capital(ism)? Or are we entering a period of entropy and perhaps implosion? Or will it be a period of social transformation and the emergence of a new type of global culture and society? Will the ever-deepening crisis of global polarization engendered by the expansion of global capital over the past thirty years be resolved by conferring further freedom via the "free market" enjoyed by capital? Or will there be a solution which comes forth from the historical dialectics of globalization, whereby concerted social action, spanning the globe, imposes new controls on capital to constrain its unbridled expansion? The future of humanity, as global and world system history teaches us, depends on the answer we give to this question. The politicization, as well as the necessary historicization of "globalization theory" is therefore far from being a mere academic problem.[10]

I suggest that we understand contemporary globalization as embodying continuity in global history, as an *intensification* of several deeply embedded patterns or tendencies. These intensifications: of Western modernity and Western capitalism; of the process of the expansion of capital accumulation on a world scale of organization; of the process of commodification of more and more spheres of life; of the process of proletarianization – or the creation of capital–wage relations as the prevailing mode of economic social relations (thus increasing the rate of exploitation of labor); of the embedded asymmetry of "North–South" (i.e. core–periphery) relations in the world system (constructed by the historic "rise of the West" to global dominance and now reproduced); and an intensification of the global polarization between rich and poor involving an ever-greater increase in global inequality.

However, at the same time, I suggest that we should understand these tendencies as subject to a dialectical process, and thereby recognize the continuing historical tension between capital versus oikos; free versus unfree labor; organization versus entropy, homogenization versus heterogenization (or fragmentation); and finally "globalization versus counter-globalization" (Gills 2001) via "the politics of resistance"(Gills 2000).

Contemporary globalization and global history are illustrative of a continued dialectic between organization and entropy inherent in globalization. The (neoliberal) states, led by the United States, coalesce to promote the world market and the globalization of production and finance and to curtail state intervention into the realm of production. They also act together to discipline any state that remains nonconformist to this neoliberal doctrine of globalization. However, this same grand coalition of (global or transnational) capital and (neoliberal) states may be engendering entropy through the erosion of class consciousness and organization; the fragmentation of identities; social polarization and marginalization of labor, and of women especially and of nonwhite or non-Europeans perhaps particularly; and via the continued degradation of the global environment. However, such entropic tendencies provoke new forms of social resistance and new forms of human consciousness and solidarities, including now on a truly global scale, against the hegemony of global capital.

This analysis gives rise to the increasing awareness of the need for "global justice" in response to the enduring realities of embedded structural asymmetries or global inequality which is now quickly emerging for many theorists and practitioners as the pivotal moral, political, and analytical concern of the era. By breaking out finally from the moral and intellectual confines of embedded Eurocentrism, the new "global" understanding of history can teach us something about the common intellectual, material, and spiritual culture and history of humanity, and therefore about our common future. The realization that we are all the inhabitants of a common planet brought about a new radical environmental consciousness which is a hopeful aspect of the emerging global politics. There is an ongoing realization that we are also all members of one common species, that is, that "races" are genetically speaking undemonstrable and a false construct based on insignificant differences given that all humans share 99.8 percent of their genes in common. The past reliance on skin color as the key differentiating criterion (of "race"), must now give way to a new consciousness of human unity and therefore to the imperative for global justice within a growing reflexive sensibility of the community of all humanity.

It is equally necessary that we should all endeavor to understand the full history of globalization, since understanding the antecedents of the contemporary phenomenon is, in effect, necessary to understand the present patterns and tensions. The next step forward therefore may be to investigate "globalization as global history" systematically in a search for enduring patterns as well as the circumstances and possibilities of social and structural transformation.

A new understanding of global history from a non-Eurocentric and therefore humancentric perspective, can thus liberate us from the many parochial "national" histories, which are themselves as much a fiction, or better, a "myth," as is the current ideological construction of neoliberal globalization. When UNESCO decided to rewrite world history textbooks several decades ago, it insisted not only on de-Europeanization and a world point of view, but also that civilization and its history be understood not from a nationalistic perspective but from one which should insist on the great and intricate interdependence of national cultures, all of which give and receive benefits in relation to the rest of the world. That project met with only limited success but must now, more than ever, be renewed with even greater vigor and determination.

We now know that globalization in some sense is a new mythology and that, as such, it is neither historically inevitable nor technologically predetermined. It is, rather, historically open, indeterminate and, above all, a thoroughly political and social process and therefore subject to human will and action and potential transformation. This hard-fought and hard-won "lesson" should become the foundation for the reconstruction of knowledge in the coming century, one in which all humanity will confront a *choice*: between possible entropic and catastrophic breakdowns environmentally, socially, economically, and politically; and alternative(s) that seek ways to break the iron cage of "realist history" and its repeated Kafkaesque nightmare scenarios of war, exploitation, and crisis, to find real and lasting solutions to the common threats to our planet home and to humanity and even to civilization itself.

Thus, historical method (or the historical mode of enquiry) must be reinvigorated, a theoretical and analytical move that goes in tandem with the historicization of globalization. This re-investigation and re-deployment of critical historical method should focus on the agency-structure problematic. This "reflective turn" should lead to an emphasis on *transformative* and *emancipatory* moments and conditions in global history, and to a critical self-awareness on the part of scholars (especially of global perspective of economy) in constructing such knowledge.

It is a basic insight of dialectical method to realize that every historical social system carries within itself the seeds of its own destruction, which is also, however, a potential for transformation. We should know that the times we are living in are certainly those of "creative destruction," not in the sense of Schumpeterian cycles of capital's expansion but rather of the demise of old structures and the potential for re-creation and transformation.

The Eurocentric impoverishment of the historical and contemporary imagination, through which humanity as a whole has been understood primarily through theories and research agendas emanating from the very particular (and possibly peculiar) experiences of "Western civilization,"[11] has remarkably and persistently succeeded in many ways over many generations. It is, nevertheless, an error of enormous proportions to reduce the rich complexity of the world to a single set of simplifications. As we enter the twenty-first century, we must resist the temptation to reproduce a monocultural Eurocentric world view with all its serious distortions. We should instead strive to identify and promote the common interest of all humanity. Only by this approach, through an understanding of the dialectics of global history, can we arrive at a truly *global* (in the sense of all-encompassing) view of globalization and global history. Renouncing all "culture-centrisms," whether of West or East, North or South, we can reach for a new level of humancentric analysis, embracing all cultural streams in the ocean of "world civilization."

Acknowledgments

I would like to acknowledge Mary Ann Tétreault and Bob Denemark for assistance in the preparation of this chapter; special thanks to Robert W. Cox, Patrick O'Brien, William H. McNeill, Steve Hobden, and John Hobson for comments on earlier draft versions of this chapter.

Notes

1 It is useful to review primitivist versus modernist and substantivist versus formalist debates in economic anthropology. In general, I tend to sympathize more with the modernist and formalist interpretations than with their opponents on the primitivist side.

I tend to agree with Ekholm and Friedman in so far as their approach to "capital-imperialism" is broadly "modernist" and compatible with my "continuity thesis." See: K. Ekholm and Jonathan Friedman in Frank and Gills (eds) 1993/6.

2 I wish to thank Robert W. Cox for making these points in comments on an earlier draft of this chapter. In private correspondence March 2000.

3 So also in the Americas. For example, see: David Hirst Thomas. 2000. *Skull Wars: Kennewick man, Archaeolgy, and the Battle for Native American Identity*, New York: Basic Books.

4 I suggest the same hypothesis for the emergence of urbanism in MesoAmerica and the Andean civilizations and for the investigation of the origins of capital in those world-historical systems. It is also possible that these civilizations may have been less detached from the "Old World" than most people think.

5 I follow Jane Jacobs (1960/1984) in viewing cities as centers of social power and economic dynamism throughout world history. In contrast to the idea of dominance of the land and agriculture in economic history, at the very least the importance of the economy of cities should not be *under*estimated. This is especially important for an accurate understanding of the medieval period in world history, even in Europe, where urbanism was admittedly somewhat weaker than elsewhere in the Eurasian world economy at the same time.

6 The "bourgeois" character of ancient commercial economies such as the Phoenicians can be taken as an example of "ancient capitalism." Phoenician cities were dedicated to capitalist activity, including production of commodities for export markets, maritime commerce, and colonization. Capital was nested in complex networks of individual, family, and state-connected enterprises. These networks encompassed the different branches of economic activity: production, commodity circulation, and credit. Private capital worked in close symbiosis with the state and its interests, and the royal family was usually engaged in commercial ventures, often in partnership with private interests (Aubet 1993).

7 The specific modern forms of capitalist practices that emerged in medieval Europe were in fact a special combination of such earlier and Oriental influences with Occidental adaptations, particularly those conventions whereby "partnerships *en commandite, maone*, privileged companies of all kinds and finally joint stock corporations were created…" (Weber 1978: 613). Abu-Lughod (1989) traces medieval Islamic contract and business practice back to pre-Islamic forms and even to Babylonian precedents. Goody (1996) makes the case that much of what the West knew of capitalist practices by the early modern period the East also knew, and probably earlier. For an interesting study of the origins of modern capitalism in East Asia see Jacobs (1958).

8 I have discussed this further in an unpublished paper, "Ascent, descent, ascent: East Asian and Western economic development comparisons" paper presented at the International Political Science Association meetings, Seoul, August 1997.

9 There is likewise a need for fresh objective comparisons between Occidental and non-Occidental institutional variants of the state. I am indebted to Randall Collins for this point.

10 For further discussion of these issues see Barry K. Gills (ed.) 2000. *Globalization and the Politics of Resistance*. Macmillan/Palgrave/St Martin's. Foreword by John Kenneth Galbraith.

11 Famously, when asked what he thought of Western civilization, Mahatma Gandhi is said to have answered, " I think it would be a good idea."

6 Mergers, stagflation, and the logic of globalization*

Jonathan Nitzan

Introduction: three mysteries

Corporate mergers, stagflation, and globalization are usually studied as separate phenomena, belonging to the fields of finance, economics, and international political economy, respectively. This chapter attempts to tie them together as integral facets of capital accumulation.

Analyzed independently, all three phenomena appear problematic, even mysterious. Take mergers and acquisitions. These are now constantly in the news, and for a good reason. Over the past decade, their value reached unprecedented levels, surpassing for the first time in history that of newly created production capacity. Yet, despite their importance, mergers and acquisitions remain enigmatic. "Most mergers disappoint," writes *The Economist*, "so why do firms keep merging?" (Anonymous 1998). According to the textbooks, there is no clear answer. Corporate merger remains one of the "ten mysteries of finance," a riddle for which there are many partial explanations but no *overall* theory (Brealey *et al.* 1992, ch. 36).

Stagflation, although presently dormant, is equally embarrassing. Most mainstream economists believe that prices should increase when there is excess demand and overheating, but stagflation – a term coined by Samuelson (1974) to denote the combination of *stag*nation and in*flation* – shows prices can also rise in the midst of unemployment and recession.[1] A similar difficulty arises with the opposite phenomenon of inflation*less* growth, such as the one experienced recently in the United States. The standard explanation rests on the disinflationary impact of accelerating productivity, although that scarcely solves the problem. The fact is that even faster efficiency gains have often failed to tame inflation in the past, so why is it that they succeed now? Frustrated, many economists seem to have finally thrown in the towel, suggesting that we now live in a "new economy" where the old rules simply no longer apply.

And globalization, too, remains perplexing to some extent. Although theories here vary a great deal, most seem to assume that in the final analysis globalization

* This article was originally published in the *Review of International Political Economy* 8(2), 2001 (http://www.tandf.co.uk). A brief epilogue is appended to reflect recent developments.

occurs because it is more efficient. Capitalist accumulators, goes the argument, are propelled by the dual need to cut costs and broaden markets; this is best achieved through integration; hence the relentless pressure toward globalization. There is, however, a little glitch in this logic. Somehow, intensifying trade and integrating production always seem to come together with various barriers, restrictions, and limitations. International political economists tend to analyze these as facets of statist protectionism, non-market *reactions* to market globalization. Yet one could equally well argue that such "protectionism" is in fact essential for accumulation, and that the logic of globalization therefore has to do not with efficiency *per se*, but with the *control* of efficiency for profitable ends.

As it turns out, some of the mist surrounding these phenomena begins to dissipate when we examine them not in isolation but together, as interrelated facets of accumulation. The following section, building on the concept of differential accumulation, outlines an alternative framework in which capital is understood as a strategic power institution. The section "Breadth and depth," articulates the various regimes of differential accumulation through which capital power is augmented, as well as sketching their broader societal implications. It identifies four distinct paths: green-field investment (external breadth), mergers and acquisitions (internal breadth), cost-cutting (internal depth), and stagflation (external depth). The remainder of the chapter develops and analyzes the interconnections between these regimes. The section "Green-field," looks at the conflicting effects on differential accumulation of green-field investment. The sections "Mergers and acquisitions," and "Amalgamation and globalization," examining a century of mergers and acquisitions in the United States, combine the logic of corporate restructuring, capitalist integration, and globalization. The sections "Cost-cutting" and "stagflation," explore the impact on differential accumulation of cost-cutting and stagflation, respectively. The final section ties up the analysis by presenting a tentative framework for understanding the pendulum of global accumulation and crisis.

Differential accumulation

This analysis is part of a larger joint investigation, by Shimshon Bichler and myself, into the nature and broader ramifications of "capital *as* power." The analysis builds on the concept of differential accumulation, with capital viewed as a strategic institution, a reflection of capitalist power over social reproduction.[2] Radical writers have long debated the relative significance for accumulation of "production" as opposed to "circulation" (for instance, Weeks 1981; Sherman 1985). Classical Marxists, preoccupied with the labor process, prioritized the former, whereas Monopoly Capital theorists, stressing the structure of ownership, shifted some of the emphasis to the latter. Less attention, however, has been paid to the categories themselves. The main problem is that the very separation between production and circulation, evident as it was in Marx's time, is no longer clear-cut: services currently account for over 70 percent of economic activity, complex production is increasingly carried out by huge corporate coalitions whose non-arm's-length transactions blur the meaning of market "circulation"; and alienation, expropriation, and capitalist power have long transcended the boundary of the factory, spilling over into consumption and into politics at large. Indeed, given that capitalist labor and capitalist ownership are two sides of the same coin, it is unclear why we need to prioritize one over the other to begin with.

The concept of differential accumulation seeks to go beyond the "production–circulation" debate. It sees capital as inherently *political*. This in turn enables us to integrate into the analysis, in addition to production and consumption, diverse phenomena such as oligopolization, ideology, religion, the state, and military conflict, as well as mergers and acquisitions, stagflation, and globalization. Most importantly, such power processes are seen not as auxiliaries to an otherwise "pure" notion of capital, but rather as essential to its understanding *from the very start*.

Capital accumulation is of course one of the more problematic concepts of political economy (Robinson 1953–54; Harcourt 1972; Bliss 1975; Obrinsky 1983). Although the issue cannot be resolved here, the thrust of the problem can be briefly outlined. The main difficulty, haunting both conservative and Marxist analyses, is excessive emphasis on "materialist" considerations. For the neoclassicists, capital is a tangible means of production measured in its own technical units. For Marxists, capital is not a physical thing but a dynamic socio-material transformation. Yet, when it comes to measurement, Marxists too resort to materialistic units of "dead labor."

The problem, first identified by Thorstein Veblen and later articulated in the Cambridge Controversies, concerns the *units* of accumulation. Neoclassical theory has never been able to explain what these units are. Marxist theory measures capital in terms of "dead labor," yet, as Marx himself openly acknowledged, once production grows in complexity it becomes difficult if not impossible to identify labor contents, even on paper; they simply do not exist (for more, see Nitzan 1992, 1998; Nitzan and Bichler 2000a).

An alternative way to tackle the issue is to build on Veblen and treat capital as a strategic institution, related to but distinct from production as such. Seen from this perspective, the magnitude of capital, measured in relative monetary terms as elaborated later, is *a crystallization of capitalist power to shape and reshape the process of social reproduction*. Much as in Marx's scheme, this power is exerted over human beings, mediated through production for profit. But in contrast to Marx, who tried to construct such power from the bottom up based on intrinsic labor values, we look at it from the top down.

On the face of it, capital appears as finance, and *only* finance. In form, it is simply the present value of expected capitalist earnings. The contents of capital, however, are political in the widest sense of the term, and the reason is not hard to see. Capitalist earnings are connected to production but the links are complicated and highly nonlinear. Owners are interested not in production *per se*, but in its effect on their relative profit. And since "too much" production is by definition detrimental to profit, it is clear that production alone – that is, without its surrounding power institutions – is too limited a basis for understanding profit and accumulation. More importantly, there are numerous institutions and processes that are linked to production remotely or not at all, yet bear heavily on profit and accumulation. Corporate collusion, patents, taxation, transfer pricing, racial discrimination, the molding of consumer "wants," brainwashing, entertainment, armed conflict, and so on and on – all have an impact on profit. And once such effects are "discounted" into asset prices, they become facets of capital.

In other words, capital embodies, or crystallizes power that emanates not only from the relations of production but also from the entire spectrum of social power in capitalism. This broader perspective suggests that a bottom-up analysis of capital, based on what Marx called the production base, is potentially too limited. A top-down approach, which incorporates from the very start all forms of power affecting profit, is possibly more revealing.

Strictly speaking, capitalists exert their power over society as a whole, so one whose profit amounts to one-hundredth of the total can be said to control 1 percent of the entire capitalist process. But such power is relevant only in relation to that of other capitalists. The real challenge is not to exert power as such, but to hold and expand it against other contenders. In a developed capitalist context, this boils down to "beating the average." And indeed, modern investors rarely if ever seek to "maximize" profit. Their ultimate goal is not absolute accumulation, but *differential* accumulation: having their profit rise faster than the average so as to make their distributive share bigger and bigger.[3]

The reason, again, is not hard to see. Like all other forms of power, capitalist power is also based on exclusion. Unlike other forms of power, though, the dynamics of capitalism – particularly the "natural right of investment" – require capitalists to exclude not only workers but also most other capitalists from accessing their sources of profit; failure to do so implies not only the shrinking of their own share, but also glut and the possible disappearance of profit altogether. In this sense, capitalist power is necessarily two-dimensional: imposing it on society both assumes and implies a pecking order among capitalists themselves.

In the same breath, one can also argue that the very purpose of capitalist enterprise, much as in Mumford's "mega machine," is to articulate, assemble, and operate such power arrangements in the first place (Mumford 1967, 1970; Nitzan 1998). And if we are to believe Veblen and Braudel, this power quest is not at all new; it lies at the very essence of capitalism and has from the very beginning (Veblen 1904; 1923; Braudel 1985).

The result is that capitalist power institutions, however different qualitatively, are always the same in one crucial respect. They all aim at, and are measured by, their relative outcome: the extent to which they generate differential accumulation. In this sense, capital is the highest form of commodification, the *commodification of power itself*.

Note that, as it stands, differential accumulation is not a deterministic law of motion. It does not have to happen. Our claim here is rather that, over time, the *quest* for differential accumulation grows into an increasingly central moment of capitalist development. That being said, there is no telling whether or not differential accumulation will succeed, or how exactly it will unfold. As a power process, it involves purposeful action against opposition, so its outcome cannot possibly be automatic. In contrast to neoclassical and some versions of Marxian economics, where unobservable concepts such as utility, factor productivity, labor value, and maximum profit are used to build "closed" deterministic models, the analysis of differential accumulation relies on an observable category – the rate of differential accumulation – in order to construct "open," contingent explanations. And, indeed, on its own, differential accumulation is a mere framework. Making it into a theory requires that we prioritize its various trajectories, explaining how and why they unfold, the circumstances under which they proceed or are held back, and their broader societal implications. The present essay is an attempt to explore some of these questions.

Furthermore, there is no assumption here that the same group of capitalists will dominate the process throughout. On the contrary, the very essence of differential accumulation is an intra-capitalist struggle simultaneously to restructure the pattern of social reproduction as well as the grid of power (see for instance, Bichler 1994–95; Nitzan and Bichler 1996, 2001). The important point in this chapter, though, is the progressive differential growth of big business *as a whole*, regardless of its particular composition. As George Orwell aptly put it, "A ruling group is a ruling group so long as it can nominate its successors. . . . *Who* wields power is not important, provided that the hierarchical structure remains always the same" (Orwell 1948: 211, original emphasis).

The centrality of differential accumulation brings to the forefront the process of *corporate centralization*. The first to emphasize this process was Marx (1909, vol. I, ch. XXV), although he never integrated it into his bottom-up theory of value and accumulation which relied heavily on the assumption of competition and the free movement of capital and labor. This limitation no longer applies in a top-down power theory of capital. If accumulation is to be understood differentially, its analysis should focus from the start not only on capital in the aggregate, but also – and indeed more so – on the large corporate groups of *dominant capital* at the core of the process. The origin of these groups, the political-economic patterns of their evolution, the means by which they expand, the broader implications of their differential growth, and the limits and contradictions imposed on that growth, are central to our understanding of capitalist development in general and its current trajectory in particular.[4]

Breadth and depth

How can dominant capital achieve differential accumulation? For the large corporation, the level of profit is the product of the number of employees times the average profit per employee. The firm can therefore raise its profit in two ways. The first, which we call "breadth," is to augment its organization by having more employees. The second, which we label "depth," is to make its existing organization a more effective appropriator so as to generate higher profit per employee.

Applying the same logic at the differential level, the implication is that a large firm will accumulate differentially by (1) expanding its employment faster than the average, (2) raising its profit per employee faster than the average, or (3) some combination of the two.[5] Each avenue – breadth or depth – can be further sub-divided into "internal" and "external" subroutes, thereby leading to a four-way taxonomy:

Table 6.1 Regimes of differential accumulation

	External	Internal
Breadth	Green-field	Mergers and acquisitions
Depth	Stagflation	Cost-cutting

1   *External breadth: green-field investment.* A firm can achieve differential accumu-lation by building new capacity and hiring new employees faster than the average. This method is labeled "external" since, from a societal perspective, it involves a net addition of employees.[6] Its upper ceiling is the extent of proletarianization. The more immediate limit comes through the negative impact it has on depth: "excessive" green-field growth creates a downward pressure on prices and hence on profit per employee.

2   *Internal breadth: mergers and acquisitions.* Strictly speaking, internal breadth involves differential earnings growth through interfirm labor mobility. This can happen when a firm adds new capacity and employment against cutbacks elsewhere, although such movements relate more to *industrial* restructuring (labor mobility between sectors) than to the *size* redistribution of firms (labor moving from small to large firms). The situation is different with corporate amalgamation via mergers and acquisitions where no new capacity is created. By taking over other companies, the firm increases its own profit relative to the average (which is virtually unaltered). We call this route "internal" since it merely redistributes control over existing capacity and employment. Merger and acquisition activity is perhaps the most potent form of differential accumulation, serving to kill two birds with one stone: it directly increases differential breadth while indirectly helping to protect and possibly boost differential depth (relative pricing power). It is limited, however, both by the availability of takeover targets and by social, political, and technological barriers.

3   *Internal depth: cost-cutting.* The purpose is to cheapen production faster than the average, either through relative efficiency gains or by relatively larger reductions in input prices. It is "internal" in that it redistributes income shares within a given price. Although cost-cutting is relentlessly pursued by large firms (directly as well as indirectly through outsourcing), the difficulty of both monopolizing new technology and controlling input prices suggests that the net effect is commonly to meet the average rather than to beat it.

4   *External depth: stagflation.* Our emphasis on stagflation rather than inflation is deliberate: contrary to conventional wisdom, inflation usually occurs with, and often necessitates, some slack. Now, for a single seller, higher prices commonly are more than offset by lost volume, but things are different for a coalition of sellers. Dominant capital, to the extent that it acts in concert,

can benefit from higher prices since, up to a point, the relative profit gains per unit outweigh the relative decline in volume.[7] Of course, for this to become a continuous process (inflation rather than discrete price increases), other firms must join the spiral. Yet, since small companies have little political leverage and are usually unable to collude, the result is to redistribute income in favor of the bigger ones who can. We refer to this method as "external," since the redistribution occurs through a (pecuniary) expansion of the pie.

What are the implications of this taxonomy? In addressing this question, it is important to distinguish the case of an individual large corporation from the broader analysis of dominant capital as a group. A single firm may successfully combine different facets of breadth and depth. Not so for dominant capital as a whole. If we look at breadth and depth not as firm strategies, but as overall *regimes* (see Table 6.1), it quickly becomes apparent that conditions which are conducive to one often undermine the other. For the sake of brevity, we group our arguments here into eight related propositions.

Proposition 1. Understood as broad regimes, breadth and depth tend to move countercyclically to one another. Breadth presupposes some measure of economic growth as well as relative political-economic stability. Depth, on the other hand, commonly implies restrictions, conflict, and stagflation. Although strictly speaking the two regimes are not mutually exclusive, they tend to "negate" one other, with more breadth associated with less depth, and vice versa.

Proposition 2. Of the two regimes, breadth is the path of least resistance. There are two reasons for this. First, it is usually more straightforward and less conflictual to expand one's organization than it is to engage in collusive increases in prices or in struggles over input costs. Second, breadth is relatively more stable and hence easier to extend and sustain, whereas depth, with its heightened social antagonism, is more vulnerable to backlash and quicker to spin out of control.

Proposition 3. Over the longer haul, mergers and acquisitions tend to rise relative to green-field investment. While both routes can contribute to differential accumulation, as capitalism spreads geographically and dominant capital grows in importance, so does the threat of excess capacity. Mergers and acquisitions alleviate the problem whereas green-field investment aggravates it.[8] The broader consequence of this shift is for chronic stagnation gradually to substitute for cyclical instability.

Proposition 4. The relative growth of mergers and acquisitions is likely to oscillate around its uptrend. Corporate amalgamation involves major social restructuring and hence is bound to run into roadblocks. The result is a wave-like pattern with long periods of acceleration followed by shorter downturns.

Proposition 5. The underlying logic of mergers and acquisitions implies progressive "spatial" unification and, eventually, globalization. For amalgamation to run ahead of overall growth, dominant capital must successively break its "envelopes," spreading from the industry, to the sector, to the national economy, and ultimately to the world as a whole. In this sense, differential accumulation is a prime mover of spatial integration and globalization.

Proposition 6. Cost-cutting is not a real alternative to an amalgamation lull. The pressure to reduce cost is ever present, but its effect is more to meet than beat the average. The principal reason is that productivity improvements are neither inherently related to corporate size nor easy to protect. Similarly, reductions in input prices are seldom proprietary and often spill over to other firms.

Proposition 7. A much more potent response to declining mergers and acquisitions is inflationary increases in profit margins. This is often facilitated by previous corporate centralization, and although the process is inherently unstable and short-lived, it can generate very large differential gains. By its nature, though, such inflation is possible only through a vigilant limitation of production with the result that inflation appears as stagflation.

Proposition 8. Over the longer term, differential accumulation depends primarily on mergers and acquisitions. In the shorter term, it can benefit from sharp stagflationary crises. The main engine of differential accumulation is corporate amalgamation, which thrives on overall growth and the successive breakup of ownership "envelopes." Occasional discontinuities in the process, however, push dominant capital toward an alternative regime of stagflationary redistribution. The result is a pendulum-like oscillation between long periods of relative political-economic stability accompanied by economic growth and low inflation, and shorter periods of heightened conflict, stagnation, and inflation.

A fuller theoretical and historical analysis of these general propositions is too wide to be undertaken here. It is nonetheless possible to highlight their significance by a brief examination of the US experience over the past century. While this experience is certainly unique to some extent, the leading role of the United States in general and of US firms in particular may offer insight into other cases as well as into the broader nature of capitalist development. Before starting our exploration, however, a word of caution. Although the United States offers the best historical data, these are not always suited for our disaggregate analysis, occasionally forcing us into rough approximations, roundabout estimates, and bare speculations. Our conclusions are therefore tentative, open to challenges, and invite further research and discussion.

Green-field growth

Employment growth is a double-edged sword for dominant capital, directly augmenting external breadth (differential employment per firm) while indirectly threatening external depth (differential pricing power). Consider first the direct impact. In general, overall employment growth augments the differential breadth of dominant capital, but the reason is largely due to the way it affects smaller firms. Large companies react to overall growth mainly by increasing their employment ranks. Smaller companies respond by growing in number (through the birth of new firms) as well as in size (by hiring more workers). This is important since newborn firms, by their very nature, tend to be smaller than the average. The implication is that, even if green-field growth is spread proportionately between dominant capital and the rest of the business universe, as long as some of this growth results in the birth of smaller firms, the net impact is to reduce average employment per firm, thus augmenting the differential breadth of dominant capital.

The evolution of this process in the United States is illustrated in Figure 6.1 (series are rebased for comparison). The data show that since 1926, the number of corporations has risen 3.6 times faster than overall employment, causing average employment per firm to drop by over 72 percent (note the logarithmic scale).[9] The process has not been even, however. During the two decades between the mid-1920s and mid-1940s, the number of firms remained relatively stable, first because of the great depression and subsequently due to World War II. Changes in overall employment were consequently reflected more or less fully in the

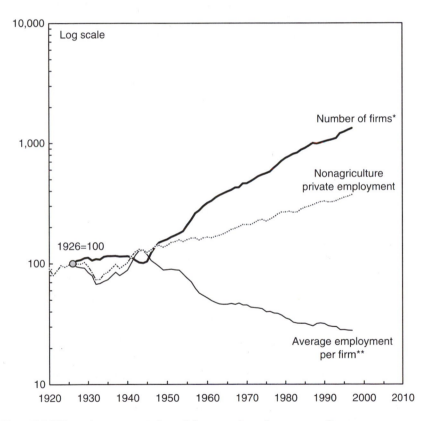

Figure 6.1 US employment, number of firms, and employment per firm.

Sources: US Internal Revenue Service; US Department of Commerce through McGraw-Hill (online).

Notes
* Corporations only, based on the number of tax returns by active corporations.
** Nonagricultural private employment divided by the number of corporations.

average size of firms that fell through the depression only to rise rapidly thereafter. In the longer run, however, this proved an aberration. Capitalism is subject to strong centrifugal forces, one of which is the inability of business enterprise to control the overall number of actors on the scene. And indeed, after the War, the number of firms started multiplying again while their average size trended down. Since large-firm employment has increased over the same period, we can safely conclude that overall employment growth boosted the differential breadth of dominant capital.

The indirect impact, operating through depth, is more complex and harder to assess. On the one hand, the multiplicity of small firms keeps their profit per employee low, partly by precluding cooperation and pricing discretion, and partly by undermining collective political action. This bears positively on the differential depth of dominant capital. On the other hand, unruly growth in the number of small firms can quickly degenerate into excess capacity, threatening to unravel cooperation within dominant capital itself. The balance between these conflicting forces is difficult if not impossible to determine.

In sum, green-field growth is no panacea for dominant capital. Although the process boosts its differential breadth, it has an indeterminate, and possibly negative effect on differential depth. The main way of counteracting this latter threat is through corporate amalgamation, to which we turn now.

Mergers and acquisitions

Our discussion in this section begins with Figure 6.2. In this figure we plot a "buy-to-build" indicator, which expresses the dollar value of mergers and acquisitions as a percent of the dollar value of gross fixed investment. In terms of our own categories, this index corresponds roughly to the ratio between internal and external breadth. (The data sources and method of computing this index are described in the Data Appendix.)

The figure illustrates two important processes, one secular, the other cyclical. First, it shows that, over the long haul, mergers and acquisitions indeed tend to become more important relative to green-field investment (Proposition 3). At the end of the nineteenth century, money put into amalgamation amounted to less than 1 percent of green-field investment. A century later, the ratio is approaching 200 percent, and rising. The trend growth rate indicated in the figure suggests that, year in, year out, mergers and acquisitions grew roughly three percentage points faster than new capacity.

Now, whereas employment associated with new capacity is added by small and large firms alike, amalgamation, almost by definition, increases mostly the employment ranks of dominant capital. The net effect of this trend, therefore, is a massive contribution to the differential accumulation of large firms.[10] The reasons for this tendency are not at all obvious. Why do firms decide to merge with, or take over other firms? Why has their urge to merge grown stronger over time? And what does it mean for the broader political economy?

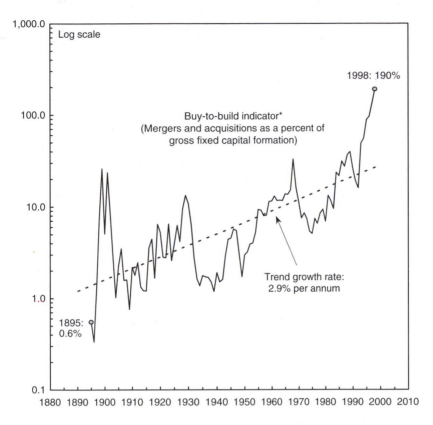

Figure 6.2 US accumulation: internal versus external breadth.

Source: See Data Appendix.

Note
* Based on splicing of separate series.

Needless to say, corporate amalgamation is a real headache for mainstream economics, whose models commonly rely on the assumption of atomistic competition. Marshall (1920) tried to solve the problem by arguing that firms, however large, are like trees in the forest: eventually they lose their vitality and die out in competition with younger, more vigorous successors. On its own, though, the forest analogy was not entirely persuasive, if only because incorporation made firms potentially perpetual. For the skeptics, therefore, Marshall had to offer an additional explanation. Even if large firms failed to die, he said, and instead grew into a corporate caste, the attendant social costs were still tolerable – first because such a caste tended to be benevolent and, second, because the costs were outweighed by the greater efficiency of large-scale business enterprise.

The rigorous spin on this latter argument was put by Coase (1937), who stated that the size of firms was largely a matter of transaction costs. Interfirm transactions, he asserted, were the most efficient since they were subject to market discipline. Such transactions, however, were not free, and therefore made sense only if their efficiency gains exceeded the extra cost of carrying them through. Otherwise, they were better internalized as intra-firm activity. Using such calculus, one could then determine the proper "boundary" of the firm which, according to Coase, was set at the point where "the cost of organizing an extra transaction within the firm become equal to the costs of carrying out the same transaction by means of an exchange on the open market or the costs of organizing in another firm" (Coase 1937: 96).

The ideological leverage of this theory proved immense. It implied that if companies such as General Electric, Cisco, or Lucent decided to "internalize" their dealings with other firms by swallowing them up, then that must be socially efficient, and that their resulting size – no matter how big – was necessarily "optimal" (e.g. Williamson 1985, 1986). In this way, the nonexistence of perfect competition was no longer an embarrassment for neoclassical theory. To the contrary, it was the *market itself* which determined the right "balance" between the benefits of competition and corporate size and, what is more, the whole thing was achieved automatically, according to the eternal principles of marginalism.

The argument is hard to refute, although that is by no means a blessing. The problem is that marginal transaction costs – much like marginal productivity and marginal utility – are unobservable so reality can never be shown as being at odds with the theory. For instance, one can use transaction costs to claim that the historical emergence of "internalized" command economies such as Nazi Germany or the Soviet Union means they were more efficient than their market predecessors. The obvious counterargument, which may well be true, is that these systems were imposed "from above," driven by a quest for power rather than efficiency. But then, can we not say the same thing about the development of oligopolistic capitalism?[11]

In fact, if it were only for efficiency, corporations should have become smaller, not larger. According to Coase's theory, technical progress, particularly in information and communication, reduces transaction costs, making the market look increasingly appealing and large corporations evermore cumbersome. Indeed, using this very logic Fukuyama (1999) recently announced the "death of the hierarchy," while advocates of the "E-Lance Economy" (as in freelance) argue that today's corporate behemoths are anomalous and will soon be replaced by small, "virtual" firms (Malone and Laubacher 1998). So far, though, these predictions seem hopelessly misplaced: amalgamation has not only continued but accelerated, including in the so-called "high-technology" sector where transactions costs supposedly fell the most.

How can that be true? Why do firms give up the benefit of market transaction in pursuit of further, presumably more expensive internalization? Are they not interested in lower cost? The riddle can be solved by using Veblen's distinction between "industry" and "business" (cf. 1904). Improved technology can certainly reduce the minimum efficient scale (MES) of production, and indeed today's largest establishments (plants, head offices, etc.) are often smaller than they were a hundred years ago. Firms, on the other hand, are business units, and since they can own many establishments, their boundaries need not depend on production as such. The real issue with corporate size is not efficiency but differential profit, and the key question therefore is whether amalgamation helps firms beat the average and, if so, how?

The conventional wisdom here is that mergers and acquisitions are a disciplinary form of "corporate control." According to writers such as Manne (1965), Jensen and Ruback (1983), and Jensen (1987), managers are often subject to conflicting loyalties which may compromise their commitment to profit maximization. The threat of takeover puts them back in line, forcing them not only to improve efficiency but also to translate such efficiency into higher profit and rising share-holder value.

This argument became popular during the 1980s, when the earnings yield on US equities fell below the yield on long-term bonds for the first time since the 1940s, giving corporate "raiders" the academic justification (if they needed one) for launching the most recent merger wave. The logic of the argument, however, was problematic. Mergers may indeed be driven by profit, but that in itself has little to do with productivity gains. To begin with, there is not much evidence that mergers are either prompted by inefficiency, or that they make the combined firms more efficient (Ravenscraft and Scherer 1987; Caves 1989; Bhagat *et al.* 1990). Indeed, as we argue later, the latent function of mergers in this regard is not to boost efficiency, but to *tame* it by keeping a lid on overall capacity growth. Moreover, there is no clear indication that mergers make amalgamated firms more profitable than they were separately, although here the issue is somewhat more complicated.

First, there is a serious methodological difficulty. Most attempts to test the effect of merger on profitability are based on comparing the performance of merged and non-merged companies (for instance, Ravenscraft 1987; Ravenscraft and Scherer 1989; Scherer and Ross 1990, ch. 5). While this method may offer some insight in the case of individual firms, it is misleading when applied to dominant capital as a whole. Looking at the amalgamation process in its entirety, the issue is not how it compares with "doing nothing" (i.e. with not amalgamating), but rather how it contrasts with the alternative strategy of green-field investment. Unfortunately, such a comparison is impossible to make since the very purpose of mergers and acquisitions is to avoid creating new capacity. In other words, amalgamation removes the main evidence against which we can assess its success.

Perhaps a better, albeit unscientific, way to tackle the issue is to answer the following hypothetical question: What would have happened to the profitability of dominant capital in the United States if, instead of splitting its investment one-third for green-field and two-thirds for mergers and acquisitions, it had plowed it all back into new capacity? As Veblen (1923: 373) correctly predicted, such a "free run of production" is not going to happen, so we cannot know for sure. But the very fact that it has not happened, together with the century-long tendency of moving in the opposite direction – from green-field to amalgamation – already suggest what the answer may be.[12]

The second important point concerns the meaning of "profitability" in this context. Conventional measures such as the earnings-to-price ratio, return on equity, or profit margin on sales, relevant as they may be for investors, are too narrow as indicators of *capitalist power* when such power is vested in and exercised by corporations rather than individuals. A more appropriate measure for this power is the distribution and differential growth of profit, and from this perspective mergers and acquisitions make a very big difference.

By fusing previously distinct earning streams, *amalgamation contributes to the organized power of dominant capital*, regardless of whether or not it augments conventional rates of return. In our view, this "earning fusion," common to all mergers, is also their ultimate goal. And indeed, by gradually shifting its emphasis from building to buying, corporate capitalism has so far been able not only to lessen the destabilizing impact of green-field cycles pointed out by Marx, but also to reproduce and consolidate on an ever-growing scale instead of collapsing under its own weight. The broader consequence of this shift has been creeping stagnation (Proposition 3), yet, as Veblen suggested, the large accumulators have learned to "manage" this stagnation for their own ends.[13]

Now, this general rationale for merger does not in itself explain the concrete historical trajectory of corporate amalgamation. Mergers and acquisitions grow but not smoothly and, indeed, the second feature evident in Figure 6.2 is the cyclical pattern of the series (Proposition 4). Over the past century, we can identify four amalgamation "waves." The first wave, occurring during the transition from the nineteenth to the twentieth century, is commonly referred to as the "monopoly" wave. The second, lasting through much of the 1920s, is known as the "oligopoly" wave. The third, building up during the late 1950s and 1960s, is nicknamed the "conglomerate" wave. The fourth wave, beginning in the early 1980s, does not yet have a popular title but, based on its all-encompassing nature, we can safely label it the "global" wave.

This wave-like pattern remains something of a mystery. Why do mergers and acquisitions have a pattern at all? Why are they not erratic, or alternatively, why do they not proceed smoothly? So far, most attempts to answer these questions have approached the issue from the micro perspective of the firm, which is precisely why they usually run into a dead end.

One of the more famous explanations is based on Tobin and Brainard (1968, 1977). The basic claim is simple: if green-field capacity is cheaper, a firm will build it from scratch; if existing capacity is cheaper, the firm will buy it from others. Extending this logic to the economy as a whole, we should therefore expect the buy-to-build ratio to be inversely correlated with the ratio of market value to replacement cost, now known as *Tobin's Q*: the less expensive existing assets are relative to new ones, the greater the proportion of "financial" to "real" investment, and vice versa.

This logic seems sensible except that, in reality, things happen to move the opposite way. Figure 6.3 depicts two series: our own buy-to-build indicator, measuring mergers and acquisitions as a percent of gross fixed investment, and *Tobin's Q*, based on the ratio of market value to net worth at replacement cost of nonfarm nonfinancial corporations (with series smoothed for easier comparison).

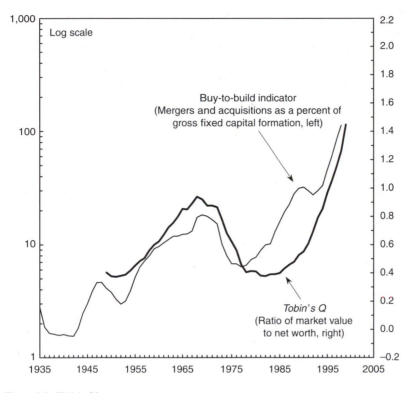

Figure 6.3 Tobin's Q?

Source: *Tobin's Q* pertains to nonfarm nonfinancial corporations, and is computed from Federal Reserve Board *Flow of Funds* data through McGraw-Hill (Online) (*Flow of Funds* codes: BS103164003L for market value, and BL102090005L for net worth at replacement cost). For the buy-to-build indicator, see Data Appendix.

Note
Series are smoothed as five-year moving averages.

According to the figure, US capitalists seem to have gone out of their minds: instead of investing in what was cheap, they systematically overspent on the expensive!

The picture looks anomalous but only because we are using neoclassical micro-economic logic to explain a complex power process. New capacity may indeed be cheap if you are the only one adding it. But if your competitors all do the same it is a different matter altogether. Under the latter circumstances, the threat of glut and falling profit makes buying existing assets much cheaper than it looks on paper. As we explain later, large firms understand this all too well and act accord-ingly.[14] In short, mergers and acquisitions, although pursued by individual firms, occur within a broader and ever-changing political economic context. It is only when making this restructuring process the center of our analysis that the general pattern of amalgamation begins to make sense.

A highly interesting attempt in this direction was offered by Lebowitz (1985), who tried to derive the tendency toward Monopoly Capitalism from the very logic of Classical Marxism. According to Marx, argues Lebowitz, the essence of accumulation is the expropriation of means of production – initially from workers but ultimately also from other capitalists – until capital becomes One, a unitary amalgam held by a single capitalist or a single corporation. The road toward such amalgamation, he continues, proceeds through horizontal, vertical, and conglomerate integration (although not necessarily following the stylized pattern in Figure 6.2). The key challenge is to show that all three phenomena are *inherent* in the inner logic of accumulation. To establish this link, Lebowitz begins by assuming, along with Marx, an intrinsic connection leading from productivity growth to accumulation. Next, he suggests that all three forms of integration increase efficiency and hence contribute to accumulation: horizontal integration creates economies of scale; vertical integration leads to more roundabout, or mechanized production runs; and conglomerate integration improves allocative efficiency through intersectoral capital mobility. To constrain any of these processes is therefore to hinder accumulation and since, according to Marx, capital works to dismantle its own barriers, it follows that all three types of integration are inevitable, and that capitalism is destined to become monopolistic.

Based on its own premises, the logic is undoubtedly elegant. The premises themselves, however, are partly incorrect as well as incomplete. The first problem concerns production. As noted earlier and argued further in the section "Cost-cutting," beyond a certain point there is no necessary connection between industrial size and efficiency/profitability, so complete productive integration cannot be traced to the inner logic of accumulation.[15] The second problem is the absence of power. Even if greater industrial integration were always more efficient and profitable, that would still leave unexplained a growing proportion of mergers which merely fuse ownership while leaving production lines separate. The difficulty is most clearly illustrated in the case of conglomerate integration: intersectoral capital movement can improve allocative efficiency only through greenfield investment but, if so, why does conglomerate consolidation almost invariably take the route of merger? The answer, by now a bit tedious, is that business consolidation is not about efficiency but the control of efficiency for differential ends. While capital is forever trying to remove the barriers on its own accumulation, this very accumulation is inherently impossible without barriers being put on others, including on most other capitalists. The act of merger fulfils both of these requirements, allowing investors to exercise their *freedom to limit*.

Seen from a differential accumulation perspective, amalgamation is a power process whose goal is to beat the average and redistribute control. Its main appeal to capitalists is that it contributes directly to differential breadth yet without undermining and sometimes boosting the potential for differential depth.[16] Thus, everything else remaining the same, it makes more sense to buy than to build. But then everything else does not, and indeed *cannot* remain the same. The reason is simple: amalgamation transforms the very conditions on which it is based.[17]

Three particular transformations need noting here. First, amalgamation is akin to eating the goose that lays the golden eggs. By gobbling up takeover targets within a given corporate universe, acquiring firms are depleting the pool of future targets. Unless this pool is somehow replenished, mergers and acquisitions eventually lead to a highly centralized structure in which dominant capital owns everything worth owning. From a certain point onward, the pace of amalgamation therefore has to decelerate. Although further amalgamation within dominant capital itself may be possible (large firms buying each other), the impact on the *group's* differential accumulation relative to the average is negligible: by this stage, dominant capital has grown so big it *is* the average.

Second, green-field growth, by adding new employment and firms, works to replenish the takeover pool to some extent. But then, and this is the second point worth noting, since green-field growth tends to trail the pace of amalgamation in both employment volume and dollar value, its effect is mostly to slow down the depletion process, not stop it. Indeed, the very process of amalgamation, by directing resources away from green-field investment, has the countervailing impact of reducing growth and hence hastening the depletion process. Thus, sooner or later, dominant capital is bound to reach its "envelope," namely the boundaries of its own corporate universe with few or no takeover targets to speak of.[18]

Third, corporate amalgamation is often socially traumatic. It commonly involves massive dislocation as well as significant power realignments, and is ultimately limited by the speed at which the underlying organizations can adapt (this last point is emphasized by Penrose 1959). The consequence is that as amalgamation builds up momentum, it also generates higher and higher roadblocks, contradictions, and counterforces.[19] Taken together, the depletion of takeover targets, the negative effect on growth associated with lower levels of green-field investment, and the emergence of counterforces, suggest that corporate amalgamation cannot possibly run smoothly and continuously (Proposition 4).

But then, why should amalgamation move in cycles? In other words, why does the uptrend resume after it stumbles? And what does this resumption mean? From the perspective of dominant capital, amalgamation is simply too important to give up. And while there may be not much worth absorbing in one's own corporate universe, *outside* of this universe targets are still plentiful. Of course, to take advantage of this broader pool dominant capital has to break through its original "envelope," which is precisely what happened as the United States moved from one wave to the other (Proposition 5).

The first, "monopoly," wave marked the emergence of modern big business, with giant corporations forming within their own original *industries*. Once this source of amalgamation was more or less exhausted, further expansion meant that firms had to move outside their industry boundaries. Indeed, the following "oligopoly" wave saw the formation of vertically integrated combines whose control increasingly spanned entire *sectors*, such as petroleum, machinery, and food products, among others. The next phase opened the whole *US corporate universe* up for grabs. Firms crossed their original boundaries of specialization to form large conglomerates with business lines ranging from raw materials, through manufacturing, to services and finance. Finally, once the national scene was more or less integrated, the main avenue for further expansion lay across international borders, hence the recent *global* merger wave.[20] So far, the global wave has been characterized by considerable de-conglomeration, with many firms refocusing on so-called "core activities" where they enjoy a leading profit position. The reason is that globalization enables additional intra-industry expansion across borders while legitimizing further domestic centralization in the name of "global competitiveness." Eventually, though, such refocusing is bound to become exhausted, pushing dominant capital back toward conglomeration, this time on a global scale. In fact, this is already happening in areas such as computing, communication, transportation, and entertainment, where technological change is rapidly blurring the lines between standard industrial classifications.[21]

Indeed, the pivotal impact of mergers is to alter not the structure of production *per se*, but the broader *structure of power*. The reason is rooted in the dialectical nature of amalgamation. By constantly pushing toward, and eventually breaking through their successive social "envelopes" – from the industry, to the sector, to the nation-state, to the world as a whole – mergers create a strong drive toward "jurisdictional integration," to use Olson's (1982) terminology. Yet this very integration pits dominant capital against new rivals under new circumstances, and so creates the need constantly to restructure power institutions, of which corporate amalgamation is itself an important dimension. Surprisingly, though, these power dynamics of mergers have drawn relatively little attention in an area where they seem to matter most, namely in the process of globalization.

Amalgamation and globalization

The gist of capitalist globalization is the spatial spread of accumulation, whose main vehicle is *the movement of capital*.[22] Most analyses of the process concentrate on its alleged cyclicality. The common view is that although capital flow has accelerated since the 1980s, the increase is part of a broader recurring pattern whose peaks were in fact recorded during the late nineteenth and early twentieth century (Taylor 1996). The standard approach to these ups and downs in capital mobility is the so-called "Unholy Trinity" of international political economy. According to this framework, there is an inherent tradeoff between state sovereignty, capital mobility, and international monetary stability, of which only two can coexist at any one time (Fleming 1962; Mundell 1963; Cohen 1993).[23] Thus, during the "liberal" Gold Standard which lasted until World War I, limited state sovereignty allowed for both free capital mobility and international monetary stability; during the interwar period, the emergence of state autonomy along with unfettered capital flows served to upset this monetary stability; after World War II, the quasi-statist system of Bretton Woods put a check on capital mobility so as to allow domestic policy autonomy without compromising monetary stability; finally, since the 1970s, the rise of neoliberalism has again unleashed capital mobility, although it is still unclear which of the other two nodes of the Trinity – state sovereignty or monetary stability – will have to go.

Why has the world moved from liberalism, to instability, to statism, and back to (neo)liberalism? Is this some sort of inevitable cycle, or is there an underlying historical process here which makes each "phase" fundamentally different? The answers vary widely.[24] Liberal interpretations emphasize the secular impact of technology which constantly pushes toward freer trade and greater capital mobility with unfortunate setbacks created by government intervention and distortions. From this perspective, postwar statism, or "embedded liberalism" as it came to be known, was largely a historical aberration. After the war, governments took advantage of the temporary weakness of capitalism to impose all sorts of restrictions and barriers. Eventually, however, the unstoppable advance of information and communication forced them to succumb, with the result being that the rate of return rather than political whim once again governed the movement of capital. Critics of this "natural-course-of-things" theory tend to reverse its emphasis. Thus, according to Helleiner (1994), the key issue is neither the expansionary tendencies of technology and markets nor their impact on the propensity of capital to move, but rather the willingness of states to let such movements occur in the first place. From this viewpoint, state regulation is not an aberration but rather the determining factor, which governments remain free to switch on and off. One of the reasons for such cyclical changes of heart, suggests Frieden (1988), is the shifting political economy of foreign debt. According to this view, during the Gold Standard, Britain became a "mature creditor," and was therefore interested in liberalization so that its debtors could have enough export earnings to service their foreign liabilities. The United States reached a similar position during the 1970s, and used its hegemonic power to reimpose liberalization for much the same reason. According to Goodman and Pauly (1995), this second coming of liberalism was further facilitated by the desire of governments to retain the benefits of transnational production. The latter required that they open the door to transnational financial intermediation, hence the dual rise of portfolio and foreign direct investment.

Plus ça change, plus c'est pareil? Perhaps, but only because much of this discussion focuses on the cyclicality of capital flow. As it turns out, this preoccupation, convenient as it may be for those skeptical of globalization, is not entirely warranted.[25] First, although the *pace* of globalization as indicated by the ebb and flow of capital movement has indeed oscillated over time, its impact on the *level* of globalization tends to be cumulative (Magdoff 1969). Thus, while skeptics such as Doremus *et al.* (1998) are correct in pointing out that most companies are still more national than global, the rapid pace of globalization suggests that the situation may not stay that way for long.[26] A second, related point is that most analyses of capital flows concentrate on *net* movements – namely, on the difference between inflow and outflow. This choice is inadequate and potentially misleading. Capitalist integration and globalization can move both ways which means that the proper measure to use here is the *gross* flow – that is, the sum of inflow and outflow (Wallich 1984). The net and gross magnitudes are the same when capital goes in only one direction, either in or out of a country. But when the flow runs in both directions the numbers could be very different. This is clearly illustrated in Figure 6.4, which contrasts capital flow with gross fixed capital formation in the G7 countries. The figure shows that since the 1980s, the relative increase of gross

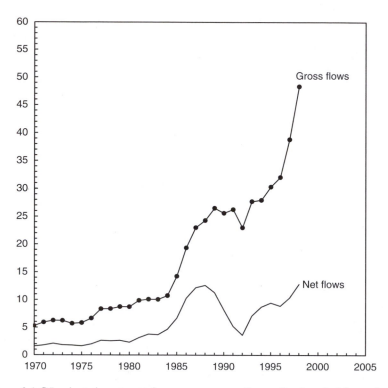

Figure 6.4 G7 private investment flows as a percent of gross fixed capital formation.

Source: International Monetary Fund, *Balance of Payment Statistics* and *International Financial Statistics* through McGraw-Hill (online).

Note
Series are expressed as three-year moving averages. Flows comprise direct and portfolio investment. Gross flows are computed as the sum of inflows and outflows. Net flows are computed separately for each country as the difference between inflow and outflow, and then converted into absolute values and aggregated. Each series denotes the ratio of overall G7 flows to overall G7 gross fixed capital formation, both in $US. Data prior to 1977 pertain to Canada, Italy, United Kingdom and the United States only.

private flows was both powerful and secular, whereas that of net flows was more limited and cyclical. As a result, by 1998, the value of gross flows reached 58 percent of green-field investment compared to only 14 percent for net flows.[27] Unfortunately, lack of historical data on gross capital movements makes it difficult to compare current developments with conditions prevailing at the turn of the century. Nonetheless, the fact that the share of gross investment in GDP was generally higher than now, and that two-way capital flow is a relatively recent phenomenon, together serve to suggest that the current pace of globalization, let alone its level, may well be at an all-time high.

The other common thread running through most analyses is that capital flow is largely a response to the more "primordial" forces of production and trade. To us, this is akin to putting the world on its head. The global movement of capital is ultimately a matter of *ownership* and hence *power* (Nitzan and Bichler 1996; Robinson and Harris 2000). Note that, on its own, the act of foreign investment – whether portfolio or direct – consists of nothing more than the creation or alteration of ownership titles.[28] Note further that the magnitude of such titles is equal to the present value of their expected future earnings. Now, since these earnings can fall as well as rise with output, and given the many "political" factors at play, it seems clear that cross-border capital flows reflect the restructuring not of global production, but of the global *politics* of production.

One of the first to approach international capital mobility as a facet of ownership and power was Hymer (1960), who argued that firms would prefer foreign investment over export or licensing when such ownership conferred differential power, or "ownership advantage" as it later came to be known. Based on this interpretation, the power of US-based foreign investors seems to have risen exponentially over the past half century, as is illustrated in Figure 6.5.

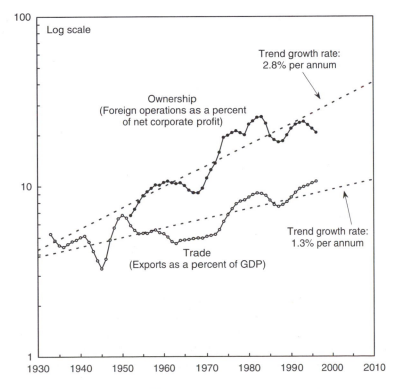

Figure 6.5 The globalization of US business: ownership versus trade.

Source: US Department of Commerce through McGraw-Hill (online).

Note
Series are shown as five-year moving averages.

The figure presents two proxies for the globalization of US business. The first, measuring the share of exports in GDP, provides a rough indication of the contribution to overall profits of trade. The second, measuring the share of foreign operations in overall net corporate profit, approximates the significance of foreign as opposed to overall investment. Up until the 1950s, the relative contribution to profit of foreign assets was similar to that of exports (assuming domestic and export sales are equally profitable, so that the ratio of export to GDP corresponds to the ratio of export profit to overall profit). Since then, the importance for profits of foreign investment has grown roughly twice as fast as that of trade, reaching 20–25 percent of the total in recent years. The faster growth of foreign profits may seem perplexing since, even with the recent resurgence of capital mobility, US trade flows are still roughly three times larger than capital flows. But, unlike trade, investment tends to accumulate, eventually causing overseas earnings to outpace those coming from exports.

This divergence serves to heighten the power underpinnings of trade liberalization. Advocates of global integration, following in the footsteps of Adam Smith and David Ricardo, tend to emphasize the central role of free trade. Unhindered exchange, they argue, is *the* major force underlying greater efficiency and lower prices. As it stands their claim may well be true. Indeed, this is one reason why dominant capital is often halfhearted about indiscriminate deregulation, particularly when it allows competitors to undermine its differential margins. Yet, despite this threat, large firms continue to support freer trade and for a very good reason. For them, it is a means to something much more important, namely free investment – or more precisely, the *freedom to impose and commodify power*.

Although difficult to ascertain with available data, the cumulative (albeit irregular) buildup of international investment has probably contributed greatly to differential accumulation by US dominant capital. The reason is that whereas exports augment the profits of small as well as large firms, the bulk of foreign earnings go to the largest corporations. It is therefore the globalization of ownership, not trade, which is the real prize. While free trade could boost as well as undermine differential accumulation, free investment tends mostly to raise it. But then, since free investment can come only in the footsteps of liberalized trade, the latter is worth pursuing even at the cost of import competition and rising trade deficits.

Foreign investment, like any other investment, is always a matter of power. The nature of this power, however, has changed significantly over time. Until well into the second half of the nineteenth century, the rapid spatial expansion of capitalism enabled profitability to rise despite the parallel increase in the number of competitors (Veblen 1923, ch. 4; Josephson 1934; Hobsbawm 1975, chs 2–3; Arrighi *et al.* 1999). As a result, there was a limited need for collusion and, indeed, most capital flows were relatively small portfolio investments associated mainly with green-field expansion (Folkerts-Landau *et al.* 1997). Eventually, excess capacity started to appear, giving rise to the progressive shift from green-field to amalgamation described in the previous section. Yet, for more than half a century the shift was mostly domestic, with mergers and acquisitions initially breaking through the various national "envelopes." It is only since the 1970s and 1980s that the process started to become truly global and to change the character of capital flow. The need to exert control has gradually moved the emphasis toward larger, "direct" foreign investment, while the threat of excess capacity pushed such investment away from green-field, with over 75 percent of the world total now taking the form of cross-border mergers and acquisitions (United Nations Conference on Trade and Development 2000: 117, figure IV.9). From a power perspective, therefore, one could say that whereas during the late nineteenth and early twentieth centuries capital mobility was largely a "choice," by the end of the twentieth century it became more of a "necessity," mandated by the combination of excess capacity and the cumulative buildup of giant firms, for which profitable expansion increasingly requires global amalgamation.

In summary, there is a long but crucial link leading from capitalism, to differential accumulation, to amalgamation, to capital mobility (Proposition 5). From this perspective, the present process of globalization is inherent in capitalist development and therefore is not easily reversible without altering capitalism or moving away from it altogether. Moreover, contrary to popular perceptions, the underlying force here is not greater efficiency but the control of efficiency, and the purpose is not aggregate but differential gain. Over time, and particularly since the 1980s, foreign investment has come to rely less on green-field and more on cross-border mergers and acquisitions, as firms increasingly break through their national "envelopes." The big winners are the large "distributional coalitions" of dominant capital. Society as a whole suffers as the emphasis progressively shifts from green-field to amalgamation, causing growth to recede and stagnation to creep in (Proposition 3).

Cost-cutting

Although mergers and acquisitions are the most effective engine of differential accumulation, they are not always feasible (Proposition 4). When merger activity recedes, dominant capital has to resort to other means or risk differential *de*cumulation. In principle, this can be done through either relative cost reduction (internal depth) or differential stagflation (external depth). In practice, the latter is much more effective (Propositions 6 and 7).

Consider cost-cutting first. The conflictual dynamics of capitalism, persistent even in the presence of oligopoly and monopoly, imply a constant pressure on firms to improve productivity and reduce input cost. This pressure, identified by the classical economists and reiterated by all subsequent schools, radical as well as conservative, seems beyond dispute. From the perspective of differential accumulation, however, cutting cost is much like "running on empty." It helps dominant capital meet the average rather than beat it.

This claim is difficult to test directly since data on productivity and input prices are rarely if ever broken down by firm size. The indirect evidence, though, seems to support our view here, if only provisionally (figures in this section are computed on the basis of data from *Fortune*, the US Internal Revenue Service, and the US Bureau of Labor Statistics). The logic is straightforward: output per employee, taken as a broad measure of "productivity," is given by the ratio of sales per employee divided by unit price (abstracting from inventory changes). Now, over the past half century, dollar sales per employee in large firms (the Fortune 500) have changed little relative to the comparable figure for the average firm: the ratio between them was 1.4 in 1954, fell gradually to 1.1 by 1969, and then rose steadily, reaching 1.7 by 1993 (although the latter increase is probably overstated due to the growing significance of outsourcing by large firms). We can also reasonably assume that prices charged by larger firms have not fallen relative to those of smaller ones since, as we show in the next section, inflation has historically worked in their favor (direct evidence, though, is again unavailable). These conjectures, along with our above definition, imply that productivity gains by dominant capital have probably been roughly equal to the economy's average.

The difficulty of achieving systematic differential cost-cutting is really not that surprising. First, even the largest firms have only limited control over their input prices, particularly given the proliferation of outsourcing; and when they do exercise such control, the benefits often spill over to other firms (a wage freeze by dominant capital groups would empower smaller firms to do the same; political pressure on OPEC by car companies to reduce oil prices would benefit all energy users; an importer winning a tariff reduction gives competing importers a free ride, etc.).[29] Second, there is no inherent reason why large firms should be better than small ones at developing new production technologies. For instance, much of the recent advances in bio-technology, information, and communication have been driven by smaller companies, some with only a handful of workers. Dominant capital has often been unable to match this flurry of innovation, in many cases finding it cheaper to let smaller companies incur the R&D cost and then buying the more promising startups, sometimes just to keep their technology from spreading too quickly.[30] Finally, production techniques, by virtue of their integrated *societal* nature, are notoriously difficult to monopolize. Unlike new products which could often be protected through patents, copyrights, and other threats, improvements in the social organization of production tend to proliferate easily, undermining the initial advantage of whoever implemented them first.

Stagflation

Unlike cost-cutting, stagflation is a highly effective means of differential accumulation. At first sight, this statement seems strange. How could large firms benefit from a crisis of rising prices, stagnating output, and falling employment? And if stagflation is indeed so "accumulation friendly," why does it not continue indefinitely? A fuller analysis of these questions is beyond our scope here, but the general thrust of the argument can be briefly outlined (for more on this subject, see Nitzan 1992; Nitzan and Bichler 2000b).

The impact on profit of raising prices and lowering volume is of course non-linear (think about the consequences for profit of moving along a downward-sloping demand curve). But recall that our concern here is not prices but *inflation*. Furthermore, we are interested in the impact of inflation not on profit but on *differential* profit. These two qualifications make a big difference. In contrast to mergers and acquisitions which are commonly pursued only by a subset of firms (the larger ones), a strategy of inflationary redistribution can succeed only within a broader inflationary context in which *all* prices tend to rise. That being said, it is also true that inflation is never uniform and hence never "neutral." Indeed, this is the whole point: inflation exists precisely because it redistributes. Paraphrasing Milton Friedman, we can safely state that "Inflation is always and everywhere a redistributional phenomenon." The key question is who benefits from such redistribution, and this cannot be answered à priori. The essence of inflation is a comprehensive destabilization and restructuring of all market relations, and although there is good reason to expect the more powerful groups to come out on top, the identity of such groups cannot be determined up front. It can only be decided in hindsight based on the distributional outcome.

In the case of the United States, this outcome, illustrated in Figure 6.6, leaves little doubt as to who the winners are. The data in the figure contrast two series.

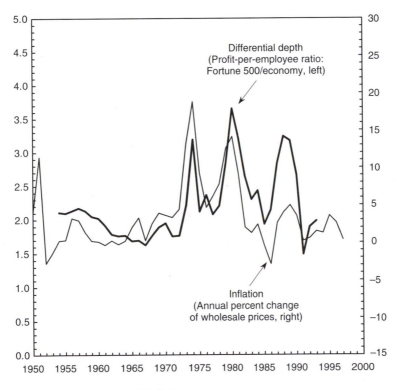

Figure 6.6 Differential depth and inflation.

Source: *Fortune*; US Department of Commerce through McGraw-Hill (online).

Note
The economy's profit per employee is computed by dividing corporate profit with inventory valuation adjustment and capital consumption allowance, less taxes, by the number of nonagricultural employees. Fortune's profit per employee is computed by dividing net profit by the number of employees.

The first is the rate of inflation measured by the annual percent change in the wholesale price index. The second is the profit-per-employee ratio, computed by dividing profit per employee in the Fortune 500 group of companies by profit per employee for the economy as a whole. The latter index corresponds to our notion of differential depth. Its fluctuations measure the extent to which dominant capital – approximated here by the Fortune 500 – is able to raise its profit per employee faster than the average.

As the figure shows, the success of dominant capital here has been tightly and positively correlated with the overall rate of inflation.[31] In other words, higher rates of inflation have played into the hands of the big players, allowing them to raise their profit per unit of organization faster than their smaller counterparts. (Further analysis reported elsewhere suggests that the link between inflation and differential depth was positively related to firm size: the larger the firm, the greater and more systematic the differential gains from inflation. See Nitzan 1992). But if the figure shows that dominant capital clearly benefited from inflation, it also suggests that this benefit was always short-lived, lasting only as long as the underlying bout of inflation. Indeed, the only way to keep such gains coming is to keep inflation going; and if the gains are to rise, inflation must accelerate. Although such increases occasionally happen, and often with the desired impact on differential accumulation, they cannot last indefinitely. As is illustrated repeatedly throughout history and across the world, inflation is a risky business. It is difficult to "manage," often degenerating into an uncontrollable spiral whose consequences – for differential accumulation and, more broadly, for the structure of capitalist power as a whole – are difficult to predict.

For this reason, inflation is more of a stop-gap option for dominant capital. In contrast to breadth, whose differential impact is slower to develop, the differential gains from inflation, which has no upper "technical" limit, are potentially huge. These gains, however, come with considerable risks which, under normal circumstances, are deemed too high. It is only when the gains from breadth dry up that dominant capital, seeing its differential accumulation undermined, moves reluctantly toward relying on inflationary redistribution. This connection between inflation and power cannot be overstated. Mainstream theory, built on a belief in competitive markets, insists that inflation and growth should go hand-in-hand.[32] This belief is usually based on a cyclical argument about supply constraints which, valid or not, is meaningful only in the short term. Over the longer haul, capacity can be increased as needed rendering material bottlenecks largely irrelevant.

The real key then becomes power. Since production provides no "natural" bottlenecks, these have to be created institutionally, through collusive and other arrangements among the key players. Regardless of their particular form, the purpose of all such arrangements is to keep overall capacity from growing too fast. The emphasis here on *overall* capacity is crucial; dominant capital may be able to keep its own production stable or even growing, but unless it manages to cap overall growth, coordination is likely to disintegrate into a price war, leading to disinflation or even outright deflation.

The upshot is simple: over the longer haul we should expect inflation and growth to be *inversely* related. Long-term growth, far from stoking the inflation fire, works to cool it off by undermining collusion. Inflation, on the other hand, requires slack and therefore tends to appear as stagflation. Before testing this proposition, however, it should be noted that the term "stagflation" has more than one interpretation. The "weak" version (see Samuelson 1974: 801) views stagflation as inflation together with unemployment and capacity underutilization. The "moderate" version (found for instance in Baumol *et al.* 1986: 83), defines it as inflation combined with slow growth or recession. Finally, the "strong" version (adopted, for example, by Parkin and Bade 1986: 618), limits stagflation only to instances in which inflation occurs with falling output. For our purpose here, the "weak" version is not very interesting: twentieth-century capitalism has been characterized by some measure of unemployment and unused capacity throughout so inflation was invariably stagflationary according to this definition. The "strong" version also is not very helpful since falling overall output is relatively rare. The most useful of the three is the "moderate" version, particularly when understood as a relationship. If growth is positively related to inflation, stagflation is clearly an anomaly. If, on the other hand, the relationship is negative, stagflation must be seen as a "normal" phenomenon, intensifying as growth declines and inflation rises and receding when growth increases and inflation falls.

As it turns out, the long-term relationship is almost invariably negative. Indeed, the evidence on this is nothing short of overwhelming (although systematically ignored by most economists). Figures 6.7 and 6.8 illustrate respectively the case of the United States over the past century or so, and of the industrialized countries since the late 1960s. The data contrast inflation and growth, both smoothed as twenty-year moving averages to accentuate their long-term pattern. The overall relationship in both figures is clearly inverse. The same long-term pattern seems to repeat itself in numerous individual countries, both developed and developing.

The negative long-term correlation between growth and inflation also helps explain the postwar schizophrenia of policy makers in capitalist countries. Their frequently stated, eternal purpose is to promote growth and assure price stability. Their unstated commitment, though, has progressively drifted in favor of differential accumulation. During breadth periods, the stated and latent goals are consistent, with high growth and low inflation allowing policy makers to do little and claim success. The problem arises when differential accumulation moves into depth and the macroeconomic scene turns stagflationary. Then the two commitments clash and the winner is almost invariably dominant capital. Policy is tightened, presumably in order to rein in inflation, but the consequence is exactly the opposite: the economy slows, which is precisely what dominant capital needs in order to keep inflation going!

Occasionally, policy tightening claims a big victory – for instance, during the early 1980s, when higher interest rates were eventually followed by disinflation. But was tighter policy here indeed the *cause* of lower inflation? As illustrated in Figure 6.2, during the early 1980s dominant capital began shifting back to breadth with a new merger wave gathering momentum. Under these circumstances, both

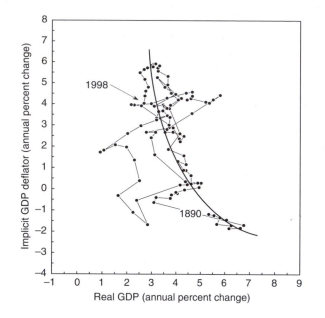

Figure 6.7 United States: long-term inflation and growth.

Sources: US Department of Commerce through McGraw-Hill (online); US President (Annual).

Note
Series are shown as twenty-year moving averages.

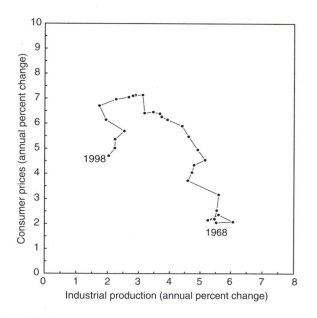

Figure 6.8 Industrialized countries: long-term inflation and growth.

Source: International Monetary Fund, *International Financial Statistics* through McGraw-Hill (online).

Note
Series are shown as twenty-year moving averages.

the need for inflation and the ability to coordinate it tend to decline. If this interpretation is correct, the real cause of disinflation was resumed breadth, with restrictive policy in fact keeping inflation higher than it would have been otherwise.

Summing up, our analysis so far suggests that of the four paths to differential accumulation, the more important are internal breadth through mergers and acquisitions, and external depth via stagflation (Proposition 8). To wrap up the discussion, we now turn to examine the relationship between the two paths and what it may mean for the future.

Are we heading for global stagflation?

Figure 6.9 contrasts our amalgamation index (the buy-to-build indicator), with a composite stagflation proxy (both smoothed as five-year moving averages). The latter proxy is constructed first by expressing unemployment and inflation as percent deviations from their respective historical means, and then averaging the two series into a combined stagflation index. (The purpose of including both inflation and unemployment is to accentuate the broader crisis aspects of depth although the pattern would have been similar had we used inflation only.)[33]

The figure highlights several interesting features. First, it suggests that, over the long haul, mergers and acquisitions were indeed the path of least resistance (Proposition 2). Whereas stagflation moved sideways, oscillating around its own stable mean, mergers and acquisitions rose exponentially relative to green-field investment (note the logarithmic scale).

Second, it shows that since the turn of the century, following the initial emergence of big business in the United States, internal breadth and external depth tended to move countercyclically, with temporary declines in the former "compensated" for by sharp increases in the latter (Propositions 1 and 8). This latter pattern is indeed quite remarkable, particularly since, as we have emphasized, differential accumulation does not have to happen and can as easily go into reverse. Yet, as the chart reveals, major declines in merger activity were almost invariably matched by intensifying stagflation, and when merger activity resumed stagflation promptly dropped.

Significantly, this inverse correlation seems to have grown tighter over time, perhaps as a consequence of the ascendancy of dominant capital and differential accumulation.[34] During the last decade of the nineteenth century, when big business was just emerging, the two series still moved in the same direction. This changed in the first decades of the twentieth century, and with dominant capital assuming the center stage, the relationship became clearly negative although still somewhat loose. From the 1930s onward, with differential accumulation becoming entrenched, the negative fit grew tighter and tighter.

What are the implications of these patterns? First, they suggest that globalization, far from contributing to growth, is likely to further exacerbate stagnation and unemployment. Considering the increasing inclination of larger firms to buy

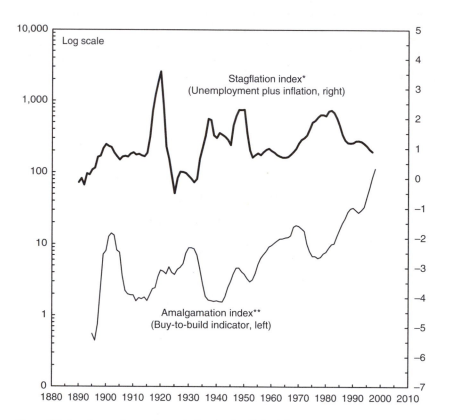

Figure 6.9 Amalgamation and stagflation in the United States.

Source: US Department of Commerce through McGraw-Hill (online), and sources listed in the Data Appendix.

Note

Series are shown as five-year moving averages (the first four observations cover available data only).

 * Average of standardized unemployment and standardized GDP deflator inflation (percent deviations from mean).

** Mergers and acquisitions as a percent of gross fixed capital formation.

capacity rather than build it, and given that giant cross-border deals now make this tendency truly global, there is little reason to expect brisk growth ahead. If anything, the downward growth trend evident for much of the postwar period is likely to continue (Proposition 3).

Second and equally important is the tendency of lulls in merger activity to trigger stagflation crises. If the logic elaborated in this chapter continues to hold, and assuming differential accumulation goes on, the end of the present merger wave should, like its predecessors, give rise to yet another stagflation crisis. This time, though, the crisis is likely to be different in both scope and duration. Contrary to previous crises whose extent was at least partly contained by national borders, this one may turn out to be truly global in both origin and magnitude. Moreover, its resolution is likely to prove much more difficult. Previous crises were defused when dominant capital broke its "envelope," moving to acquire firms outside its original universe. This time, there are no more "envelopes" to break. Dominant capital now makes the world its playing field. When this field no longer yields enough takeover targets, where can the large companies go? And if, after this merger wave ends, there is indeed no new universe to conquer, what will bring stagflation to an end?

As these lines are written this scenario may seem far-fetched. The global pool of takeover targets – including the privatization of state-owned firms and public services – remains vast. Moreover, half of the world's population still lives pretty much outside the capitalist fold. Their proletarianization promises plenty of new green-field investment, which will in turn continue to generate new takeover targets. Nonetheless, the analysis suggests that as dominant capital gets closer to its ultimate, global "envelope," capitalism will become increasingly prone to stagflation crises. The more immediate barrier on further global amalgamation will likely be regulatory or financial. In many sectors global amalgamation is approaching "antitrust thresholds" as they are now called, and in some of them – including information and telecommunications – it has already triggered regulatory intervention (Hargreaves *et al.* 2000; Pretzlik and Lewis 2000). Also, much of the current merger drive has been financed by a rising stock market. If and when the boom turns to bust, this too could bring amalgamation to a temporary halt.

The ultimate barrier, however, is the contradiction inherent in a system built on *ever-increasing* power. Over the past several centuries, this contradiction was obscured by the "horizontal" dimensions of markets – equal exchange, free opportunity, democracy, and growing output. Yet markets, important as they may be, are merely a mechanism of capitalism. The essence of capitalism is differential accumulation and the relative expansion of power. This contrast between means and end is crucial. Conceived merely as a market system, capitalism could function indefinitely, at least in principle. But as a social order built on *augmenting* power, it is necessarily self-limiting and therefore finite. From this perspective, the key issue is not the level or rate of profit but its distribution: whereas the former can always be increased, no capitalist can ever own more than the entire profit pie. And so, if large companies continue to spend on amalgamation twice as much as they do on new capacity, eventually – although we cannot say when – there will be nothing more for them to conquer. The resulting corporate oligarchy, reminiscent of Jack London's description in *The Iron Heel* (1907), may be able to increase its profit but not its relative power. Differential accumulation can disintegrate at any time. At that point, however, it *must* come to an end, and with it capitalism as we know it.

Epilogue (August 2002)

Since this article was first published in early 2001, the "hype" surrounding the breadth phase has been punctured. The merger boom, having reached a historical peak, collapsed together with the stock market; the world entered a recession; and hopes for "peace dividends" in a high-tech global village have been dashed by low-tech terrorism, massive military "retaliations" and rising security budgets. Do these developments mark the beginning of a new depth phase? The answer is not yet clear. Some of the key ingredients of depth – specifically, stagnating production, political tension, and growing conflict – are clearly here. The main challenge for dominant capital, however, is to use these developments as a basis for inflationary redistribution, and that has not yet happened. Stagflation has recently resurfaced in certain peripheral countries such as Argentina and Israel. But it is only when such stagflation takes hold of the developed countries that we can announce the dawn of a new depth regime.

Data Appendix

There are no systematic historical time series for mergers and acquisitions in the United States (other countries have even less). The series constructed in this chapter and plotted in Figures 6.2, 6.3, and 6.9, are computed on the basis of various studies, which often use different definitions covering different universes of companies.

The dollar values of mergers and acquisition for the 1895–1919 period are taken from Nelson (1959, table 14: 37), whereas those covering the 1920–29 period come from Eis (1969), as reported in *Historical Statistics of the United States* (US Department of Commerce. Bureau of the Census 1975, vol. 2, table V38-40: 914). Both data sets cover manufacturing and mining transactions only, and thus fail to reflect the parallel amalgamation drive in other sectors (Markham 1955).

Data for the 1930–66 period are from the US Federal Trade Commission, reported in *Historical Statistics of the United States* (1975, vol. 2, table V38-40: 914). These data, again covering only manufacturing and mining, pertain to the number of transactions rather than their dollar value. Significantly, though, the number of mergers and acquisitions correlates closely with the value ratio of mergers and acquisitions to green-field investment during previous and subsequent periods for which data on both are available (the 1920s and 1960–80s). In our computations, we assumed a similar correlation to have existed during 1930–66 and hence used the former series (with proper re-basing) as a proxy for the latter ratio.

From 1967 onward, we again use value data which this time cover all sectors. Figures for 1967–79 are from W.T. Grimm, reported in Weston (1987, table 3.3: 44). For 1980–83, data are from Securities Data Corporation, comprising transactions of over $1 million only. The last series, covering the period from 1984 to the present and coming from the same source, consists of transactions of $5 million or more. The latter two data sets are reported regularly in the US Department of Commerce's *Statistical Abstract of the United States* (Annual).

In constructing our indicator for the ratio of mergers and acquisitions to gross fixed investment, we divided, for each year, the dollar value of mergers and acquisitions by the corresponding dollar value of gross fixed capital formation (taken from the *Historical Statistics of the United States* (1975) and from various issues of the *Statistical Abstract of the United States*). For the 1930–66 period, we spliced in the number of deals linked to prior and later value ratios.

Acknowledgment

I would like to thank Shimshon Bichler, Marc-André Gagnon, Mehran Nakhjavani, Mary Ann Tétreault, and three anonymous referees for their critical comments. Research for this chapter was partly supported by a SSHRC grant.

Notes

1 During the late 1970s, a new branch of macroeconomic theory emphasizing supply shocks claimed to have solved the mystery of stagflation by blaming it on extra-market forces such as wicked oil sheikhs and greedy labor unions (for instance, Blinder 1979; Bruno and Sachs 1985). By pushing up the cost of raw materials and labor, these "aliens" cause deficient supply (rather than excess demand), which in turn has the double impact of raising prices while lowering production. Such cost-push explanations are not entirely misguided, but they are rarely brought to their logical conclusion and are therefore necessarily partial. The problem is that neoclassicists consider profit to be a cost of production on a par with wages and rent. But if that is true, why is it possible to have a "wage shock" and an "oil shock" but not a "profit shock"? Another solution to the stagflation riddle is favored by the expectations school (cf. Phelps 1968; Lucas 1972; Friedman 1976). It returns to Hume's classical dichotomy and argues that inflation is a "nominal" phenomenon, dependent exclusively on expectations and liquidity, and hence consistent with either stagnation or growth which are "real" phenomena. The problems with this latter theory are numerous, including the fact that its key explanatory variables – expectations and the "natural rate of unemployment" – cannot be observed directly and often end up being "determined" so to speak by the econometric fit (see Nitzan 1992).
2 The political essence of capital is emphasized in Bichler (1986) and developed more fully in Bichler (1991). For the concept, implications, and applications of differential accumulation, see Nitzan (1992); Nitzan and Bichler (1995); Bichler and Nitzan (1996a,b); Nitzan and Bichler (1996); Nitzan (1998); Nitzan and Bichler (2000a,b); and Nitzan and Bichler (2001).
3 Conventional theory celebrates the iron law of profit maximization, although it is not very clear why. For one, the concept holds little water in the real world. As Hall and Hitch (1939) showed more than half a century ago, few if any capitalists know what maximum profit means or how to achieve it, and as many studies before and since have suggested they instead use "markup pricing" to achieve a "target rate of return" (for instance, Brown 1924; Kaplan *et al.* 1958; and Blair 1972). The marginalists could not accept this heresy. Led by Machlup (1946), they lashed back, arguing that regardless of what businessmen said, in the end markup formulae were nothing more than

real-world techniques for maximizing profit – although they themselves were still unable to show exactly what that "maximum" was (Robinson 1966: 78–9). Many theorists refuse to be bothered by such earthly debates but the situation is hardly better in the "higher world" of textbooks. As it turns out, maximum profit is indeed "workable" in the extreme cases of perfect competition and monopoly. But then what about the entire range of "imperfections" between these (nonexistent) ideal types? The problem, first identified by Cournot (1838), is one of oligopolistic interdependence which, in its "unrestricted" form, makes maximum profit indeterminate even in the mind of the economist. Game theory has solved this problem a million times over but only by assuming certain predetermined rules. Sadly, real firms are free to ignore such rules, so the enigma of maximum profit remains.

4 By focusing here on the corporation rather than its ultimate owners, we bypass the long debate on the separation of ownership from control first identified by Marx and later intensified with the publication of Berle's and Means's *The Modern Corporation and Private Property* (1932). The harsher critiques of the "separation thesis," such as Zeitlin (1974), contested its conclusions as being based on "pseudofacts." Control, they argued, has never truly been separated from ownership. Less hostile critiques, like Baran and Sweezy (1966) and more recently Screpanti (1999), accepted that ownership is increasingly separate from control but maintain that this merely turns the corporation into a more effective "profit machine." One way or the other, we concur with Veblen that the corporation itself, regardless of who runs it, was historically necessary for the survival of capitalism. Without this institution, which for Marx signaled the imminent "abolition of capital as private property within the framework of capitalist production itself" (1909, vol. III: 516), the centrifugal forces of competition and excess capacity would have probably killed the bourgeois order long ago. Any analysis of capitalism must therefore have the corporation as a central building block.

5 Strictly speaking, differential accumulation requires not a positive rate of growth but a positive difference between rates of growth. Dominant capital can therefore accumulate differentially even with its own profit falling, provided that the average declines even faster. This understanding is assumed throughout the chapter.

6 For any given firm, green-field investment can of course draw on interfirm labor mobility as well as on new employment. From an aggregate perspective, however, labor movement between firms is properly classified as internal breadth.

7 Corporate capitalism, although always conflictual, is rarely if ever competitive in the sense of firms being "price-takers." The view taken here is that the very existence of profit presupposes power which normally requires some measure of both collusion and exclusion, tacit or otherwise (Nitzan 1998). The success of such collusion/exclusion is reflected, if only indirectly, in differential profit margins, or in what Kalecki (1943a) called the "degree of monopoly" (for alternative concepts of competition and their relation to profit, see Ochoa and Glick 1992).

8 The notion of excess capacity, associated mainly with Monopoly Capital writers such as Kalecki (1971), Steindl (1952) and Baran and Sweezy (1966), is admittedly problematic. Here, we use it to denote the potential threat to prevailing profit margins from higher resource utilization. To illustrate, since World War II, US margins, measured by the combined profit and interest share of GDP, have been positively related to the rate of unemployment (Nitzan and Bichler 2000a, figure 2: 80). In this context, a move from higher to lower unemployment increases utilization and threatens margins.

9 Our measurements here are not strictly consistent in that we contrast the number of corporations with overall nonagricultural private employment (which also includes proprietorships and partnerships), rather than with corporate employment only (for which data are not publicly available). Based on a comparison of revenue

data, and assuming these are roughly proportional to employment trends, corporate employment over the period has grown by 17 percent more than overall nonagriculture private employment. Correcting for this difference implies that average employment per corporation over the period has fallen by 67 percent, compared with 72 percent indicated in the chart. This bias is clearly too small to alter the overall picture.

10 The effect on relative employment growth is probably somewhat smaller than what is implied by the dollar figures. Amalgamated companies often end up shedding some workers, and also merger and acquisition data include divestitures, which reduce rather than raise employment. Correcting for these qualifications, however, would not likely alter the overall trend.

11 For more on the contrast between power and efficiency arguments, see Knoedler (1995).

12 A glimpse into what such a "free run" might have looked like is offered by the recent experience of Japan, a country where the merger medicine for green-field is still socially prohibited: "The underlying problem facing many Japanese companies," writes the *Financial Times*, "is that they have misallocated capital over a long period. Instead of regarding it as a scarce resource to be used as efficiently as possible, they have pursued engineering excellence.… Japanese production lines are often models of automated efficiency, but less attention has been paid to whether the goods on them should be produced at all. Many companies have poured cash into project that will never generate a return above the cost of capital" (Abrahams and Harney 1999).

13 Controlled stagnation is also used as a stick against labor, contributing to the political supremacy of capital by preventing full employment. In the immediate postwar years, this goal was achieved mainly through what Kalecki (1943b) termed the "political business cycle," with governments propping up the economy, only to step on the brakes as soon as employment became "too high." In time, the mechanism was perfected into a full-fledged "political trend," as Steindl (1979) later called it, with tight neoliberal policies aimed at maintaining unemployment "naturally" high. On the surface such policies seem to sacrifice accumulation for the more primordial goal of keeping capitalists in the driver's seat, although in practice the loss is often more apparent than real. First, policy-induced stagnation shifts income from profit to interest, but does not necessarily undermine the overall income share of capital. Second, for dominant capital, redistribution from labor and smaller firms could more than compensate for the negative impact on profit of stunted growth. Finally and no less importantly, the greater "stability" associated with stagnation translates into falling risk premia and a corresponding rise in asset prices.

14 In this context, *Tobin's Q* turns from a cause to a consequence, with mergers and acquisitions driving up asset prices and therefore the ratio of market value to replacement cost.

15 Economies of scale, impressive as they were in Marx's time, are not a timeless iron law, but rather are historically and technologically contingent. Diseconomies of scale can be just as important. There is no reason to believe that completely centralized planning, capitalist or otherwise, is most efficient. Also with regard to roundabout processes – longer production runs may be more efficient but only up to a point, beyond which they almost always run into organizational barriers.

16 Note that the act of merger itself has no effect on depth. It works only indirectly, through increasing corporate centralization, and even that is merely a facilitating factor. Consolidation makes it easier for firms to collude but that does not imply that collusion will actually take place or that it will be effective.

17 This is also why most macro studies of mergers and acquisitions, such as Mitchell and Mulheirn (1996), Weston *et al.* (1998) or Winston (1998), are usually insufficient. Although they acknowledge the role of structural changes such as increased competition,

technical change, and deregulation, they tend to treat them more as external "shocks" to which amalgamation is then a "response."

18 A typical illustration of this process is provided by the food business. During the 1980s, the sector went through rapid amalgamation. In 1981, a $1.9 billion merger between Nabisco and Standard Brands created Nabisco Brands, which then merged in a $4.9 billion deal with R.J. Reynolds to create RJR Nabisco. A few years later, KKR, which earlier had acquired Beatrice for $6.2 billion, paid $30.6 billion to take over RJR Nabisco in what was then the largest takeover on record. Elsewhere in the sector, Nestlé took over Carnation ($2.9 billion) and Rowntree ($4.5 billion); Grand Metropolitan acquired Pillsbury ($5.7 billion) and Guinness ($16 billion); Phillip Morris bought General Foods ($5.7 billion) and Kraft ($13.4 billion); BCI Holdings took over some Beatrice divisions ($6.1 billion); and Rhône-Poulenc bought Hoechst ($21.9 billion). By the end of the 1980s, the merger flurry had died down. According to a recent report in the *Financial Times*, food companies are very cheap, yet "shareholders have deserted food stocks...partly because of the absence of genuinely attractive acquisition targets" in an industry whose "biggest problem has been minimal sales growth." During the 1990s, there were a few more big transactions, such as the $14.9 billion acquisition of Nabisco by Philip Morris, but these were mostly reshuffles of assets among the large players. The experience of reaching the "envelope" was aptly summarized by a Bestfood executive whose company had been taken over by Unilever: "I have been to Bentonville, Arkansas [home of Wal-Mart's head-quarters], and I would like to say that it is not the end of the world, but you can see it" (Edgecliffe-Johnson 2000).

19 The effect of such counterforces can be dramatic. The 1933 Glass–Steagall Act, for example, reversed an earlier diversification trend by US banks, preventing them from owning nonfinancial corporations, a limitation which is only now relaxed.

20 The process is of course hardly unique to the United States. For example, "Before [South Africa] started the progressive unwinding of exchange controls in 1994," writes the *Financial Times*, "large companies were prevented from expanding overseas. With capital trapped at home, they gobbled up all available companies in their industries before acquiring companies in other sectors and becoming conglomerates" (Plender and Mallet 2000). For analyses of differential accumulation, business consolidation, and globalization in South Africa and Israel, see Nitzan and Bichler (1996, 2001).

21 For instance, information, telecommunication and entertainment companies such as Cisco, Lucent, Microsoft, AOL-Time Warner, NewsCorp, Hutchison, and Vivendi now increasingly integrate computing (hardware and software), services (consulting), infrastructure (cables and satellite), content (television, movies, music, and print pub-lishing) and communication (internet and telephony), while leisure firms like Carnival Cruise own shipping lines, resort hotels, airlines, and sports teams. Companies like General Electric and Philip Morris have never abandoned conglomeration and continue spreading in numerous directions.

22 Globalization of course has other dimensions, but these are secondary to our purpose here.

23 The rationale is based on the external account identity between current and capital balances. If the international monetary system were to remain stable while states retain domestic sovereignty over exports and imports, capital movements must be controlled in order to "accommodate" the resulting current account imbalances. In the absence of such capital controls, states would have to give up their policy autonomy or else the mismatch between the current and capital balances would upset international monetary stability.

24 For views and reviews, see Cerny (1993), Helleiner (1994), Sobel (1994), and Cohen (1996).

25 For more on the globalization debate, see Gordon (1988), Du Boff *et al.* (1997), Sivanandan and Wood (1997), Burbach and Robinson (1999), Hirst and Thompson (1999), Radice (1999), and Sutcliffe and Glyn (1999).

26 According to the *World Investment Report*, the share of transnational production in world GDP has risen from 5.3 percent in 1982, to 6.6 in 1990, to 10.1 percent in 1999, while the average "transnationality" of the world's top 100 transnational corporations increased to 54 percent in 1998, up from 51 percent in 1990 (United Nations Conference on Trade and Development 2000, table I.1: 4 and table III.2: 76). (UNCTAD's "Transnationality Index" is defined as the average of the ratios of foreign to total assets, foreign to total sales, and foreign to total employment.)

27 Note that the series in Figure 6.4 is based on quarterly data and therefore fails to reflect shorter "hot money" movements. Their inclusion would have further widened the disparity between gross and net flows.

28 The popular perception that "direct" investment creates new productive capacity, in contrast to "portfolio" investment which is merely a paper transaction, is simply wrong. In fact, *both* are paper transactions whose only difference is relative size: investments worth more than 10 percent of the target company's equity are commonly classified as direct, whereas those worth less are considered portfolio.

29 The challenge to differential accumulation of "universal" cost was summarized neatly by Andrew Grove, Chairman of Intel: "How do you build a company," he asks "when your buyers are infinitely knowledgeable and where your suppliers maintain a level playing field for your competitors? What remains your competitive differentiator or your source of value or whatever academic cliché you want to wrap around it?" (Byrne 2000).

30 "Big American companies," writes *The Economist*, "fear that innovation is the secret of success – and that they cannot innovate." Indeed, their "terror" is that "innovation seems to work best outside of them," with the result that "Much of today's merger boom is driven by a desperate search for new ideas," with trading in intangible assets reaching $100 billion in 1998, up from $15 billion in 1990 (Anonymous 1999). "Nobody holds out for organic growth any more," declares Sir Richard Sykes, chairman of Glaxo SmithKline which in 1999 controlled 7.3 percent of the world market for pharmaceuticals. According to a recent *Financial Times* survey in which he is cited, the reason has little to do with "efficiency gains." Indeed, "Those wary of mergers argue there is no evidence of scale contributing to greater efficiency. Ed Scolnick, chief scientist at Merck, found absolutely no correlation between the size and productivity of his company's research laboratories. The relative success of small biotechnology companies suggests that scale in research may even be a disadvantage." Of course, this is hardly a reason not to merge. As Jim Niedel of Glaxo points out in the same article, "doubling up" [via merger] allows companies to screen twice as many compounds, not to mention the resulting increase in "salespower" (Pilling 2000). In our terminology, it contributes to both internal breadth and external depth.

31 *Fortune* stopped reporting aggregate employment after 1993, but the relationship in the figure is likely to have remained positive for the rest of the decade. Note that the profit-per-employee ratio is the product of the sales-per-employee ratio and the markup ratio (the latter being ratio between the net profit share of sales in the Fortune 500 and in the economy as a whole). Now, as indicated in the section "Crosscutting," the sales-per-employee ratio remained fairly stationary throughout the period. The markup ratio, on the other hand, was positively and highly correlated with inflation throughout the 1954–98 period. Given the relationship between these two series, the implication is that the correlation between inflation and profit-per-employee depicted in the figure also continued to be positive after 1993.

32 Supply-shock explanations of stagflation are in this sense outside the mainstream since they acknowledge, if only half-heartedly, the existence of market power.

33 Inflation fluctuates much more than unemployment and therefore dominates the combined stagflation index. The correlation coefficient between the combined index and its inflation component, both expressed as five-year moving averages, is 0.93.

34 The thirty-year moving correlation between the stagflation and amalgamation indices (with the latter expressed as deviations from trend) rose gradually from a negative 0.11 in 1927 to a negative 0.9 in 1998.

7   Global dreams and
local anger

From structural to acute violence
in a globalizing world

Peter Uvin

This chapter studies the impact of structural violence on communal, acute violence. I define structural violence here, provisionally, as the "extent to which fundamental human needs tend to be frustrated and human development tends to be inhibited as a result of the normal workings of a society's institutions" (Gil 1986: 129; see also Christie 1997: 315). The connection between structural violence and acute violence seems intuitively evident, but it has not often been explicitly analyzed. In an earlier book on the Rwandan genocide, I studied these relations at the micro-level (Uvin 1998). In this chapter, I set out to examine the relationship between structural and acute violence at a more general, conceptual level, against the backdrop of the globalization of the world political economy. The chapter has two aims then: to analyze the mechanisms by which conditions of structural violence favor eruptions of acute violence (primarily of a communal nature), and to explore the impact of globalization on this process.

This chapter is divided into three major parts. The first part defines structural violence; the second discusses its relation to globalization; and the third aims to outline its impact on acute violence. I draw on a wide literature from the fields of political science, anthropology, sociology, and, rarer for an International Political Economy (IPE) article, psychology, and public health. These eclectic choices are explained by the multifaceted nature of the social dynamics of violence, and by the fact that scholars in these disciplines have provided important understandings of some of these dynamics. Much of this literature builds on a deep social engagement: whether we look at the work of public health specialists Paul Farmer and R. G. Wilkinson, anthropologists Nancy Scheper-Hughes and Philippe Bourgois, psychologists David Gil and Michael Simpson, or peace scholars Johan Galtung and John Burton, through it all there runs a common thread of an engaged, humanistic political position. This essay, then, also seeks to highlight the major contributions of these engaged scholars.

Structural violence

The term "structural violence" is believed to originate with Johan Galtung, the father of peace research and one of the foremost social scientists of the second half of the twentieth century. In 1969, he began this project by defining "violence" as "those factors that cause people's actual physical and mental realizations to be below their potential realizations." As such, violence can be built into the social structure and functioning of society, "show[ing] up as unequal power and consequently as unequal life chances." One example: "in a society where life expectancy is twice as high in the upper class as in the lower classes, violence is exercised even if there are no concrete actors one can point to directly attacking others, as when one person kills another" (Galtung 1969: 168, 169, 171).

This was Galtung's attempt to incorporate the notion of "positive peace" into the work of peace researchers. Indeed, in the late 1960s, against the backdrop of the Vietnam War and an increased questioning of North–South differentiation, "traditional peace research" (of which Galtung was also widely acknowledged to have been a father, along with figures such as Kenneth Boulding in the United States) was under heavy attack by a new generation of radical, mainly European peace scholars. One of their prime complaints was that traditional peace researchers focused solely on negative peace, that is, the absence of war, elevating this situation uncritically to an absolute ideal. This, the critics argued, neglected what they called positive peace, that is, social justice. In situations of high exploitation and inequality, is the absence of overt war truly the best possible outcome? Or might overt violence occasionally be required to render social structures more humane and just? Galtung's development of the concept of structural violence was an attempt to respond to these criticisms without abandoning peace defined as the absence of violence as the primary goal of activists. It was through this concept also that Galtung would move from an initial focus on disarmament to later work on international development (Lawler 1995: chapter 3, 150).

The new concept proved very popular during the 1970s, a time of radical thinking in much of academia especially around issues of Third World development and social change. The concept of structural violence became deeply enmeshed in the radical politics of the period. For some, such as Angela Davis, Frantz Fanon, Jean Ziegler, and Herbert Marcuse, structural violence was intrinsic to peripheral capitalism and thus could only be ended by a revolution. For others, it served as a mobilizing concept. Gernot Köhler and Norman Alcock (1976), for example, calculated that the annual mortality worldwide due to structural violence produced casualty rates much higher than those resulting from international wars. Critics of the concept – and the broader theoretical framework within which it was embedded – reproached its radicalism as well as its vagueness and the difficulty of operationalizing it.

By the 1980s, research on structural violence – even the simple use of the term – had declined dramatically. The political and intellectual climate had undergone a radical shift: structural adjustment and liberalization had come to dominate the development agenda. Radical paradigms such as Marxism and dependency theory lost legitimacy following the economic failure of import-substitution policies. The remaining progressive scholars shifted their forces to micro-level concerns such as self-help and grassroots organization – or moved to an entirely different intellectual space, that of postmodernism.

Still, the concept of structural violence did not disappear entirely. A recent database search shows that, in the 1990s, the term "structural violence" still was regularly used in the social sciences, particularly (social) psychology and public health. It is employed by critical scholars to describe social situations that are characterized by a combination of inequality, insecurity, repression, arbitrariness, and racism. As such, the term has been used to describe living conditions in Brazil, apartheid South Africa (Gil 1970; Van der Merwe 1989; Hoffmann and McKendrick 1990: 20; Simpson 1993: 603; Ramphele 1997), Haiti (Farmer 1996: 263), communities of indigenous peoples in Latin America (Scheper-Hughes 1992; MacGregor and Rubio 1994) and the poor in inner city America (Kaljee *et al.* 1995; Bourgois 1995). Many of these situations, it should be noted, are also characterized by high degrees of acute violence. Some writers use related terms such as "institutional violence" (Khiddu-Makubuya 1994: 145, writing about the conditions facing the poor in Uganda), "social-structural violence" (Gil 1986: 127), or "silent violence" (Spitz 1978, analyzing the political causes of famine) to describe the same set of relationships.

While acute violence is usually both visible and socially condemned, structural violence is not (Galtung 1969; MacGregor and Rubio 1994: 48). Nancy Scheper-Hughes calls these situations "small genocides," observing that "the paradox is that they are not invisible because they are secreted away and hidden from view, but quite the reverse. As Wittgenstein noted, the things that are hardest to perceive are often those which are right before our eyes and therefore simply taken for granted" (Scheper-Hughes 1996: 889). The mechanisms of structural violence are "normal." The invisibility of structural violence extends even to those who are subjected to it (Macgregor and Rubio 1994: 49; von Wallenberg Pachaly 1995: 223; Bourgois 1996: *passim*; Farmer 1996: 280).

In this chapter, I define structural violence as the joint occurrence of high inequality, social exclusion, and the humiliation characteristic of symbolic violence. It is the coexistence of all these factors – and, unfortunately, they do coexist for many of the world's people – that renders a situation one of structural violence. Inequality alone does not constitute structural violence. It must be accompanied by exclusion and humiliation. These three factors neither can be reduced to one another, nor do they necessarily follow one from another. Even though much discrimination occurs together with symbolic humiliation, major variations may be observed. Similarly, people who are humiliated are often at the bottom of the economic ladder; but this is not always the case.[1]

Of the three elements of structural violence, inequality is the most easily recognizable and measurable; from a variety of disciplinary perspectives, economic inequality has been studied and related to other social dynamics such as economic growth, violence, and disease (I will come back later to some of this). Social exclusion is a more recent, hard-to-quantify concept, albeit one that makes intuitive sense. Humiliation or symbolic violence is probably the most surprising element on the list: it almost never appears on the research agendas of International Relations (IR) or IPE scholars, and only rarely is analyzed by other social scientists. Both the latter concepts, then, deserve some elaboration.

Social exclusion

Social exclusion was defined by an International Labor Organization/United Nations Development Program team as a property of societies in which "the rules which enable and constrain access and entitlements to goods, services, activities and resources are unjust in the sense that certain categories of people are denied opportunities which are open to other persons who are comparable. Social exclusion is a property of society if racial, sexual, and other forms of discrimination are present, if the markets through which people earn a livelihood are segmented, or if public goods, which in theory should be available to everyone, are semi-public" (1996: 11; see also Silver 1994: 543–5). Social exclusion, then, refers to social structures and actions that actively deny rights and entitlements to certain categories of marginalized people.

Many authors who describe structural violence provide examples that belong to the category of social exclusion. Bruno Kapferer (1994: 87), after defining the concept, enumerates the following examples of structural violence: "the violence of bureaucratic decisions, which follow rules without consideration for the particular case; or the denial of educational opportunity except to privileged groups, or of employment except to those with appropriate contacts." Felipe Macgregor and Marcial Rubio (1994: 50) argue that the structural violence Indians face in Bolivia includes matters such as "the inefficient administration of justice,... [and] discrimination in relation to gender."

Social exclusion may be social, regional, sexual, and/or ethnic in character. It is usually deeply embedded in the routine functioning of society. Indeed, one of the first tasks of those fighting it is to "denaturalize" it, to render it visible. In poor countries, social exclusion usually takes the form of unequal access to the state, to development projects, and to education, thereby reproducing the privileges of a small elite (for a case study of Rwanda, see Uvin 1998: part III).

Humiliation

Structural violence should not be defined solely in material or economic terms, as if life could be reduced to these aspects only. Over the decades, many scholars of violence have studied its intangible aspects such as mental and emotional harm, denial of dignity and integrity, and the "destruction of the individual in a psychological or spiritual sense" (Hoffmann and McKendrick 1990: 4–5). Galtung himself, in his more recent work, lists the following basic needs categories that are diminished by structural violence: survival, well-being, freedom, and identity (1990: 292). Coming from a different perspective, Robert Chambers (1995), father of the rapid, participatory, rural appraisal approach to development research, has recently synthesized decades of work with local communities throughout the world. He argues that, from the point of view of the poor, "the condition of deprivation" reaches far beyond lack of income to include social dimensions. It is characterized by social inferiority, isolation, physical weakness, vulnerability, seasonal deprivation, powerlessness, and humiliation. And recent work by a World Bank team on the "Voices of the Poor" reveals that poor people's definitions reveal important psychological aspects of poverty. Poor people are acutely aware of their lack of voice, power, and independence, which subject them to exploitation. Their poverty also leaves them vulnerable to rudeness, humiliation, and inhumane treatment by both private and public agents (Narayan *et al.* 2000: 26). In this chapter, I will synthesize these features under the term "humiliation," defined by Avishai Margalit in his fascinating book *The Decent Society*, as "any sort of behavior that constitutes a sound reason for a person to consider his or her self-respect injured" (1996: 1, 9).

Coming from multiple traditions within social science, human needs theorists have long agreed that all human beings have genetically programmed, inherent, basic needs for identity/recognition, security, and autonomy/self-determination (Gil 1986: 127–9, 1996: 78). The *eminence grise* of the human needs school, John Burton (1997: 2, 17), writes that "members of the human race have shared physical characteristics and needs, such as for food and shelter. Less obvious, and frequently ignored, are shared needs for social recognition as individuals and as members of identity groups within a society. Denial of physical needs can be a source of conflict. The denial of psychological and social needs is probably a far more important cause of conflict." Similarly, Christie writes about human needs for security, well being, self-determination, and identity, noting that violence against these human needs can be built into the structure of society and become a major cause of acute violence (1997: 316). A quote from Erich Fromm reflects well the basic tenets of this school of thought:

> It would seem that the amount of destructiveness to be found in individuals is proportionate to the amount to which expansiveness of life is curtailed. By this we do not refer to individual frustrations of this or that instinctive desire, but to the thwarting of the whole of life, the blockage of the spontaneity of the growth and expression of man's sensuous, emotional, and intellectual capacities … . Destructiveness is the outcome of unlived life.
>
> (Fromm 1941)

Since the 1970s, another school of thought, focusing specifically on the Third World, has argued that the modernization ideology underlying the development enterprise destroyed people's "traditional" values, communities, and their sense of self-worth.[2] This approach was meant as a powerful critique against development. It was taken up by some Third World intellectuals and advocates of indigenous peoples who describe a set of ideas and associated behaviors by governments and international agencies – whether "development ideology," or "Westernization," or "consumerism" – as inherently violent. They argue that this violence plays itself out at the level of minds, identities, and cultures – not bodies and buildings. In this context, the terms "cultural violence" (MacGregor and Rubio 1994: 52; Staub 1999), "symbolic violence" (a term from Bourdieu: see Calhoun *et al.* 1993), and even cultural genocide have been employed (see Stover 1990; United Nations 1995; Levene 1999, all of whom use the term in the context of indigenous peoples).

The concrete modalities through which humiliation is transmitted include top-down authoritarian interaction between the state and the people (Kapferer 1994: 60), condescending behaviors by elites, both local and foreign (Colin and Losch 1990: 88; von Benda-Beckmann 1993: 122; Simpson 1993: 605; Albo 1994: 133–4; Uvin 1998: chapter 5; Narayan *et al.* 2000: 31, 33); and the systematic denial of local knowledge and culture (Albo 1994: 129; Uvin 1998: chapter 5). A key variable here is the extent of external penetration of local relations; in other words, local communities, even very poor ones, that are able to maintain a degree of social and cultural autonomy suffer much less from humiliation than those which cannot.

Globalization and structural violence

In this section, I analyze the impact of globalization on structural violence and its components: income inequality, social exclusion, and humiliation. Globalization is considered here from the perspective of the way people live their lives and conceive of their social relations; such a definition will by necessity "interrelate multiple levels of analysis – economics, politics, culture and ideology" (Mittelman 1996: 427). From this perspective, globalization is not only or even principally a matter of financial flows and sites of production, but also, and perhaps more, a matter of consumption, culture, knowledge, taste, perception, and expectation. Globalization is a qualitative process of compression of space and time affecting all people in the world, albeit unequally. It manifests itself in what people consume, how they make money, what they dream, wear, smoke, and eat, where they travel, what and how they learn, where they pollute, and to whom they compare themselves. Globalization, then, contains an important conceptual/psychological component which various authors have described as "a growing consciousness of the world as a single place," a "fundamental change in sensibility… [including a] "global level of comparison;" or "a basic change in the way…actors think and operate across the globe" (quotes respectively from Scholte 1996: 46; Robertson 1992: 179; and Biersteker 1998: 17).

During the last decade, a vast and lively debate about the nature, causes, and consequences of globalization has taken place: is it an unavoidable, almost natural phenomenon, or is it man- and policy-made? Can states – or individuals – shape it or are they shaped by it (Barber 1995; Hirst and Thompson 1999)? Is it a new phenomenon or a repeat of the past? I will not take positions on these debates here. All I want to do is to explore globalization's impact on structural violence. Globalization is about countries' and people's insertion into capitalism, and consequently displays all the features that capitalism has historically displayed, but on a larger scale. It comes as no surprise, then, that "globalization represents an expansion and deepening of long-established structures of inequality in political economy" (Youngs 1997: 16). Regardless of the potential promise of globalization, and of the extent to which it has actually elevated the economic growth rates of some people in some countries, all evidence indicates that globalization has contributed to greater inequality within countries worldwide (United Nations Development Program 1999: 3). This seems to be the case both for those countries that are beneficially inserted into the dynamics of globalization (the OECD, some Asian and South American countries, Eastern Europe and much of the former Soviet Union), and for those, such as most of sub-Saharan Africa, that have been bypassed by it (Milanovic 1998; United Nations Development Program 1999). Liberals and conservatives argue that in the long run everyone will benefit from globalization and, following standard economic theory, that income inequality will subsequently decline. However, this has clearly not happened yet and it does not seem likely to happen soon. It is at best a promise for the long run.

With regard to social exclusion, globalization has a significant positive potential: women finding gainful employment outside of the home; local and international NGOs creating coalitions to resist oppression; new emancipatory ideas becoming more widespread; information flowing in ways that are uncontrolled by repressive governments; even the pressure from Bretton Woods and post-Bretton Woods institutions to modify patterns of clientelism and corruption – all these factors may act as countervailing forces against current dynamics of social exclusion, especially those located in elites' control over the state.

However, much of globalization's potentially beneficial impact on social exclusion has yet to be realized. The reasons for that are multiple and deep-seated. First, repressive states and reactionary individuals also benefit from globalization. In the case of states, moreover, the convention of sovereignty continues to protect the capacity of those in power to defend the status quo. Second, privately controlled mechanisms of social exclusion, those not based on state power, tend to become strengthened as a result of globalization. There is no reason to assume that unchecked private power is any less creative of structural violence than unchecked public power. Finally, while states often are agents of exclusion and discrimination, historically, in many countries, they also have been key tools for positive social change. The erosion of their power without introducing other accessible and potentially accountable and inclusive platforms for governance thus reduces that possibility.

In the discussion so far, I adopted a traditional state-centric perspective from which globalization is seen as influencing the dynamics of structural violence indirectly, through its impact on the national polities and economies where people live and engage in social struggles. It is possible, however, to argue that globalization affects structural violence directly, by itself, within societies. This comes from taking a global perspective in which people are seen as world citizens occupying places in a global division of labor, power, wealth, information, consumption, and prestige. It is then possible to study how dynamics of inequality, social exclusion, and humiliation emerge directly from the structure and functioning of the globalized world political economy.

Until recently, the global perspective constituted a more theoretical than real exercise. For the purposes of ethical argument, it was possible to talk about the absolutely stunning degree of global inequality or the injustice of global social exclusion. One could reflect on the injustice of global social exclusion by considering the fact that some people, by virtue of being born in the Third World, had dramatically lower life expectancies than those born in the rich countries, often dying from easily preventable or curable diseases. These reflections, while factually correct, were by and large ethical or conceptual arguments. They did not reflect the real-life perceptions or dynamics of the world's poor. Most people in poor countries did not have the faintest idea of the wealth and the life chances available to those in rich countries (the same holds, to a lesser extent, from the opposite perspective). The humiliation that could emanate from the international system was by and large limited to rare interpersonal contacts such as between colonial administrators and "barbarians" (Coetzee 1980).

Technological changes occurring over the last few decades have changed that dramatically. The key aspect here again is not so much the usually discussed increase in global financial exchanges. Rather, it is the combination of widening worldwide inequality with a global awareness of, and aspiration to emulate, Western standards of living and modes of consumption.

Global society is stunningly inegalitarian. Among the most often mentioned comparisons are these: fewer than 100 persons, two-thirds of whom are US citizens, own as much of the world's resources as the 2.4 billion poorest of the world who make up 41 percent of the globe's population. In addition, "the assets of the three richest people are more than the combined GNP of all least developed countries" (United Nations Development Program 1999: 37). All data show that inequality between countries has risen greatly during the last decades (as it has within countries, as I noted earlier). The gap between the average per capita income of citizens of the rich countries as compared to those of the poor countries has risen from $3,800 in 1950 to $9,600 in 1980 and $19,800 in 1990 (Seligson 1993: 3); in 1998, the gap reached $25,000 (based on World Bank 2000: 231). UNDP (1999: 35–7) provides the following data: "the income gap between the fifth of the world's people living in the richest countries and the fifth in the poorest was 74 to 1 in 1997, up from 60 to 1 in 1990 and 30 to 1 in 1960." At present growth rates, it will take hundreds of years for most of the world's poor countries and people to cross the gap between the rich and poor (Morawetz 1993: 9); others will never get there.

These data are not theoretical: people throughout the world are acutely aware of these inequalities and of how the odds are stacked against them. Marshall Wolfe (1995: 90), discussing "exclusion from the consumer culture," rightly says that: "people throughout the world are now exposed to messages concerning diversified and continually changing norms for consumption. They have internalized such norms to an extent that hardly could have been expected a few decades ago, when 'the revolution of rising expectations' became a current cliché, and that is altogether out of keeping with the capacity of the majority to respond." This change in expectations is only one result of longstanding deep trends including the growth of upper and middle classes in many Latin American and Asian, and to a lesser extent, African countries; the growth in advertising and the massive spread of television; further increases in migration; and dramatic increases in voluntary travel between rich and poor countries, whether for tourism or for education.

In consequence, the staggering inequality that characterizes global society goes hand-in-hand with the deep and constant humiliation. As the seductive goals of (over)-consumption and freedom (whether sexual, geographic, or material) expand for a privileged minority, and as images glorifying these freedoms and consumption cultures are incessantly spread via omnipresent mass media, tourists, and aid workers, the large mass of the world's population is ever more deeply reminded of its inferiority, ignorance, and insignificance. In an odd way, the development enterprise plays a key role here: which Third World village does not have a resident American volunteer, digging latrines in her Tommy Hilfiger tee-shirt and listening to her Sony disc-man; which person does not see the four-wheel-drive vehicle of a major aid agency speed by on its way to somewhere more important than here?

Finally, seen from below, global society is characterized by massive social exclusion. The vast majority of the world's population can never aspire to the lifestyles and opportunities open to those promoting the global liberal discourse. From a global perspective, the "developed" life is primarily a matter of birth and privilege. For most of the world's population, mechanisms of social exclusion function as blatantly as they did in, say, the Middle Ages, while the rhetoric surrounding them denies their existence. The liberal discourse and associated practices that dominate at the global level (and are enforced daily by major multilateral, bilateral, and private institutions in the center) are obviously untrue: for many of the world's people, a lifetime of hard work and innovation leads at best to remaining as poor as they are today, and at worst to further impoverishment. This is more than an image: people throughout the world are deeply aware of the inequality and the exclusion, and they profoundly resent it.

In short, dramatically increasing inequality between states as well as within them, together with a global awareness of each other's divergent opportunities and the essentially one-way and top-down nature of communication with the rest of the world, all create a situation of astonishing structural violence from the perspective of those at the bottom of the global pecking order.

From structural to acute violence

That conditions of structural violence are conducive to outbreaks of acute violence seems intuitively obvious. But concretely, what are the transmission belts between the two? From the literature, four kinds of relations can be distinguished. The first two are essentially mirrors of each other. One is the proposition that those upon whom structural violence is exerted will resist it and rebel against their lot, using acute violence to change the structures that oppress them. The other is the observation that those who benefit from structural violence will use all means necessary, including acute violence, to safeguard their privileges (Gil 1996: 77; Burton 1997: 33; Schwebel 1997: 333). In both cases, acute violence takes place between the underdogs and the top dogs, between those suffering from structural violence and those exercising or benefiting from it. This is a well known and understood process that has been described by many social scientists (Horowitz 1985; Stavenhagen 1990; Gurr 1993; Fein 1995). Models of conflict designed to detect early warning of conflict currently *en vogue* in foreign policy and development aid circles, for example, are mostly built on this basic insight: they measure impoverishment, discrimination, and mobilization around grievances by marginalized groups, and expect violence to result as these indicators rise.

However, other mechanisms exist by which structural violence can be expected to lead to acute violence *among the underdogs* themselves. One is the possibility that under conditions of intense resource competition among the excluded that follows from structural violence, there is bound to be fierce and bloody competition among the poor for a share of the remaining available slices from a small pie (Schwebel 1997: 340). The later years of South African apartheid seem a text-book example of this, with various ethnic groups and their leaders confronting each other violently in order to capture the last crumbs that fell from the table of the apartheid system.

In addition, the frustration, anger, and destruction of social capital engendered by structural violence may not lead to attempts to change the structures of oppression themselves. Rather, through projection mechanisms that build on deep personal identities and social sanctions, they trigger violence against other, "inferior" social groups. In other words, rather than revolting against the "top dogs," people who are subjected to structural violence often vent their anger against minority groups who serve as scapegoats. This is all the more likely to occur if and when there is a long history of describing and treating these minority groups as outside of the social body, as strangers or as profiteers, etc. David Gil (1996: 81) describes this clearly when he writes that "most often, [violence] is not directed against the sources, agents, and beneficiaries of societal violence, but displaced onto other targets." In the same vein Burton (1997: 34) writes about "the transfer of anger by those who feel deprived, not against those responsible, for they are not accessible, but against others within a community also suffering, such as other minorities, and even others who live in the same locality." Violence in much of the postcolonial world – including Rwanda in the 1990s – is principally of the latter type (Spencer 1992: 265; Uvin 1998). The rest of this chapter focuses on the connection between structural violence and violence between the underdogs. I emphasize this relationship for two reasons: first, it is intuitively less evident and less studied, and at least for the case of sub-Saharan Africa which is my area of specialization (and which is, sadly, a region haunted by great acute and structural violence), acute violence between underdogs is by far the most common response to structural violence.

We can distinguish two basic transmission belts by which structural violence leads to acute communal violence between underdogs: one is social, and consists of the loss of the sense of society and the social capital that ordinarily constitute brakes on possible dynamics of violence. The other is psychological, consisting of the need for projection and scapegoating that results from the humiliation and loss of self-respect engendered by structural violence.

Decrease in legitimacy and social capital

In sociology, there is a longstanding tradition of linking income inequality to violent crime (Blau and Blau 1982; Messner and Tardiff 1986; Kennedy *et al.* 1998b; Kawachi *et al.*, 1999; see too the economists Bourguignon 1999; Benabou 2000). Scores of statistical analyses at the levels of countries, provinces, cities, etc. have borne out this relationship, which is close to undisputed among sociologists and criminologists.[3]

More recently, a fascinating literature on the effects of income inequality has emerged in the field of public health. A growing body of empirical research suggests that the greater the disparity in income within a given society, the lower the average life expectancy. In other words, independently of absolute levels of income, countries that display more income inequality have higher mortality rates than countries where income inequality is lower (Farmer *et al.* 1996; Bobak *et al.* 1998; Kennedy *et al.* 1998a; Kawachi *et al.* 1999; for criticism, see Judge *et al.* 1998).[4]

What are the connections between income inequality on the one hand, and crime and morbidity on the other? A series of studies points to psychological distress, feelings of hopelessness, and the destruction of social capital as crucial variables. Some studies provide data suggesting that high levels of income inequality and social exclusion lead to hopelessness, depression, and other forms of psychological distress, which in turn, either directly or indirectly (through violence, drugs, and other risky behaviors) increase morbidity and mortality (Engel 1968; Krieger *et al.* 1993; Wilkinson 1997; see Fiscella and Franks 1997 for a dissenting viewpoint). Others argue that high income inequality weakens the relation of individuals to the larger society, destroys social trust and social capital, and creates social disorganization – all of which are conducive to higher mortality (Wilkinson 1996; Bobak *et al.* 1998: 277; Kennedy 1998: 14–15; see too Putnam 1995; Vilas 1997: 61; Silver 1998: 67).

One specific way that structural violence contributes to the depletion of social capital is through the process of impunity, the flip side of social exclusion. In many countries in the world, and especially from the perspective of the poor and marginalized, impunity is a matter of daily life. When judicial procedures see the highest bidder prevail; when entry into secondary and tertiary education is the result of money and influence rather than knowledge and perseverance; when the best jobs are allocated not on the basis of competence but of connections; when cases of manifest incompetence or abuse of power end in the promotion of their perpetrators; when laws are flouted and corruption is rife, people lose their faith in the system, become cynical, and are easily tempted to break laws themselves. As Arthur Ripstein (1997: 94) states: "If the state does nothing in response to acts which are both unjust and humiliating, it allows those who do wrong to overstep the bounds of their role as citizens. Criminal acts [thus] become official.... Unpunished crimes gain their status as official acts from the fact that the state purports to protect people against them. When it fails to protect, it acquiesces." Not surprisingly, then, impunity and exclusion lead to an accumulation of anger directed at the institutions and representatives of the state – for it is they who embody the discourse that has lost its meaning, transmit, and/or condone the humiliation, and benefit from the results of exclusion.

This is how structural violence lowers barriers against acute violence. As social capital erodes; as the norms of society lose legitimacy; as people's knowledge bases are reduced to slogans; as progress becomes a meaningless concept; as communities are riven by conflict and jealousy; as segments of society show their contempt for the rules of decency; as high inequality destroys any notion of community; and as desperation and immiseration grow, people become increasingly immune to social constraints on the use of violence. This argument differs from the often heard observation that communal violence, whether in Rwanda or in East-Central LA, is the result of opportunism. It is true that opportunistic behavior has been observed in every case of mass violence anywhere (Tambiah 1997: 1178; Uvin 1999 for Rwanda); but when stated as a causal generalization, as is often the case, this is little more than a politically convenient platitude (Feagin and Hahn 1973: 127ff., discussing the "riffraff theory" of violence). Hence, we need to be more precise.

Opportunism cannot, by definition, be the prime explanation for the occurrence of violence. For opportunism to exist, there must be processes in which opportunists can insert themselves to do their dirty work (Goldhagen 1996: 382). What I want to capture here is the extent to which structural violence produces a greater propensity as well as more structures of opportunity from which to consider the use of violence by underdogs. The mechanisms are various. One is desperation. Societies characterized by great structural violence are societies with many desperate people who, if given the opportunity to steal or settle grievances with impunity, may choose to do so. As Kasozi (1994: 200), discussing Uganda, writes: "Social discipline deteriorated in the face of such living conditions. To survive, people disregarded rules, procedures, morals." A second mechanism is ignorance: uneducated, illiterate people who are never exposed to broad information, asked to reflect independently, or encouraged to ask critical questions, are highly susceptible to arguments that justify violence. A third one is anger – anger at the "systemic injustice" of which the underdogs are victims; anger at the people as well as the whole system that produces structural violence and allows it to perpetuate itself. A fourth, closely related, mechanism follows – the loss of general social capital. Laws or ethical rules matter less and simple opportunity becomes more important. As Khiddu-Makubuya (1994: 161) also writing about Uganda says, under conditions of structural violence "governments with violent tendencies have not lacked supporters, henchmen and operatives whose lowest common denominator is socio-economic opportunism and desire for economic gain....Many poor and deprived people have jumped on the bandwagon of violence in the hope of obtaining political and economic justice."

Scapegoating and projection

It is hard for most of us to imagine how tense and frustration-ridden a society must be in which the large majority of the population is shown daily the lifestyle of the "developed" and exhorted to achieve it, but is, at the same time, structurally excluded from this "good life" and from most chances of achieving it. Taken together, great inequality, closure of life chances, and social exclusion cohere into a profoundly powerful force acting on many of the world's people. This impossibility, this closing-off, this violent force not only affects people's material lives, but also cannot fail to have a profound impact on their sense of self-worth, the nature of their social relations, and their sense of citizenship (Schwebel 1997: 338). As Galtung (1990: 294) writes, "A violent structure leaves marks not only on the body but also on the mind and the spirit."

More concretely, structural violence is characterized by, and leads to, a profound sense of frustration and personal inadequacy. People cannot live with these feelings and need ways to discharge and overcome them. Human beings have a profound need to make sense of life, to establish self-respect. As Daniel Christie (1997: 325) writes: "Ethnocentrism, the belief in in-group superiority over out-group, can serve multiple needs for those who would practice it, including the need for security and identity." And George Eaton Simpson and J. Milton Yinger (1953: 61) wrote almost half a century ago:

> Prejudice is an attempt to find meaning, to explain. ... Prejudice may be an attempt to enhance one's self-esteem or to remove a threat to self-esteem. In a culture that stresses the opportunities each person has for success but prevents success (by its own definition) for a great number, it is not surprising to find a great many people creating a shadowy image of success by placing themselves, categorically, above all members of inferior groups.

Racist prejudice can serve as a means for ordinary people subjected to structural violence and humiliation to make sense of their predicament and to explain their ever-growing misery through projection and scapegoating. In many countries, "state-supplied" racism – often directed at upwardly mobile or professionally visible minority groups[5] – provides poor people with a sense of value, as well as an "explanation" for the mal-development they face daily in their lives. As Simpson and Yinger (1953: 83) stated in their seminal work on prejudice: "The designation of inferior groups comes from those on top – an expression of their right to rule – as well as from frustrated persons often near the bottom, as an expression of their need for security." Everywhere in the world, young, frustrated men are the ones most vulnerable to violent ethnic appeals (Bardhan 1997: 1386; Tambiah 1997: 1178).

Ervin Staub, one of the foremost psychologists to have studied "the roots of evil," similarly describes how devaluation of others and scapegoating serve as strategies to cope with the stress of persistent life problems, frustration, and lack of self-esteem (Staub 1989: chapter 3, 1990). "The frustrated, seeking a concrete target to strike out against and allies with whom they can identify, may find both by selecting scapegoats – in particular, those who are seen as threatening their security" (Schwebel 1997: 342). And, on a more social level, Horowitz (1985) has brilliantly demonstrated how ethnicity may provide people with legitimacy, self-respect, and a claim to social inclusion.

To sum up, one of the key social science questions of our time has been why ethnicity is the preferred form of so many violent conflicts. This is all the more so as, with few exceptions, most ethnic conflicts do not take place between top dogs and underdogs but rather within the latter category. One widely accepted possibility is that ethnicity is easily mobilizeable because it is both a strong, primary attachment for people and at the same time eminently fluid and malleable by political entrepreneurs (Bourgois 1989: conclusion; Bardhan 1997: 1388). Our analysis of structural violence allows us to formulate an additional argument: because so much structural violence is exerted as an attack on people's sense of self-respect and human identity, their revolt against it will be along identity lines as well (Christie 1997: 319; Loury 1999: 10). In other words, the violence that is inflicted on people's identities is as acute and as painful as the discrimination and the exclusion that affect their material lives. Not surprisingly, then, resistance is often felt and articulated at the level of identity.[6]

Conclusion

This chapter described the connections between structural violence on the one hand, and war and acute violence on the other, most notably those kinds of violence that have dominated the world scene during the last decades, for example, civil war and communal violence. The concept of structural violence provided a framework incorporating the deep connections between politics (social exclusion), economics (inequality), and the social-psychological dimensions of life (humiliation). The advantage of using the structural violence lens resides in the holistic framework it provides, allowing a sharper focus on the social and psychological dynamics that lead to acute violence than is provided by conventional IR and IPE models. Indeed, I believe that the notion of humiliation or symbolic violence and its link with globalization is a key aspect of this analysis. Beyond finance and trade, globalization is about attitudes, expectations, and symbolic culture, and the consequent deeply felt exclusion and humiliation of those – the very large majority of the world's population – excluded from its (perceived) benefits. Symbolic politics matter deeply, and ought to be taken more seriously in security and development studies than has been the case in the past.

The concept of structural violence allows us to see the multi-dimensional nature of the dynamics that lead to communal violence, how they are tightly interwoven, and how they mutually influence one another. At the economic level, great inequality combined with the closure of life chances create deep misery and a desperate need for actions that carry the promise of change. At the political level, dynamics of social exclusion and impunity destroy social capital and the legitimacy not only of states and governments, but also of the laws and institutions that usually serve to deter violence. At the socio-psychological level, symbolic violence, ignorance, and humiliation produce dynamics of scapegoating and projection that usually occur along identity lines. All these dynamics reinforce one another.

Structural violence may lead to other forms of acute violence than the communal, intra-underdog variety described in this chapter. One was mentioned earlier: political violence that seeks to reverse the status quo and overthrow the top dogs. But structural violence can also be channelled into unstructured, individual forms of violence, including the public criminality of gang violence and drug trafficking (Gil 1986: 128; Crutchfield 1989; Bourgois 1996: chapter 3; Kennedy *et al.* 1998b); the semi-public sphere of witchcraft and religious fundamentalism (Beaujard 1995); the private sphere of domestic violence against women and children (Gil 1986; Simpson 1993: 605; Bourgois 1996: chapter 6); and the personal, individual space of drug abuse, risky sexual behavior, and suicide (Gil 1996). In many contemporary cases, these spheres combine, as is suggested in the dramatic instance of Sierra Leone, where criminality, opportunism, drug abuse, sexual violence, and ethnic conflict are occurring together in what can only be called a total collapse of all that makes humans social and ethical.

The social sciences do not have a grand theory to explain, let alone predict, which of these various spheres will be the site where the results of structural violence will become manifest. As William Miller says, writing about one aspect of structural violence:

> Whether rage rather than despair attends humiliation will depend on who or what is perceived to have caused it, or on who or what can plausibly be blamed for causing it, and on what the possibilities of remedying it may be. We should expect rather wide-ranging cultural variation, depending on the rules and practices regarding blame, the permissible objects of blame, the extent to which blame is appropriately focused inward or projected into others.
>
> (Miller 1993: 160; see also Ross 1993 for similar
> arguments about "cultures of conflict")

Beyond these cultural factors, political scientists would add, among others, the objectives of political entrepreneurs (Adam 1990) and the presence of publicly sanctioned targets of opportunity (Allport 1954); sociologists include the extent to which groups of underdogs are crosscut by significant other social divisions (Lijphardt 1968) and the nature of communal and family ties (Ramphele 1997: 1191); political economists examine the opportunity structure of alternative modes of economic gain (Collier 2000); and psychologists analyze the availability of memories of intergroup conflict (Volkan 1994) as well as prevailing modes of socialization as to how conflict should be resolved (Ross 1997).

Finally, in the light of current events, it is interesting to touch briefly on religious terrorism. One strand of scholarly explanation describes religious terrorism as the result of the humiliation felt by people who feel rejected by the global consumer society. In search of integrity and self-respect, they strike against what they believe to be the ultimate symbol of, if not the key power behind, the order that excludes them – often the United States (Gopin 2000; Juergensmeyer 2000; Stern 2002). Religious terrorism, then, seems to be a hybrid form of violence that merges calculated violence against the perceived top dogs with emotional violence against those who are different. This case brings home the important lesson that *all* forms of violence take place against socially constructed enemies: whether for the purposes of communal, religious, political, and even certain forms of criminal and personal violence, the enemy has to be named and blame attributed. This is where political entrepreneurs come into the picture as well as pre-existing ideologies of differentiation, truth, and salvation. Structural violence, then, is always only part of the explanation, requiring simultaneous attention to human agency, and social and historical dynamics of society.

Acknowledgment

The author thanks Jose Itzigsohn, Frederic Lapeyre, Hilary Silver, Heinz Sonntag, and, especially, Mary Ann Tétreault, for their comments. Intellectual encouragement from Craig Murphy is also gratefully acknowledged.

Notes

1 For example, Jews in pre-Nazi Europe and Tutsi in pre-genocide Rwanda.
2 Marglin and Marglin (1996); for a postmodern version of this argument, see Escobar (1995) as well as much of the work in contemporary gender, ethnic, and postcolonial studies.
3 Note that at the individual level, the relations are more debated and uncertain (see Crutchfield 1989).
4 These correlations are strong and statistically significant in most studies, even after adjustment is made for median income and poverty. These correlations have been identified in studies comparing rich countries only, studies including both rich and developing countries, and studies focusing entirely on subpopulations in the United States or Russia.
5 I thank Mary Ann Tétreault for this observation.
6 As Stephen Blank (1994) argues for the case of the post-Soviet Eastern European states, under conditions of anomie and widespread frustration, nationalism provided the anchoring point around which a sense of community and social order was forged (see also Hobsbawm 1991).

Part IV
Repair of the world

8 Globalization, "new" trade theory, and a Keynesian reformist project

Hartmut Elsenhans

In modern economics, there are currently two bodies of theory that argue in favor of a supply-side reinforcement of investment spending as opposed to mass consumption and thus in favor of adjustment to globalization by cutting wages and government spending: endogenous growth theory (EGT) (Romer 1986, 1987, 1990, 1994; Segerstrom 1991; Caballé and Santos 1993; Grossman and Helpman 1994) and strategic trade theory (STT) (Krugman 1991, 1993). EGT deals with the empirical fact that the decline of capital productivity assumed by standard neoclassical growth theory, has never and probably will never occur. Drawing on previous work (Crafts 1996), it searches for an additional factor of production which is assumed to create further increases in productivity, identifying here the role of human capital and technology. In order to maintain competitiveness, capitalist enterprises and all territorial (national) economies have to maximize the productivity of investment by optimizing the mix of investment in physical capital (plant and equipment) and human capital (training and education). The post-Keynesian observation of stable capital–output ratios (Domar 1961; Bicanic 1962; Mayor 1968; Helmstädter 1969: 48–60) was the basis for the argument about rising real wages as a condition for capitalist growth. The same observation is used in EGT to justify austerity in the name of efficiency. This appropriates Keynes to maintain that the rise in household incomes is based on human capital that households must reproduce by spending on education and training. STT is closely linked to EGT. It maintains that the welfare of a nation depends on its capacity to operate at the technical frontier, which yields Schumpeterian innovation rents. Just as in EGT, in order for a country to maintain a competitive position on the technical frontier, consumption has to be curtailed in favor of investment in physical and human capital.

In opposition to these theoretical approaches, I argue that disappointment and maldistributed welfare gains from contemporary globalization are due not to its extent but rather to perverse policies and certain characteristics. The result is a race to the bottom that cannot be addressed by wage cuts. The essential instrument driving the cost competitiveness of catching-up economies is devaluation. This option is only open to lagging economies, and not to those with a surplus in their balance of trade or even in their balance of payments.

From a global economic perspective, wage cuts in particular economies do not increase their competitiveness because they are compensated by exchange rate improvements, and are therefore useless. Hence, there is room to maneuver at the national level. This maneuverability is based on productivity increases, as EGT assumes, but productivity increases are not necessarily the result of a restriction on consumption. A constant capital-to-output ratio can be shown to depend on increasing mass incomes, reducing financial surpluses to levels of investment that allow the rate of accumulation to be kept in line with the rate of technical progress (Elsenhans 2000f). In addition, a leading economy will have high levels of productivity in a wide variety of sectors. Its comparative advantage may therefore not lie entirely in the technologically most promising sectors, despite its "being first" here as well. Indeed, it may have less of a leading role here than in older sectors. According to Ricardo's law of comparative advantage, such an economy will specialize in backward sectors. In a global economy where all participating economies are capitalist, specialization in backward sectors does not lead to permanent decline or even to a loss of employment. Yet comparative advantage in future growth sectors may also be achieved by noncapitalist economies, despite low productivity in these sectors because of even lower average productivity. Despite the multiplier effects they create (employing additional workers creates new jobs in local-market-oriented industries through the demand of these workers for locally produced goods), if the marginal product of marginal labor in nonexport branches of production – which are important for overall employment levels – of underdeveloped economies is less than what this labor must earn for its survival, export drives may not lead to full employment, and therefore will not lead to overall wage increases. The consequent lack of development of internal markets in turn undercuts the prosperity of nonexport-oriented branches of production. Such economies can devalue indefinitely, as was shown during the Asian crisis, without their export surpluses leading to full employment.

The conclusion is that globalization is not the problem but rather its limited capacity to transform noncapitalist modes of production into capitalist ones through striving to achieve full employment.

Globalization and imperfect competition

Globalization, which I define as the reduction of transaction costs for transnational economic relations, trade, and long-term (including foreign direct investment (FDI)) and short-term capital movements, is said to disempower labor. Capitalism appears to be triumphant, yet capitalists are interpreted as power brokers operating in markets that are characterized by imperfect competition (see Jonathan Nitzan, Chapter 6 this volume). Imperfect competition implies some sort of monopoly. In Anglo-Saxon academia, this approach is particularly prominent and seems to be indebted to two theoretical heritages. Barbara Jenkins, in her analysis of cultural dominance in Chapter 4 refers to one of its origins: Gramsci and his psychological explanation of the political stability of capitalism despite political majorities of workers whose objective interests do not correspond with those of capitalists. The other is the realist approach to international relations (Elsenhans 2000e). Economic power replaces political power in zero-sum games between companies. This approach is taken by Nitzan in his analysis of differential accumulation.

The "invisible hand" of Adam Smith implies, however, that the pursuit of capital's selfish interests may result in situations that are not consistent with the immediate interests of capitalists. The standard neoclassical textbook theory of wage determination may be quoted here. Let us assume with Nitzan that differential accumulation is the main aim of capitalists. In that case, individual capitalists have to invest in productivity growth if they want to beat their competitors, and they may also engage in power games to control markets. As long as technical efficiency leads to a marginal product of labor above marginal cost, employment will increase. If technical progress increases the marginal product of labor, real wages will rise in line with rising marginal product if there are no or only weak barriers to entry to markets. This clearly is not in the interest of private capitalists, however, although it may be a condition for the proper functioning of a capitalist system (Elsenhans 1983).

The contention that capital can control strategic outcomes at the macro-economic level implies market imperfections. The conviction that macro-economic outcomes correspond to capitalists' interests is often associated in theory-building with the assumption that monopoly capitalism is the predominant form of capitalism. Critiques of globalization normally insist not only that globalization increases economic exchange, but also that it increases economic transnationalization through the growth of multinational enterprises. The existence and visibility of these enterprises is considered proof of increasing market imperfections (as an example see Markusen and Venables 1998). Yet, it seems reasonable to assume that, unless the number of companies is drastically reduced, the integration of the three major markets of the West – the United States, the European Union, and Japan – has, in fact, greatly increased competition between major global players which have given up their claims to protected spheres of economic influence. In Western Europe most believe that globalization has led at least temporarily to increasing competition. This does not mean that the share of the largest companies in worldwide sales is reduced. The critiques do not target size; they target monopoly power in pricing. Concentrating on a limited market makes it possible to charge prices which raise the profit rate above the average profit rate. Protected national markets have been an important instrument of such monopoly power. Being able to charge high prices in protected markets and sell at prices lower than average but higher than marginal costs in foreign markets is at the root of Hilferding's (1910/1968: 439) theory of imperialism, one of the three seminal theories of imperialism, the others being Lenin's (1917/1964) and Luxemburg's (1912/1923).

Oligopolistic firms losing market power in protected national markets is a good indicator of the influence of globalization on the conditions of competition among major players. The share of the six largest German automanufacturers in total automobile sales in the Federal Republic of Germany has decreased only slightly due to the extremely powerful competitive position of major German car-makers. In 1988 it was 69.2 percent, and in 1995, 67.5 percent, despite mergers and acquisitions of smaller firms in Germany which normally should have led to a rise in the share of these six largest producers. The share in total sales of the hundred largest machine-makers in Germany was 38.2 percent in 1988, 36.7 percent in 1995, and 36.5 percent in 1998. The share in total sales of the six largest chemical producers in Germany decreased from 40.3 percent in 1980 to 33 percent in 1995, and only 27.9 percent in 1998 (Statistisches Bundesamt 1990: 178, 1997: 196, 2000: 184). Concentration through mega-mergers can therefore be explained as a reaction to intensified competition (Weizsäcker 1999; Lenel 2000) because the conditions of competition in global markets correspond more closely to perfect competition than those in protected national markets (Wiesenthal 1998: 21).

Thus, the Gramscian view of capitalist hegemony in the mind of labor probably plays a lesser role than the historical fact that capitalists are less powerful as a privileged class than precapitalists were or less powerful than the contemporary noncapitalist privileged classes are. Indeed, this is the reason why capitalist structures are generally accepted by most organizations representing the opposite camp, namely labor – not only capitalist wage labor, but also other forms of labor such as self-employed small- and medium-scale producers in agricultural and "informal" small-scale industrial sectors of the "South." For these producers, the debate about capitalism does not focus on its overall characteristics or its potential contradictions with competing, less materialistic value systems, but on the position of labor within capitalism. This argument is in complete disagreement with Przeworski (1980: 135, 1985: 183), who argues that workers give their consent to capitalist arrangements in the industrialized world because they expect higher wages. They do expect higher wages, but they also prefer capitalism for at least two other reasons: it involves less wasteful exploitation, which noncapitalist privileged classes have often justified in the name of socialism (Konrád and Szelényi 1978: 109), and it promotes political equality and democracy. The market is an efficient instrument for controlling privileges and exploitation. Any alternative pattern of globalization, at least for most modern labor around the world, requires an instrumentalization of the market, including the acceptance of property rights for means of production as being delegated and not natural or god-given. The constitution of the Federal Republic of Germany, accepted by the Western allies in 1949, explicitly states the limited nature of property rights. To regain ideological hegemony labor must instrumentalize the market, not reject it.

Theoretical approaches centered around a description of how power is concentrated in the hands of capitalists – which is sometimes deplored and vehemently condemned – weakens the position of labor in its struggle with capital if viable alternatives to a market economy are not presented. Any worldwide coalition of labor and international solidarity, such as the one advocated by Alejandro Colás in Chapter 9 this volume, cannot expect to make advances on the basis of noble values if the projects planned are not realistic. The cultural hegemony of capitalism in a Gramscian sense seems to function by discrediting any alternative to the rules set by capitalists to impose their own immediate interests.

Globalization or the law of comparative costs

The theory of an inevitable race to the bottom with respect to wages and labor conditions implies that specialization depends on absolute cost advantages. In reality, specialization depends on comparative advantage or comparative costs.

As to the law of comparative costs, an economy increases its welfare through specialization even if it produces all products with a lower factor deployment than its potential trading partners. According to EGT and its emphasis on human capital, the physical capital endowment as formulated in the Heckscher–Samuelson–Ohlin theorem (Ohlin 1927; Samuelson 1948; Heckscher 1970) does not apply, but, rather, the Ricardian formulation (Ricardo 1817/1951: 135ff.) Ricardo's example assumes, for reasons of politeness, that Portugal produces both textiles and wine more productively than England, but that England's backwardness is less in textile than in wine production. In order to avoid confusion, let us use Ricardo in the manner presented in standard textbook introductions. In this example, England produces both textiles and wine more productively than Portugal, but England's advantage in productivity is higher in textiles than in wine. This reformulation takes into account a certain implication in Ricardo's thinking, namely that England's comparative advantage is in the dynamic branch where an "improvement in arts and machinery" (Ricardo 1817/1951: 141) occurs. Even the most superficial observer in Ricardo's day would have been expected to agree intuitively with England's specialization in textiles, but not necessarily with Portugal's specialization in wine.

If England has a comparative advantage in textiles, it will specialize in this product as long as Portugal engages in free trade. Suppose that England and Portugal have equal international labor costs, and that labor is ultimately the only factor of production. English and Portuguese consumers would initially buy only English textiles and wine. Portuguese wine and cloth merchants would offer Portuguese escudos on the exchange market in order to buy English pounds. Under a gold standard, there would be a drain of bullion out of Portugal, decreasing the general price level, whereas the inflow of bullion into England would raise English prices. If a gold standard does not exist, the supply of Portuguese currency on foreign exchange markets would lead to exchange rate adjustments. The price of Portuguese products would fall as long as some Portuguese products, those where Portugal's backwardness is lowest in relative terms, become internationally competitive. If wine is a luxury product and textiles a wage good, then the new pattern of specialization would make English real wages constant and real wages in Portugal rise.

The mechanism of adjusting price levels in international currency shows that international labor-cost differentials depend not on wage movements but on exchange rates (Elsenhans 1997a, 1999b,c, 2000b). There are two implications to this argument. First, devaluation is the instrument through which comparative advantage is transformed into cost competitiveness. Second, the implied absence of purchasing-power parity between countries with different levels of economic development implies a subsidy from the nonexport-oriented part of the economy to the export-oriented part, as long as·the former is not stimulated by the effects of either growing internal demand or growing export opportunities.

The most comprehensive treatment of devaluation as an instrument for promoting manufactured exports is the World Bank report by Zafiris Tzannatos (1997). IMF data on exchange rates do not control for the inflation rate, the rate of productivity increases, or the effect of administered prices, such as for rice in East Asia, on wage goods. Simply observing the exchange rates published by the IMF gives little indication of the real exchange rate. Price indices are often lacking or not very representative. Tzannatos's study accounts for increases in productivity in wage goods and export products, as well as the rate of inflation, and concludes as follows: "With the solitary exception of Korea's real wage movements relative to productivity, all other countries maintained their wage–productivity gap at the same level (with some fluctuations) for the last two decades [...] All countries depreciated with respect to the Japanese yen. Some depreciated rather aggressively" (Tzannatos 1997: 2–3). In other words, the nominal exchange rates of the newly industrialized countries declined little in relation to a declining dollar but massively in relation to their main competitor, the Japanese yen. But US data reflect a massive decline of the Korean exchange rate during the 1970s and the 1980s from 251.4 (index 100 = 1992) to 88.6 in 1985, that is, until the decline of the dollar against the yen that started with the Plaza Agreement (United States Bureau of Labor Statistics 1998: 28).

Devaluation is an instrument for promoting exports of manufactured products and, for this reason, has been advocated since the 1960s (Seers 1964: 236). Korea devalued its currency in 1964, just at the start of its export offensive (Kim 1971: 19). Bernd Stecher (1972: 7), an author at the Kiel Institute, and Daniel Schydlowsky (1972: 283) drew initial conclusions, which were later confirmed by others (see Bradford 1987: 310; Edwards 1989: 3; Cypher 1991; Tenkate 1992: 665). Ultimately, the World Bank joined this consensus (Page *et al.* 1993: 136); UNCTAD (1992: 7) had backed devaluation even earlier. The experience of the Newly Industrialized Countries (NICs) is summarized by Frédéric Atlan *et al.* (1988).

François Bourguignon *et al.* (1991: 1503) showed that devaluation is more socially beneficial than fiscal or wage restraint. China did not devalue during the Asian crisis of 1997, although it had done so in the 1980s (Woo and Tsang 1988: 44). East Asia's greater capacity to devalue (low import content of luxury consumption) in comparison to Latin America was a major difference that explains the greater success of East Asia in export-led growth (Agosin and French-Davis 1995: 39; Shafaeddin 1995: 17). Rates of devaluation of 500 percent are reported by Rodríguez Céspedes (1983: 163) for Latin America, quite comparable to the Asian crisis or the African structural adjustment programs. These were ineffective due to comparative advantage in price inelastic and income inelastic raw materials (Rittenberg 1986; Fontaine 1994: 689).

If devaluation is the instrument for becoming sectorally competitive without necessarily leading to full employment, there has to be absence of purchasing-power parity between developed industrialized countries and underdeveloped ones. The purchasing power of a wage paid in an underdeveloped economy, especially in an export-oriented one, is much higher in the local economy than if converted into international currency at the prevailing rate (Yotopoulos and Lin 1993: 11; Narrasiquin 1995: 325; Guillaumont-Jeanneney and Hua 1996; Lafay 1996: 948, 963; Weliwita 1998; Doganlar 1999). The purchasing power of a salary in an underdeveloped country is 5–10 times higher than the purchasing power of the same salary in an industrialized country if exchanged at the going exchange rate (Chen *et al.* 1994). A brief glance into any of the recent world development reports by the World Bank suffices to show that GNP per capita at the prevailing exchange rate and GNP at purchasing-power parity diverge the more the country is (at least initially) export-oriented. GNP per capita in mainland China in 1999 was $780, but at purchasing-power parity it was $3,291. The corresponding values for India are $450 and $2,149. In Vietnam, a country just beginning its export offensive, GNP per capita in 1990 was $370, whereas at purchasing-power parity it was $1,755. Even in the Republic of Korea, GNP per capita in 1999 was $8,490, whereas GNP per capita at parity was $14,637. In contrast, for upper-middle income countries, there was no divergence, and in high-income countries GNP per capita at prevailing exchange rates was about 20 percent higher than at purchasing-power parity (World Bank 2000: 274–5).

The often quoted wage differentials, in the range of 70:1 between leading industrialized countries and backward catching-up countries, are calculated on the basis of exchange rates. Any social scientist with experience in empirical research will realize that survival on one-seventieth of American wages is not possible at American price levels. It is obvious that such low international wages are achieved by an implicit subsidy to wage laborers in export sectors of low-income countries. These workers make purchases from local wage-goods-producing sectors, especially agriculture. The benefit of an agricultural surplus sold locally goes not only to local wage laborers, but also cheapens exports to consumers in the industrialized world. It has been calculated that India may raise its level of employment through devaluation without increasing its foreign export earnings (Krishnamurty and Pandit 1996: 75).

Devaluation is a powerful instrument for subsidizing the economic transformation of a catching-up economy. Subsidies in the form of low-priced nontradables are perfectly legal, and benefit nearly all catching-up economies that use them. Japan and West Germany greatly relied on this mechanism in the 1950s and 1960s. Thus, Korean authors rightly argued that exploitation in the sense of Emmanuel's (1969: 109–11) unequal exchange is a powerful growth-inducing mechanism (Suh 1987: 111). Incidentally, even Marx (1867/1972: 12) was aware of this, insisting on the lack of capitalist exploitation in Continental Europe as a source of its misery.

But not all countries following the strategy of devaluation-driven growth will be able to achieve full employment. The Japanese success story cannot necessarily be replicated. Export drives may be too weak to transform an economy and raise its marginal product of labor to the level of income required for subsistence. This point is made by the theory of labor-surplus economies with structural unemployment (Lewis 1954; Georgescu-Roegen 1960; Fei and Ranis 1964).

Cutting wage costs in the leading industrialized countries would therefore not result in competitiveness. The argument that Germany has to lower wages because of unemployment – the international price of German labor was admittedly much higher than the price of American labor in 1998 (but is no longer in 2002 due to the appreciation of the dollar),[1] not to mention Third World labor – implies that Germany should solve its unemployment problem by means of another export drive. But Germany's balance of trade surplus was already at a record high in 2000, and further nearly doubled in 2001 to reach 94 billions of Euros (Deutsche Bundesbank 2002). Any further wage restraint would simply be compensated by higher exchange rates (Elsenhans 1997a).

There are limits to devaluation-driven growth with full employment. Just as an overextension of investment spending creates inflationary processes, an over-extension of export surpluses leads to imported inflation or wage increases due to scarcity of labor, as it did at the end of the 1960s in West Germany. Today's successfully catching-up economies cannot avoid currency appreciation. They have to revalue their currencies, as Japan did in the 1980s.

The operation of this adjustment process explains why similar levels of inter-nationalization can generate different outcomes in the technically leading countries and different behavioral patterns among their working classes. The current "globalization" process (increasing shares of transnational, as compared to non-transnational, economic transactions) has only recently reached pre-1913 levels (Gosh 1995: 126; Bovenberg and Gordon 1996: 1057; Irwin 1996: 41–4; Verdier 1998: 13ff.; Theurl 1999). The data are irrefutable (Feldstein 1994: 685; UNCTAD 1994: 120f.; Bairoch 1996; Bergeljik and Mensik 1997: 166). Neither the share of FDI in total local capital formation nor the share of foreign trade in GNP is significantly higher today than it was before 1913. No economy has yet matched Great Britain's shares of capital exports in gross capital formation: 1860–69, 29.5 percent; 1890–99, 25.8 percent; and 1905–14, 53.5 percent (Cairncross 1953: 180; Deane and Cole 1967: 308; Kenwood and Lougheed 1971: 40). The annual average outward flow of FDI as a percentage of gross fixed capital formation for the developed industrial world was 5.7 from 1987 to 1992, and 9.7 percent in 1997. For the European Union these figures were 8.3 and 14.8 percent, due mainly to capital flows between EU countries, which have come to represent an increasingly integrated economy with a single currency, and they were relatively high only for small countries with large multinational enterprises, such as Sweden (1997, 40.6 percent). For the United States, outward and inward flows of FDI over the last ten years were less than 10 percent of gross fixed capital formation (1987–92, 3.9 percent, 1997, 9.7 percent, Japan 1987–92, 3.6 percent, 1997, 2.2 percent, UNCTAD 1999: 501–2).

The higher share of multinational enterprises in world production today in comparison to their share during the last pre-World War I decade may represent a greater degree of concentration in the contemporary pattern of globalization but not a more intensive globalization. Competition policy – and not globalization – is the issue at stake. Competition policy is greatly supported by more open markets, as shown earlier. I might add that, with respect to the power of global enterprises and their use of state governments, there is no study dealing with the influence of today's transnational corporations on political decision making comparable to Hallgarten's (1935) analysis of imperialism prior to World War I.

The only aspect of the current globalization process that decisively surpasses pre-1913 levels is short-term financial movements. These are, however, not an indicator of globalization, but of its absence. In a gold-currency system, hence in a truly globalized international financial system, there is no need for mechanisms to protect against the risk of fluctuations in exchange rates, the focal point of contemporary short-term financial market operations. A gold-currency system has fixed exchange rates. Today's currency system resembles the medieval economy where unclear accountabilities for non-gold currencies led to financial disorder. It was replaced by the uniform adoption of the gold standard with the rise of globalization in the late nineteenth century, even by Britain, which until 1873 had had a gold and sterling mix backing its currency.[2]

To be sure, communication and transport costs have decreased but if that were the problem, the Tobin tax would be quite sufficient to deal with it. Eric Helleiner (1995) and Gerald Epstein and Herbert Gintis (1995) have shown that other forms of transaction costs affect long-term investment and that the reduction of communication costs affects only short-term capital movements and not the real economy. Thus, we do not need less globalization but rather a financial system where Keynesian credit money can be produced only by those able to assume a clear political and social responsibility, just as in the case of the nation-state.

The lack of theoretical agreement with respect to the global economy is demonstrated by the situation today in comparison with the 1930s. In the 1930s, the responsibility of the nonmarket economy and the state for overall growth was admitted worldwide. Decolonization became possible because it was recognized that only a democratically responsible state could impose development policies.

Nowadays, not even the G-7 countries can agree on how to deal with valueless money injected into the economy to stimulate economic growth.

The specific nature of the present globalization process is, however, not the absence of a reliable financial regime comparable to the gold standard in the late nineteenth century. Pre-1913 globalization levels did not trigger the fears which prevail today; they led to a cheapening of raw material imports, through which real incomes of labor in the industrial countries increased (the famous labor aristocracy). This did not endanger jobs because low-wage countries did not become competitive in price- and income-elastic products, with the exception of Indian textiles in the late nineteenth century.

Globalization today is characterized by devaluation-based competitiveness in income and price-elastic goods from economies that cannot overcome structural labor surpluses despite their export drives. It is this new competitiveness, and not the movement of financial resources, that creates anxiety. The relocation of production sites was accompanied by enterprises engaging in blackmail in the latter part of the nineteenth century, as shown by Marx: "It has become fashionable among English capitalists to describe Belgium as a paradise of workers, because freedom of work and, what amounts to the same, freedom of capital have not been stunted by trade unions or factory laws" (Marx 1867/1972: 700). But Marx expected a rapid transformation of the low-technology low-wage economies. It is Hobson (1902/1938: 313) who, to my knowledge, first saw the danger of competition from low-wage countries when he wrote: "... the investors and business managers of the West appear to have struck in China a mine of labor power richer by far than any of the gold and other mineral deposits which directed imperial enterprise in Africa and elsewhere."

The decisive factor is whether or not multiplier effects from additional exports in a catching-up economy transform this economy into a capitalist one. Assume that there are economies that cannot overcome structural labor surpluses despite export drives. In such economies, the low price of export products is the result of export workers being supplied with basic necessities from sectors of local production which – either because of their quality or low productivity in their manufacturing – are not competitive on the world market at prevailing exchange rates.

Nineteenth-century globalization was characterized by marginality-ridden economies with no chance to become competitive in price and income-elastic (manufactured) goods. Economies that participated in the export of manufactured goods were characterized by parallel growth, with slightly higher growth rates in some catching-up countries and a limited degree of falling behind in the industrial world. I have termed this pattern the convoy model of globalization (Elsenhans 1998: 17–24; 1999c: 439–41). The falling-behind economy is relatively productive in comparison to a technically innovative economy, particularly in technically more backward sectors. The rise in the export surplus of a leading economy with a subsequent rise in its national price level (gold currency) or in the international prices of its factors of production (flexible exchange rates) provides the less innovative economy with new export opportunities and possibilities for import substitution, so that it cannot fall behind indefinitely if its productivity in less innovative sectors and, ultimately, its marginal productivity are relatively high in comparison to the technically leading economy. But high marginal productivity also means that the less innovative country cannot overtake the leading economy through unlimited currency devaluation (and hence a reduction of the costs of its national factors of production in international currency), because it would soon achieve export surpluses on the basis of old products.

Suppose, however, that economies which exhibit the two following characteristics are participating in the globalization process:

1   the marginal product of a substantial part of their labor force is below the cost of subsistence, so that a substantial part of this labor force cannot secure entitlement to jobs and income because it is not surplus-producing (I refer to this as marginality, Elsenhans 1995b: 193–9);

2   there is a surplus in agriculture sufficient to feed all available labor provided that this labor receives entitlement as formulated by Sen (1981).

Such an economy can create entitlement for its marginal labor by devaluing its currency, even to a level where the incomes of export workers are not sufficient to pay for wage goods necessary for their survival from the world market. In this case, the wage goods are supplied from the local agricultural surplus.

It is clear that the challenge presented by contemporary globalization does not stem from low-wage countries. The real challenge is presented by economies, which have been successful in sectoral development on the basis of exports and a surplus in their agriculture, allowing them to accept very high rates of devaluation. If these countries achieve full employment following devaluation the challenge disappears, as was the case in Taiwan and South Korea. The internal market expands, leading to higher real incomes, higher imports, etc., and ultimately forcing these economies to conform to the convoy model.

This analysis shows that attempting to adjust to globalization by means of wage cuts and a reduction of fiscal expenditures is unrealistic. Additional export workers in catching-up economies can be fed from the surplus of local wage-goods production, while wage cuts in the industrially leading countries merely lead to further devaluation in these economies. The dramatic devaluations following the Asian crisis of 1997 and the subsequent recovery of most East and Southeast Asian economies have shown that there is still ample room for maneuvering with exchange-rate depreciations. The international cost of labor may even approach zero if the economy concerned makes economic transformation through full employment, as opposed to high export earnings, its top priority, provided that it can produce locally the wage goods for its export workers.

Productivity advances on the basis of endogenous growth

Endogenous growth theory is rarely discussed in International Political Economy (IPE). IPE deals with economic questions primarily by discussing the interest of capitalist enterprises in making a profit. It treats profit as the surplus which accrues to industrialists because of their ownership of the means of production. Profit, however, is a very special category of surplus or earnings. Michal Kalecki (1971: 13) has shown that under perfect competition profit depends on investment spending and not on the productivity increases which result from investment. Profit is not just a residual like rent, but income created through demand by labor for consumption goods in excess of labor income from consumption goods production (Elsenhans 1996b: 3–7).

The individual enterprise wants earnings on its balance sheet. These may be the result of investment spending, and also of market imperfections, that is rent. Profit as a special category of earnings distinct from rent depends not only on power and competitiveness but also on the overall state of the economy. IPE does not mention structural factors such as the dependence of profit on investment spending and the relative insignificance of investment spending for productivity growth, as demonstrated by the stability of the capital–output ratio and the importance of complementary factors of growth (Elsenhans 2000d). Yet, whether globalization inevitably leads to greater inequality because of the requirements for financing the accumulation process or not is a function of the requirements for accumulation and productivity growth. Its political consequences are closely linked to movements of the capital–output ratio, as shown by the body of theories which link the demise of capitalism to the rising organic composition of capital, and hence to technical progress.

Endogenous growth theory deals with the role of technical progress in economic growth within the framework of neoclassical economics. It integrates the findings of post-Keynesianism and other heterodox discussions into neoclassical models. It was devised in order to explain why the growth linked to capital accumulation did not lead to a decline in capital productivity – a question first tackled long ago (Bortkiewicz 1907: 445–67), and reformulated half a century later (Okishio 1961), becoming the subject of considerable debate with a substantial body of literature (Roemer 1979; Van Parijs 1980; Bowles 1981). This finding is of great importance for all political and sociological discussions of capitalism. As technical progress results in constant capital productivity, the increase in accumulation leads to gains in production which can only be absorbed under very heroic assumptions[3] and only by the capitalist sector as assumed by Lenin (1899/1956: 54, 69, 283, 1897/1951: 32). Neoclassical economics admits that wages have to rise – when full employment is achieved, which also occurred in the United States after twenty-five years of restructuring – in line with productivity increases because of the scarcity of productive labor. The claim that capitalists are unable to invest in technologies which do not raise the profit rate at constant wages also implies that capitalist growth requires increasing mass incomes, at least in the long run.

This link between capitalism and permanent social reform can be refuted if it can be shown that the source of a stable capital–output ratio and stable capital productivity is a sector of production that has been overlooked and, which also requires remuneration. For Bortkiewicz and Okishio there is little doubt that stability in the capital–output ratio and hence the stability of the marginal efficiency of capital is due to technological progress. The issue then becomes how to promote it. The solution proposed by EGT is to introduce a new factor of production whose contribution is to maintain technical efficiency. The decline in capital productivity predicted by neoclassical economics is thus counteracted by the increasing importance of this new factor of production.

Suppose that a comparison is made between the car traffic of two cities. The number of cars and passengers is identical in both cases, but the speed of traffic is not. In attempting to explain higher speeds in one of the cities, one may first consider the hypothesis that more powerful cars are being used in that case. In economic terms, this explanation would correspond to having more physical capital in an enterprise. If after comparison this explanation has to be rejected, two other hypotheses may be advanced. The explanation corresponding to EGT would be that infrastructure as an invisible factor not produced by driving is better in one case than in the other. Such infrastructure could be produced by a specific and multifaceted innovation system comprised of the households that improve the streets in their neighborhoods and the local government that builds larger overpasses. In contrast, the Keynesian explanation would be twofold. On the one hand, drivers evoke infrastructure-improving investment by means of their demand. Even private companies will be willing to invest in improvements when drivers are willing to pay for their services. On the other hand, social equality results in a great many people going in the same direction at the same time so that car pooling becomes possible, reducing the amount of infrastructure required.

This opposition between EGT and Keynesian interpretations can be demonstrated by considering the debate over the effect of rising mass incomes on growth. That the more egalitarian societies of the Third World have experienced higher rates of growth is admitted even by leading economists at the World Bank (Birdsall *et al.* 1995: 482; Alesina and Perotti 1997). The World Bank advocates an orthodox interpretation of the East Asian model, which it labels "shared development" (Page *et al.* 1993: 157ff.).

This orthodox position was first formulated as follows. Food intake increases (at the lowest levels of absolute income) with increasing mass incomes, reducing undernourishment and leading to a rise in labor productivity (Wheeler 1980: 450–1, Strauss 1986; Deolalikar 1988; Fogel 1994: 386). But many societies have resolved the food supply problem without a decisive increase in labor productivity, including societies that have achieved high levels of agricultural surpluses as evidenced by the extent of their nonagricultural construction projects, for example, Ancient India. Even Gunder Frank has argued that Asia was richer than Europe but was unable to transform its surplus into demand for standardized industrial products for consumption by middle classes (Frank 1998: 300f.). The link between economic growth and rising demand by the poor, even the rural poor, for simple products is no longer really disputed. The informal sector thrives where agriculture is prosperous, and there is a low concentration of land ownership (Adelman 1984; Gray and Singer 1988: 403; Dutt 1991: 348).

The alternate version of supply-driven growth where growth is linked to equality focuses on human-capital formation. Human capital is a construct which regards labor skills as produced via an accumulation process comparable in a sense to the construction of new machinery. But no one has yet been able to clearly identify and describe the specific factors of this production process. There is no clear link between the level of formal education in a society and productivity growth. An important mechanism of human-capital formation is learning by doing, the result of a joint production process where learning does not incur additional costs for ·the enterprise, just as sulfur does not incur costs to an oil refinery because it is a byproduct of the production process. Such human-capital formation has long been used to justify protection for learning-intensive industries against foreign competitors.

In order to justify higher incomes for the poor based on the productivity increases expected from human-capital formation, it has to be assumed that the poor will invest more in upgrading their skills if they receive higher incomes (Birdsall *et al.* 1995: 482; Alesina and Perotti 1997). At the start of the Industrial Revolution, however, industrial laborers were recruited from the lowest strata of rural society with the lowest level of skills (Bendix 1956: 36–8; Thompson 1968: 309f.). There are considerable reserves of skills today in the informal sectors of Asia and

North Africa, especially in the metal-working sectors, which are important for investment-goods production. But these potential supplies are not utilized to enhance growth because of a lack of demand for the products of these industries.

The main difference between human and physical capital is its treatment on the company balance sheet. A company that has above average rates of return has disembodied factors of productivity growth, hence human capital. That it outperforms others is explained by the presence of this factor. If this company is sold, its owners will acquire an amount of money that corresponds to the earning capacity of a similar amount of unspecified property with similar risk characteristics. The new owner will enter the purchase price of the company into his statement of assets and liabilities as an asset treated statistically similarly to the physical capital which he amortizes.

The spurious character of human capital is demonstrated by Mankiw (1995: 294), who cavalierly declares that all increases in real wages should be credited finally to human capital on the basis of a low minimum wage in the United States and high differences between this minimum wage and all other wages. Under this assumption, human capital in precapitalist societies with their vagrant and marginal populations would have to be estimated as enormous, whereas egalitarian societies of the East Asian type, those with limited spreads in labor earnings due to the excellence of their educational systems and thus, according to EGT, the excellence of their innovation systems, are characterized by low human-capital formation, as argued by Collins and Bosworth (1996: 157–9). There is no manipulation of reality that a neoclassical economist would not accept to save the theoretical structure of neoclassical economics against the realities of the world.

There is a major objection to the explanation that the productivity of physical capital is increased by households investing in their own human capital. If, assuming sufficient aggregate demand and conditions of competition, enterprises can develop new products and new technologies, which they are able to sell profitably, they will react to a scarcity of labor by financing appropriate training measures. Everything depends on efficiency: are enterprises or households more efficient in producing skills? Households do not invest in skills under competitive conditions but they could increase their human capital by increasing their spending on education. Less efficient households simply have to spend more to avoid incurring sanctions from the market but there is no real competition for improvement. Anyone can engage in "self exploitation." There is a striking parallel here to the mechanisms for maintaining positive growth rates in "real socialism."[4]

The private entrepreneur cannot spend on technical progress by reducing his wage bill, but only by incurring additional outlays. Spending on "inefficient" technical progress is curtailed and overall efficiency increases. Capitalism deprives households of the investment function, and therefore eliminates both the necessity and the possibility of economic agents producing with inefficient technologies. It is therefore logical that spending on skill acquisition and technical progress by entrepreneurs should be characterized by a lower cost–performance ratio than the same spending by households and the state. Obviously, the same type of reasoning can be applied to state outlays for human-capital formation, with one qualification, however: this state outlay may become necessary because of the public-goods character and indivisibilities of the "training and education" product.

The point of contention between EGT and the Keynesian perspective is not the importance of skills or technical progress, but the question of how to promote them. These views diverge with respect to which elements are automatically produced by the decentralized decisions of enterprises and households, and which elements require monitoring by nonmarket institutions, that is, the state. In a Keynesian world, a full-employment level of aggregate demand forces entrepreneurs to compete for scarce labor, to introduce the best available technologies, and even to develop better technologies themselves. The discovery process is left to entrepreneurs who are willing to bear the risks. The wasteful use of resources is minimized as enterprises strive to attain the highest levels of technical development. It is assumed that these decisions are made under conditions of imperfect knowledge. They require trial-and-error processes in which forecasts of future levels of employment and demand may be inaccurate. When entrepreneurs perceive possibilities for technical innovation at some point in the growth process, they invest in a herd-like manner. The threat of macroeconomic imbalances is dealt with by global demand management (fiscal and monetary policies). In this perspective, entrepreneurs do not really need supporting institutions for discovering new products and new technologies.

In order to defend the foundations of the neoclassical model, EGT has to claim the existence of a nonmarket-based coordination process for the formation of its most important asset, human capital. In line with the neoclassical theory of employment and wage determination, EGT supposes that entrepreneurs hire labor according to the technically possible levels of marginal product, but questions the readiness of entrepreneurs to share the costs of setting up indivisible institutions for promoting technical progress due to the potential problem of free-riders. But the level of marginal product which the wage rate has to reach in order for the economy to achieve full employment is not only dependent on technical characteristics, but also on effective demand (Irsch 1979: 46–9, 70). The EGT model has implications which its proponents probably did not intend. It assumes entrepreneurs to be efficient in fulfilling the politico-economic conditions of full employment (a full-employment investment-demand level). But it considers their capacity to innovate as limited. It has to be complemented by other institutions such as technical research agencies. It is difficult to deny that there is a free-rider problem in the creation of additional demand through investment spending much greater than in the creation of additional skills. The individual entrepreneur cannot expect that the wages he pays will become purchasing power for his own products (Rosenstein-Rodan 1943). Indeed, any enterprise that pays high wages creates purchasing power for other enterprises and therefore suffers structurally from a free-rider problem.

Demand-oriented Keynesian models identify aggregate demand and investment outlay as the key elements in the growth process. Because entrepreneurs cannot form coalitions for raising average wages, empowerment of labor is essential for maintaining capitalist growth. This is why globalization has become a problem; the pattern it presently follows disempowers labor worldwide (Elsenhans 1981, 1987).

Technology promotion and homogeneity of demand

There is a fundamental reason why a more egalitarian distribution of income promotes growth and – by necessity, not by chance – higher capital productivity. The correlation was pointed out long ago by critics of neoclassical economics (Strassmann 1956; Elsenhans 1975), and its possibility has been admitted even by authors of the EGT school (Murphy *et al.* 1989). It implies that the competitive position of egalitarian economies should be enhanced at the international level for two reasons. First, the level of real wages is not the basis of international labor costs in an economy. Rising real wages in poor countries with sufficient agricultural surplus do not affect the international price of that labor. Second, an egalitarian demand creates internal markets for new products at a more rapid rate than if the consumption of these products were restricted to tiny minorities. This favors innovation in production technologies for lowering costs, and creates a comparative advantage for these products on the world market.

Suppose, as EGT does, that there are economies of scale in a typical line of industrial production. This assumption is irrefutable for any science or knowledge-based production.[5] Even the simplest technical device is characterized by a certain economy of scale, for example, a hammer used to pound nails (as opposed to pounding nails without one). Humans invent tools and instruments because they perceive economies of scale.

Let us assume that in the case of an egalitarian distribution of demand there is a less diversified demand and, in the case of a less egalitarian distribution, a more diversified demand. Optimal plant sizes may in both cases be small enough to allow maximum economies of scale in any consumption-goods production. In the case of an egalitarian distribution of income, a larger number of optimally sized plants satisfy the demand for one out of a class of products than in the case of an inegalitarian distribution. Therefore, the demand for similar equipment is higher where demand is more egalitarian, if different products are produced by different machinery. Savings on the cost of machinery depend on designing machines for specific production processes (Young 1928). The more full-capacity utilization is reached by utilizing the machinery for a small number of operations, the more specialized this machinery can become.

This effect is much more significant in science-based industries. There is, however, no fundamental difference between the invention of tools and the development of new, science-based technology for improving productivity. In both cases sunk costs prevent new technology from being initially more productive than older, less advanced technology. Only with full-capacity use of new machinery do unit costs decrease. The more new machinery is used, the larger the number of goods or services across which to distribute the sunk costs of its development. Expectations of such scale economies offset the risk of choosing a higher cost technology in developing such a machine. Equality of distribution favors innovation.

It may be argued that a nonmarket innovation system based on supply-side support for new technologies is superior to a demand-driven innovation process. Let us therefore distinguish two sources for improving efficiency: a demand-dependent one and an effort-dependent one. The demand-dependent path is stimulated by rising demand, which triggers demand-induced investment. Let us assume that the rate of growth of innovation is a linear function of the rate of growth of income. The effort-dependent form of improving efficiency is based on a subsidy. But it also has to lead to a product which is in demand, otherwise it would be wasteful. Furthermore, enterprises are unwilling to spend on R&D if they do not perceive profitability. A promising candidate for nonmarket support is therefore one that cannot be sold profitably at first unless its price in relation to real incomes decreases, either because it is subsidized or because real incomes increase, but which promises to be profitable in the future.

Making new products available earlier requires financing, and thereby reduces the purchasing power of households and enterprises. The reduction of purchasing power reduces the demand for all products, even subsidized ones, but the subsidized product can compensate for this lower demand by means of its subsidy. It can be shown (see Appendix) that the best environment for a successful supply-side innovation-promoting industrial policy is a fairly advanced (with respect to skills), but still technologically backward economy with the following characteristics: it is engaged in a catching-up process on the basis of imitation; it has an internal mass market capable of absorbing important shares of the products at least initially; and its lean, state-led innovation system has succeeded in concentrating on technologies with spillovers to other industries and which benefit from growing markets either at home or abroad. Industrial policy may contribute by widening the time horizon of entrepreneurs and customers, supporting (i.e. artificially cheapening) initially unprofitable products until sufficient demand develops to induce entrepreneurs to take over the production of these products.

The link between industrial policy and equality of demand is, in a sense, paradoxical. On the one hand, industrial policy will be more successful the more egalitarian the distribution of demand. On the other hand, industrial policy creates possibilities for rent seeking, and therefore unleashes tendencies for a less egalitarian income distribution. EGT views the second factor, increased rent seeking, as merely a problem of the organizational inefficiency of institutions at the meso- or micro-level, and of the degree of entrepreneurial freedom. Entrepreneurs are, however, not directly interested in competition and profit. They are interested in earnings, and, as Nitzan shows in Chapter 6 this volume, will try to earn as much as possible. According to macroeconomic textbook assumptions drawing on Kalecki (1971: 13), the amount of profit realized *ex post* by all enterprises together after the production round is over corresponds to the amount of investment outlays. This is because enterprises are able to sell products at a profit only if, in addition to the demand financed from wages in consumption-goods production, an additional demand for consumption goods drives up the prices and earnings of these goods above the costs of labor incurred directly or indirectly in their production. The proposed strategy of EGT therefore implies the threat of rent. Thus, when EGT approaches the issue of nonmarket structures for the promotion of programs to enhance human capital, it deals with the problem of how to create efficient rent-based structures which are not tied to market mechanisms. At best, EGT can be thought of as a theory for explaining how an economy can channel resources into sectoral technical progress by manipulating relative prices. Relative prices are closely linked to comparative advantage so that, in reality, EGT is a theory of nonmarket-based manipulation of relative prices with the aim of shifting comparative advantage, especially in favor of catching-up economies.

The importance of being first

There is a close link between EGT and STT. Both try to provide comparative advantage to economies capable of promoting technical competence by nonmarket institutions, seeking comparative advantage in branches of production where outlets are expected to grow. EGT demonstrates the *possibility* of "being first" by means of state interventionist manipulation of relative prices, hence comparative advantage. STT argues the *necessity* of doing so (Krugman 1987 versus Bhagwati 1989). The argument is linked to the old infant-industry-protection school, but its real precursor is Hilferding's theory of imperialism, developed in the early twentieth century. By reserving the internal market and charging world-market prices which are below average but above marginal costs, an economy can concentrate on the most dynamic industries with the highest technical spin-offs (Hilferding 1910/1968: 421ff.).

The body of theories in favor of protectionism can be reduced to two basic arguments: (1) any market-oriented production results in a tradable product and in the skill-upgrading of laborers; (2) the cost–benefit calculation of patterns of specialization differs depending on whether or not the skills created by a production process are taken into account. Including these capacities in calculations of costs and benefits is difficult since they are, by definition, not valued on the market. Thus, the optimization of costs in relation to growth perspectives depends on uncertain expectations. A narrow cost–benefit approach, which can be imposed by the market, may prompt the abandonment of branches with great potential for skill-upgrading in favor of branches with less such potential. Economies suffering from Dutch disease (high export earnings in low-skill branches like raw materials production) are afflicted by this very pattern of specialization (Enders and Herberg 1983; Wijnbergen 1984; Parvin and Dezhlaakhsh 1988; Ansari 1989).

A technologically leading country can maintain its technological superiority through trade specialization provided that its advance in productivity in new products is at least as high as its advance in productivity in older products. This was the underlying assumption of the product cycle theory (Vernon 1966). If this condition is not fulfilled, high productivity in old products leads to a high exchange rate and comparatively high costs for these new products. Even if a country is first in launching a product, it will dominate the world market only if it has not only the highest productivity but also comparative advantage in the production of this product, that is, if its technical advances in manufacturing the product are higher than the country's average level of technical advance (which may be quite high due to the effects of learning by doing in older branches).

Strategic trade theory suggests dealing with the competitive edge of devaluation-driven export economies by shifting comparative advantage to those industries where backward countries cannot compete technically despite theoretically unlimited devaluation. It is unlikely that the limited share of such products in total world demand would allow a major part of today's industrially leading countries to take refuge in this pattern of specialization.[6] Since the strategy depends on state-led shifts in comparative advantage, it creates political structures for more state interventionism. In addition, with increasing wage spreads between different branches, demand expansion through employment growth in a leading sector may not be sufficient to create full employment in the other sectors of the economies engaged in this adjustment path (Elsenhans 2000b: 31–7).

Endogenous growth theory and STT are responses to the challenges of globalization that are strictly limited to a "national" level. They show how to improve the competitive edge of one currency area *vis-à-vis* another one. In a neoclassical world of full employment, they are meaningless. In a Keynesian world, where global equilibria are possible with unemployment, they enable adherents to enjoy higher levels of employment than others. Yet, both systematically neglect the global level. They are meaningless in a neoclassical setting because the latter implies that there is full employment and, because of full employment, automatic equalization of factor productivities across branches of production. This leads first to homogeneous differences in productivity levels between national economies without complete factor mobility at the international level (nationally segmented labor markets) and then, through the operation of the Heckscher–Ohlin–Samuelson mechanism (Ohlin 1927; Samuelson 1948; Heckscher 1970), to convergence of factor productivities in both catching-up economies and leading economies. In a Keynesian world, the technically backward economy will not necessarily enjoy the possibility of raising the prices of products of technically backward sectors where it has a comparative advantage. If workers and enterprises in the technically more advanced branches also can carry out technically less advanced activities with a higher rate of physical productivity, and if there is insufficient demand for the products of the technically more advanced branches, they may shift to technically less advanced activities.

Moreover, in a Keynesian world STT strategies are destructive at the global level for the following reason. They imply solving the employment problem by means of foreign trade surpluses. Foreign trade surpluses lead to the indebtedness of deficit economies, a problem that cannot be tackled without devaluation. Devaluation implies reduced purchasing power for the devaluing country relative to its productive capacity. It exports at lower unit prices, and it buys less from the world market. Any improvement in terms of trade for the more advanced countries, as implied in devaluation, has the same effect as productivity increases. It raises the production capacity of the world economy relative to its consumption capacity. EGT in its practical consequences – that is, limiting expansion of mass consumption in order to finance technical improvement – and STT explicitly reinforce underconsumptionist tendencies at the global level.

The solution to the challenge of globalization: make the world safe for the welfare state

The Keynesian alternative does not consist in national economies trying to escape the consequences of devaluation-driven growth by catching-up underdeveloped and marginality-ridden economies, but in transforming the new participants in the international economy so that they are able or even forced to conform to the convoy model. This requires neither an alignment of Third World wages to levels prevailing in the industrially leading countries, nor the transfer of so-called "social standards" to the export sectors of the South, but only the elimination of marginality. Any serious development strategy involves overcoming marginality.

Import-substitution industrialization as conceived by Rosenstein-Rodan (1943), Nurkse (1953), or Hirschman (1958) consisted in mobilizing financial surpluses for not-yet-profitable investment to compensate for the narrowness of internal markets with the aim of creating productive employment in industry to absorb the labor surplus. Agrarian reform, the flagship of reformist modernization strategies of the 1960s, involved internalizing marginal labor on owner-operated farms so that the rents from highly productive labor time accrued to farm families, which also had to mobilize their own very-low-productivity marginal labor in order to produce what they needed for subsistence (Elsenhans 1996a: 96f.)

Nongovernmental development agencies, economically speaking, channel rents from the richest strata of the world population (in foreign countries and their own countries) to the poor in order to increase their negotiating power on labor markets structured by marginality (Elsenhans 1995a). Even export-led growth is a form of mobilizing rent, as devaluation implies the transfer of resources from wage-goods-producing sectors to the workers of the export sector. Because of devaluation their wages may not be high enough to buy their wage goods from the world market. Using estimations of the number of poor persons in the South as an indicator of marginality, which is about 1–1.2 billion people, the $50 billion of current development assistance could be used to increase the per capita incomes earned by these marginals. This could be accomplished by means of an artificial industry "producing" otherwise useless goods, which would be bought by Western development agencies. This artificial industry – for example, the gathering of a certain type of stone thrown from helicopters into remote areas – would entitle marginals to income in exchange for their services. These incomes would, in exchange, "supply" the West with a good conscience – such as it already hopes to achieve with current development assistance programs. The results would be more positive than today's development assistance, which mostly benefits elites without empowering the poor (Elsenhans 1991: 281–284). Some may argue that such an artificial industry is a *reductio ad absurdum*. On the contrary, it is a rational position for negotiation which the West could propose if "elites" in the South continue to block the trickling down of financial assistance from the West to their own poor.

The proposal implies consumption of otherwise investible resources. It is therefore opposed to an understanding of growth which insists on investment as the main source of productivity increases. Because of the Anglo-Saxon focus on the priority of saving, profit, and therefore investment to be paid from savings and profits, there was an implicit opposition to the adoption of Keynesianism by the larger American public from the very beginning of the "mid-century order." In Keynesianism, investment is triggered by consumption. With insufficient investment, spending on public investment creates incomes for consumption. This represents the easiest way to increase consumption administratively. But in the presentation of Keynesianism to an American public with little grasp of Keynesian theory, investment is justified in a depression not only in order to use otherwise idle resources but, ultimately, to contribute to productivity growth. However, from a strictly Keynesian perspective, productivity increases arise not from deficit spending by the state but from the reestablishment of the basic mechanisms of neoclassical growth. Productivity increases, in the version of Keynesianism adopted by the larger American public, are expected from the very quality of investment financed by deficit spending. To Americans, deficit spending increases productivity, whereas in Keynesianism it is the administratively simplest way to create demand. Proposing an artificial industry is not the best way to promote the efficient use of scarce resources. But given the fact that an efficient use of scarce resources may not be possible due to political structures in rent-based Third-World economies, my artificial industry may well be the most efficient solution economically, provided that it is able to undo all forms of elitist self-privileging entrenched in the political structures of these societies.

Institutional frameworks and endogenous growth

EGT and STT introduce factors complementary to the accumulation of what they call physical capital. The economy is no longer autonomous from society and the political system, which, in the neoclassical world, had only served to set a framework for its operation. Institutions are transformed into a factor of production in order to be incorporated into the formal structure of the neoclassical production function. At the same time, this implies an amorphous (embeddedness of the market, "postwar-embedded" capitalism) and narrowly circumscribed (knowledge-intensive and knowledge-creating agencies) concept of institutions. Since Adam Smith (1776/1996: 79–81), the structure of demand and hence – in his words – the "thriving of the economy" has been shown to depend on the bargaining power of labor and thus, ultimately, on the structure of the politico-economic system.

With the perspective of EGT as his starting point, Richard Grabowski (e.g. 1994: 183, 1995: 67) has shown that the emergence of a market economy depends on the institutionalization of rules of exchange. This institutionalization is greatly supported by an intensification of market exchanges because a greater number of transactions lessens moral hazard. Using Korea and Japan as examples, he shows that this intensification is linked to rising mass incomes in agriculture (Grabowski 2000: 243). I extend this argument even further by maintaining that the market needs no other embeddedness than the support of profit through rising mass incomes (Elsenhans 2000a). Rising mass incomes create artificial scarcity for the surplus-appropriating classes. This forces them to behave as competitive capitalists who, by means of innovation, adapt all other structures to the requirements of competition instead of such behavior being adopted for cultural reasons. Capitalism does not disembed the economy from society in the manner described by Polanyi (1944: 230f.) Rather, this disembeddedness becomes possible because new mechanisms of embeddedness are created through the scarcity of labor. Without these mechanisms, profit cannot emerge. The mechanisms of the new embeddedness of capitalism, that is, rising mass incomes during most of the eighteenth and nineteenth century, were the condition for the transition to capitalism of today's developed countries (Elsenhans 1983, 1997b).

With rising wages, labor eliminates all forms of surplus appropriation not channeled into the spending of private enterprises on the net investment ultimately sanctioned by final demand. If consumption increases to the level of production capacity of the consumption goods sector, entrepreneurs will increase investment spending to add production capacity. They create wages without additional consumption goods but with the consequence of forced savings (Kaldor 1955: 95). It is, therefore, labor which creates the incentive for investment. The historical unity of the third estate in its struggle against precapitalist forms of appropriation of surplus (i.e. rent) in the transition to capitalism had its basis in this natural alliance between profit and rising mass incomes against rent.

A model that focuses on the relation between capitalist growth and rising mass incomes can do with a relatively simple set of institutions. Because inflexibilities on the labor market arise when full employment is approached, a noninflationary growth of mass incomes depends on the capacity to manage the distributional conflict between capital and labor in such a way as to ensure that there is neither permanent unemployment nor an overheating of economic activity. The appropriateness of this focus is confirmed by the present institutional setup of bourgeois societies, which basically reflects the opposition between labor and capital (Mitra 1999: 226). Political science has long discussed the effectiveness of various approaches to managing this conflict, for example, the theory of Rhenan capitalism (Albert 1991: 119f.; Boyer 1996), of neocorporatism (Schmitter 1974; Lehmbruch 1979) or the East Asian models of integrating labor into the set of goals of a particular enterprise (Gospel 1988: 113; Kenney and Florida 1988: 145; Levine and Ontsu 1991: 103).

Anyone who has ever tried to explain the nature of European party systems to students in noncapitalist countries is struck by one major characteristic. The party systems of all capitalist industrial countries are characterized by a cleavage between more labor-friendly and more business-friendly "camps" struggling over property rights and macroeconomic policies. In rentier societies, in contrast, the central political conflict is over the access of various rentiers to surplus. Rentier societies are characterized by a political struggle over the centralization or decentralization of surplus appropriation. Capitalist bourgeois societies normally experience great difficulties when confronted with problems outside the capital–labor conflict. This can be demonstrated by a standard constant in foreign policy research. Foreign policy is not attractive to voters and, therefore, often leads to multi-partisan cooperation, with the so-called "foreign policy elites" having disproportionate influence.[7]

The struggle over resources for the production of complementary inputs to physical capital is "embedded" in the conflict between labor and capital. In the case of market failure, the state channels resources. The amount, efficiency, and management of these resources is determined by the structure of nonstate organizations, often referred to as "civil society." The tendency in the nineteenth century and in the post-1945 period toward the convergence of capitalist systems, which differ quite considerably in their social structures and foundations, especially in their patterns of civil society (Dollar and Wolff 1988; Wolff 1991; Alam 1992; Costello 1993; Williamson 1996: 291), is proof of the wide variety of possible institutional setups as long as labor remains empowered and entitled through full-employment policies. The argument of culturally determined differences in business attitudes has limited empirical foundations. It draws on the political theory of modernization, which had described bureaucracies fed from rents. These bureaucracies, in addition, were not controlled by capital and labor. Rarely has the theory of modernization described real entrepreneurs in underdeveloped countries, the informal sector entrepreneurs.

Some remarks on the perspectives of the world system

The challenge presented by the current processes called globalization rests mainly in the circumstances surrounding these processes and the patterns they follow. Globalization does not lead to a disempowerment of labor simply because there is a reduction of transborder transaction costs. It is rather the failure of capitalism to transform the economies of the rest of the world into capitalist ones which disempowers labor in the already capitalist world where it was first empowered. The growth of employment in the not-yet-capitalist world does not lead to the empowerment of labor there, although the possibility is certainly not excluded (Fields 1994). Marx and Engels shared the views of contemporary globalization fans. They expected the bourgeoisie to be capable of converting the rest of the world economy to capitalist structures based on the self-interests of typical bourgeois citizens.

A mixture of success and failure precludes capitalism from eliminating other modes of production and helps it maintain its isolated character in a world where the conditions for its growth exist. The argument of this chapter is that there is a link between capitalist accumulation and scarcity of labor. Capitalism requires rising mass incomes (Elsenhans 1983). Because labor is relatively powerless in underdeveloped economies with widespread marginality, labor risks being disempowered in the developed capitalist economies of the West whenever this disempowered labor in the South becomes competitive at the international level. I have shown that the possibility of indirectly subsidizing export production through surpluses in wage-goods production leads to such a situation.

The disempowerment of labor in the North through the discovery of a "gold mine" of disempowered labor in the South is occurring at a time when the macroeconomic focus of economics is declining. Neoclassical thinking has deprived Keynesianism of its clout by integrating major findings of Keynesianism into EGT. Both theories, STT and EGT, are supply-side-oriented, and neglect the possibility of fundamental imbalances between production and consumption capacity due to the deficient empowerment of labor. Thus, the world economy has to deal with the threat of underconsumption in the wake of devaluation-driven export-oriented industrialization in marginality-ridden economies – to be sure, the majority of the world – while academic economists are almost exclusively preoccupied with supply-side problems.

The demonization of the current pattern of globalization can be reversed by rediscovering the macrolevel, essential if the democratic process is to recover a margin of maneuverability anywhere in the world. This reflection should, however, also take into account other circumstances discrediting a leftist reform strategy, which accepts market regulation as an efficient mechanism but which does not follow market orthodoxy because of the possibility of unemployment equilibria if the spontaneous tendencies of the market are followed.

The empowerment of labor in capitalism has implications for the behavior required of labor as households and income maximizers. Labor has to be flexible to react rapidly to wage fluctuations in various branches and enterprises. It has to favor short-term perspectives and spend its income on consumption goods in order to contribute to full-capacity utilization. Yet, with capitalism maturing and mass incomes increasing, flexibility decreases and households react to crises by increasing their propensity to save.

As productivity increases, so does the division of labor and the specialization of skills. There are increasingly fewer workers who possess the full complement of skills necessary to produce a product for one firm who could be employed without retraining by another. Productivity increases depend on linking different skills, ultimately, firm-specific skills. The same labor has very different productivities when it moves from one plant to another, as shown by the East German experience (Klodt 1991: 99). Yet, where labor markets are inflexible, there is inflationary pressure and adjustment costs are high. The alternatives are to maintain flexibility by threatening labor with high rates of unemployment, the Anglo-Saxon solution, or by implementing compensatory programs for flexibility. High levels of employment and a reliable welfare state increase flexibility, as was evident in postwar West Germany, where flexibility was never higher than during the period of long-term full employment which lasted until the 1970s (Pietsch 1978: 257–63).

Most Western countries lack a culture of flexibility. Managers treat inside information as private property, allowing them to charge monopoly prices for their own services. Managerial incomes vary worldwide. If there were a permanent rotating system of managers for each managerial post there would be several, equally qualified applicants, and market imperfections would be reduced. Strong tax discrimination against inflexible high-income earners could increase the availability of a surplus of formally well-trained labor which also has acquired informal qualifications by training on the job.

My model of the embeddedness of capitalism in rising mass incomes implies that additional purchasing power be spent on actually produced goods and services. If, however, additional purchasing power is used for savings, entrepreneurs face rising costs without additional demand. In a world of rising mass incomes, the importance of the immediate satisfaction of material needs decreases in relation to the importance of the satisfaction of future needs, for which there can be no real guarantee due to the uncertainty of the future. Households that try to guarantee their future purchasing power may increase their private savings. But by increasing their savings, they do not get a direct future claim on the product they do not consume today (Sinn 2000: 406). Instead, they get a monetary asset which, like all other monetary assets reserved for future markets, competes for the goods the economy will make available in the future. Saving households participate in a race to secure a share in an unknown amount of future purchasing power. Suppose that all savings are transformed into effective demand at the same time. In the German case, where total accumulated savings of private households are now a multiple of annual national consumption, the only possible consequences are inflation and balance of trade deficits with devaluation (Elsenhans 1999d, 2000b).

That these savings have increased capacity is at least contradicted, if not disproved, by EGT itself: productivity growth is not dependent on the amount of spending on investment. In an EGT world characterized by increasing savings and constant capital productivity, there are not enough assets in relation to the demand of households and enterprises for property (Buchanan and Wilmeth 1998: 12ff.). Financial markets present only a temporary solution to this dilemma. As long as households and enterprises evaluate their earnings from assets on financial markets on the basis of increasing stock prices, the rise in such assets depends only on the supply of cheap money to the stock market, that is, additional savings. The "real" economy will be characterized by sluggish growth because cheap money associated with such a situation, and spending out of speculative earnings (for luxuries), will not fully compensate low increases in mass demand. The money households save today is only valuable in the sense that it is a share of a global volume of money in the future (a form of differential accumulation in the household sector comparable to the one described by Nitzan in Chapter 6 this volume). Its purchasing power is determined by the future capacity of production. Any race to increase savings is therefore relatively useless for the future and harmful for the present.

Overcoming the challenges of the specific pattern of globalization today requires an expanding world economy. Increasing exports of manufactures only leads to slow growth in mass demand and wage-goods production in typical underdeveloped economies. The most demand increases therefore have to come from the developed industrial economies. These economies could engage in such demand-oriented growth processes and draw the underdeveloped world into capitalist transformation, but their immediate interests are in generating trade surpluses for maintaining employment. The social forces behind such a model, labor and capital in the export sectors of the developed world, are economically and politically the most powerful actors in these economies and the most efficient ones economically. Labor and capital that cannot benefit from exports find it difficult to publicly support claims for expansion of the internal market because their higher wages are considered as endangering their jobs. The underconsumptionist tendencies unleashed by devaluation-driven export-oriented industrialization are also reinforced by strategies of the developed capitalist countries, particularly those that are technically less efficient (Elsenhans 1981, 1987).

These trends in the world economy are occurring at the same time that the macro-level is being neglected in favor of the micro-level, not only by financial elites and political decision makers, but also in academic discussions. Before the fall of the Berlin Wall (although to a gradually decreasing degree), even the intellectual supporters of big business had to admit that the West could not afford major employment crises because of the danger that West European working classes would withdraw their political loyalty. Moreover, the West, in its relations with nonaligned countries, was forced for similar reasons to accept oil-price increases and attempts to promote a New International Economic Order in the 1970s.

In the 1930s – in stark contrast to the situation today – there emerged a shared agreement among the democracies in the West and their colonial or semicolonial spheres of influence worldwide about the capacity of society to "appropriate" its own destiny through democratic processes. The forces which expressed this vision in the United Nations and in national liberation movements in Asia, Africa, and later on in Latin America, were victorious in World War II as well as in the process of decolonization. With the fall of the Berlin Wall, it became clear that changes in the postwar period had generated an ideological climate in which the left had no economic project and no economic model of its own. The forces of labor had failed to win hegemony in Gramscian terms. They had rejected the Keynesian implications of a politico-economic analysis of capitalism, which acknowledged the contribution of rising mass incomes to welfare and efficiency by upholding the whip of competition. The market was not considered an instrument. Instead, intellectuals on the petit-bourgeois left were able to exercise their political and ideological hegemony, and morally denounced capitalism using

Marx's political economy – but not his method. Marx's method consisted in using the most modern formulation of economics and putting this in a wider politico-economic and social context. The Marxists of the late 1960s almost completely neglected the development of economic thought since Marx, and often Marx himself. By demonizing capitalism, the original Marxist proposal to discover possibilities of transformation in the contradictions of the existing world was neglected by modern-day Marxists. Instead, they simply advised rejecting the existing world.

The result is an undifferentiated and universal denunciation of globalization, which is unable to offer an alternative strategy to the most modern variants of neoclassical economics, the ones formulated in EGT and STT, that is, cut your costs and increase your productivity in order to take the lead in new products. The global race towards cost reduction cannot lead to anything but a concerted "beggar-thy-neighbor" drive toward an underconsumptionist crisis. One cannot avoid supposing that many critics of globalization ultimately feel comforted by the tendency to such crises because these confirm their arguments and offer hope for a radically different world economy. Yet, it is highly improbable that anything will arise other than bureaucratism if the market is not allowed to play its role. In sum, the total rejection of a capitalist world economy excludes the opportunity of exploiting the positive aspects of globalization, channeling it into a pattern where undeniable productivity increases can benefit the largest possible number of people via worldwide social reform.

Appendix

Total production consists of the subsidized and unsubsidized sector so that

$$a_s + a_r = \bar{a}_s + \bar{a}_r = 1, \tag{1}$$

where a_s is the share of the subsidized sector in total production before introduction of the subsidy, $\bar{a}_s$ is this share of the subsidized sector after introduction of the subsidy, and a_r, $\bar{a}_r$ the corresponding shares of the unsubsidized sector.

The subsidy reduces the price of the product and may contribute to greater sales. Productivity will increase because of the increase in sales. Productivity in the subsidized sector before the subsidy is represented by y_s, with $\bar{y}_s$ the productivity after the subsidy, so that the subsidy increases production if

$$a_s y_s \leq \bar{a}_s \bar{y}_s. \tag{2}$$

Let us suppose that all investment in technical progress in the unsubsidized economy is due to the reactions of entrepreneurs to market forces, so that we can consider demand-driven technical progress as depending only on the growth of demand in the unsubsidized sector. The subsidy reduces total demand for the unsubsidized sector as well as the demand-induced growth of productivity in this sector so that

$$a_r y_r > \bar{a}_r \bar{y}_r. \tag{3}$$

For overall growth to occur, the following condition has to hold:

$$\frac{\bar{a}_s \bar{y}_s}{a_s y_s} > \frac{a_r y_r}{\bar{a}_r \bar{y}_r}. \tag{4}$$

This inequality can be fulfilled on the basis of various mechanisms, among others:

- The rate of productivity growth in the unsubsidized sector does not substantially decrease despite a decrease in demand. The subsidized sector introduces a new technology with large spillovers into the unsubsidized sector so that there is also an increase in productivity growth in the unsubsidized sector, instead of withheld productivity growth.
- Productivity increase in the subsidized sector is not only higher, but is considerably higher than the withheld productivity increase in the rest of the economy. We may assume that $\bar{a}_s / a_s > a_r / \bar{a}_s$ as it is not reasonable to expect more than half of production to be efficiently subsidized, so that $\bar{y}_s / y_s$ compensating $y_r / \bar{y}_r$ occurs only with high rates of productivity increase in the subsidized sector. The rate of productivity increase in the subsidized sector must therefore be quite substantial, especially if $y_r / \bar{y}_r$ is relatively high, which is considered to indicate demand-dependent technical progress.

Hence, with regard to the possibilities of demand-dependent productivity growth, industrial policy is efficient only if high increases in the rates of productivity growth can be achieved in the subsidized sector through subsidies. A leading economy is characterized by the gradual character of technical improvement. It is therefore quite efficient in improving technology on the basis of inducements which result from rising mass demand. In such a mass-demand-driven economy with high productivity increases due to economies of scale, industrial policy rarely seems to be efficient, whereas it may seem quite capable of performing in an economy where, because of inequality of income, demand-driven productivity increase is low. Moreover, it is easier for a backward economy to determine where actual growth is highest in leading countries and to imitate them, than for a leading country to forecast the technological frontier of the future, so that industrial policy is particularly efficient in catching up by means of imitation (Leff 1985: 347f.; Paqué 1995: 251).

If we assume that productivity increases depend not only on the discovery of a product but also on the discovery of less costly processes for its manufacture, industrial policy is facilitated by an egalitarian distribution of income. The prevailing cost price of a subsidized product (p_s) may be defined as follows:

$$p_s = \frac{FC_s + (VC_s/\alpha) - S_s}{Q_s},\qquad (5)$$

where FC_s represents fixed costs, especially the R&D outlay for the discovery of the product, VC_s represents the variable costs, α the productivity increase due to economies of scale with $\alpha' > 0$ (so that productivity grows with increasing scale), S_s the subsidy paid to the subsidized sector under consideration, and Q_s the quantity of products produced.

We can conclude from (5) that the cost price decreases more rapidly the larger the quantities produced, as FC_s does not increase, and VC_s does not increase in line with the quantity produced because of $\alpha' > 0$. The price impact of a given level of subsidization decreases with increasing quantities produced. Therefore, the subsidy allows reducing the price for a limited demand. The larger the quantity, the less the effect of the subsidy, but the more important the effect of economies of scale. The extent that effort-dependent technical progress can lead to more growth is thus dependent upon the degree to which the subsidized sector can increase its own productivity. Overall productivity increases are greatly supported by economies of scale based on rising mass demand. Growth through effort-dependent technical progress is achieved more easily with a more egalitarian distribution of income.

Notes

1 For a regular publication of comparative wages adjusted to exchange rates see US Department of Labor, Bureau of Labor Statistics, Office of Productivity and Technology: International Comparisons of Hourly Compensation Costs for Production Workers in Manufacturing. http://stats.bls.gov

2 I have dealt elsewhere with how the unclear guarantee for credit money leads to the emergence of a new rentier class (Elsenhans 2000c).

3 The period before the collapse of a system characterized by all increases in production being invested and the rate of growth of capital being higher than the rate of growth of national income depends on the initial parameters. The model is extensively presented in Elsenhans 1994: 423–7, 1995b. If there is an unlimited supply of technical progress, mass incomes will not necessarily rise, because the increase in labor productivity necessary to supply a rapidly rising capital stock with at least constant rates of return may be sufficient. Hence, real wages may be stable or even decrease in the case of rapid productivity increases, as, in this case, the Leninist solution of the internal market growing exclusively from the demand for investment goods does not lead to a decline in the profit rate. Whenever the implied high increases of the rate of increase of labor productivity growth are not achieved, the system collapses.

4 This was accomplished in real socialism by increasing the share of investment in national income and simultaneously accepting a decreasing productivity of investment, Elsenhans 2000e.

5 This was demonstrated already in the eighteenth century by Boulton in his analysis of the development of the steam engine, see Williams (1964: 131).

6 It should be mentioned that most categorizations of tradables according to technological levels are based on crude branch categories of international trade statistics which grossly overstate the importance of high technology products. On the problem of such definitions see Maurer (1994: 309), Schmitt-Rink (1988: 159–61), and IFO (1994: 147).

7 See, among others, Zimmermann (1973), Hurwitz and Peffley (1987), Holsti (1992), and Powlick (1995). An example is France's war in Algeria, which in 1958 had caused a deadlock in the representative party system, as nearly all organizations, parties, and associations had become deeply divided. A slowly growing majority in favor of ending the war through negotiations was not able to manifest itself at the level of institutionalized political forces; see Elsenhans (2000d: 946–92).

9 Exploitation and solidarity
Putting the political back into IPE

Alejandro Colás

Introduction

One striking feature of contemporary international political economy (IPE) is the virtual absence of any sustained discussion of problems and concepts associated with moral theory or political philosophy. For all the rich and varied contributions of IPE to the study of global capitalism and political structures such as the state or international organizations it gives rise to, there are arguably few, if any, studies that self-consciously cross the boundaries between IPE and international political theory. A random overview of the key textbooks in IPE reveals little or no direct engagement with notions such as distributive justice, exploitation, fairness, obligations, or rights.[1] For their part, political philosophers who have engaged with the moral issues thrown up by the workings of global capitalism, are generally loath to develop analyses of the dynamics of this system.[2] Sophisticated and challenging as some of the "new normative theories" in International Relations have been, they rarely seek to explain the very phenomena – global economic inequality, disparities in state power, global social hierarchies – they aim to condemn.[3]

This mutual neglect between IPE and political philosophy is doubly perplexing. First, because it is surely incontrovertible that global capitalism – or if one wishes, the world economy – generates a range of socio-economic and political problems that require both explanation and evaluation. Short of advocating a hard-nosed positivism, few scholars would claim that one can disengage the analysis of global capitalism from a normative assessment – both diagnostic and prescriptive – of its social and political impact on our daily lives.[4] Second, and more important, the normative silences of IPE are disconcerting in that the language and concerns of political philosophy have from the very outset been prominent in the study of political economy. From its origins in the eighteenth century through to the contemporary debates on the "social" or "moral" economy, the study of political economy has been associated with some of the central problems of political philosophy. Be it the Scottish Enlightenment's emphasis upon "virtue," Marx's concern with "alienation," or more recent discussions regarding "entitlements," political economy has found it difficult to escape its status as a "moral science."[5] As one recent textbook on political economy has usefully noted, "[a] main difficulty of political economy, common to different approaches, lies in the tendency to gloss over the separateness of the two spheres of the economic and the political, absorbing one into the other. A main theme of our survey is the importance of understanding and appreciating the categorical distinction between politics and economics, and the dangers of making one or the other dominant in both realms" (Caporaso and Levine 1992: 6).

Clearly, the academic division of labor goes some way in explaining this intellectual replication of the separation between the economic and the political under capitalism. Moreover, it is indeed a tall order to follow the classical political economists (Marx's critique included) in combining normative and analytical concerns when explaining and evaluating global capitalism. Neither of these considerations, however, should dissuade those of us who perceive an interconnection between morality and economics from at least pursuing what appears as a logical and necessary objective. One broad, overarching aim of this chapter, therefore, is to reestablish and explore the connection between political philosophy and the global reproduction of capitalism. More specifically, I wish to discuss how two concepts – exploitation and solidarity – can serve to explain the workings of global capitalism and illuminate future possibilities for the radical transformation of this system. In essence, my argument is that capitalist relations of production represent the central articulating feature of the contemporary global economy. Such relations generate social and political antagonisms which in turn open possibilities for solidary action both within and across particular states. Thus, in line with the tradition of classical political economy, I want to make a case for the tight connection between the analytical conception of exploitation and the normative aspiration to solidarity.

This neat progression from the identification of a global mode of production (capitalism) and its attendant class antagonisms, to holding out the prospect of international or transnational solidarity must, however, be severely qualified. For capitalism has historically reproduced itself on a global scale through the mediation of precapitalist structures (states, empires, households, kinship networks, and so forth) with their own distinctive modes of exploitation and oppression. A second claim of this essay, therefore, is that capitalism is globally articulated with noncapitalist modes of production in ways that complicate the simple identification of class interests as a source of international or transnational solidarity. Contrary to Marx's and Engels's prediction in 1848, and contrary indeed to the wilder speculations of some globalization theorists today, capitalism has not "created a world after its own image." It rather has grafted its own logic upon preexisting social and political hierarchies to engender a profoundly divided and heterogeneous, yet highly interconnected totality we have come to call the global economy.[6]

These basic arguments will be pursued in three stages. First, the notions of exploitation and solidarity as they are used in this essay are set out, thereby highlighting the inherently political nature of seemingly "economic" concepts such as "market exchange" or "exploitation." Second, a cursory and necessarily schematic account of contemporary global capitalism as a differentiated mode of production will be offered. Here, I retrieve some of the key insights of the so-called "articulation of the modes of production" school of the 1970s, arguing that they are especially relevant to the analysis of contemporary global capitalism. The concluding section draws together the threads of the preceding discussion with particular reference to the potentialities of internationalist solidarity in the contemporary world. While upholding the view that the class interests generated through the global process of capitalist exploitation still offer the sturdiest base for the construction of international solidarity, a case will be made for an internationalism that is also keenly aware of the noncapitalist forms of exploitation and oppression that continue to be an integral part of the global capitalist economy. It is with this ambitious agenda in mind that I now turn to a more tentative discussion of exploitation and solidarity as two phenomena expressive of the interface between the normative and the analytical dimensions of contemporary global capitalism.

Exploitation and solidarity under global capitalism

The term "exploitation" means "to make use of something." It can be understood in at least three senses: in neutral, technical terms, "the exploitation of wind power"; as a purely moral condemnation, "the exploitation of someone else's disadvantage"; and in an economic fashion, "the exploitation of wage-labor."[7] Each of these three conceptions of exploitation can be understood in isolation – it is unnecessary for example, that the exploitation of a disadvantage be tied to socio-economic circumstances: a person might be exploited because he or she is mentally or physically disabled. Moreover, the third form of exploitation (economic exploitation) is arguably unique to capitalism – feudal or tributary exploitation rests on the extraction of surplus through political, military, and juridical (i.e. extra-economic) coercion. The definition of exploitation adopted in this essay, however, combines all three meanings. In what follows, I shall be chiefly concerned with *capitalist* exploitation as a process that is at once neutral and unjust in that it encompasses both the generation of surplus value through what appears as a purely economic exchange[8] between capital and labor, and the systematic limitation of freedom and equality of workers through this exchange. From this perspective, exploitation serves simultaneously as a descriptive, explanatory, and condemnatory category in the analysis of capitalism. In order to illustrate this claim, I shall provide a brief and, for many, familiar summary of capitalist exploitation.

The defining feature of capitalism as a mode of production – the valorization of capital by commodified labor – occurs through an exchange between workers and capitalists. This unique accomplishment of capitalism was effected historically through the forceful and generally violent dispossession of direct producers from their means of subsistence, a process which Marx famously labelled "primitive" or "primary" accumulation. With the unfolding of this process, whole populations acquired the "double freedom" of the capitalist market: they were relieved of their means of reproduction (land, tools, access to commons, and so forth), discharged from feudal obligations, and were now formally free to sell their labor-power in the capitalist market in exchange for a wage. Within the capitalist market (the sphere of circulation) this social relation appears as a free and equal exchange between the two parties. Yet, at the same time, the value produced by the worker under the capitalist mode of production is necessarily higher than that of the wage he or she is paid. Thus, once we analyze the wage relation from the vantage of the sphere of production, what appeared as a free and equal exchange now reveals itself to be a compelled[9] and unequal exchange from which the capitalist pockets unpaid labor as profit.

From an "economic" perspective, both sets of relations are exploitive in the sense that they are necessary for the generation of surplus value. Yet while exploitation within the sphere of circulation is legitimated through bourgeois law and cannot therefore properly be called unjust (a capitalist wage contract involves two formally free and equal parties), once we enter the sphere of production, exploitation acquires an unjust character in that it is premised upon the appropriation by the capitalist of the unpaid labor of the worker. This by itself might justify the claim that capitalist exploitation not only has an "economic" meaning but also a "moral" or "political" one. But underlying the second view of exploitation is the further claim that capitalist wage relations deny workers the possibility of freedom (self-realization) and equality. By compelling workers to sell their labor-power as a commodity, capitalism both restricts the possibilities of workers' human self-realization and subjects them to systematic subordination *vis-à-vis* the capitalist class. In both these respects, the notion of exploitation helps to illustrate the close connection between the reproduction of capitalism and the concerns of justice.

This brief and necessarily schematic definition of exploitation is plainly far from uncontroversial. In the Marxist literature alone, the idea of exploitation has generated fascinating but inconclusive debates surrounding the place of, *inter alia*, the labor theory of value, property relations, methodological individualism, and theories of justice in the elucidation and application of the concept. Outside Marxist circles – most prominently in feminist and environmental approaches to the issue – the notion of exploitation is extended to include noneconomic relations between men and women, humans and nature, and indeed among past, present, and future generations. Aside from the obvious limitations of space and competence, I shall not address these contending theories because the principal aim of this essay is not to defend a particular conception of exploitation, but rather to argue that this notion should be at the heart of a renewed engagement between economics and political philosophy in the analysis of contemporary global capitalism. This notwithstanding, it may be useful to state for the record that the conception of exploitation deployed below is heavily informed by the writings of Norman Geras (1985; 1992) and Ellen Meiksins Wood (1995b). From Geras I take the notion that exploitation is both an analytical and normative concept that serves to ground a Marxist theory of justice. With Meiksins Wood I emphasize that capitalist exploitation is above all about social relations of production so that (i) *pace* Analytical Marxism, unequal distribution of wealth through differentiated property relations cannot in itself be seen as exploitive, and (ii) *contra* feminist and ecologist arguments, where a distinction must be made between, on the one hand, capitalist exploitation as an unjust social relation premised on the generation of surplus value and, on the other, oppression and resource exhaustion as instances, respectively, of unequal gender and natural relations which do not by themselves generate surplus value, and which therefore stand outside strictly capitalist, "economic" exploitation. (The point of this distinction is neither to diminish the importance or incidence of gender oppression and ecological degradation, nor indeed to suggest that they are unconnected to the production of surplus value. Rather, my aim is to emphasize the uniqueness of the wage relation as the defining feature of exploitation under capitalism.)

The relevance of these considerations for the analysis of global capitalism will, I hope, become apparent in the next section of the chapter. To anticipate, however, outlining the specificity of capitalist exploitation is crucial in order to grasp its complex coexistence and interaction with noncapitalist forms of oppression and exploitation under global capitalism. I argue below that contemporary capitalism is still reproduced globally through the noncapitalist exploitation and oppression of sizeable sectors of the world's population. This inevitably raises difficulties for any class-based project of internationalist solidarity, the idea to which I now turn.

In its most basic formulation, solidarity refers to a sense of unity among individuals which arises either out of shared socio-historical experiences or, in a weaker form, out of empathy, and which binds these individuals in the collective pursuit of a specific political goal. Because the concept has been deployed in a variety of different contexts and for very distinct purposes, I focus more narrowly on international solidarity (the term "international" is used loosely to include socio-economic and political relations between and across states) as a principle that suggests individuals have moral obligations beyond the particular political/cultural boundaries of state, nationality, ethnicity, religion, or color.

Over the past two decades, the idea of international solidarity has been increasingly invoked with reference to the globalization of capitalism. Cosmopolitan political theorists such as Charles Beitz, Thomas Pogge, and Brian Barry have argued that an increasing global economic interdependence warrants the corresponding global application of solidary principles of justice such as wealth redistribution or fair trade.[10] Like many of their counterparts in IPE, liberal cosmopolitans conceive of capitalism exclusively as a market, not a mode of production, and consequently view exploitation (insofar as they use the term) as an unequal exchange between states in the sphere of circulation rather than as an unjust relation of production among classes. Yet, as was pointed out earlier, capitalist exchange cannot by itself be deemed unjust until we consider it as part of a broader process of value-creation and appropriation. To use a very crude example: the terms of trade between say, the European Union (EU) member states and their Maghrebi "partners" may be asymmetrical but they are not unjust. Tunisia and Morocco have entered into a "free trade" agreement with the EU which, from the market perspective, is no less just than the work contract between myself and my university. It is only when we consider such agreements in the wider context of (international) capitalist social relations that the exploitation of say, Maghrebi garment workers, can be condemned as unjust – not because European traders and consumers stand to benefit from cheap clothing (which we may do), but because capitalists (be they European or Maghrebi) necessarily appropriate a portion of the value created by the garment workers. In short, while liberal cosmopolitans are right to emphasize how international "economic inter-dependence" creates unequal and asymmetrical relations between states, they err in suggesting that such relations are necessarily exploitive and unjust. Global capitalist relations, I have argued, can only properly be deemed unjust once we consider exploitative relations between classes – a consideration which only the socialist version of cosmopolitanism takes into account when addressing the plausibility of international solidarity.

Historically, the socialist understanding of international solidarity has been premised on two basic assumptions: humanity is the ultimate reference point of any moral reasoning, and social class is the key galvanizing agent of international solidarity. Simplifying somewhat, the first premise arises from the radical Enlightenment and its emphasis upon the fundamental equality of human beings, while the second assumption derives from the Marxist understanding of capitalism as a universalizing force that increasingly pits one class (the proletariat) against another (the bourgeoisie) on a global scale. The contradiction inherent in simul-taneously positing a universal humanity and a universal class has, in the socialist tradition, generally been resolved by suggesting that only the solidary action of the working class in the transcendence of capitalism can guarantee the fulfilment of our universal human potential. Thus, the socialist conception of international solidarity uniquely claims that our universal humanity can only be realized through the concerted political action of the exploited classes on a global scale. From such a vantage point, nationality, culture, ethnicity, and other particularist affiliations are neither naturalized nor considered irrelevant to our human expe-rience. Unlike liberal cosmopolitanism, the socialist variant understands inter-national solidarity neither as a global application of the "difference principle" nor as a scheme arising out of "justice as impartiality." Rather, it argues that inter-national solidarity should be rooted in the particular interests of exploited classes, and geared toward the transcendence of the very system that generates international injustice, namely capitalism. From this perspective, the moral defense of our shared humanity must take account of existing socio-economic and political divisions when translating our moral convictions into political solidarity.

These considerations are important for the overall argument of this chapter in two respects. On the one hand, they reemphasize the claim that there is a necessary interconnection between political philosophy and IPE: no normative theory of international relations can afford to talk of international solidarity without addressing the socio-economic conditions under which this principle becomes both desirable and plausible. Likewise, it would appear churlish for even the most hardened empiricist IPE scholar to reject the possibility that international solidarity could be a palliative for the inequalities and injustices wrought by global capitalism. In other words, the idea of international solidarity, like that of exploitation, offers an instance of how we can bring at least one understanding of "the political" back to the forefront of IPE. On the other hand, however, the notion of international solidarity, and its socialist variant in particular, leads directly to the vexed questions of how internationalist solidarity may be successfully grounded in the future; what role social class can play in such a project; and indeed how far contemporary forms of exploitation encourage the global articulation of class solidarity. However unwieldy these questions seem, and regardless of how tentative their answers might be, they should certainly be addressed. A good starting point in this endeavor is the reconsideration of global capitalism as a "differentiated" and "articulated" mode of production.

Global capitalism as a differentiated mode of production

The origins, development, and character of global capitalism is arguably the central, most contested issue in contemporary IPE. Thus rather than attempting the futile exercise of surveying and evaluating each of the myriad accounts available, the approach adopted here sets off from two basic assumptions. The first is that global capitalism is a historically specific mode of production, that is, a distinct social combination of forces and relations of production for the purpose of generating economic surplus. It is important to underline this seemingly straightforward assumption because there is a strong tendency among social theorists concerned with global capitalism (non-Marxist and those who claim to be influenced by Marxism alike) to reduce this system to only one of its constitutive domains: the market, or sphere of circulation. This impoverishes our understanding of global capitalism both analytically and normatively as it obscures the centrality of social relations of production in the definition of capitalism, as well as limiting the possibility of moral condemnation explored above. As numerous scholars have indicated (Laclau 1971; Brenner 1977; Skocpol 1977; see also Denemark and Thomas 1989), "Neo-Smithian" or "circulationist" approaches to global capitalism like those of André Gunder Frank or Immanuel Wallerstein turn capitalism into a world-system of exchange propelled by the mercantile quest for profit through trade at the expense of investigating the productive relations that underpin this historically specific mode of surplus extraction and appropriation.[11] Clearly, trade and the circulation of finance and money capital have in the past been essential, and today are increasingly powerful components of global capitalism – often significantly shaping the modes of surplus extraction across the world. Yet as Eric Wolf succinctly put it in his magisterial account of modern world history: "What we must be clear about...is the analytical distinction between the employment of wealth in the pursuit of further wealth, and capitalism as a qualitatively different mode of committing social labour to the transformation of nature" (Wolf 1997: 298). It is here that a Marxist definition of capitalism departs from other radical interpretations like that expounded by Barry K. Gills in this volume. For while the former (among which I include myself) identify the *differentia specifica* of capitalist society as its capacity (indeed necessity) to reproduce itself through the value-form, the latter tend to emphasize, as Gills does here, that "The underlying material basis of capital, is, simply put, the storing of a surplus" (Gills, Chapter 5, this volume).[12]

The second major assumption made here is that capitalism has historically reproduced itself across the globe in variegated forms. Contrary to the more evolutionist passages in the *Communist Manifesto* and other earlier writings of Marx and Engels, capitalism has not compelled "[a]ll nations, on pain of extinction, to adopt the bourgeois mode of production." Instead, it has encountered forms of socio-political and economic resistance and collaboration in the course of its expansion which have led to an uneven extension of capitalist social relations, and indeed to an uneasy coexistence with noncapitalist social relations in many parts of the world. Eric Wolf, again, provides a lucid summary of how the combined and uneven reproduction of capitalism since the nineteenth century engendered a "differentiated" mode of production on a global scale:

> The outcome of this process was a complex hierarchical system controlled by the capitalist mode of production, but including a vast array of subsidiary regions that exhibited different combinations of the capitalist mode with other modes. The carrier industries of the capitalist mode dominated the system, but these rested upon variable and shifting supports that were often embedded in different modes of production.
>
> (Ibid.: 296–7)

This characterization of global capitalism as a "differentiated" mode of production in turn reveals a third particularity in the study of the system, namely the tension between understanding global capitalism as an abstract (though, of course, no less real) system of value-creation and accumulation, and analyzing it as a concrete historical mode of production; between identifying the "laws of motion" of capital and dissecting the varying historical and geographical expressions of capitalism. Clearly, these two avenues are not incompatible as they in fact represent different levels of abstraction available for the analysis of the single totality that is global capitalism. Precisely because of this, however, it is important to uphold such a distinction and analyze global capitalism as a complex system that is at once dominated by the boundless quest for surplus value and historically capable of satisfying this imperative in combination with other, noncapitalist forms of surplus extraction or exploitation. One now forgotten but arguably still pertinent attempt at explaining this complex unfolding of global capitalist expansion is the so-called Articulation of the Modes of Production "school" (henceforth AMP).

The notion of "articulation" or "combination" of modes of production emerged in the 1970s among Marxist scholars concerned with what they perceived as the paradoxical coexistence of free wage labor and forms of unfree labor under the capitalist mode of production (Foster-Carter 1978; Miles 1986; Brewer 1989). As Adian Foster-Carter's useful summary suggests, the AMP literature sought to address

> [t]he paradox of capitalism's relation to other modes of production being conceived not (or not simply) as *succession* or *evolution* [but one where] capitalism

neither evolves mechanically from what precedes it, nor…necessarily dissolve[s] it. Indeed, so far from banishing pre-capitalist forms, it not only co-exists with them but buttresses them, and even on occasions devilishly conjures them up *ex nihilio*.

(Foster-Carter 1978: 51)

This apparent paradox was generally resolved by the AMP theorists with reference to Althusser and Balibar's distinction between the capitalist mode of production as a historically particular arrangement of the relations and forces of production, and a social formation as a concrete historical instance of a "society" that contained both capitalist and noncapitalist social relations (Althusser and Balibar 1970). Though the former can explain qualitative epochal changes in forms of social organization (as in the difference between a feudal and a capitalist mode of production), it cannot hope to capture the manifold historical and geographical expressions of the capitalist mode of production in actual societies – hence the recourse to the concept of "social formation."

In their analyses of diverse social formations, some AMP theorists addressed historical experiences such as the transition from feudalism to capitalism in Europe or the imposition of capitalist social relations upon colonized populations (e.g. Rey 1973). Others focused more narrowly upon the contemporary expressions of "articulated" capitalism existing in apartheid South Africa or in modern Peru (e.g. Wolpe, ed. 1980).[13] Overall, however, they seemed to agree that historically, capital has expanded internationally by grafting its own logic upon precapitalist modes of production. Sometimes this was achieved without resort to violence and through various contractual agreements; for the most part, however, it was accomplished through direct military domination of subjected peoples. Yet far from representing a conjunctural use of extra-economic coercion in the process of creating a market of free wage earners (Marx's "primitive" or "original" accumulation discussed before), in many regions of the world extra-economic domination and exploitation became a permanent feature of capitalist reproduction. Thus, one relevant insight of the AMP "school" resides in its emphasis upon the "external" imposition of capitalist social relations across the globe through violent, military, and juridico-political (i.e. extra-economic) mechanisms ranging from outright colonial domination to more surreptitious "unequal treaties":[14]

[In the non-western world] pre-capitalist modes did not evolve naturally to meet the needs of capitalism, so capitalist relations of production could not arise from within. These areas could (and did) engage in exchange, and were drawn into the world market, but exchange reinforced the hold of pre-capitalist ruling classes and strengthened resistance to the implantation of capitalist relations of production.

(Brewer 1989: 234)

The upshot in terms of contemporary global capitalism is that, in many regions of the world, precapitalist structures of kinship, ethnicity, and religion still play a significant role in the social organization of production and its attendant legal and political institutions.

Using the analytical and historical insights of the AMP perspective, it is possible to envisage global capitalism as a mode of production that generates variegated social formations across the world through its historical development in articulation with other modes of production, and through its contemporary incorporation of different modes of exploitation. As the first truly global mode of production, capitalism imposes its overarching logic of capital accumulation upon all peoples in the world, but it does so in the context of particular social formations that often include precapitalist modes of exploitation.

A contemporary example of this might be the global food market where, as several recent studies have noted, capitalist and noncapitalist relations of exploitation coexist at the site of production, with the latter sometimes deliberately reintroduced for both economic and political reasons. One such instance, documented in Miriam Wells's influential study, was the resurgence of sharecropping during the 1970s and 1980s in the California strawberry sector, decades after this mode of exploitation had been replaced by wage labor.[15] Another case is that of agricultural restructuring in the Caribbean where according to a recent study by Laura Raynolds

> [f]irms in the most dynamic agro-export sectors…are increasing their competitive flexibility by establishing multiple informal labour processes which tap various pools of politically and economically vulnerable workers […] These enterprises take advantage of female subordination in the economy and the household to employ women in low-wage jobs and access their unpaid family labour.
>
> (Raynolds 1997: 129)

A third instance is evocatively analyzed in Jenny B. White's study of women's labor in contemporary Istanbul (White 1994). Focusing on squatter settlements where garment production serves as a major source of income, White uncovers a complex set of exploitive relations which hinge on the combination of wage relations mediated through the capitalist market and what the author identifies as forms of "reciprocal exploitation" or "collective usufruct" predicated on solidary kinship relations. Under these conditions, "The surplus value produced by the individual labor of these women is appropriated by the [kinship] group as a whole and by the intermediary in particular, but also by the merchants who resell their products locally and on the world market" (ibid.: 198).

It is no doubt possible to recount similar and more drastic instances of the articulation of modes of production in the global economy. (Without wishing to underplay the importance of empirical backing, I take it as unnecessary to present here a detailed empirical account of such instances of articulation.) The relevant conclusion for the purposes of this essay is simply that global capitalism can incorporate different modes of exploitation, thus complicating the project of international solidarity premised on a common class experience. If workers across the world are exploited in significantly different ways, the prospect of harnessing their everyday experience of material reproduction – let alone the more "cultural" manifestations of this reproduction in myriad "identities" – to the project of international socialist solidarity becomes increasingly unrealistic. This is a question to which I shall return toward the end of this chapter. For the moment, however, I shall conclude this part of the discussion by highlighting three areas where the AMP approach to global capitalism may be useful to those of us concerned with the character of exploitation and the possibility of solidarity under contemporary capitalism.

The first key advantage of the AMP approach is that it allows us to account for extra-economic forms of oppression and domination as integral parts of global capitalism. This is of both conceptual and political significance. On the one hand it addresses the seemingly paradoxical coexistence of, for example, capitalism and slavery in the Caribbean islands or capitalism and debt peonage among Amerindians in nineteenth- and early-twentieth-century Guatemala. In both instances, the existence of a global capitalist market clearly served as a backdrop and stimulant to the production of sugar and coffee in these regions.[16] Yet the modes of exploitation adopted by the propertied classes in these cases varied through time and place, so that, for example, indentured and slave labor and wage labor and debt peonage respectively alternated as the dominant forms of exploitation, largely as a result of very particular conjunctures generated by the combination of class antagonism, state power, and calculations of economic efficiency (McCreery 1983; Knight 1988; see also Miles 1986). On a more political plane, an understanding of global capitalism informed by the AMP approach offers a clearer perspective on the politics derived from the complex juxtaposition of race and class (i.e. it raises the difficult and well-worn issue of how socialists are to speak to workers who simultaneously suffer the wages of racism and capitalism).

Second, thinking in terms of a global capitalism differentiated through varying local social formations encourages us to reflect on the origin and nature of different modes of political domination, or different expressions of state sovereignty. In order to explain the diversity of forms the sovereign state has taken through-out modernity (from Absolutism through to popular democracies) it seems essential to consider the history of the antagonism between classes thrown up by specific social formations. This would suggest, for instance, that the divergent forms of political domination in, say, the Middle East, can in large measure be explained with reference to the historical articulation of capitalism with precapitalist modes of production and exchange which in turn generate class interests peculiar to that specific social formation. The initial installation and subsequent longevity of dynastic monarchies in the Arabian peninsula (and the corresponding lack of civil liberties of the indigenous population, let alone the sizeable population of "guest workers") might be explained through an analysis of how British imperialism grafted (and the USA later sustained) the general dynamics of capitalist exchange and production upon preexisting social relations, and how this specific combination has produced rentier social formations with very particular class antagonisms and indeed, interclass alliances.[17]

Last, and perhaps most importantly, the adoption of an AMP approach does not preclude reference to the increasing power of trade, money, and finance capital within the global economy, nor to the significant changes in the modes of regulation and regimes of accumulation across the world. It does, nonetheless, guard against the conflation of global capitalism with the sphere of circulation, and constantly alerts us to the dialectic nature of global capitalism – at once capable of "battering down all Chinese walls" and preserving (often reinventing) old modes of exploitation. For again, it is only with reference to some notion of global capitalism as a differentiated or articulated mode of production that we can begin to make sense of and mobilize against the kind of contradictory predicament faced by many peoples in the world today – a predicament neatly captured by John Saul and Colin Leys with specific reference to Africa:

> [a]fter 80 years of colonial rule and almost four decades of independence, in most of [Africa] there is some capital but not a lot of capitalism. The predominant social relations are still not capitalist, nor is the prevailing logic of production. Africa south of the Sahara exists in the capitalist world, which marks and constrains the lives of its inhabitants at every turn, but it is not of it.
> (Saul and Leys 1999: 13)

The possibility of international solidarity

The central aim of this chapter has been to think through two concepts – exploitation and solidarity – which in my view can help both to explain and radically transform the aforementioned predicament faced by large sections of the world's population. In doing so, a secondary objective of this essay has been to emphasize the necessary interconnection between the concerns of "economics" and those of "politics." More specifically, I have suggested that all but the most dogmatic of positivists must recognize that notions of justice, rights, freedom, distribution and, of course, exploitation and solidarity, are central to the study of IPE. Likewise, a case has been made for international theories of justice to anchor their prescriptions to the actual analysis of global capitalism; for the need to explain our social world before we set out to condemn it. The upshot of this exercise is simply to reimbue IPE with the political urgency of its classical proponents. To be perfectly clear: the claim here is not an epistemological one to the effect that all truth claims about the global economy are somehow relative, socially constructed, or value-laden, but rather an ontological proposition about global capitalism itself, as a social system permeated by all kinds of values that any critical social theory must attempt to lay bare. Clearly, the preceding sections of this chapter have invoked Marx and the Marxist tradition as the most fertile reference point in this endeavor, but there is plenty of scope for a critical engagement with other traditions in IPE as well. With these summary considerations in mind, I now turn to a final assessment of the possibilities of international solidarity in the context of a differentiated global capitalism.

The central unanswered question underlying this essay is this: what are the possible grounds for invoking international solidarity under global capitalism? The short answer, in a cosmopolitan vein, is simply our shared humanity. If we start from the central premise of IPE, namely that the spread of global capitalism has forged an inescapable socio-economic and political interconnection between all peoples and regions of the world, then it surely follows that we can apply some criteria of basic human needs to the whole of the global economy. In the same way that political economy is concerned with the distribution of wealth for the satisfaction of needs in a domestic setting, so IPE can be said to address these issues in the global realm. At one level, then, we can simply assert that obligations of solidarity are due to fellow humans whose basic needs are not secured, simply on the basis of the global socio-economic and political interconnections generated by the world economy.

This straightforward answer, however, begs two further questions that ultimately render it superficial and idealistic: first, are these obligations to international solidarity premised on justice or on charity (i.e. on principles that are to be enforced through the relevant international political structures or on the voluntary action of concerned groups and individuals); and second, if it is principles of justice that are to ground international solidarity, which social groups and institutions are to be the agents of this solidarity?

I have argued that a preliminary response to these questions revolves around the concept of exploitation. In this view, international solidarity has to be rooted in principles of justice and not charity (i.e. on mutual obligation and not on discretionary hand-outs), and it is most likely to succeed as a class-based project. By focusing on global capitalism as a differentiated mode of production, I have suggested, we can both uncover injustices generated by this system and identify potential sources of international solidary action against such injustices. The experience of class exploitation is central to this enterprise in two key respects. First, as was argued above, it is capitalist relations of exploitation that globally articulate and therefore reproduce unjust relations, not only between workers and capitalists, but also between men and women or between one ethnic group and another. While "extra-economic" forms of exploitation and oppression (such as the sexual division of labor and racial or ethnic hierarchies) plainly predate the advent of capitalism, it has been my claim that the historical expansion of capitalism offers a mixed record of both reinforcing and undermining (and some-times reinventing) such unjust relations. To paraphrase and invert the above quote from Saul and Leys: sexism and racism might not be of the capitalist world, but they are certainly in it. One consequence of this for the purposes of our discussion is that neither justice nor solidarity can be invoked in the contemporary world without reference to the ways in which global capitalism articulates "economic" and "extra-economic" exploitation and oppression. The point is not to pit one against the other but rather continually to reexamine ways in which, say, wage relations and the sexual division of labor interact and reinforce each other in producing global injustices.

A second and related way in which class exploitation is central to the project of internationalist solidarity is that it offers concrete agents – class organizations – capable of realizing this aspiration. Now clearly, international class solidarity is neither the only example of internationalist agency nor is its record unblemished.

Feminist, environmentalist, pacifist, and indeed religious "fundamentalist" and even fascist movements have all expressed forms of international solidarity. Moreover, like any other project that aims to transcend socio-political boundaries of gender, nationality, religion, and so forth, working-class or socialist internationalism has often foundered upon the reality of state interest, nationalist chauvinism and, in some instances, outright racism (Colás 1994). But drawing lessons from history should not preclude critically analyzing the structures and processes that dominate the present international system. In this chapter, I have argued that global capitalism is the structure and class exploitation is the process which fundamentally shape our socio-economic and political world. It is within this context that social class becomes the sturdiest foundation for international solidarity, as it is simultaneously the one irremovable social relation necessary for the reproduction of the current system (global capitalism) and the most universal of social cleavages. This conception of solidarity is clearly challenged by alternative sources of international solidarity – religious, ethnic, gender-based, and so forth. But the claim made here is not one about the empirical preponderance of one form of solidarity over another. That, in many respects, is an open question. It is about the structural sources of global injustice and the most appropriate political strategy for overcoming them. While racism and sexism are structurally unnecessary for the reproduction of the wage relation, the existence of a class of direct producers and a class of appropriators clearly is. Likewise, while a sexual division of labor exists in all societies today, it does so in forms that are more substantially differentiated than that of class exploitation. So long as this is the case, it is unlikely that interclass solidarity based on faith, ethnic affiliation, or sex will by themselves do away with the unjust exploitive relations that define global capitalism.[18] Again, it is important to reiterate that sexual or racial oppression and class exploitation, far from standing in opposition to each other, combine in the most insidious fashion under contemporary global capitalism. It is precisely because of this perverse articulation of myriad forms of domination, I have argued, that distinctions must be drawn between capitalist and noncapitalist ("economic" and "extra-economic") modes of exploitation and oppression in the world today. The notion of a differentiated or articulated global capitalism provides us with the analytical tools to unmask these complex combinations of power and identify those social forces with the greatest potential of carrying out international solidarity action against the very system that sustains these unjust power relations.

Acknowledgment

Many thanks to Mary Ann Tétreault and Kenny Thomas for their extensive and constructive comments on the original draft of this chapter.

Notes

1 Texts consulted are: Gilpin 1987; Gill and Law 1988; Hettne 1995; Lake and Frieden 1995; Murphy and Tooze 1991; Spero and Hart 1997. The term "exploitation" only appears indexed in Gilpin, and in one contribution to the Hettne volume.

2 For a useful summary of some of these views see Brown 1992. See also Thompson, 1992; Attfield and Wilkinns 1992 and chapter 12 of Doyle 1997.

3 Some notable exceptions to this general trend, coming from very different ideological perspectives include David Held's sophisticated discussion of "nautonomy" in the context of projects for "cosmopolitan democracy" in Held 1995; the recent work of David Harvey in Harvey 1996 and 1999; Martha Nussbaum's discussion of the impact of the global economy on human development in Nussbaum 2000; and Nobel laureate Amartya Sen's life-long engagement with the relationship between ethics and economics, perhaps best captured in his collected essays in Sen 1999. Retrospectively, the work of Karl Polanyi is in many respects a model of how the normative concerns inherent in political economy can be rendered explicit. See especially Polanyi 1958.

4 Peter Uvin makes a similar claim in this volume.

5 See, among others, Fitzgibbons 1995; Hont and Ignatieff 1983; Hutchison 1988; Naredo 1987; Lukes 1986 and an excellent chapter on "justice-centered approaches" to political economy in Caporaso and Levine 1992. Also of interest in this context are Appleby 1978 and Wood 1994.

6 Peter Uvin develops this same point in this volume with relation to the inequalities engendered by the "structural violence" which accompanies capitalist globalization.

7 An extremely useful reader on the subject is Nielsen and Ware (eds), 1997.

8 Perhaps the clearest contemporary exposition of this crucial Marxian insight is that offered by Ellen Wood in Meiksins Wood 1995a: 40: "Capitalism is uniquely capable of maintaining private property and the power of surplus extraction without the proprietor wielding direct political power in the conventional sense. The state – which stands apart from the economy even though it *intervenes* in it – can ostensibly (notably, by means of universal suffrage) belong to everyone, producer and appropriator, without usurping the exploitative power of the appropriator. The expropriation of the direct producer simply makes certain direct political powers less immediately necessary to surplus extraction. This is exactly what it means to say that the capitalist has economic rather than extra-economic powers of exploitation."

9 Under capitalism, workers have no choice but to offer their labor-power for sale in order to survive.

10 Representative texts include: Beitz 1999; Barry 1989; Pogge 1992; and Hutchings 1999.

11 This is also true of the recent, empirically rich studies inspired by the "global commodity chain" literature. See, for example, Gereffi and Korzeniewicz 1994 and McMichael 1996.

12 Whilst the "storing of surplus" has of course existed in different social formations throughout human history, the systematic subsumption of whole societies to the law of value is achieved for the first time after Europe's "dual revolution" at the turn of the nineteenth century. As we shall shortly see, all this need not preclude analyzing the role of noncapitalist forms of exploitation under capitalism, but instead aims to tighten our definition of relevant abstractions such as "capital" and "value" when considering their actual operation under concrete social formations.

13 Some of these texts are collected in Wolpe 1980. See also Rey 1973.

14 For a historical study of the former see, for example, Geschiere 1985. See also Penvenne 1995.

15 Wells's theoretical conclusion was that "[m]odern sharecropping not only is congruent with advanced commodity production but also stems from the social dynamics of mature capitalism and uses an apparent throwback to earlier labor processes to support the contemporary penetration of capital into agriculture" (Wells 1984). For an excellent summary and original reconsideration of sharecropping under capitalism see Kayatekin 1996/97.

16 There is in this respect some degree of overlap between the AMP approach to global capitalism and the world-systems theory of Immanuel Wallerstein.

As Denmark and Thomas (1988) usefully point out, Wallerstein's emphasis on the "world-system" level of analysis challenges more orthodox Marxist understandings of capitalism as a nationally confined mode of production. Yet whereas the former famously emphasizes the structural constraints to capitalist development generated by a regionalized worldwide division of labor, the latter leaves open to the mediating forces of class and the state the possibility of capitalist development in specific regions of the world. In other words, the AMP approach, whilst recognizing, like world-system theory, the persistence of precapitalist modes of exploitation under global capitalism, unlike the latter allows for a historically and geographically contingent resolution of the apparent incompatibility between wage labor and other forms of exploitation.

17 For an up-to-date analysis of how these particularities play themselves out in one of the more dynamic societies in the peninsula see Tétreault 2000. For a consideration of the "invention" and subsequent persistence of dynastic monarchies in that region see Kostiner 2000.

18 Most world religions have a strongly developed sense of international solidarity, but it is characteristically premised on charitable principles. In the instances where capitalism is explicitly linked to injustice (as in the case of Catholic "liberation theology"), this is normally done with reference to some conception of class solidarity. Likewise, most forms of interclass ethnic solidarity address the injustices generated by capitalism not through the transcendence of this system, but rather through the encouragement of petty-bourgeois capitalism. See for example, Marable 1998 and James 1998.

10 The globalization of human affairs

A reconsideration of science, political economy, and world order

Clark A. Miller

> Scientists and engineers have played a central role in refashioning the material and social worlds of modernity. They have provided key resources with which human beings and institutions imagine, and in part realize, particular visions of progress. These resources can also destabilize identities, threaten security, and arouse resistance. For example, in biomedicine, genetic breakthroughs may allow us to remake the human body, profile individuals and populations, and commodify nature in unprecedented ways; in the information sciences new technologies promise to provide ready access to vast realms of information, facilitate new forms of human interaction and consumption, and enable new forms of state and corporate surveillance; in the military sphere, new technologies may offer unprecedented accuracy and striking power to the armed forces of postindustrial states. These new knowledges and technological forms are materializing at the same time that processes of globalization are mobilizing novel flows of capital, commodities, ideas, technologies, and human migration across borders – and so giving rise to new types of social and technoscientific experimentation.
>
> (A conference announcement at the turn of the millennium)

Science and technology stand at the center of the modern world order – both political and economic. Since World War II, nations have increasingly turned to scientific and technological research and development to provide for their national security (Dennis 1994). The regulatory authority of the state depends implicitly on the generation of statistical information about society and the economy, and on science advice concerning health, safety, and environmental risks (Ezrahi 1990; Jasanoff 1990, 1986; Beck 1992; Porter 1995; Rueschemeyer and Skocpol 1995). The modern firm is first and foremost an agent of technological production (Chandler 1977; Noble 1977; Hughes 1983). Yet, in seeking to understand processes of global change now taking place, students of international political economy have left largely unexamined the activities of scientists, engineers, and others in society who are responsible for the production of new knowledges and technologies. Although scientific and technological changes have been recognized as fundamental components of globalization, scholars have traditionally assumed that they take place outside the realm of social analysis, that is, that they are independent drivers of society and the economy. Nothing could be further from the truth.

Science and technology are powerful agents of social change that are deeply intertwined with other social and economic institutions. They are also human institutions that are open to study, analysis, and investigation by social scientists. Long ago, as Peter Taylor notes in his essay in this volume, scholars of international political economy recognized that "international politics and international business could not sensibly be studied in isolation of each other" (Taylor, Chapter 3 this volume). So, too, I would argue, we now need to recognize that the production and distribution of power and wealth cannot sensibly be studied in isolation from the production and distribution of ideas and technologies. Put in slightly different terms, as we strive to understand the transition from a world order centered around the nation-state to what comes after, it is essential that we focus attention on the changing organization of knowledge and its application.

The connections between changes in science and technology and broader processes of globalization take two principal forms. First, advances in science and technology open up new ways of understanding and acting in the world, prompting people to rethink fundamental notions such as sovereignty, identity, agency, causality, and power (for an explicit rendering of this argument in the case of science, technology, and the law, see Jasanoff 1995). Scientists and engineers have been deeply involved in the conceptual reimagination of nature and society as being made up of global systems – that is, systems that can be understood and managed on scales no smaller than the planet itself – and in the construction of novel technological systems that span the globe. As much as anything else, globalization is a process of rethinking the often taken-for-granted assumptions and frameworks that guide individual and collective interpretation and behavior. Increasingly people perceive themselves as part of a global community, a world market, and a single planet, and they act accordingly. Scientific laboratories, engineering research programs, and other expert institutions operate as critical sites in the production and dissemination of this new global imagination and its attendant technologies.

Second, as society has sought to reconfigure political values, behaviors, and institutions to respond to processes of globalization, science and technology have emerged as key resources in legitimizing global governing arrangements. Responding to the globalization of ideas about the environment, for example, people have begun to create new environmental regimes to coordinate global regulatory processes. Scientists and engineers play key roles in these regimes, and not only as sources of knowledge and information. The objectivity of science is often seen as a powerful voice of political neutrality able to span the divergent national cultures and perspectives of diplomatic participants. Much as national governments have drawn on the perceived political neutrality of "objective" experts and expert knowledge in policymaking since the early twentieth century, international institutions have increasingly followed in their footsteps in the post-World War II era (analyses of the role of experts in liberal democracy can be found in Hays 1959; Jasanoff 1990; Porter 1995; analyses of the role of experts in international affairs can be found in Haas 1990, 1992; Litfin 1994; Jasanoff and

Wynne 1998; Miller and Edwards 2001a). To paraphrase Yaron Ezrahi's classic study of science and American democracy, the case study I present illustrates the extent to which science and technology are now used "to ideologically defend and legitimate … modes of public action, of presenting, defending, and criticizing the uses of political power" in international regimes (Ezrahi 1990: 1).

This chapter explores these two connections between changes in world order and changes in science and technology through a case study of the globalization of environmental politics and the role of scientists in both creating the underlying conceptual foundations for this transformation and establishing formal inter-governmental institutions of environmental governance. The study documents the evolution of international regimes dealing with the atmosphere from the creation of the World Meteorological Organization in 1947 to the signing and ratification of the UN Framework Convention on Climate Change in the 1990s. In the first part of the chapter, I examine how scientists in these regimes helped to transform people's views of the atmosphere so that it is now represented and understood as a global commons – and how this cognitive shift depended, in turn, on scientists' involvement in broader transformations of political and economic order in the postwar era. Together, processes of scientific, technological, political, and economic change ultimately gave rise to conditions under which scientists could visualize and investigate the atmosphere as a global system.

In the second part of the chapter, I turn my attention to the formal roles that scientists have played in international institutions. Here I show that, quite apart from the new ideas about nature they brought to diplomatic negotiations, the formal role of experts and expert knowledge in global policymaking has been the subject of normative debates about the proper structure of global governance. Examined closely, debates about meteorology and climatology appear very similar to a broad range of other discursive sites where, as Sheila Jasanoff has aptly put it, "society is busily constructing its ideas about what constitutes legitimate knowledge, who is entitled to speak for nature, and how much deference science should command in relation to other modes of knowing" (Jasanoff 1995: xv). Indeed, global environmental regimes constitute one of the first places where such issues have been examined rigorously, and in public view, in global society. As such, they serve as important sites of experimentation in efforts to create the constitutional basis of global governance.

Rethinking globalization

Globalization is most frequently defined in terms of the growing interdependence of individuals and communities around the world as flows of goods and people increase (see, e.g. Keohane and Nye 2001, chapter 10). Common measures of globalization point to the growth of international monetary and trade flows, the reach of transnational corporations and nongovernmental organizations, and the expansion of travel and communications networks. At best, this definition is inadequate. Globalization cannot merely encompass the geographic scope of human relations. In terms of the extent of its reach, the British Empire was certainly global – yet the imperial era is rarely discussed as an era of globalization (among the exceptions is Schwartz 2000). Globalization is something that is taken to be happening now, today. Measures of the density of global-scale human relations also fail to address the problem adequately. Even assuming a monotonic increase in human interdependence on planetary scales, one is left with the problem of threshold. Where on this curve does the world begin (or reach) the stage of globalization?

The onset of globalization is frequently equated to the emergence of issues that encompass the entire planet, for example, AIDS, ozone depletion, and persistent organic pollutants (see, e.g. Rosenau 1992). Here again, however, the definition is inadequate. How does one decide when a particular issue is truly "global"? What is it that makes the outbreak of AIDS in the 1980s "global" as compared to outbreaks of diseases such as malaria and smallpox in the 1950s? Certainly, the World Health Organization has been involved in addressing all three. Similarly, why were the elimination of DDT and other persistent organic pollutants like dioxin and PCBs treated as national problems in the 1960s but today are viewed as global problems? Moreover, this definition fails adequately to account for the fact that World War II was clearly understood by people around the world as a global war. Indeed, at the war's end, the creation of the United Nations as a global governing institution was seen as necessary to ensure a global peace. How do these events of half a century ago, fit into our understanding of globalization?

The basic problem with both of these approaches is that they do not account for the central role of ideas in defining globalization. What differs between the 1970s and the 1990s is not so much the magnitude or the scope of people's interactions with one another around the world but rather how people understand those interactions. During the 1980s and 1990s, as it has at other times such as during the years immediately following World War II, the idea that large parts of human affairs encompass the planet as a whole proliferated in the public discourses of many cultures. What explains this remarkable convergence in how diverse groups of people imagine and conceptualize the world they inhabit? How deep does this convergence go? What consequences has this idea had for how people interpret, value, and identify with the social, economic, and political institutions in which they participate? And how, in turn, are people changing their institutions to meet the challenges they perceive as haunting this new "global" community? These are the kinds of questions raised by the dynamic transformations taking place in human affairs as we embark on the twenty-first century.

To address these questions, the scope of our inquiries into political economy needs to expand. In 1660, John Wilkins adopted the term "Physico-Mathematicall-Experimentall Learning" to describe the science being carried out by the newly created British Royal Society. Wilkins's use of the triplet "Physico-Mathematicall-Experimentall" referred his readers to the amalgamation of Aristotelian physics, the mixed mathematics of the Jesuit colleges, and the experimental tradition of Robert Boyle that constituted the new science (Dear 1995). Each formed an indispensable and irreducible part of the whole. The phrase "political economy" has something of this character, denoting recognition of the independent, yet interconnected character of political and economic institutions in modern life. Politics and economics, the phrase implies, both shape world order, yet neither can be simply reduced to the other.

The argument I want to make in the rest of this chapter extends this same concept to a third set of powerful modern institutions. Politics and economics have become deeply entwined over the past century with the institutions of, as some have called it, "technoscience." To be sure, this is widely recognized among political economists, especially by those whose attention is focused on the dynamics of globalization (e.g. Rosenau 1992). The tendency of many such scholars, however, is to accord science and technology rather trivial explanatory value, treating them either as autonomous, external variables or as wholly determined by political and economic forces. As scholars in the emerging interdisciplinary field of science and technology studies have demonstrated, however, both approaches are mistakes. Science and technology are products of human achievement and organization whose current state is historically and culturally dependent (see, especially, Jasanoff *et al.* 1996). They influence and are influenced by their extensive interactions with other institutions in society. They cannot, however, be reduced to epiphenomena of either politics or economics.

Consider two short examples: the industrial revolution and the green revolution. During the industrial revolution, the creation of the factory and other large-scale, technological systems transformed the means of production and the nature of work. In turn, the organization of government also changed so as to provide for the regulation of these new enterprises whose scale vastly surpassed those of previous eras. Emergent from these processes were two institutions that today are central to modern society: the business corporation and the administrative state. Also emergent from the same processes of change were concurrent alterations in the organization of the production of knowledge and expertise which created both the professions and the modern research university. Put differently, to understand why corporations and states take the form they do requires an understanding of the creation of a class of professional managers and the universities to train them as well as an understanding of processes of political and economic change (Hays 1959; Galambos 1970; Layton 1971; Noble 1977; Hughes 1989; Rueschemeyer and Skocpol 1995).

The changes in agricultural production in the United States during the first half of the twentieth century and around the world since the 1950s (changes collectively termed "the green revolution") also altered the production of wealth and power in society. Increasingly, only a small fraction of the population makes its living from working the land, and current land ownership patterns differ markedly from their predecessors. These changes have occurred in large part as the result of modern plant breeding techniques and mechanized farming. However, these technologies did not just appear nor were they adopted automatically by farmers, governments, and corporations. The creation and adoption of green revolution technologies around the world involved significant changes in the relationship between agricultural scientists, government agencies, and corporations that created the modern agricultural extension service in the United States and the international agricultural research institutes of the CGIAR system throughout the tropics.[1] Political and economic forces were central to these changes, but so were the desires of agriculturalists to make plant breeding into a science and to help feed a hungry world (Fitzgerald 1990; Perkins 1997).

Globalization is as much about the emergence and application of new ideas as it is about new economic, social, and political arrangements. Such ideas are frequently constituted, circulated, organized, and institutionalized by scientists, engineers, and other expert communities. Yet, processes of knowledge production, validation, and application are not entirely independent of other aspects of society. As they develop and acquire credibility, experts and their "knowledges," like the climate scientists, observation networks, and computer models I discuss next, become intertwined with economic, social, and political arrangements. Advances in science and technology prompt citizens, officials, and markets to reconsider important norms and institutions in society. Simultaneously, changes in the distribution of wealth and power open new opportunities to create and disseminate knowledges and technologies. In this way, changes in science and technology become coupled with broader changes in world order. In the language of science studies, science and technology are co-produced with political and economic arrangements.

Reimagining the environment

One important area in which changes in the production and distribution of wealth and power are occurring in tandem with changes in the production and distribution of knowledge and know-how is the globalization of the Earth's environment.[2] Of considerable importance in the emergence of global environmental consciousness and the creation of international environmental regimes have been changing scientific ideas about the Earth's atmosphere. Since the early 1970s, scientists, concerned citizens, and diplomats have worked to forge international agreements to address problems of climate change and ozone depletion. Their efforts center on the idea that the Earth's atmosphere constitutes a global commons. Specifically, two new terms have emerged in scientific and political discourses to represent facets of the atmosphere that can be understood and managed on scales no smaller than the globe itself: the *ozone layer* and the *climate system*. Only by investigating the institutional contexts in which these ideas were constructed and acquired credibility among experts and other policymakers, I contend, can we begin to fully understand the forces that are shaping contemporary political landscapes (see also Jasanoff 2001).

Underpinning the construction of ideas about the ozone layer and the climate system is a dramatic change in people's conceptual frameworks.[3] Until the 1970s, scientists and lay observers alike characterized people's interactions with the atmosphere in predominantly local terms. In 1941, for example, the first US government assessment of human–climate interactions defined climate as follows: "the climate of a place is merely a build-up of all the weather from day to day" (Hambidge 1941: 4). This definition supports the kind of conceptual framing of climate underlying the notion that Boston and Miami have different climates.

As reflected in the definition of climate adopted by the 1992 UN Framework Convention on Climate Change, however, the conceptual framing of climate that guides international efforts to combat climate change is quite different. The Framework Convention adopts an alternate definition of the climate as an integrated, global system comprising "the totality of the atmosphere, hydrosphere, biosphere, and geosphere and their interactions" (Mintzer and Leonard 1993: 338). From this perspective, climate is not specific to an individual locale but rather encompasses the planet as a whole.

This shift in perspective has had important political consequences and has the potential to catalyze important economic transformations as well. Minimally, the idea that a climate system exists and is threatened by emissions of carbon dioxide and other greenhouse gases has generated an enormous amount of political activity coalesced around what international relations scholars term the climate regime. Climate scientists, government officials, and representatives of business and nongovernmental organizations meet regularly several times a year in a host of new international governing institutions, including the Intergovernmental Panel on Climate Change (IPCC) and the institutions created by the Framework Convention: the Conference of Parties and the Subsidiary Bodies for Implementation and Scientific and Technological Advice. Participants in these regimes have contributed to the development of new norms of interaction in global society, including the need to regulate economic activity to reduce greenhouse gas emissions and to provide new resources to poor people allowing them to adopt environmentally friendly technologies. The ultimate objective of the regime is simple even if its implementation is not: to transform human economies into a form that does not interfere with the natural functioning of the climate system.

To fully understand these political and economic changes, I argue, it is necessary to explain how the conceptual framing of the atmosphere as a global system arose and acquired credibility and persuasiveness among diverse scientific, policy, and public audiences. Put differently, why did various groups stop imagining climate as a local phenomenon and start imagining it in global terms? To answer this question requires historical investigation of changes in the organization of meteorology as a discipline and its relationship to international politics. These changes began during the years following World War II and have continued up to the present.

The creation of the WMO

Scientific views of the climate are intimately tied up with scientific practices for investigating atmospheric phenomena. Until recently, climatologists studied the climate by taking long-term (usually 30-year) averages of weather data in a particular place or region. Scientific instruments for studying the collective energetics and dynamics of the atmosphere became available to climatologists only after World War II with the creation of a worldwide network for exchanging meteorological data. Subsequently, data from this network helped to catalyze and foster the development of other new scientific instruments – computer models of atmospheric dynamics – to manage the data stream and use it to generate depictions of the worldwide climate system (Edwards 2001). Today, the representations constructed by the latest generation of such models, so-called general circulation models or GCMs, play key roles in the ongoing political dynamics of the climate regime (Edwards and Schneider 2001).

Scholars of political economy who investigate the emerging climate regime typically take scientists' changing views of the atmosphere as unproblematic and in need of no further explanation (O'Riordan and Jaeger 1996; Victor 2001). Yet, closer examination reveals that the construction of scientists' views of the atmosphere as a global system and the adoption of these views by policy audiences entailed a great deal of political and economic work. The postwar global expansion of networks for exchanging meteorological data took place as part of the political transformation of international relations that created the United Nations and other multilateral international organizations. It was driven both by the normative agenda of a small group of meteorologists who sought to bring the benefits of weather forecasting to people everywhere, and by the economic and political agenda for expanding international trade through the construction of new civil aviation networks. Both agendas met resistance. Ultimately, the construction of a global atmospheric observation network required convincing governments to cooperate in the cross-calibration of meteorological instruments and scientists to become deeply involved in world politics, in order to persuade policy makers in countries around the world that there were benefits to be gained from international cooperation and harmonization.

The creation of worldwide meteorological data networks after World War II was accomplished through the activities of the World Meteorological Organization (WMO). Both the establishment of the WMO and its efforts to extend meteorological data networks around the world entailed scientific, technological, and political changes. Driven by the desire to enhance the safety of rapidly expanding civil air transportation networks, the United States and Europe committed significant new resources in the early postwar era to the construction of better weather observation and data exchange networks. To coordinate these networks, meteorologists argued strongly for the creation of an intergovernmental organization made up of representatives of national weather services from around the world. In 1947, the World Meteorological Convention was signed authorizing such an institution and, in 1951, the first meeting of the new WMO was held.[4]

WMO programs brought important changes for meteorological cooperation. Prior to World War II, the heads of national weather services had coordinated their activities through the International Meteorological Organization, a private, scientific association. The shift to an intergovernmental arrangement imposed new institutional restrictions that were sharply opposed by some participants. The WMO joined the fledgling United Nations system, bringing not only bureaucratic considerations, such as voting membership on the basis of legal sovereignty and the requirement that the WMO work in all of the UN languages, but also the exclusion of some countries from the organization entirely (e.g. Spain and the People's Republic of China). As many meteorologists had feared, WMO meetings became sites where, on occasion, broader geopolitical dramas were played out.

Yet, the intergovernmental status of the WMO also brought dramatically expanded resources. The WMO became an active participant in UN and bilateral technical assistance programs that provided significant resources for extending meteorological networks to developing countries. WMO experts planned, and sometimes even implemented, the construction of weather observation and forecasting services in countries where none previously had existed (e.g. Libya).[5] In the process, they found themselves arguing that benefits of broader participation in the international system be extended to developing countries. During the International Geophysical Year, WMO participants also guided the development of new research networks in the uninhabited lands and oceans of the world where ongoing observations had not occurred before.[6] Together with the launch of the first meteorological satellites in the 1960s, these networks underpinned what the WMO titled the World Weather Watch – a program to make the benefits of weather observation and forecasting available to people all around the planet.

Through technical assistance and International Geophysical Year (IGY) programs, meteorologists had created a network that could also provide them with a real-time picture of global atmospheric dynamics. The first computer models of the general circulation of the entire atmosphere were built in the 1960s from data and information emerging from this rapidly expanding network (Edwards 2001). Indeed, some of the earliest such models used what would later be called "the carbon dioxide problem" or "global warming" as a tool for investigating model dynamics. Throughout the 1960s and 1970s, scientific interest in these models expanded rapidly until, by the early 1980s, many climatologists asserted the superiority of computer models of the so-called "climate system" over other methods of understanding the climate (see, especially, NRC 1979, 1982).

Despite this shift in scientific perceptions, however, the view of climate as a local or regional phenomenon remained pervasive in political discourse. In the early 1970s, the US Central Intelligence Agency and State Department expressed considerable concern over the possibility that regional climatic change could create security threats by engendering social and political instability (CIA 1974). In 1979, discussions at the World Climate Conference were heavily dominated by statistical investigations of local climates around the world (WMO 1979). Indeed, as late as 1983, the US National Academy of Sciences encouraged responding to increasing carbon dioxide concentrations in the atmosphere as "changes in local environmental factors – rainfall, river flow, sea level…to which nations and individuals adapt" (NRC 1983: 16).

Major changes in the political framing of climate change did not occur until 1988, when governments, working with the WMO and the UN Environment Programme, agreed to the creation of a new body to address climate change, the Intergovernmental Panel on Climate Change (IPCC). Assigned the task of summarizing expert knowledge about the climate, scientists affiliated with the IPCC deliberately centered their attentions on the behavior of the climate system and distanced themselves from discussions of the weather. In successfully making this shift, they drew implicitly on the rhetorical power of depictions of the global atmosphere adopted by negotiators during the completion of the Montreal Protocol the year before. Ultimately, the IPCC's vision of the global climate system shaped the negotiation of the UN Framework Convention on Climate Change, which defines its ultimate goal in explicitly systemic terms:

> The ultimate objective of this Convention ... is to achieve ... stabilization of greenhouse gas concentrations in the atmosphere at a level that would prevent dangerous anthropogenic interference with the climate system.[7]
>
> (Mintzer and Leonard 1993: 339)

Expertise and global governance

The events recounted in the previous section show why it is important to expand studies of political economy to incorporate investigations of scientific and technological change. The idea that the global commons is now at risk has helped empower discourses of change in international political economy, at a minimum, encouraging the creation of new institutions like the climate and ozone regimes. Within these regimes, participants are working to transform the norms and practices of such foundational arrangements in international relations as the sovereignty of the nation-state and the primacy of nationalism as the sole legitimate form of political identity (cf. Litfin 1998). They are also working to transform the modern economy so that it no longer poses a threat to the atmospheric system. We have observed that the emergence and credibility of the idea that the atmosphere constitutes a global system at risk from human activities has entwined processes of cognitive change with processes of economic and political change in postwar global society for at least half a century.

If studies of political economy ignore these connections, they may miss critical factors that help account for political and economic change. Consider, for example, relationships between climate modeling and the politics of the climate regime. The framing of global environmental issues has had important consequences for how regulatory decisions are made within the regime. Because climate change is seen as a global problem, negotiations today involve around 160 countries. An alternative approach might have sought to negotiate a treaty among the three countries, the US, China, and Russia, whose territories contain the vast majority of the world's coal reserves. Similarly, negotiators have sought to create a global market for emissions permits instead of pursuing differentiated local approaches to emissions reductions. Climate modeling has played an important role stabilizing this framing of climate as a global problem in preference to others. The adoption of a global framing by climate modelers, in turn, reflects important aspects of the societal contexts in which climate modeling is carried out (Shackley 2001). Since climate modeling is almost completely dominated by experts and institutions in the United States, Europe, and Japan, model framing tends to reflect issues of concern to these nations (e.g. research into global ecological limits and the potential climatic changes in the United States Midwest) as opposed to issues of concerns to others (e.g. research into strategies for altering consumption patterns in the North or into the potential impacts of climate change on the Southeast Asian Monsoon – see Kandlikar and Sagar 1997). While climate scientists have not deliberately skewed their results (or allowed negotiators to do so) to achieve certain political outcomes for their own countries, their choices have not been without political and economic significance.

In this section, I argue for the existence of a second, equally important connection between the institutions of technoscience and global political economy. The evolution of international regimes surrounding the atmosphere, from the early history of the WMO to the creation of the ozone and climate regimes in the 1980s and 1990s, illustrates the central, albeit changing, place of expertise in the ideological underpinnings of the multilateral system of international governance that characterizes postwar international relations. In a recent volume, John Ruggie and his colleagues documented the emergence and stabilization of the multilateral form of international governance in the early postwar era (Ruggie 1993). The early success of this form of governance depended, I contend, on the commitment of the United States to a particular view of the relations between experts and liberal forms of governance (and, minimally, the acquiescence of other countries to following American leadership).

In her contribution to the Ruggie volume, Anne-Marie Burley argues that the creation of the UN Specialized Agencies mirrored the construction (a decade earlier) of similar, expert-run regulatory agencies in the New Deal United States (Burley 1993). The creation and early operation of agencies like the WMO centered on the construction and expansion of transnational epistemic communities (on the definition of epistemic communities, see Haas and Adler 1992; for a parallel analysis to mine for the Bretton Woods Institutions, see Ikenberry 1992). In turn, experts working in these agencies helped forge a broader system of international peace and prosperity for the postwar world.

By building expert institutions, American foreign policy officials sought to build on what they saw as the unique capacity of experts to overcome the limits of political conflict and to create effective international institutions for managing world affairs (Berkner 1950). At the core of each of these new institutions lay a cognitive commitment to a global system whose better management would help contribute to the success of international cooperation. As articulated by US officials, the objectives of the 1947 World Meteorological Convention were to enhance international cooperation in weather science so as to increase understanding of the atmosphere, strengthen better weather forecasts, improve agricultural production, make air and sea travel safer, and ultimately establish a more secure world order.[8] The International Monetary Fund (IMF) was created along similar lines to help manage the system of currency exchange, the World Health Organization to address worldwide public health concerns, and the Food and Agriculture Organization to manage the production and distribution of the world's food resources.

In each case, expert bureaucracies were created to facilitate cooperation in the production and use of knowledge about relevant global systems. Experts were viewed not only as sources of specialized knowledge and skills but also as agents uniquely situated to overcome the barriers of national difference. Their distinctive moral character was seen as exempting them from the political problems faced by their diplomatic partners in the new organizations and enabling them to promote intergovernmental harmonization of technical practices.[9] Although the Cold War, which frequently generated conflicts in expert forums as deep as any found in other sites of East–West interaction, severely challenged this perspective, American scientists and diplomats continued throughout the postwar period to foster the creation of institutions that treated scientists as unique and exempt from considerations of sovereignty or political difference (Greenaway 1996). Over time, as we saw in the previous section, additional areas of responsibility were added to the roles of experts in international organizations, particularly through the creation of large-scale technical assistance programs and efforts like the IGY to coordinate international scientific research.

Today, experts play many varied roles in international relations. While the United Nations General Assembly and Secretariat witnessed a substantial decline in power and influence in world affairs over the second half of the twentieth century, many UN Specialized Agencies remain extremely important at the turn of the twenty-first century in the construction of new global governing arrangements. The stature of institutions like the IMF and World Bank hardly needs mention. Over the past decade, the Food and Agriculture Organization, in partnership with the World Trade Organization and the Convention on Biological Diversity, has worked to generate rules and principles governing the trade and patenting of genetic material, particularly with regard to the use and safety of genetically modified crops (Gupta 2000). Likewise, the WMO is a key player in the ongoing negotiations of the ozone regime and less central but nonetheless also important in the climate regime.

At the same time, experts have become increasingly prevalent in new organizations created since 1970. Although the United States and many European nations declared themselves against creating large new international bureaucracies in the late 1960s and 1970s, subsequent years saw the initiation of an array of new institutions for international environmental cooperation (Haas *et al.* 1993). The most successful of these have centered on regional or global systems viewed as in need of coordinated management, such as the regional seas programs, protection of Antarctica, trade in endangered species, ozone depletion, and climate change. Much of the demand for these regimes was created by the emergence of epistemic communities with specific ideas about how to manage these resources as international commons (Peterson 1988; Haas 1990, 1992; Litfin 1994). In every case, the underlying treaty that created a governing regime also explicitly provides for expert advisory institutions as a formal requirement. Likewise, the World Trade Organization vests its central regulatory authority – the power to strike down national health, consumer safety, or environmental laws that are seen as masquerades for the creation of trade barriers – in expert panels empowered to rule on whether or not the laws are grounded on sound scientific principles.

As experts have acquired new roles in managing planetary affairs, however, skepticism has also deepened regarding the organization of expertise and its integration into international diplomacy. Not surprisingly, as the power of experts has grown within global governing regimes, other participants in these regimes such as governments, industry groups, and nongovernmental organizations have become increasingly conscious of the need to pay careful attention to the organizing rules and principles that govern international expert bodies. Soon after US and European governments established the IPCC in 1988, for example, developing country governments began to object to the panel's framing of climate change. IPCC scientists portrayed climate change as a problem of ecological thresholds – the planetary environment was being pushed to its limits by greenhouse gas emissions. In contrast, developing countries viewed climate change as a problem of overconsumption (in the North) and a lack of access on the part of developing countries to new technologies that would enable them to develop in environmentally friendly ways (cf. Jasanoff 1993).

The unwillingness of the IPCC to consider issues of equity and technology transfer (ostensibly because its activities were scientific) led developing countries to reject a 1990 proposal by UNEP to allow the IPCC to oversee negotiations for a climate treaty. Instead, the United Nations created a separate organization – the Intergovernmental Negotiating Committee – in which the negotiations took place. During these negotiations, disputes about the IPCC continued. US and European governments favored attaching the IPCC to the treaty regime as the official scientific advisory body while developing countries rejected any mention of the IPCC. The compromise enshrined in the 1992 Framework Convention on Climate Change established the Subsidiary Body for Scientific and Technological Advice (SBSTA) as a kind of legislative subcommittee with the authority to call upon scientific organizations – including the IPCC, if it so chooses – to provide regime participants with expert advice.

Since then, SBSTA has functioned as an important site for a number of difficult negotiations over how to properly organize global expert advisory processes and institutions. In this, SBSTA has become a model for the governing arrangements incorporated into other global environmental treaties, including the 1992 Convention on Biological Diversity and the 1994 Convention to Combat Desertification. At stake in the decisions of SBSTA and its counterparts in other regimes are important issues such as who counts as an expert, what standards govern the production of policy-relevant scientific knowledge, and how much weight will be given to science as compared to other modes of knowing. Authors such as Sheila Jasanoff and Brian Wynne have argued that such considerations can have enormous impact on the distribution of power and legitimacy within domestic regulatory processes (Wynne 1982; Jasanoff 1990). Increasingly, it is becoming apparent that states and other participants in global governing regimes are also taking these issues very seriously as sites of power and influence in world affairs.

What has emerged, then, in the late twentieth century is a situation of considerable flux in our understanding of nature and science and their relationship to global governance. The future evolution of globalization depends in great measure not only on the flow of goods and materials around the world but also on the flow and uptake of ideas among the world's peoples. Formal expert advisory institutions such as those described here constitute only one part of a complicated story. Of comparable importance to the climate regime are institutions like the

International Research Institute for Climate Prediction (IRI) at Columbia University. Designed to reach out to people in their daily lives and to transform their actions on the basis of a global understanding of the atmosphere, IRI is developing programs to provide forecasts of changes in the climate system, such as El Niño events, on time scales of a few seasons or years. If they succeed in establishing themselves as what Bruno Latour describes as an "obligatory point of passage" in the flow of ideas, IRI will help to reshape world order in ways that could bypass states and international negotiations altogether (Latour 1987). The pervasive influences of modern communications technologies like CNN and the internet on what ideas achieve currency and credibility around the world also should not be discounted. What seems clear is that social scientists need to pay close attention to the social processes in which knowledge is produced and consumed to fully understand globalization.

Conclusion: technoscience and political economy

Writers in the tradition of "epistemic communities" argue that science is a powerful agent in contemporary international relations (e.g. Haas 1990, 1992). In this chapter I have tried to go one step further, arguing that the internal dynamics of science and its relations with other social institutions must be understood if we are to fully understand the evolution of global political orders. Scientists and engineers, like diplomats and international businessmen, need to be seen as important players on the global stage. Science, in this sense, is deeply political.

In his famous treatise, *On War*, Carl von Clausewitz defines war as "a continuation of policy by other means": "We see, therefore, that War is not merely a political act, but also a real political instrument, a continuation of political commerce, a carrying out of the same by other means" (Clausewitz 1968: 119).

In much the same way, I suggested earlier in the paper, political economists have treated the market as an extension and continuation of the domain of politics. My claim in this paper is that the internal dynamics of the scientific community and its relations to other institutions in society also carry fundamental implications for the distribution of power and wealth, the making of public choices, and constitution of social order. Thus, science, too, is politics by other means. But it is important to think carefully about precisely what that implies. I do not mean, for example, that science is merely political. Scientists do not necessarily act in ways that are similar to other kinds of political agents. Theories and categories that political scientists apply to institutions like the Congress, the Presidency, interest groups, or new social movements will not, therefore, simply apply wholesale to science. I also do not mean to imply that science is *entirely* political. There are many reasons to pursue scientific research (and to study science as a social institution) that have little or nothing to do with influencing things that we normally consider to be political. Even when motivated by desires that are not conventionally understood as political, however, scientists' actions may nonetheless unintentionally shape politics. Finally, I do not mean to imply that science is an epiphenomenon of other political institutions. I do not suggest that we can understand the production of scientific knowledge as the outcome of processes driven solely by the state, interest groups, or other political agents.

Rather, I argue that science is a social institution (indeed, it is a diverse array of often quite distinctive social institutions) whose internal dynamics and relations with other social institutions are deeply embedded in the dynamics of world order. In consequence scientific worldviews and technological systems form a critical part of the constitutional basis of emerging global society. As I have argued here, the construction, validation, and application of ideas that take place in expert communities fundamentally shape globalization. Changes in world order depend on which ideas acquire prominence and credibility among experts as well as among citizens, markets, and political officials. As I showed in the second part of the chapter, experts are also increasingly important participants in the structuring of global governing arrangements. As scholars of international political economy seek to understand and critically evaluate new, interconnected forms of social, economic, and political order that emerge through processes of globalization, they must pay increasing attention to the way in which these arrangements are also tied into the organization of knowledge production and application. Put differently, we need to explore how ideas acquire credibility and solidity, as well as power and authority, as they are taken up into the construction of new forms of order.

Notes

1 CGIAR stands for the Consultative Group on International Agricultural Research of the World Bank, which was established in 1971 to formalize the system of international agricultural research institutes created in the 1950s and 1960s by US plant breeders, diplomats, and private foundations.
2 The material for this and subsequent sections is drawn, in part, from previous writings on this subject. For detailed treatments, see Miller and Edwards (2001b); Miller (2001 a,b); Miller (2000); Miller (forthcoming).
3 In what follows, I discuss principally the case of climate change. For a useful discussion of the politics of the ozone layer, see Litfin (1994); Benedick (1991).
4 Documentation of the negotiation and early activities of the WMO can be found in IMO (1947) and WMO (1951a–d).
5 Early issues of the *WMO Bulletin* contain extensive discussions of the technical assistance programs of the WMO.
6 WMO activities during the IGY are described at length in Van Miegham (1955a,b), US National Committee for the International Geophysical Year (1956), and Berkner (1959).
7 For another discussion of the political and scientific dimensions of the IPCC, see Boehmer-Christiansen (1994).
8 In a 1947 speech of welcome to delegates negotiating what would become the World Meteorological Convention, written in close collaboration with F.W. Reichelderfer, chief of the US Weather Service, US Assistant Secretary of State Garrison Norton remarked: "In our welcome to you, we therefore have in mind a broader future than the science of meteorology alone. Certainly, we are interested in your technical success and in the new constitution for the World Meteorological Organization which you will consider here. But we also believe that your achievements will contribute in some measure to the aims of permanent world peace and prosperity towards which the nations of the world are working" (Norton 1947: 374).

9 In the same speech, Norton also remarked: "I hope you can always keep foremost in your mind the technical and scientific nature of your work so that your relationships may be as free as possible from the obstacles and problems of political science." He went on to praise meteorologists' "global outlook," their "appreciation of international cooperation," and their ability "in the search for scientific truths" to avoid "the more uncertain and unselfish motives that complicate and hinder co-operation in some fields of international interest" (Norton 1947: 373).

Part V

Conclusion

11 Alternative directions in the study of the global political economy

Robert A. Denemark

Susan Strange contributed the first chapter to the first volume of the *International Political Economy Yearbook*, published in 1985. In it she urged International Political Economy (IPE) toward maturity, toward a separation from the stultifying effects of its erstwhile parents (international relations with its state-centric bias and economics with its narrow view of human motivation). She counseled the need for attention to a wider array of less tainted subdisciplines, to the question of "who benefits?", to questions of concern to more than just the policy makers of hegemonic states, to cross-ideological fertilization and attention to values. She warned us to take neither the accuracy of existing data for granted, nor the neutrality of the questions they were gathered to answer.

At her passing in 1998, Strange was memorialized in the fifty-year retrospective edition of *International Organization*, the most important IPE journal in the United States. One must question whether it was a fitting tribute. All but one of that issue's seventeen contributors came from the fields of international relations and economics, and the last few lines of the volume read "... the field needs to move in the direction of formulating parsimonious models and clearly refutable null hypotheses, and toward developing empirical techniques that will allow those hypotheses to be more directly confronted by the data. This, admittedly, is easier said than done."[1] The study of the global political economy has indeed matured, as attested by the sophistication of the literature and the many insights offered. But there has also developed an orthodoxy, the "politics of international economic relations" approach, against which Strange railed to the end of her life.

Strange's call for attention to fresh perspectives, a healthy heterodoxy, and openness to normative concerns animated this volume. Final chapters are fitting places to ask whether the work has been successful, and here I consider the insights we have offered in this volume regarding units of analysis (both spatial and temporal), fundamental relationships, hegemony, the disaffected, and globalization. In keeping with Strange's vision, the treatments in the various chapters show considerable independence. I also look at what this volume suggests for the road ahead. The transdisciplinary scholarship offered here is clearly useful. Nonetheless, there are issues that we have not addressed and elements of praxis that remain underdeveloped. Finally, we consider what scholars outside the mainstream might do to help build a better understanding of the global political economy.

Odysseys of place and time

Traditional international relations focuses on states or state systems, while neoclassical liberal economics is tethered to the rational value-maximizing individual. In contrast, at least three very different sets of understandings about how to legitimately conceptualize the global political economy emerge from these readings. For Alex Colás, building on the literature of the 1970s on articulated modes of production, "social formations" are central. Colás offers no simple linear model of "precapitalist" forms evolving into "capitalist" forms in a lockstep historical progression. Instead we find an acknowledgment that capitalism does not so much destroy as overpower other social orders. The result is a social formation in which an uneasy relationship emerges between very different modes of appropriation of labor power. The social formation is at once a local and a systemic phenomenon, where domestic politics presents a strange fusion of symptoms with multiple levels of power and exploitation. At the heart of it all rests the capitalist wage relation, which must be overcome for any sort of justice to prevail. Herein lies a twin challenge. Since multiple forms of exploitation overlap, multiple and fragmented responses may be expected to emerge. Movements centered on race, caste, gender, and class do not merge easily. The cobbling together of any solidarity in response, particularly at the global level, is likely to be horribly difficult. Adding to the difficulty is Colás's belief that no movement in response can be successful if it fails to confront the class politics that rests at the absolute heart of exploitation.

For Peter Taylor, the relevant unit is the modern world-system with its capitalist world economy. This Wallerstenian perspective understands the system as having emerged in the long sixteenth century with the advent of European domination and traditional capitalism. For Wallerstein and Taylor, however, modes of appropriation of labor power do not so much coexist as evolve into a complex set of relations designed to exploit, in whatever form might be handy, workers in various parts of the globe. From this perspective we are dealing not so much with "social formations" where separate systems interact, as with a single capitalist system that has actively appropriated noncapitalist forms of domination. These forms become part of a capitalist world economy, which must be understood as a unit if one is to comprehend the functioning of its parts. This system is further reinforced by various visions of itself propagated by hegemonic actors. Each new hegemon brings with it a new sense of the system that projects its own special image of the social order. The US version projects a global system of sovereign nation-states dominating our view of the world. Mosaic "political" maps and "state-istics" crystallize a world of "embedded statism." Hence the capitalist world economy is also revealed as an idea, a metageography whose nature goes uncontested as a matter of "common knowledge."

Barry Gills offers the third and perhaps the most revolutionary sense of the nature of the system. It is a world system, but it is neither of modern origins nor does it depend on capitalism as its defining dynamic. Gills proposes that we move back through time in search of continuities regarding the accumulation of capital. He finds a good many. Capitalist relations of production are again but one aspect of the modern world, and are not considered historically unique in imposing a drive for ceaseless accumulation. Instead, Gills identifies a set of dialectical processes that transcend capitalism. Tensions between capital and *oikos*, free and unfree labor, and organization and entropy are the triumvirate that have defined social life for millennia. To focus too much on only their latest manifestation is to surrender our perspective, our ability to understand longer term trends, the nature of the past, the present, and the future. For Gills, the sixteenth century with its eurocentric core and its over emphasis on capitalism is too recent and too prosaic a starting point.

For all of the sometimes vitriolic debate that has emerged on these issues among authors in the critical tradition (see Denemark and Thomas 1988; Frank 1991, 1998; Frank and Gills 1993/6; Wallerstein 1993, 1995b, 1999; Arrighi *et al.* 1999; Denemark 1999, 2000), each of our chapters focuses on offering an alternative to the atomistic individual or the national state as the core of analysis. These chapters open a discussion of how to understand the global political economy in terms of both time and space.

Odysseys of money and power

For all their ostensible disagreements, Colás, Taylor, and Gills all identify capital as resting at the core of global processes. Capital is not viewed in the traditional terms that inhere in international relations and liberal economics, that is, as a store of value and medium of exchange. It is instead a relationship that ties resources and individuals together in ways that may be manipulated so as to provide or reinforce the power of some groups over others. The various ways in which this might take place are discussed in greater depth by Jonathan Nitzan, Hartmut Elsenhans, and Spike Peterson. For Nitzan, capital is the inherently political commodification of power. One can better understand this relationship by abandoning the idea that owners seek maximum profits and recognize that they instead seek the relative gains of what Nitzan calls "differential accumulation." This search for relative gains is a historical constant that transcends the capitalist system. There are many ways to earn greater differential returns, and these modalities help us understand the economic swings between periods of relatively stable growth when new investments, mergers and acquisitions dominate corporate strategy, and the much more unstable and problematic stagflation strategies.

Elsenhans takes a very different view. The capitalist class is really not so powerful as, for example, dominant strata prior to the advent of capitalism. Neither is capitalism, with its emphasis on market processes, the real problem. Indeed Elsenhans sees market processes as the best practical alternative to the over-bureaucratization of both economic and political life. The real battle is ideological and concerns distribution. Elsenhans rejects currently popular endogenous growth and strategic trade theories that stress low wages and high levels of human capital. He views real growth as a function of demand: the more demand, the more production required to satiate that demand, and therefore the more growth. To Elsenhans, the view that neoclassical liberals take regarding growth is particularly stultifying. The low wages and high levels of inequality they favor actually depress demand and are self-defeating. The empirical evidence for this, in all manner of societies, seems particularly clear and is either ignored or explained away. After cataloging some of the evidence Elsenhans (178) declares that "There is no manipulation of reality that a neoclassical economist would not accept to save the theoretical structure of neoclassical economics against the realities of the world." Elsenhans's frustration is evident, and comes from his belief that capitalism need not be so exploitive as its current manifestations appear. His own radical proposals offer a vision and a program for growth with equity. Capitalist exploitation to the contrary, "worldwide social reform" is possible.

Peterson provides the broadest critique of capital as a relationship by pointing out what we ignore as a result of the prevailing ideology. The nature of productive relations, the traditional stuff of IPE, consumes our attention and allows the "reproductive" and the "virtual" economies to go unnoticed. Reproduction concerns the fundamental, gendered, and mostly unpaid labor that goes into the creation of affective relations, home, and family. An array of nonmarket relationships are understood from her perspective to lack market status exactly because dominant forces have an incentive to keep them off the books. Doing so facilitates exploitation at various levels of society, even in the productive market itself where persons traditionally charged with "nonmarket" tasks find their labor power devalued when they attempt to join the wage-labor force. Broader still is the virtual economy, an economy of signs, constructed desires, perceptions, and (misplaced) trust in which disembodied capital emerges in the hands of "producers" (investors, financiers) who do no more than appropriate what they hope will be a claim over a future stream of money income.

Odysseys of mind and control

In traditional international political economy the term "hegemony" usually refers to a set of power attributes deemed sufficient to provide their holder with the ability to make and enforce a given set of rules. But for Peterson, hegemony is about ideas and her virtual economy is very much a function of closely guarded and self-consciously reinforced ideas by those who benefit from a given set of conceptualizations. Following Antonio Gramsci, Robert Cox, and even Michel Foucault, hegemony is defined rather consistently in this volume as a set of beliefs that appear unproblematic, beyond question, and are accepted as "common sense." This is a distinctly untraditional definition of hegemony that sheds significant light on a variety of processes in the global political economy.

While Peterson reveals the "reproductive" and the "virtual" forces of the global political economy, Barbara Jenkins goes into greater detail as to how those forces are created and protected. A given market culture is not natural, but is created by a "culture industry" using the technology of mass production to impose a model of norms, desires, and behaviors that serve its interests. Popular media are controlled by less than two dozen firms headquartered in advanced countries and capable of forcibly opening other societies to their pre-scripted messages through liberalizing institutions like the WTO and NAFTA. Cultural commodification destroys local art, but not before appropriating anything in it that looks potentially profitable. The media and the message are that there is no alternative to the market, and "denying the rigors of market logic brings fruitless pain" (Jenkins 78). We are homogenized and demobilized, even to the point of readily accepting the myths that enslave us. While there are a few contradictions and bright spots inherent in the cosmopolitan nature of the new world art, in the fusion that emerges in transnational practice and in the cultural responses that build as a result of this crushing homogeneity the outlook is fairly dim.

Nowhere is the essentially social, contested, and variable nature of the ideas that underpin hegemony more galling than in the study of science. In a "modern" world it is argued that knowledge yields power. The task of science is to discover objective laws about how things work, master those forces, and reap the attendant benefits. This may be the model of science and technology in modernity, but in a "postmodern" world it is argued that power yields knowledge. The ability to dominate others, propagate those explanations of complex phenomena that suit the propagator's needs, and reap the attendant benefits is the model of the virtual and the ideational in postmodernity. Clark Miller identifies science as a key social dynamic, resting precariously between the modern and the postmodern in that it both affects and is affected by the society in which it is embedded. In his chapter the definition of "climate" played a significant role in the manner in which that concept was studied, as well as in the political fight to broaden our vision of the relevant environment. That broader vision was dependent in part on the existence of a specific material interest in safer global trade and travel, part of the Cold War. Likewise, the broader definition also brought with it new political concerns and programs that the scientific community was then in a far better position to champion.

The odysseys of the wretched of the earth

Traditional studies in international relations and economics treat normative concerns with some distaste. Both fancy themselves as sciences, if not value-free then at least aspiring to something akin to neutrality. If there is a dominant ethos in international relations it is the unfortunate truth that might makes right, and in economics we are dealing with a prescriptive science that counsels adherence to the same precepts in lieu of reality (as with game theory, see Rapoport 1960: 226–7). The chapters in this volume differ from that perspective to a level of unanimity rarely seen among such a diverse group of critical scholars. The study of global political economy is and should be normatively based. While the various authors make no attempt systematically to list the oppressed, their plight animates the entire work.

Nobody is more direct than Alex Colás who argues that a new normative sense must inspire our studies of the global political economy. Gills speaks of the need to develop a new "humancentric" analysis. Peterson and Jenkins argue poignantly about the subjugation of women. Peterson goes so far as to adopt the term "feminization" as a synonym for a broader range of those exploited, regardless of their gender, in the formal, informal, or virtual economy. Taylor, Elsenhans, and Nitzan speak of capitalist exploitation. Mary Ann Tétreault's introduction reinforces the problems of exploitation across the full range of issues, while Miller strips the myth of objectivity from even the "hard" scientific endeavor.

The chapter that ties the problem of exploitation to more specific forms of violence was written by Peter Uvin. Uvin seeks to reintroduce the concept of structural violence, popular some three decades ago, to the debate. Structural violence exists when fundamental human needs and capacities are frustrated by social structures. In a more idealistic era this gap between legitimate needs and their realistic fulfillment was sufficient in and of itself to raise concern. In a more cynical age, the existence of haves and have-nots is more likely to be taken as axiomatic. But Uvin ties structural violence directly to acute violence by chronicling the path from frustration via inequality, exclusion, and humiliation, to the kind of very palpable violence that constitutes terror and genocide. In the wake of recent events, explanations of motives for such actions should sound a responsive chord.

The globalized odyssey

It is difficult to escape the term "globalization" in current scholarship, and in this regard the present volume might be considered fairly traditional. "Globalization" appears in numerous chapter titles and, given the lack of a standard understanding, the authors here join an already existing fray. The insights that emerge come in two forms. First, we find a set of understandings of globalization that are unique. Taylor and Gills are most relevant in this regard. Second, we find a set of analyses of how globalization, more typically defined as an intensification of various cross-border interactions, affects the nontraditional processes discussed in other contexts. Peter Taylor defines globalization as a "moment" in which our old conceptualization of the world, our current embedded statist "metageography," is beginning to give way before new forces. This statist metageography may be seriously out of date, and a new system of globalized flows of goods and services, and of relations between nodal cities as opposed to allegedly sovereign nation-states, may constitute its emerging nature. Globalization is the term we use for these processes and this period of transition.

For Gills, globalization is a methodological issue. His argument for a very long-term perspective renders suggestions that globalization is substantially a "new" phenomenon problematic at the very least. There have been several instances of serious increases or declines in the nature of relations across existing borders, however conceived. Elsenhans happily provides excellent sources of support in this regard, noting the higher relative levels of international investment that existed just over one century ago. Gills argues that globalization needs to be historicized, in part to strip contemporary analysis of its embedded Eurocentrism, and in part to allow us to consider other periods of intensification or "pulsations" in the global political economy. Where Taylor stresses what may be emerging in the here and now, Gills would have us consult the longest *durée* in the hope of finding some additional theoretical and empirical perspective.

Other authors are quick to answer the challenge of "globalization" and its implications by considering the effects of increases in speed, scale, and complexity on a variety of processes. Peterson laments that such intensification invites exploitive metanarratives, while Jenkins explores the institutions that go about creating just such a set of myths. Peterson and Miller are both concerned with the role that science and technology play in facilitating such global metanarratives. Colás laments the greater scope of exploitation as it inhibits solidarity. Nitzan sees the extension of the relevant market as facilitating the more harmful modes of differential accumulation, merger and acquisition (over green-field investment), and stagflation (over cost-cutting).

Elsenhans argues that the reduction in transaction costs that defines globalization provides additional impetus for the fostering of self-defeating growth policies. As liberal economics counsels a response to globalization that stresses a self-induced and self-inflicted reduction in wages and social support, effective demand, the engine of growth, will decline more globally than locally. This trend is strengthened by the greater incorporation of unorganized labor, weak in and of itself and used as a lever to weaken labor in those areas where it had been organized. The disempowering of labor across societies will lead to higher levels of inequality and lower wages, Elsenhans's prescription for lower rates of growth with increased inequality. And finally there is Uvin's analysis of globalization as spreading both the objective conditions for and subjective perceptions of greater inequality, of greater social exclusion, and of greater humiliation. These are the elements that turn structural violence into killing fields of various sorts.

The intellectual odyssey

This volume speaks of other issues as well: the breaking down of false intellectual boundaries, the construction of a counter-hegemonic project, and an openness to the future. As regards intellectual boundaries, this small volume includes authors from several disciplines and countries. It is important to break down the artificial barriers that separate students of various social processes. Born in the nineteenth century, these separate social science disciplines emerged with the differentiation of the policy-relevant social sciences from their roots in history. The historian's ideographic bias was an inappropriate foundation from which to formulate useful social laws. Modern economics, sociology, and political science eventually emerged, and were joined by anthropology so that "oriental" and other "backward" societies could be subjected to their own scientific scrutiny (Wallerstein *et al.* 1996). This differentiation is by no means illogical. The study of society as a whole is far too large to digest. Without breaking it into smaller, more focused sets of phenomena, our vision would have remained perpetually cloudy. The creation of special disciplines with their own favored vocabularies, literatures, and sets of analytical tools, allowed progress to be made. But this progress came at a considerable cost in terms of the ability of those ever-more specialized students to bring the insights that their hard work garnered back to the broader questions we face. We fractured human knowledge in an attempt to gain some leverage over the whole, and ended up unable to profit from the results. Transdisciplinary work remains difficult. Even Karl Popper, hardly a progressive contributor to a discipline that Strange (1985: 16) characterized as suffering from "collective autism" argued "...we are not students of some subject matter but students of problems... And problems may cut right across the borders of any subject matter or discipline" (cited in Serafini 1989: 81).

Have we made progress in breaking down these barriers to comprehensive knowledge that were created in great part to make the study of society manageable? I would argue that we have begun to do so. This volume includes chapters that consider remarkably similar sets of problems from remarkably different perspectives. There is no single acceptable method of analysis. Concern for a set of problems: the vicissitudes of globalization, the processes of global capitalism, and the building of progressive social theory, ties these chapters together. Deep history, linguistic analysis, cultural studies, class analysis, normative concerns, rich description, and data analysis inhabit these pages, and the authors have taken one another's contributions seriously. Jenkins (p. 164) concludes her chapter by suggesting that "It is imperative that political economists break down the false barriers between disciplinary fiefdoms..." She echoes Taylor's explicit call for "transdisciplinarity," and more implicit calls by various others to take a broader view.

The counter-hegemonic project?

Globalization is not inevitable, and it is not necessarily permanent. Our methods tell us that globalization should bring with it the seeds of its own destruction, but the nature of any such contrary forces are impossible to identify at this early date. Indeed, the counter-hegemonic pickings appear slim. Powered by capital, in command of science and technology, and fortified by culture, the dominant neoliberal synthesis appears impregnable. The forces of TINA (There Is No Alternative) seem pervasive. Saying so is not the same as committing the sin of excluding agency. Exploitation may be defined as the theft of agency from a subject population. To suggest that individuals are offered little room to maneuver is not to deny their agency, it is to define their exploitation. Nonetheless, there are a few bright spots. Miller speaks of the progressive elements of science, Jenkins of the progressive responses to cultural fusion and the search for new forms of community, Gills of the building of a humanocentric analysis, and Colás the continuing search for solidarity. Elsenhans warns of criticism without alternatives, and offers a sophisticated program designed to foster growth and equality for those in both advanced and peripheral countries.

Toward the future

There is always more that could have and should have been said. This volume fails to consider Nature, perhaps the most important issue around which some tangible level of resistance has emerged. Little is said of religious movements beyond Tétreault's introduction and a passing mention by Jenkins. Yet, for better or worse, these appear to be the dominant form of resistance to globalization. The movement of humans across borders, away from violence, in search of a better life or because the market for those with significant skills makes it so worthwhile, gets scant notice as well. No doubt there are scores of other critical issues to consider. Neither is praxis significantly advanced except by Elsenhans, who warns that endless criticism without the offering of alternatives is self-defeating. His admonition should be taken to heart.

I suggest that we might also act in a progressive manner in our role as producers of scholarship. This volume brought together individuals of various, sometimes incompatible, ontological and epistemological proclivities. They aimed their critical abilities not at each other but at understanding the global political economy. Indeed, what sense does it make for underrepresented positions to take constant aim at one another? We should become less concerned with berating one another over matters of method than we are about identifying problems of common concern and using our various analytics to address them. The more light we generate and the more puzzles we solve, the more we focus on the identification of what has been ignored and what is in fact a problem; the less we focus on our differences, the more we shall learn from and enrich our various analyses. Chris Chase-Dunn once suggested in a talk that "We can sit around and insult one another's intellectual grandparents, or we can read what each of us has to say and see what parts of it make sense and fit together. That way we might actually learn something." It is sound advice.

Note

1 The final article in the collection is "Dental Hygiene and Nuclear War: How International Relations Looks from Economics" by Barry Eichengreen. I have long been a fan of Eichengreen's fine historical and contemporary work on the global financial system. I quote him here simply to point out that the editors of *International Organization* provided him with the opportunity to offer a powerful "last word" in an important retrospective, and what he chose to say was likely not the type of advice of which Strange would have approved.

Bibliography

Abrahams, Paul and Alexandra Harney. 1999. "High Output, Low Profits." *Financial Times*, June 2: 15.

Abu-Lughod, Janet L. 1989. *Before European Hegemony: The World System A.D. 1250–1350*. New York: Oxford University Press.

——. 1990. "Restructuring the Premodern World-System." *Review*, XIII(2): 273–86.

Adam, Heribert. 1990. "Exclusive Nationalism versus Inclusive Patriotism: State Ideologies for Divided Societies." *Innovation*, 3(4): 569–87.

Adams, Henry Brooks. 1895. *The Law of Civilization and Decay*. London: Sonnenschein.

——. 1943. *The Law of Civilization and Decay: An Essay on History*. New York: Alfred A. Knopf.

Adelman, Irma. 1984. "Beyond Export-led Growth." *World Development*, 12(9): 937–49.

Adorno, Theodor. 1972. "The Culture Industry: Enlightenment as Mass Deception." In *Dialectic of Enlightenment*, eds, Max Horkheimer and Theodor Adorno. New York: Herder and Herder.

Agger, Ben. 1992. *The Discourse of Domination: From the Frankfurt School to Postmodernism*. Evanston, IL: Northwestern University Press.

Agnew, John. 1993. "The Territorial Trap," *Review of International Political Economy*, 1: 53–80.

Agosin, Manuel R. and Ricardo French-Davis. 1995. "Trade Liberalization and Growth: Recent Experiences in Latin America." *Journal of Interamerican Studies and World Affairs*, 37(3): 9–58.

Aitkens, Rob and Barbara Jenkins. 2000. "Jumping Borders with Pleasure: Chicano Cultural Resistance to Neo-Liberalism." *Studies in Political Economy*, 63: 87–110.

Alam, M. Shahid. 1992. "Convergence in Developed Countries: An Empirical Investigation." *Weltwirtschaftliches Archiv*, 128(2): 189–201.

Albert, Michel. 1991. *Capitalisme contre capitalisme*. Paris: Editions du Seuil.

Albo, Xavier. 1994. "Ethnic Violence: the Case of Bolivia." In *The Culture of Violence*, eds, Kumar Rupesinghe and Marcel Rubio C. Tokyo: United Nations University Press, pp. 119–43.

Alesina, Alberto and Roberto Perotti. 1997. "Welfare State and Competitiveness." *American Economic Review*, 87(5): 921–40.

Alexander, Jeffrey C. 1982. *Theoretical Logic in Sociology*, Berkeley, CA: University of California Press, pp. 1–2.

Alexander, Peter and Rick Halpern. 2000. *Racializing Class, Classifying Race: Labour and Difference in Britain, the USA, and Africa*. New York: St Martin's Press.

Allport, Gordon W. 1954. *The Nature of Prejudice*. New York: Anchor Books.

Al-Mughni, Haya. 2000. "Women's Movements and the Autonomy of Civil Society in Kuwait." In *Feminist Approaches to Social Movements, Community, and Power.* vol. 1. *Conscious Acts and the Politics of Social Change*, eds, Robin L. Teske and Mary Ann Tétreault. Columbia: University of South Carolina Press, pp. 170–87.

Althusser, Louis and Etienne Balibar. 1970. *Reading Capital London*: New Left Books.

Åman, Jan. 1996. In the proceedings of a Symposium entitled "Form Follows Anything: Architecture, Power, Politics." October 3–6, at Färgfabriken, Stockhom, Sweden: 9.

Amin, A. and K. Robins. 1990. "The Re-emergence of Regional Economies? The Mythical Geography of Flexible Accumulation." *Environment and Planning D*, 8(1): 7–34.

Amin, Samir. 1976. *Unequal Development*. Translated by Brian Pearce. New York, NY: Monthly Review Press.

——. 1988. *Eurocentrism*, London: Zed Press.

Ammoore, Louise Richard Dodgson, Randall Germain, Barry K.Gills, Paul Langley, and Iain Watson. 2000. "International Political Economy and the Call to History." *Review of International Political Economy*, 7(1): 53–71.

Anderson, Perry. 1974. *Passages From Antiquity to Feudalism*, London: New Left Books.

Anonymous. 1998. "The Trouble With Mergers, Cont'd." *The Economist*. November 28: 17.

——. 1999. "Fear of the Unknown." *The Economist*. December 4: 61–2.

Ansari, Mohammed I. 1989. "The Dutch Disease: The Canadian Evidence." *Weltwirtschaftliches Archiv*, 125(4): 804–13.

Appadurai, Arjun (ed.). 1996. *Modernity at Large: Cultural Dimensions of Globalization.* Minneapolis: University of Minnesota Press.

——. 1988. *The Social Life of Things: Commodities in Cultural Perspective.* New York: Cambridge University Press.

Appleby, Joyce O. 1978. *Economic Thought and Ideology in Seventeenth-Century England.* Princeton, NJ: Princeton University Press.

Arrighi, Giovanni, Kenneth Barr, and Shuji Hisaeda. 1994. *The Long Twentieth Century.* London: Verso.

——. 1999a. "The Transformation of Business Enterprise." In *Chaos and Governance in the Modern World System*, eds, G. Arrighi and B. J. Silver. Minneapolis and London: University of Minnesota Press, pp. 97–150.

——. 1999b. "The World According to Andre Gunder Frank," *Review*, XXII(3): 327–54.

Ash, Timothy Garton. 2002. "On the Frontier." *New York Review of Books*, November 7: 60–1.

Ashcraft, Richard. 1996. "Religion and Lockean Natural Rights." In *Religious Diversity and Human Rights*, eds, Irene Bloom, J. Paul Martin, and Wayne L. Proudfoot. New York: Columbia University Press, pp. 195–212.

Atlan, Frédéric, Faadhel Lakhoua, Egidio Luis Miotti, Carlos Quenano, Quê Phuong Tran, and Nathalie Ricoeur-Nicolai. 1998. "Le rôle des taux de change dans les économies émergentes." In *Revue économique*, 49(1): 9–26.

Attfield, Robin and Barry Wilkinns. 1992. *International Justice and the Third World.* London: Routledge.

Aubet, Maria Eugenia. 1987/1993. *The Phoenicians and the West: Politics, Colonies and Trade.* Cambridge: Cambridge University Press.

Augelli, Enrico and Craig Murphy. 1997. "Consciousness, Myth, and Collective Action: Sorel, Gramsci, and the Ethical State." Paper presented at the annual meeting of the International Studies Association, March, Toronto.

Austin, J. L. 1962. *How to do Things with Words.* Cambridge, MA: Harvard University Press.

Ayubi, Nazih N. 1995. *Over-stating the Arab State: Politics and Society in the Middle East.* London: I. B. Tauris.

Babha, Homi. 1994. *The Location of Culture*. London: Routledge.

Bairoch, Paul. 1996. "Globalization, Myths and Realities: One Century of External Trade and Foreign Investment." In *States Against Markets. The Limits of Globalization*, eds, Robert Boyer and Daniel Drach. London: Routledge, pp. 173–92.

Ball, Terence. 1987. "Introduction." In *Idioms of Inquiry*, ed., T. Ball, Albany, NY: State University of New York Press, pp. 1–10.

Ball, Terence, James Farr, and Russell Hanson (eds). 1989. *Political Innovation and Conceptual Change*. New York, NY: Cambridge University Press.

Baran, Paul. A. and Paul M. Sweezy. 1966. *Monopoly Capital. An Essay on the American Economic and Social Order*. New York: Modern Reader Paperbacks.

Barber, Benjamin R. 1995. *Jihad vs McWorld. How Globalism and Tribalism are Reshaping the World*. New York: Random House.

Bardhan, Pranab. 1997. "Method in the Madness? A Political-Economy Analysis of the Ethnic Conflicts in Less Developed Countries." *World Development*, 25(9): 1399–407.

Barnet, Richard J. and John Cavanagh. 1994a. *Global Dreams: Imperial Corporations and the New World Order*. New York: Simon and Schuster.

——. 1994b. "Creating a Level Playing Field." *Technology Review*, May/June: 23–9.

Barnet, Richard J. and Ronald E. Muller, 1974. *Global Reach*. New York: Simon and Schuster.

Bar-On, Dan. 1999. *The Indescribable and the Undiscussable: Reconstructing Human Discourse After Trauma*. Budapest: Central European University Press.

Barry, Brian. 1989. "Humanity and Justice in Global Perspective." In *Democracy, Power and Justice: Essays in Political Theory*. Oxford: Clarendon Press, pp. 434–62.

Bartlett, C. J. 1984. *The Global Conflict, 1800–1970*. London: Longman.

Baudrillard, Jean. 1975. *The Mirror of Production*. Translated by M. Poster. St Louis, MO: Telos Press.

Baumol, W. J., A. S. Blinder, and W. M. Scarth. 1986. *Economics. Principles and Policies – Macroeconomics*. Canadian edition. Toronto: Academic Press Canada.

Beaujard, Philippe. 1995. "La violence dans les sociétés du sud-est du Madagascar." *Cahiers d'Etudes Africaines*, 35(2–3): 563–98.

Beaverstock, Jonathan V., Smith, Richard G., and Taylor, Peter J. 1999. "A Roster of World Cities." *Cities*, 16: 445–58.

Beck, Ulrich. 1992. *Risk Society: Towards a New Modernity*. Newbury Part, CA: Sage Publications.

Beechey, Veronica. 1987. *Unequal Work*. London: Verso.

——. 1988. "Rethinking the Definition of Work." In *Feminism of the Labor Force: Paradoxes and Promises*, eds, Jane Jenson, Elisabeth Hagen, and Ceallaigh Reddy. New York: Oxford University Press, pp. 45–62.

Beer, Francis A. and Robert Hariman (eds). 1996. *Post-Realism: The Rhetorical Turn in International Relations*. E. Lansing, MI: Michigan State University Press.

Beitz, Charles R. 1999. *Political Theory and International Relations*. 2nd edition Princeton, NJ: Princeton University Press.

Benabou, Roland. 2000. "Unequal Societies: Income Distribution and the Social Contract." *American Economic Review*, 90(1): 96–129.

Benda, Vaclav, Simecka, Milan. Jirous, Ivan M. Dienstbier, Jiri. Havel, Vaclav. Hejdanek, Ladislav. Simsa, Jan. 1988. "Parallel Polis; or An Independent Sociey in Central and Eastern Europe: An Inquiry." *Social Research*, 55: 211–26.

Benda-Beckman, Franz von. 1993. "Scapegoat and Magic Charm: Law in Development Theory and Practice." In *An Anthropological Critique of Development. The Growth of Ignorance*, ed., Mark Hobart. London: Routledge, pp. 116–34.

Bendix, Reinhard. 1956. *Work and Authority in Industry*. Berkeley: University of California Press.

Benedick, R. 1991. *Ozone Diplomacy: New Directions in Safeguarding the Planet*. Cambridge, MA: Harvard University Press.

Bennett, Tony. 1999. "Useful Culture." In *Representing the Nation*, eds, David Boswell and Jessica Evans. New York: Routledge, pp. 380–94.

Bentley, J. H. 1993. *Old World Encounters: Cross-Cultural Contacts and Exchanges in Pre-Modern Times*. Oxford: Oxford University Press.

Bergeljik, Peter and Nico W. Mensik. 1997. "Measuring Globalization." *Journal of World Trade*, 31(3): 159–68.

Berger, John. 1972. *Ways of Seeing*. London: British Broadcasting Corporation and Penguin Books.

Berger, Peter and Thomas Luckmann. 1967. *The Social Construction of Reality*. New York, NY: Anchor Books.

Berkner, Lloyd V. 1950. *Science and Foreign Relations*. Washington, DC: Department of State.

——. 1959. *Reminiscences of the International Geophysical Year*. No. 354. New York, NY: Columbia University Oral History Research Office.

Berle Jr, A. A. and G. C. Means. 1932/1967. *The Modern Corporation and Private Property*. Revised edition New York: Harcourt, Brace & World.

Berlin, Isaiah. 1962. "Does Political Theory Still Exist?" In *Philosophy, Politics, and Society*. 2nd series, ed., I. Berlin. Oxford, England: Basil Blackwell.

——. 1969. "Two Concepts of Liberty." In *Four Essays on Liberty*. Oxford: Oxford University Press, pp. 118–72.

Berman, Marshall. 1988. *All that is Solid Melts into Air*. New York: Penguin.

Bernstein, Richard J. 1976. *The Restructuring of Social and Political Theory*. Philadelphia, PA: University of Pennsylvania Press.

——. 1983. *Beyond Objectivism and Relativism*. Philadelphia, PA: University of Pennsylvania Press.

——. 1985. "Introduction." In *Habermas and Modernity*, ed., R. Bernstein. Cambridge, MA: MIT Press, pp. 1–32.

——. 1991. *The New Constellation: The Ethical–Political Horizons of Modernity/Postmodernity*. Cambridge, England: Polity Press.

——. 1992. "The Resurgence of Pragmatism." *Social Research*, 59(4): 813–40.

Bhagat, Sanjai, Andrei Shleifer, and Robert W. Vishny. 1990. "Hostile Takeovers in the 1980s: The Return to Corporate Specialization." *Brookings Papers on Economic Activity: Microeconomics*, 1–85.

Bhagwati, Jagdish. 1989. "Is Free Trade Passé After All?" *Weltwirtschaftliches Archiv*, 125(1): 17–44.

Bicanic, Rudolf. 1962. "The Threshold of Economic Growth." *Kyklos*, 15(1): 7–28.

Bichler, Shimshon. 1986. "The Political Economy of Military Spending in Israel. Several Aspects of the Activities of Dominant Capital Groups." Unpublished Master's Thesis, Political Science, Hebrew University, Jerusalem.

——. 1991. "The Political Economy of Military Spending in Israel." Unpublished Doctoral Dissertation, Political Science, Hebrew University, Jerusalem.

——. 1994–1995. "Political Power Shifts in Israel, 1977 and 1992: Unsuccessful Electoral Economics or Long Range Realignment?" *Science & Society*, 58(4): 415–39.

Bichler, Shimshon and Jonathan Nitzan. 1996a. "Military Spending and Differential Accumulation: A New Approach to the Political Economy of Armament – The Case of Israel." *Review of Radical Political Economics*, 28(1): 52–97.

Bichler, Shimshon and Jonathan Nitzan. 1996b. "Putting the State in its Place: US Foreign Policy and Differential Accumulation in Middle-East 'Energy Conflicts'." *Review of International Political Economy*, 3(4): 613–66.

Biersteker, Thomas. 1989. "Critical Reflections on Post-Positivism in International Relations." *International Studies Quarterly*, 33(3): 263–7.

——. 1998. "Globalization and the Modes of Operation of Major Institutional Actors." *Oxford Development Studies*, 26(1): 15–31.

Biology and Philosophy. 1993. Special Issue: "Integration in Biology," 8(3).

Birdsall, Nancy, David Ross, and Richard Sabot. 1995. "Inequality and Growth Reconsidered: Lessons from East Asia." *World Bank Economic Review*, 9(3): 477–508.

Bishop, Ryan and Lillian Robinson. 1998. *Night Market: Sexual Cultures and the Thai Economic Miracle*. New York: Routledge.

Blair, John M. 1972. *Economic Concentration: Structure, Behavior and Public Policy*. New York: Harcourt, Brace Jovanovich.

Blank, Stephen. 1994. "The Return of the Repressed? Post-1989 Nationalism in the 'New' Eastern Europe." *Nationalities Papers*, 22(2): 405–25.

Blau, Judith R. and Peter M. Blau. 1982. "The Cost of Inequality: Metropolitan Structure and Violent Crime." *American Sociological Review*, 27: 15–26.

Blaut, James M. (ed.). 1992. *1492: The Debate on Colonialism, Eurocentrism and History*. Trenton NJ: Africa World Press.

——. 1993. *The Colonizer's Model of the World: Geographical Diffusionism and Eurocentric History*. New York: Guilford Press.

Blinder, Alan S. 1979. *Economic Policy and the Great Stagflation*. New York: Academic Press.

Bliss, C. J. 1975. *Capital Theory and the Distribution of Income*. Amsterdam and Oxford: North–Holland Pub. Co.

Bloch, M. 1967. "Natural economy or money economy: a pseudo-dilemma." In *Land and Work in Medieval Europe, Papers by Marc Bloch*, ed., J. E. Anderson. London, pp. 230–43.

Bloch, R. Howard and Stephen G. Nichols. 1996. "Introduction." In *Medievalism and the Modernist Temper*, ed., R. H. Bloch and S. G. Nichols. Baltimore, MD: Johns Hopkins University Press.

Bobak, Martin, Hynek Pikhart, Claude Hertzman, Richard Rose, Michael Marmot. 1998. "Socioeconomic Factors, Perceived Control and Self-Reported Health in Russia." A Cross-Sectional Survey. *Social Science and Medicine*, 47(2): 269–79.

Boehmer-Christianson, S. 1994. "Global Climate Protection Policy: The Limits of Scientific Advice." *Global Environmental Change*, 4(2): 140–59.

Bohman, James. 1991. *New Philosophy of Science*. Cambridge, MA: MIT Press.

Bordo, Susan. 1993. *Unbearable Weight: Feminism, Western Culture, and the Body*. Berkeley: University of California Press.

Boris, Eileen. 1996. "Sexual Divisions, Gender Constructions." In *Homeworkers in Global Perspective*, eds, Eileen Boris and Lisa Prugl. New York: Routledge, pp. 19–37.

Boris, Eileen and Elisabeth Prugl (eds). 1996. *Homeworkers in Global Perspective*. New York: Routledge.

Bortkiewicz, L. von. 1907. "Wertrechnung und Preisrechnung im Marxschen System, 3. Teil." *Archiv für Sozialwissenschaft und Sozialpolitik*, 25(2): 455–89.

Bottomore, Tom (ed.). 1991. *A Dictionary of Marxist Thought*. Oxford: Blackwell Publishers.

Bourdieu, Pierre. 1984. *Distinction: A Social Critique of the Judgement of Taste*. New York: Routledge & Kegan Paul.

Bourdieu, Pierre and Alain Darbel. 1969. *L'Amour de l'art: Les Musées d'art européens et leur public*. Paris: Editions de minuit.

Bourgois, Philippe I. 1989. *Ethnicity at Work. Divided Labor on a Central American Banana Plantation*. Baltimore: Johns Hopkins University Press.

——. 1995. *In Search of Respect. Selling Crack in El Barrio*. Cambridge: Cambridge University Press.

Bourguignon, Francois. 1999. *Crime, Violence and Inequitable Development*. Paper presented at the World Bank Conference on Development Economics. Washington, DC: April.

Bourguignon, François, Jaime de Melo, and Christian Morrison. 1991. "Poverty and Adjustment: Issues and Evidence from the OECD Project." *World Development*, 19(11): 1485–508.

Bovenberg, A. Lans and Roger H. Gordon. 1996. "Why is Capital so Immobile Internationally? Possible Explanations and Implications for Capital Income Taxation." *American Economic Review*, 86(5): 1057–76.

Bowles, Samuel. 1981. "Technical Change and the Profit Rate: A Simple Proof of the Okishio Theorem." *Cambridge Journal of Economics*, 5(2): 183–6.

Boyer, Robert. 1996. *The Seven Paradoxes of Capitalism. Or is a Theory of Modern Economies Still Possible?* Paris: CEPRMAP, October.

Bradford, Colin I. 1987. "Trade and Structural Change: NICs and Next Tier NICc as Transitional Economies." *World Development*, 15(3): 299–316.

Braidotti, Rosi. 1994. *Nomadic Subjects: Embodiment and Sexual Difference in Contemporary Feminist Theory*. New York: Columbia University Press.

Braudel, Fernand. 1984. *Civilization & Capitalism, 15th–18th Century*. Trans. from the French and Revised by Sian Reynolds, 3 vols. New York: Harper & Row.

Brealey, Richard, Stewart Myers, Gordon Sick, and Ronald Giammarino. 1992. *Principles of Corporate Finance*. 2nd Canadian edition. Toronto: McGraw-Hill Ryerson Limited.

Brenner, Robert. 1997. "The Origins of Capitalist Development: A Critique of Neo-Smithian Marxism." *New Left Review*, 104(July–August): 25–92.

Brewer, Anthony. 1989. *Marxist Theories of Imperialism*. London: Routledge.

Broad, Dave. 2000. "The Periodic Casualization of Work: The Informal Economy, Casual Labor, and the *Longue Durée*." In *Informalization: Process and Structure*, eds, Faruk Tabak and Michaeline A. Crichlow. Baltimore and London: The Johns Hopkins University Press, pp. 23–46.

Brown, Chris. 1992. *International Relations Theory: New Normative Approaches*. London: Harvester Wheatsheaf.

Brown, D. 1924. "Pricing Policy in Relation to Financial Control." *Management and Administration*, February: 195–8; March: 283–6; April: 417–22.

Bruce, Steve. 1993. "Fundamentalism, Ethnicity, and Enclave." In *Fundamentalisms and the State: Remaking Politics, Economics and Militance*, eds, Martin Marty and R. Scott Appleby. Chicago: University of Chicago Press, pp. 50–67.

Bruno, Michael and Jeffrey Sachs. 1985. *Economics of Worldwide Stagflation*. Cambridge, MA: Harvard University Press.

Buchanan, Neil H. and Harvey D. Wilmeth. 1998. *Unified Economic Theory: Conceptual Foundations and Policy Implications. Fifth Post Keynesian Workshop: Full Employment and Price Stability in a Global Economy*. Knoxville: MS July.

Burbach, Roger and William I. Robinson. 1999. "The Fin De Siecle Debate: Globalization as Epochal Shift." *Science & Society*, 63(1): 10–39.

Burch, Kurt. 1995. "Invigorating World-systems Theory as Critical Theory: Exploring Philosophical Foundations and Postpositivism." *Journal of World System Research*, 1(1): 1–107.

——. 1997. "Constituting IPE and Modernity." In *Constituting International Political Economy*, eds, K. Burch and R. Denemark. Boulder, CO: Lynne Rienner Publishers, pp. 21–40.

Burch, Kurt. 1998. *"Property" and the Making of the International System: Constituting Sovereignty, Political Economy, and the Modern Era*. Boulder, CO: Lynne Rienner Publishers.

——. 2001. "Toward a Constructivist Comparative Politics." In *Constructivism and Comparative Politics*, ed., D. Green. Armonk, NJ: M. E. Sharpe.

Burley, A. M. 1993. "Regulating the World: Multilateralism, International Law, and the Projection of the New Deal Regulatory State." In *Multilateralism Matters: The Theory and Praxis of an Institutional Form*, ed., J. G. Ruggie. New York, NY: Columbia University Press, pp. 125–56.

Burton, John W. 1997. *Violence Explained: The Sources of Conflict, Violence and Crime and their Prevention*. Manchester: Manchester University Press.

Butler, Judith. 1997. *The Psychic Life of Power*. Stanford: Stanford University Press.

Byrne, John A. 2000. "Visionary vs. Visionary." *Business Week*, August 28: 210–12.

Bystydzienski, Jill M. and Joti Sekhorn. 1999. "Introduction." In *Democratization and Women's Grassroots Movements*, eds, Jill M. Bystydzienski and Joti Sekhorn. Bloomington: Indiana University Press, pp. 1–21.

Caballé, Jordi and Manuel S. Santos. 1993. "On Endogenous Growth with Physical and Human Capital." *Journal of Political Economy*, 101(6): 1042–67.

Çağatay, Nilufer and Sule Ozler. 1995. Feminization of the Labor Force. *World Development*, 23(11) November: 1883–94.

Cairncross, Alec Kirkland. 1953. *Home and Foreign Investment 1870–1913. Studies in Capital Accumulation*. Cambridge: Cambridge University Press.

Calhoun, Craig J., Edward LiPuma, and Moishe Postone. 1993. *Bourdieu : Critical Perspectives*. Chicago: University of Chicago Press.

Callinicos, Alex. 1999. *Social Theory: A Historical Introduction*. New York, NY: New York University Press.

Cameron, Rondo. 1976. Book review of *The Modern World-System*. *Journal of Interdisciplinary History*, 7(1): 140–4.

Caporaso, James A. (ed.). 2000. *Continuity and Change in the Westphalian Order*. Malden, MA: Blackwell Publishers.

Caporaso, James A. and David A. Levine. 1992. *Theories of Political Economy*. Cambridge: Cambridge University Press.

Cardoso, Fernando Henrique and Enzo Faletto. 1979. *Dependency and Development in Latin America*. Translated by Marjory M. Urquidi. Berkeley, CA: University of California Press.

Carrington, William J. and Enrica Detragiache. 1998. "How big is the brain drain?" Working Paper 98/102. International Monetary Fund, Washington, DC.

Castells, Manuel. 1996. *The Rise of Network Society*. Oxford: Blackwell.

——. 2000. *The Rise of the Network Society*. 2nd edition, Oxford: Blackwell.

Castells, Manuel and Alejandro Portes. 1989. "World Underneath: The Origins, Dynamics, and Effects of the Informal Economy." In *The Informal Economy: Studies in Advanced and Less Developed Countries*, eds, Alejandro Portes, Manuel Castells, and Lauren A. Benton. Baltimore: Johns Hopkins University Press, pp. 11–37.

Caves, Richard. 1989. "Mergers, Takeovers, and Economic Efficiency: Foresight vs. Hindsight." *International Journal of Industrial Organization*, 7: 151–74.

Central Intelligence Agency (CIA). 1974. *Potential Implications of Trends in Food, Population, and Climate*. Washington, DC: US Government Printing Office.

Cerny, Philip G. 1990. *The Changing Architecture of Politics: Structure, Agency, and the Future of the State*. London: Sage.

—— (ed.). 1993. *Finance and World Politics*. Aldeshot, England: Edward Elgar.

——. 1994. "The dynamics of financial globalization: technology, market structure, and policy response." *Policy Sciences*, 27: 319–42.

——. 1995. "Globalization and the Changing Logic of Collective Action." *International Organization*, 49(4): 595–625.

——. 1996. "What Next for the State?" In *Globalization: Theory and Practice*, eds, Eleonore Kofman and Gillian Youngs. London: Pinter, pp. 123–37.

Chambers, Robert. 1995. *Poverty and Livelihoods. Whose Reality Counts?* Sussex: Institute for Development Studies, Discussion Paper no. 347.

Chandler, Jr. Alfred D. 1977. *The Visible Hand: The Managerial Revolution in American Business*. Cambridge, MA: Belknap Press.

Chant, Sylvia. 1997. *Women-Headed Households: Diversity and Dynamics in the Developing World*. New York: St Martin's Press.

Chase-Dunn, Christopher. 1981. "Interstate System and Capitalist World-Economy: One Logic or Two?" *International Studies Quarterly*, 25(1): 19–42.

——. 1982. "Commentary." In *World-Systems Analysis: Theory and Methodology*, eds, T. Hopkins and I. Wallerstein. Beverly Hills, CA: Sage, pp. 181–5.

——. 1989. *Global Formation*. Cambridge, MA: Basil Blackwell.

——. 1992. "The Comparative Study of World-Systems." *Review*, XV(3): 313–33.

Chase-Dunn, Christopher and Thomas D. Hall (eds). 1991. *Core/Periphery Relations in Precapitalist Worlds*. Boulder, CO: Westview Press.

——. 1992. "World-Systems and Modes of Production: Toward the Comparative Study of Transformations." *Humboldt Journal of Social Relations*, 18(1): 81–117.

——. 1993a. "Comparing World-Systems." *Social Forces*, 71: 851–86.

—— (eds). 1993b. "The Unity and Disunity of Indian Ocean History from the Rise of Islam to 1750: The Outline of a Theory and Historical Discourse." *Journal of World History*, 4(1): 1–21.

——. 1994. "The Historical Evolution of World-Systems." *Sociological Inquiry*, 64(3): 257–80.

——. 1997. *Rise and Demise: Comparing World-Systems*. Boulder, CO: Westview Press.

Chaudhuri, K. N. 1985/1997. *Trade and Civilisation in the Indian Ocean: An Economic History from the Rise of Islam to 1750*. Cambridge: Cambridge University Press.

——. 1990. *Asia Before Europe: Economy and Civilisation of the Indian Ocean from the Rise of Islam to 1750*, Cambridge: Cambridge University Press.

Chen, Haichun, M. J. Gordon and Zhiming Yan. 1994. "The Real Income and Consumption of an Urban Chinese Family." *Journal of Development Studies*, 31(1): 201–13.

Childe, Gordon. 1942. *What Happened in History*. Harmondsworth: Pelican.

Chin, Christine B. N. 1998. *In Service and Servitude: Foreign Female Domestic Workers and the Malaysian 'Modernity' Project*. New York: Columbia University Press.

Chirot, Daniel. 1980. "Book Review" of *The Capitalist World-Economy* (Wallerstein, 1979) and *National Development and the World System* (Meyer and Hannan, eds). *Social Forces*, 59(2): 538–43.

Christie, Daniel J. 1997. "Reducing Direct and Structural Violence: The Human Needs Theory." *Peace and Conflict: Journal of Peace Psychology*, 3(4): 315–32.

Clausewitz, Carl von. 1968. *On War*. London: Penguin.

Cloud, Kathleen and Nancy Garrett. 1997. "A Modest Proposal for Inclusion of Women's Household Human Capital Production in Analysis of Structural Transformation. *Feminist Economics*, 3(1): 151–77.

Coase, Ronald H. 1937/1996. "The Nature of the Firm." In *The Economic Nature of the Firm: A Reader*, eds, L. Putterman and R. S. Kroszner. Cambridge: Cambridge University Press, pp. 89–104.

Cochran, Molly. 1999. *Normative Theory in International Relations: A Pragmatic Approach.* New York, NY: Cambridge University Press.

Cock, Jacklyn. 1980. *Maids and Madams: A Study in the Politics of Exploitation.* Johannesburg: Ravan Press.

Coetzee, J. M. 1980. *Waiting for the Barbarians.* New York: Penguin Books.

Cohen, Benjamin J. 1993. "The Triad and the Unholy Trinity: Lessons for the Pacific Region." In *Pacific Economic Relations in the 1990s: Cooperation or Conflict*, eds, R. Higgott, R. Leaver and J. Ravenhill. Boulder, CO: Lynne Rienner Publishers, pp. 133–58.

——. 1996. "Phoenix Rise: The Resurrection of Global Finance." *World Politics*, 48(2): 268–96.

——. 1998. *The Geography of Money.* Ithaca, NY: Cornell University Press.

Cohen, Rina. 1994. A Brief History of Racism in Immigration Policies for Recruiting Domestics. *Canadian Woman Studies/Les Cahiers de la Femme*, 14(2): 83–6.

Colás, Alejandro. 1994. "Putting Cosmopolitanism into Practice: the Case of Socialist Internationalism" *Millennium: Journal of International Studies*, 23(3): 513–34.

——. 2002. *International Civil Society.* Cambridge, UK: Polity.

Colin, Jean-Philippe and Bruno Losch. 1990. "Touche pas à mon planteur. Réflexions sur les 'encadrements' paysans à travers quelques examples ivoriens." *Politique Africaine*, 40: 83–99.

Collier, Paul. 2000. Economic Causes of Civil Conflict and their Implications for Policy. In *Managing Global Chaos*, eds, Chester A. Crocker and Fen Osler Hampson, with Pamela Aall. Washington, DC: US Institute of Peace.

Collins, Susan M. and Barry P. Bosworth. 1996. "Economic Growth in East Asia: Accumulation versus Assimilation." *Brookings Papers on Economic Activity*, 2: 135–203.

Connolly, William. 1981. *Appearance and Reality in Politics.* New York, NY: Cambridge University Press.

——. 1983. *Terms of Political Discourse.* Princeton, NJ: Princeton University Press.

Cook, Terry. 1984. "A Reconstruction of the World: George R. Parkin's British Empire map of 1893." *Cartographia*, 21(4), 53–65.

Corbridge, Stuart, and Nigel Thrift. 1994. "Money, Power and Space. Introduction and Overview." In *Money, Power and Space*, eds, Stuart Corbridge, Nigel Thrift and Ron Martin. Oxford: Blackwell, pp. 1–25.

Cosgrove, D. 1994. "Contested Global Visions: One-world, Whole-world, and the Apollo Space Photographs." *Annals of the Association of American Geographers*, 84(2): 270–94.

Costello, Donna M. 1993. "A Cross-Country, Cross-Industry Comparison of Productivity Growth." *Journal of Political Economy*, 101(2): 207–22.

Cournot, Augustin. 1838/1929. *Researches Into the Mathematical Principles of the Theory of Wealth.* Trans. N. T. Bacon. New York: Macmillan.

Cox, Robert W. 1981. "Social Forces, States, and World Order: Beyond International Relations Theory." *Millennium*, 10(2): 126–55.

——. 1987. *Power, Production and World Order: Social Forces in the Making of History.* New York: Columbia University Press.

———. 1991. The Global Political Economy and Social Choice. In *The New Era of Global Competition*, eds, Daniel Drache and Meric S. Gertler. Montreal: McGill-Queen's University Press, pp. 335–50.

Crafts, Nicholas F. R. 1996. "The First Industrial Revolution: A Guided Tour for Growth Economists." *American Economic Review*, 86(1): 197–206.

Crossan, John Dominic. 1998. *The Birth of Christianity: Discovering What Happened in the Years Immediately After the Execution of Jesus*. San Francisco: Harper Collins.

Crutchfield, Robert D. 1989. "Labor Stratification and Violent Crime." *Social Forces*, 68(2): 489–512.

Currier, Carrie. 1999. Sex and the International Political Economy: Unmasking Biases and Establishing Connections in Southeast Asia's Sex Industry. Unpublished paper.

Curtin, Philip D. 1984. *Cross-Cultural Trade in World History*. Cambridge: Cambridge University Press.

Cusack, Mary Frances. 1868/1995. *An Illustrated History of Ireland: from AD 400 to 1800*. London: Bracken Books.

Cypher, James M. 1991. "La política de México para la promoción de exportaciones: Un nuevo patrón de acumulación?" *Revista Mexicana de Sociología*, 53(3): 81–111.

Dasgupta, Partha. 1993. *An Inquiry into Well-Being and Destitution*. Oxford, England: Oxford University Press.

Davis, Ann. 1997. "Class, Gender, and Culture: A Discussion of Marxism, Feminism, and Postmodernism." In *Gender and Political Economy*, eds, Ellen Mutari, Heather Boushey, and William Fraher IV. Armonk, NY and London: M.E. Sharpe, pp. 92–111.

Davis, Mike. 1992. *City of Quartz*. New York: Vintage.

Deane, Phyllis and W. A. Cole. 1967. *British Economic Growth 1688–1959. Trends and Structures*. Cambridge: Cambridge University Press.

Dear, P. 1995. *Discipline and Experience: The Mathematical Way in the Scientific Revolution*. Chicago, IL: Chicago University Press.

De Certeau, Michel. 1984. *The Practice of Everyday Life*. Berkeley: University of California Press.

De Grazia, Victoria and Ellen Furlough (eds). 1996. *The Sex of Things: Gender and Consumption in Historical Perspective*. Berkeley: University of California Press.

Denemark, Robert. 1999. "World System History: From International Politics to the Study of Global Relations." In *Prospects for International Relations*, ed., D. Bobrow. Malden, MA: Blackwell Publishers, pp. 43–75.

———. 2000. "Cumulation and Direction in World System History." In *World System History: The Social Science of Long-Term Change*, eds, R. Denemark, Jonathan Friedman, Barry K. Gills and George Modelski. London: Routledge, pp. 299–312.

Denemark, Robert and Kenneth P. Thomas. 1988. "The Brenner-Wallerstein Debate." *International Studies Quarterly*, 32(1): 47–65.

Denemark, Robert and Jonathan Friedman, Barry K. Gills and George Modelski (eds). 2000. *World System History: The Social Science of Long Term Change*. London: Routledge.

Dennis, Michael. 1994. "'Our First Line of Defense' Two University Laboratories in the Postwar American State." *Isis*, 85(3): 427–55.

Deolalikar, Anil B. 1988. "Nutrition and Labor Productivity in Agriculture: Estimates for Rural South India." *Review of Economics and Statistics*, 70(3): 406–13.

Der Derian, James. 1992. *Antidiplomacy: Spies, Terror, Speed and War*. Cambridge, MA: Blackwell Publishers.

Der Derian, James and Michael J. Shapiro (eds). 1989. *International/Intertextual Relations*. Lexington, MA: Lexington Books.

Derrida, Jacques. 1977. *Of Grammatology*. Trans. by G.C. Spivak. Baltimore, MD: Johns Hopkins University Press.

Deutche Bundesbank. 2002. *Monthly Report*, March, vol. 54. http://www.bundes bank.de/vo/vo_mb.en.php (accessed 06.05.2003).

Diamond, Jared. 1997. *Guns, Germs, and Steel: The Fates of Human Societies*. New York: W. W. Norton.

Didion, Joan. 2000. "God's Country." *New York Review of Books*, November 2: 68–70, 72–6.

Diebert, Ronald. 1997. *Parchment, Printing and Hypermedia: Communication in World Order Transformation*. New York: Columbia University Press.

Dietrich Rueschemeyer and Theda Skocpol. 1995. *States, Social Knowledge, and the Origins of Modern Social Policies*. Princeton: Princeton University Press.

Division for the Advancement of Women (DAW): United Nations. 1999. *World Survey on the Role of Women in Development*. New York: United Nations.

Dodd, Nigel. 1999. *Social Theory and Modernity*. Malden, MA: Polity Press.

Doganlar, Murat. 1999. "Testing Long-run Validity of Purchasing Parity for Asian Countries." *Indian Journal of Economics*, 79(314): 277–84.

Dollar, David and Edward N. Wolff. 1988. "Convergence of Industry Labor Productivity among Advanced Economies 1963–1982." *Review of Economics and Statistics*, 70(4): 549–58.

Domar, Evsey D. 1961. "The Capital–Output Ratio in the United States: Its Variation and Stability." In *The Theory of Capital*, eds, F. A. Lutz and D. C. Hague. New York, London: Macmillan, St Martin's Press, pp. 95–117.

Domhoff, G. William. 1996. *State Autonomy or Class Dominance? Case Studies on Policy Making in America*. Aldine DeGruyter.

Doremus, Paul N., William W. Keller, Louis W. Pauly, and Simon Reich. 1998. *The Myth of the Global Corporation*. Princeton, NJ: Princeton University Press.

Dos Santos, Theotonio. 1970. "The Structure of Dependence." *American Economic Review*, 60(2): 231–6.

Doty, Roxanne. 1996. *Imperial Encounters: The Politics of Representation in North–South Relations*. Minneapolis, MN: University of Minnesota Press.

Doyle, Michael W. 1997. *Ways of War and Peace*. New York and London: W.W. Norton.

Drucker, Peter F. 1986. "The Changed World Economy." *Foreign Affairs*, 64(4): 768–91.

——. 1997. "The Global Economy and the Nation-State." *Foreign Affairs*, 76(5): 159–71.

Dryzek, John S. 1995. "Critical Theory as a Research Program." In *The Cambridge Companion to Habermas*, ed., S. K. White. New York, NY: Cambridge University Press, pp. 97–119.

Dryzek, John S. and Jeffrey Berejikian. 1993. "Reconstructive Democratic Theory." *American Political Science Review*, 87(1): 48–60.

Du Boff, Richard D., Edward S. Herman, William K. Tabb, and Ellen Meiksins Wood. 1997. "Debate on Globalization." *Monthly Review*, 49(6): 27–43.

Du Gay, Paul. 1996. "Organizing Identity: Entrepreneurial Governance and Public Management." In *Questions of Cultural Identity*, eds, Stuart Hall and Paul du Gay. London: Sage, pp. 151–69.

Duncan, Carol. 1993. *The Aesthetics of Power*. New York: Cambridge University Press.

——. 1995. *Civilizing Rituals: Inside Public Art Museums*. New York: Routledge.

Dunn, John. 1985. *Rethinking Modern Political Theory: Essays 1979–1983*. New York, NY: Cambridge University Press.

Dutt, Amitava Krishna. 1991. "Stagnation, Income Distribution and the Agrarian Constraint: A Note." *Cambridge Journal of Economics*, 15(3): 343–51.

Eagleton, Terry. 1991. *Ideology: An Introduction.* New York, NY: Verso.

The Economist. 1997. October 18.

———. 1998. *Pocket World in Figures 1999.* New York: John Wiley & Sons, Inc.

———. 1999a. August 28.

———. 1999b. *Pocket World in Figures.* New York: John Wiley & Sons, Inc.

Edgecliffe-Johnson, Andrew. 2000. "Feeding Frenzy." *Financial Times.* June 8: 14.

Edwards, Sebastian. 1989. "Exchange Rate Misalignment in Developing Countries." *World Bank Research Observer,* 1(1) 3–21.

Edwards, P. 2001. "Representing the Global Atmosphere." In *Changing the Atmosphere: Expert Knowledge and Global Environmental Governance,* eds, C. A. Miller and P. N. Edwards. Cambridge, MA: MIT Press, pp. 31–66.

Edwards, P. and S. Schneider. 2001. "Self-Governance and Peer Review in Science-for-Policy." In *Changing the Atmosphere: Expert Knowledge and Global Environmental Governance,* eds, C. A. Miller and P. N. Edwards. Cambridge, MA: MIT Press, pp. 219–46.

Eichengreen, Barry. 1996. *Globalizing Capital: A History of the International Monetary System.* Princeton, NJ: Princeton University Press.

———. 1998. "Dental Hygiene and Nuclear War: How International Relations Looks from Economics." *International Organization,* 52: 4, pp. 993–1012.

Eis, Carl. 1969. "The 1919–1930 Merger Movement in American Industry." *The Journal of Law and Economics,* 12(2): 267–96.

Eisenstadt, S. N. 1963. *The Political Systems of Empires.* Glencoe, IL: The Free Press, pp. 993–1012.

Eisenstein, Zillah R. 1998. *Global Obscenities: Patriarchy, Capitalism, and the Lure of Cyberfantasy.* New York: New York University Press.

Ekholm, K. and J. Friedman. 1982. "'Capital' Imperialism and Exploitation in Ancient World Systems." *Review,* 4(1): 87–109; also in Frank and Gills (eds). 1993/6. *The World System* op. cit., London: Routledge, pp. 59–80.

Elsenhans, Hartmut. 1975. "Overcoming Underdevelopment. A Research Paradigm." *Journal of Peace Research,* 12(4): 293–313.

———. 1981. "Social Consequences of the NIEO. Structural Change in the Periphery as Precondition for Continual Reforms in the Centre." In *Elements of World Instability: Armaments, Communication, Food, International Division of Labor,* eds, Egbert Jahn and Yoshikazu Sakamoto. Frankfurt am Main/New York: Campus, pp. 86–95.

———. 1983. "Rising Mass Incomes as a Condition of Capitalist Growth: Implications for the World Economy." *International Organization,* 37(1): 1–38.

———. 1987. "Absorbing Global Surplus Labor." *Annals of the American Academy of Political and Social Science,* 492: 124–35.

———. 1991. "Problems Central to Economic Policy Deregulation in Bangladesh." *Internationales Asienforum,* 22(3/4): 259–86.

———. 1994. "Rent, State and the Market: The Political Economy of the Transition to Self-sustained Capitalism." *Pakistan Development Review,* 33(4): 393–428.

———. 1995a. "Marginality, Rent and Non-Governmental Organizations." *Indian Journal of Public Administration,* 41(2): 139–59.

———. 1995b. "Überwindung von Marginalität als Gegenstand der Armutsbekämpfung." In *Bevölkerungsdynamik und Grundbedürfnisse in Entwicklungsländern: Schriften des Vereins für Socialpolitik 241,* ed., Hans Bernd Schäfer. Berlin: Duncker & Humblot, pp. 193–221.

———. 1996a. "A Welfare Capitalist World System or the Feudalisation of the Global System." In *Changing Global Political/Ideological Context and Afro-Asia Strategies for Development,* ed., B. Ramesh Babu. New Delhi: South Asian Books, pp. 57–130.

Elsenhans, Hartmut. 1996b. *Eléments pour une théorie de l'importance de la demande dans la crois-sance capitaliste. Textes de Recherche 33*. Paris: IEDES.

——. 1997a. "Globalization: Myths and Real Challenges." *Journal of the Third World Spectrum*, 4(2): 1–22.

——. 1997b. "Rent and the Transition to Capitalism." *Asien-Afrika-Lateinamerika*, 25(6): 651–86.

——. 1998. "Europäische Einigung unter dem Druck der Globalisierung." *Berichte. Forschungsinstitut der IWVWW*, 8(66): 11–34.

——. 1999a. "Autonomy of Civil Society, Empowerment of Labor, and the Transition to Capitalism." In *Bureaucracy – Citizen Interface: Conflict and Consensus*, eds, Randhir B. Jain and Renu Khator. New Delhi: B.R. Publishing Corporation, pp. 15–60.

——. 1999b "Globalisation and the European Integration Process." *International Studies*, 36(3): 217–35.

——. 1999c. "Globalization or Dutch Disease: Its Political and Social Consequences." in *Technological Diffusion in the Third World. New World Order Series*, vol. 16 (Part I), eds, Hans Wolfgang Singer, Neelambar Hatti, and Rameshwar Tandon. New Delhi: B.R. Publishing Corporation, pp. 425–69.

——. 1999d. "Individualistische Strategien der Haushalte zur Zukunftssicherung: Grundlage für den Niedergang des wohlfahrtsstaatlichen Kapitalismus." *Comparativ. Leipziger Beiträge zur Universalgeschichte und vergleichenden Gesellschaftsforschung*, 9(3).

——. 1999e. "Rent and Technology Distortion: The Two Cul-de-Sac of State Correction and Market Orientation in IAC and IBC." *Journal of the Third World Spectrum*, 6(1): 33–56.

——. 2000a. "Einbettende Strukturen oder steigende Masseneinkommen als Ursache von Wachstum durch Marktwirtschaft." In *Die politische Konstitution von Märkten*, eds, Roland Czada and Susanne Lütz. Opladen: Westdeutscher Verlag, pp. 73–88.

——. 2000b. "Globalisation in a Labourist Keynesian Approach." *Journal of Social Studies*, 89 July–September: 1–66.

——. 2000c. "Die Globalisierung der Finanzmärkte und die Entstehung einer neuen Rentenklasse." In *Vom Ewigen Frieden und vom Wohlstand der Nationen. Dieter Senghaas zum 60. Geburtstag*, ed., Ulrich Menzel. Frankfurt am Main: Suhrkamp, pp. 518–42.

——. 2000d. *La guerre d'Algérie 1954–1962. La transition d'une France à une autre. Le passage de la IV à la Ve République*. Paris: Publisud.

——. 2000e. "Political Economy or Economic Politics? The Prospects of Civil Society in an Era of Globalization." *Indian Journal of Public Administration*, 46(4).

——. 2000f. "The Rise and Fall of Really Existing Socialism." *Journal of Social Studies*, 87 January–March: 1–16.

——. 2001. *Das Internationale System zwischen Zivilgesellschaft und Rente*. Münster: Lit.

Elson, Diane and Ruth Pearson. 1981. "The Subordination of Women and the Internationalization of Factory Production." In *Of Marriage and Market: Women's Subordination in International Perspective*, eds, K. Young, C. Wolkowitz and C. McCullagh. London: CSE Books, pp. 144–66.

Emmanuel, Arghiri. 1969. *L'échange inégal. Essai sur les antagonismes dans les rapports économiques internationaux*. Paris: Maspéro.

——. 1972. *Unequal Exchange: A Study of the Imperialism of Trade*. Trans. by Brian Pearce. Additional comments by Charles Bettelheim. New York, NY: Monthly Review Press.

Enders, Klaus and Horst Herberg. 1983. "The Dutch Disease: Causes, Consequences, Cures and Calmatives." *Weltwirtschaftliches Archiv*, 119(3): 473–95.

Engel, G. L. 1968. "A life-Setting Conducive to Illness. The Giving Up–Given Up Complex." *Annals of Internal medicine*, 69: 293–9.

Enloe, Cynthia. 1990. *Bananas, Beaches and Bases: Making Feminist Sense of International Politics*. Berkeley: University of California Press.

Epstein, Gerald and Herbert Gintis. 1995. "International Capital Markets and National Economic Policy." *Review of International Political Economy*, 2(4): 693–718.

Escobar, Arturo. 1995. *Encountering Development : The Making and Unmaking of the Third World*. Princeton: Princeton University Press.

Evans, Peter. 1979. *Dependent Development*. Princeton, NJ: Princeton University Press.

Ezrahi, Y. 1990. *The Descent of Icarus: Science and the Transformation of Contemporary Democracy*. Cambridge, MA: Harvard University Press.

Farmer, Paul. 1996. "On Suffering and Structural Violence: A View from Below." *Daedalus*, 125(1): 261–83.

Farmer, Paul, Margaret Connors, and Janie Simmons. 1996. *Women, Poverty and AIDS. [or :?] Sex, Drugs and Structural Violence*. Monroe: Common Courage Press.

Fatton, Robert. 1995. *Predatory Rule: State and Civil Society in Africa*. Boulder: Lynne Rienner.

Fay, Brian. 1975. *Social Theory and Political Practice*. Boston, MA: Allen and Unwin.

——. 1987. *Critical Social Science*. Ithaca, NY: Cornell University Press.

Featherstone, Liza and Doug Henwood. 2001. "Clothes Encounters: Activists and Economists Clash over Sweatshops." *Lingua Franca*, March: 26–33.

Feagin, Joe R. and Harlan Hahn. 1973. *Ghetto Revolts; the Politics of Violence in American Cities*. New York: Macmillan.

Fei, John C. H. and Gustav Ranis. 1964. *Development of a Labor Surplus Economy. Theory and Policy*. Homewood, IL: Irwin.

Fein, Helen. 1995. "More Murder in the Middle: Life-Integrity Violations and Democracy in the World, 1987." *Human Rights Quarterly*, 17(1): 79–106.

Feldstein, Martin. 1994. "Tax Policy and International Capital Flows." *Weltwirtschaftliches Archiv*, 130(4): 676–97.

Ferguson, Niall. 2001. *The Cash Nexus: Money and Power in the Modern World, 1700–2000*. New York: Basic Books.

Ferguson, Yale H. and Richard W. Mansbach. 1988. *The Elusive Quest*. Columbia, SC: University of South Carolina Press.

Feyerabend, Paul. 1975. *Against Method: Outline of an Anarchist Theory of Knowledge*. New York, NY: New Left Books.

Fields, Gary S. 1994. "Changing Labor Market Conditions and Economic Development in Hong Kong, the Republic of Korea, Singapore and Taiwan China." *World Bank Economic Review*, 8(3): 395–414.

Finnemore, Martha. 1996. *National Interests in International Society*. Ithaca, NY: Cornell University Press.

Firat, A. Fuat. 1994. "Gender and Consumption: Transcending the Feminine." In *Gender Issues and Consumer Behavior*, ed., Janeen Arnold Costa. Provo, UT: Association for Consumer Research, pp. 205–28.

Fiscella, Kevin and Peter Franks. 1997. "Does Psychological Stress Contribute To Racial and Socioeconomic Disparities in Mortality?" *Social Science and Medicine*, 45(12): 1805–9.

Fitzgerald, D. 1990. *The Business of Breeding: Hybrid Corn in Illinois, 1890–1940*. Ithaca, NY: Cornell University Press.

Fitzgerald, Frances. 1973. *Fire in the Lake: The Vietnamese and the Americans in Vietnam*. Boston: Atlantic-Little Brown.

Fitzgibbons, Adam. 1995. *Adam Smith's System of Liberty, Wealth and Virtue: The Moral and Political Foundations of the Wealth of Nations.* Oxford: Clarendon Press.

Fleming, Marcus J. 1962. "Domestic Financial Policies Under Fixed and Under Floating Exchange Rates." *IMF Staff Papers,* November 9: 369–80.

Fleming, Matthew H., John Roman and Graham Farrel. 2000. The Shadow Economy. *Journal of International Affairs,* 53(2): 387–409.

Flyvbjerg, Bent. 2001. *Making Social Science Matter.* New York, NY: Cambridge University Press.

Fogel, Robert W. 1994. "Economic Growth, Population Theory, and Physiology: The Bearing of Long-Term Processes on the Making of Economic Policy." *American Economic Review,* 84(3): 369–95.

Folkerts-Landau, David, Donald Mathieson, and Garry J. Schinasi. 1997. *International Capital Markets. Developments, Prospects, and Key Policy Issues.* Washington, DC: International Monetary Fund.

Fontaine, Jean-Marc. 1994. "Financement, échanges et investissement: le cercle vicieux de l'Afrique subsaharienne." *Tiers Monde,* 35(139): 684–700.

Foster-Carter, Aidan, 1978. "The Modes of Production Controversy." *New Left Review,* 107 (January–February): 47–77.

Foucault, Michel. 1972. *The Archeaology of Knowledge and the Discourse on Language.* Translated by A. M. S. Smith. New York, NY: Pantheon Books.

——. 1980. *Power/Knowledge,* ed., C. Gordon. New York: Pantheon.

——. 1991. "Governmentality." In *The Foucault Effect: Studies in Governmentality,* eds, Graham Burchill, Colin Gordon, and Peter Miller. Hertfordshere: Harvester Wheatsheaf.

——. 1995. *Discipline and Punish: The Birth of the Prison.* Trans. by Alan Sheridan. New York: Vintage.

Fox, Richard Wightman and T. J. Jackson Lears (ed.). 1983. *The Culture of Consumption: Critical Essays in American History, 1880–1980.* New York: Pantheon.

Frank, André G. 1990. "A Theoretical Introduction to 5000 Years of World System History." *Review,* XIII(2): 155–248.

——. 1993. "Bronze Age World System Cycles." *Current Anthropology,* 34(4): 383–429.

——. 1994. "The World Economic System in Asia before European Hegemony." *The Historian,* 56(2): 260–76.

——. 1998. *ReOrient.* Berkeley: University of California Press.

Frank, André G. and Barry K. Gills. 1991. "Transitional Ideological Modes: Feudalism, Capitalism, Socialism," *Critique of Anthropology,* 11(2): 171–88.

——. 1992. "The Five Thousand Year World System: An Interdisciplinary Introduction." *Humboldt Journal of Social Relations,* 18(1): 1–79.

——. 1993/6. *The World System: Five Hundred Years or Five Thousand?* London: Routledge.

——. 1995. *The World System: Five Hundred or Five Thousand Years?* New York, NY: Routledge.

Frieden, Jeffrey A. 1988/1995. "Capital Politics: Creditors and the International Political Economy." In *International Political Economy. Perspectives on Global Power and Wealth,* eds, J. A. Frieden and D. A. Lake. New York: St Martin's Press, pp. 282–98.

Friedman, Milton. 1976. *Inflation and Unemployment: The New Dimension of Politics.* The 1976 Alfred Nobel Memorial Lecture. London: The Institute of Economic Affairs.

Friedmann, Harriet. 1990. "Rethinking Capitalism and Hierarchy." *Review* XIII(2): 255–64.

Fromm, Erich. 1941. *Escape from Freedom.* New York, Rinehardt.

Frost, Mervyn. 1996. *Ethics in International Relations: A Constitutive Theory.* New York, NY: Cambridge University Press.

Fukuyama, Francis. 1999. "Death of the Hierarchy." *Financial Times*, June 13: I.

Fuller, Steve. 1988. *Social Epistemology*. Bloomington, IN: Indiana University Press.

——. 1989. *Philosophy of Science and its Discontents*. Boulder, CO: Westview.

Gadamer, Hans-George. 1975. *Truth and Method*. New York, NY: Seabury Press.

Galambos, L. 1970. "The Emerging Organizational Synthesis in Modern American History." *Business History Review*, 44: 279–90.

Gallaher, Carol. Forthcoming. "The Religious Right Reacts to Globalization." In *The International Political Economy Yearbook*. vol. 13, eds, Mary Ann Tétreault and Robert A. Denemark. Boulder: Lynne Rienner.

Galtung, Johan. 1969. "Violence, Peace, and Peace Research." *Journal of Peace Research*, 6(1): 167–91.

——. 1990. "Cultural Violence." *Journal of Peace Research*, 27(3): 291–305.

Gardiner, Jean. 2000. "Gender and Family in the Formation of human capital." In *Towards a Gendered Political Economy*, eds, Joanne Cook, Jennifer Roberts, and Georgina Waylen. London: Macmillan, pp. 61–75.

Gasiorowski, Mark J. 1991. *U.S. Foreign Policy and the Shah: Building a Client State in Iran*. Ithaca, NY: Cornell University Press.

Geertz, Clifford. 1973. *The Interpretation of Cultures*. New York, NY: Basic Books.

George, Jim. 1994. *Discourses on Global Politics*. Boulder, CO: Lynne Rienner Publishers.

Georgescu-Roegen, Nicholas. 1960. "Economic Theory and Agrarian Economics." *Oxford Economic Papers*, 12(1): 1–40.

Geras, Norman. 1985. "The Controversy about Marx and Justice." *New Left Review*, 150 (March–April): 47–88.

——. 1992. "Bringing Marx to Justice: An Addendum and Rejoinder." *New Left Review*, 195 (September–October): 37–70.

Gereffi, George and Marie Korzeniewicz (eds). 1994. *Commodity Chains and Global Capitalism*. Westport, CT: Praeger.

Geschiere, Peter, 1985. "Imposing Capitalist Dominance through the State: The Multifarious Role of the Colonial State in Africa." In *Old Modes of Production and Capitalist Encroachment*, eds, W. van Binsbergen and P. Geschiere. London: Routledge and Keegan Paul.

Gibson, James William. 1986. *The Perfect War: The War We Couldn't Lose and How We Did*. New York: Vintage.

Giddens, Anthony. 1979. *Central Problems in Social Theory*. Berkeley, CA: University of California Press.

——. 1984. *The Constitution of Society: Outline of a Theory of Structuration*. Berkeley, CA: University of California Press.

——. 1990. *The Consequences of Modernity*. Stanford, CA: Stanford University Press.

——. 1999. *Runaway World: How Gobalization is Reshaping our Lives*. London: Routledge.

Gil, David G. 1970. *Violence Against Children*. Cambridge: Harvard University Press.

——. 1986. "Sociocultural Aspects of Domestic Violence." In *Violence in the Home*, ed., M. Lystad. New York: Brunner/Mazel, pp. 124–49.

——. 1996. "Preventing Violence in a Structurally Violent Society: Mission Impossible." *American Journal of Orthopsychiatry*, 66(1): 77–84.

Gill, Stephen. 1988. *American Hegemony and the Trilateral Commission*. Cambridge: Cambridge University Press.

—— (ed.). 1993. *Gramsci, Historial Materialism and International Relations*. Cambridge: Cambridge University Press.

Gill, Stephen. 1994. Knowledge, Politics, and Neo-Liberal Political Economy. In *Political Economy and the Changing Global Order*, eds, Richard Stubbs and Geoffrey R. D. Underhill. New York: St Martin's Press, pp. 75–88.

——. 1997. "Finance, Production and Panopticism." In *Globalization, Democratization and Multilateralism*, ed., Stephen Gill. London: Macmillan/UNU Press: 51–75.

Gill, Stephen and David Law. 1988. *The Global Political Economy: Perspectives, Problems and Policies*. Baltimore, MD: Johns Hopkins University Press.

Gills, Barry. 1989. "International Relations Theory and the Processes of World History: Three Approaches." In *The Study of International Relations: The State of the Art*, eds, Hugh C. Dyer and Leon Mangasarian. London: Macmillan, pp. 103–54.

——. 1993. "Hegemonic Transitions in the World System." In *The World System: Five Hundred Years or Five Thousand?*, eds, Frank and Gills. London, New York: Routledge, pp. 115–40.

——. 1995. "Capital and Power in the Processes of World History." In *Civilizations and World Systems: Studying World-Historical Change*, ed., Stephen K. Sanderson. Walnut Creek, London, New Delhi: AltaMira Press (Sage), pp. 136–62.

——. 1996. "The Continuity Thesis in World Development." In *The Underdevelopment of Development: Essays in Honour of Andre Gunder Frank*, eds, Sing C. Chew and Robert A. Denemark. Thousand Oaks, London, New Delhi: Sage Publications, pp. 226–45.

Gills, Barry K. and Andre Gunder Frank. 1990. "The Cumulation of Accumulation: These and Research Agenda for 5000 Years of World System History." *Dialectical Anthropology*, 15(1): 19–42. (And in Christopher Chase Dunn and Thomas D. Hall (eds). 1991. *Precapitalist Core Periphery Relations*. Boulder, CO: Westview Press, pp. 67–111.

——. 1992. "World System Cycles, Crises, and Hegemonial Shifts, 1700 BC to 1700 AD." *Review*, XV(4): 621–87.

Gills, Dong-Sook. 2001. "Globalization and Counter-Globalization." In *Women and Work in Globalizing Asia. Women's Work in Asia*, eds, D. S. Gills and N. Piper. London: Routledge Curzon.

Gilpin, Robert. 1981. *War and Change in World Politics*. New York: Cambridge University Press.

——. 1987. *The Political Economic of International Relations*. Princeton, NJ: Princeton University Press.

Girard, Rene. 1979. *Violence and the Sacred*. Trans. Patrick Gregory. Baltimore: Johns Hopkins University Press.

Glenn, Evelyn Nakano. 1986. *Issei, Nisei, War Bride: Three Generations of Japanese American Women in Domestic Service*. Philadelphia: Temple University Press.

Godfried, Nathan. 1987. *Bridging the Gap Between Rich and Poor: American Economic Development Policy Toward the Arab East, 1942–1949*. Westport, CT: Greenwood Press.

Goldberg, Ellis. 1992. "Smashing Idols and the State: The Protestant Ethic and Egyptian Sunni Radicalism." In *Comparing Muslim Societies: Knowledge and the State in a World Civilization*, ed., Juan R. I. Cole. Ann Arbor: University of Michigan Press, pp. 195–236.

Goldfrank, Walter. 1990. "Current Issues in World-Systems Theory." *Review*, XIII(2): 245–55.

Goldhagen, Daniel Jonah. 1996. *Hitler's Willing Executioners: Ordinary Germans and the Holocaust*. New York: Alfred Knopf.

Golub, Stephen S. 1994. "Comparative Advantage, Exchange Rates, and Sectoral Trade Balances of Major Industrial Countries." *IMF Staff Papers*, 41(2): 286–313.

Goodman, John B. and Louis W. Pauly. 1995. "The Obsolescence of Capital Controls? Economic Management in an Age of Global Markets." In *International Political Economy. Perspectives on Global Power and Wealth*, ed., J. A. Frieden and D. A. Lake. New York: St Martin's Press, pp. 299–317.

Goodman, R.F. and W.R. Fisher (eds). 1995. *Rethinking Knowledge: Reflections Across the Disciplines*. Albany, NY: State University of New York Press.

Goodman, Robert. 1995. "Introduction." In *Rethinking Knowledge: Reflections Across the Disciplines*, eds, R. F. Goodman and W. R. Fisher. Albany, NY: State University of New York Press, pp. i–xvii.

Goody, Jack. 1996. *The East in the West*. Cambridge: Cambridge University Press.

Gopin, Mark. 2000. *Between Eden and Armageddon. The Future of World Religions, Violence, and Peacemaking*. Oxford, England: Oxford University Press.

Gordon, David. 1988. "The Global Economy: New Edifice or Crumbling Foundations?" *New Left Review*, 168: 24–64.

Gosh, Atish R. 1995. "International Capital Mobility Amongst the Major Industrialized Countries: Too Little Or Too Much." *Economic Journal*, 105(428): 107–28.

Gospel, Howard F. 1988. "The Management of Labor: Great Britain, the U.S., and Japan." *Business History*, 30(1): 104–16.

Gould, Carol C. 1988. *Rethinking Democracy: Freedom and Social Cooperation in Politics, Economy, and Society*. New York: Cambridge University Press.

Gouldner, Alvin. 1970. *The Coming Crisis of Western Sociology*. New York, NY: Avon Books.

Gourevitch, Philip. 1998. *We Wish to Inform You that Tomorrow We will be Killed with our Families: Stories from Rwanda*. New York: Farrar Straus and Giroux.

Grabowski, Richard. 1994. "Peasant Agriculture and the Distribution of Power in PreWar East Asia." *Canadian Journal of Development Studies*, 15(2): 171–91.

———. 1995. "Economic Development and the Rise of the Market System." *Studies in Comparative International Development*, 30(3): 49–69.

———. 2000. "Integrated National Markets, Industrialization, and Broadly Based Agricultural Growth." *Asien-Afrika-Lateinamerika*, 28(3): 241–64.

Gramsci, Antonio. 1971. *Selections from the Prison Notebooks of Antonio Gramsci*, ed. and trans., Q. Hoare and G.N. Smith. London: Lawrence and Wishart.

Gray, Patricia and Hans Wolfgang Singer. 1988. "Trade Policy and Growth of Developing Countries: Some New Data." *World Development*, 16(3): 395–403.

Greenaway, Frank. 1996. *Science International*. Cambridge, UD: Cambridge University Press.

Greenwald, Maurine Weiner. 1980. *Women, War, and Work: The Impact of World War I on Women Workers in the United States*. Westport, CT: Greenwood Press.

Grossman, Grene and Elhanan Helpman. 1994. "Endogenous Innovation in the Theory of Growth." *Journal of Economic Perspectives*, 8(1): 23–44.

Guillaumont-Jeanneney, Sylviane and Ping Hua. 1996. "Politique du change et développement des exportations manufacturées en Chine." *Revue économique*, 47(3): 851–60.

Gunder Frank, André. 1966. "The Development of Underdevelopment." *Monthly Review*, 18: 17–31.

Gupta, Aarti. 2000. "Governing trade in genetically modified organisms: The Caragena Protocol on Biosafety." *Environment*, 42(4): 22–33.

Gurr, Ted R. 1993. *Minorities at Risk. A Global View of Ethnopolitical Conflicts*. Washington, DC: US Institute of Peace Press.

Haas, Peter. 1990. *Saving the Mediterranean: The Politics of International Environmental Cooperation*. New York, NY: Columbia University Press.

——— (ed.). 1992. "Knowledge, Power, and International Policy Coordination." *International Organization*, 46(1).

Haas, Peter and Emmanuel Adler. 1992. "Introduction : Epistemic Communities and International Policy Coordination." *International Organization*, 46(1): 1–36.

Haas, Peter, R. Keohane, M. Levy (eds). 1993. *Institutions for the Earth: Sources of Effective International Environmental Protection*. Cambridge, MA: MIT Press.

Habermas, Jürgen. 1971. *Knowledge and Human Interests*. Trans. by J. Shapiro. Boston, MA: Beacon Press.

——. 1975. *Legitimation Crisis*. Trans. by T. McCarthy. Boston: Beacon Press.

——. 1979. *Communication and the Evolution of Society*. Boston, MA: Beacon Press.

——. 1984. *The Theory of Communicative Action*. Trans. by T. McCarthy. Boston, MA: Beacon Press.

——. 1987. *The Philosophical Discourse of Modernity: 12 Lectures*. Trans. by F. Lawrence. Cambridge, MA: MIT Press.

——. 1988. *On the Logic of the Social Sciences*. Trans. by S W. Nicholson and J. Stark. Cambridge, MA: MIT Press.

——. 1991. *The Structural Transformation of the Public Sphere: An Inquiry into a Category of Bourgeois Society*. Trans. Thomas Burger and Frederick Lawrence. Cambridge: MIT Press.

Hagen, Elisabeth and Jane Jenson. 1988. "Paradoxes and Promises." In *Feminization of the Labor Force: Paradoxes and Promises*, eds, Jane Jenson, Elisabeth Hagen, and Ceallaigh Reddy. New York: Oxford University Press.

Hall, Barbara Welling. 2000. "Power and Powerlessness in the Help Fund: Women, Russia, and the Spirit of Totalitarianism." In *Feminist Approaches to Social Movements, Community, and Power*, vol. 1, *Conscious Acts and the Politics of Social Change*, eds, Robin L. Teske and Mary Ann Tétreault. Columbia: University of South Carolina Press, pp. 246–64.

Hall, R. L. and C. J. Hitch. 1939. "Price Theory and Business Behaviour." *Oxford Economic Papers*, (2): 12–45.

Hall, Stuart. 1997. "The Global and the Local: Globalization and Ethnicity." In *Culture, Globalization and the World-System: Contemporary Conditions for the Representation of Identity*, ed., Anthony King. Minneapolis: University of Minnesota Press, pp. 19–40.

Hall, Thomas D. and Christopher Chase-Dunn. 1994. "Forward into the Past: World-Systems before 1500." *Sociological Forum*, 9(2):295–306.

Hallgarten, Wolfgang. 1935. *Vorkriegsimperialismus. Die soziologischen Grundlagen der Außenpolitik europäischer Großmächte bis 1914*. Paris: Edition Météore.

Hambidge, G. 1941. "Climate and Man – A Summary." In *Climate and Man*, eds, G. Hambidge, M. J. Drown, F. W. Reichelderfer, Louis H. Bean, Joseph B. Kincer, Larry F. Page, C. G. Rossby, Charles F. Sarle, C. Warren Thornthwaite, Edgar W. Woolard. Washington, DC: US Government Printing Office.

Hamman, Harry. 1998. "Remodeling International Relations: New Tools from New Science?" In *International Relations in a Constructed World*, 173. eds, V. Kubalkova, N. Onuf, and P. Kowert. Armonk, NJ: M.E. Sharpe, Inc.

Harcourt, Geoffrey C. 1972. *Some Cambridge Controversies in the Theory of Capital*. Cambridge: Cambridge University Press.

Hardin, Russell. 1987. "Rational Choice Theories." In *Idioms of Inquiry: Critique and Renewal in Political Science*, ed., T. Ball. Albany, NY: State University of New York Press, pp. 67–91.

Hardt, Michael and Antonio Negri. 2000. *Empire*. Cambridge, MA: Harvard University Press.

Hargreaves, Deborah, Richard Waters, and James Harding. 2000. "Regulating the Unknown." *Financial Times*, September 7: 14.

Hartmann, Heidi. 1981. "The Unhappy Marriage of Marxism and Feminism: Towards a More Progressive Union." In *Women and Revolution*, ed., Lydia Sargent. Boston: South End Press.

Harvey, David. 1989. *The Condition of Postmodernity: An Enquiry into the Origins of Cultural Change*. Cambridge, MA: Basil Blackwell.

——. 1995. "Globalization in Question." *Rethinking Marxism*, 8(4): 1–17.

——. 1996. *Justice, Nature and the Geography of Difference*. Oxford: Basil Blackwell.

——. 1999. *Spaces of Hope*. Edinburgh: Edinburgh University Press.

Havel, Václav. 1989. *Living in Truth*, ed., Jan Vladislav. London: Faber and Faber.

——. 1990. *Disturbing the Peace: A Conversation with Karel Hvížd'ala*. Trans. Paul Wilson. New York: Alfred A. Knopf.

Hawley, John Stratton (ed.). 1994. *Fundamentalism and Gender*. New York: Oxford University Press.

Hays, S. P. 1959. *Conservation and the Gospel of Efficiency: The Progressive Conservation Movement, 1890–1920*. Cambridge, MA, Harvard University Press.

Heckscher, Eli. 1970. "The Effect of Foreign Trade on the Distribution of Income." In *Readings in the Theory of International Trade*. New York: American Economic Association, pp. 272–301.

Heeren, A. H. L. 1833. *Historical Researches into the Politics, Intercourse, and Trade of the Principal Nations of Antiquity. Asiatic Nations*, vol. 1. Oxford: D.A. Talboys.

Held, David. 1980. *Introduction to Critical Theory*. London, England: Hutchinson.

——. 1995. *Democracy and the Global Order: From the Modern State to Cosmopolitan Governance*. Cambridge: Polity Press.

Held, David, Anthony McGrew, David Goldblatt, and Jonathan Perraton. (eds). 1999. *The Global Transformations Reader*. Stanford: Stanford University Press.

——. (eds). 1999. *Global Transformation: Politics, Economics, and Culture*. Cambridge: Polity Press.

Helleiner, Eric. 1994. *States and the Reemergence of Global Finance: From Bretton Woods to the 1990s*. Ithaca, NY: Cornell University Press.

——. 1995. "Explaining the Globalization of Financial Markets: Bringing States Back In." *Review of International Political Economy*, 2(2): 315–42.

——. 1999. "Historicizing territorial currencies." *Political Geography*, 18: 309–40.

Helmstädter, Ernst. 1969. *Der Kapitalkoeffizient. Eine kapitaltheoretische Untersuchung*. Stuttgart: Gustav Fischer, pp. 48–60.

Hennessey, Rosemary. 2000. *Profit and Pleasure: Sexual Identities in Late Capitalism*. New York and London: Routledge.

Hernstein, Richard J. and Charles Murray. 1996. *The Bell Curve: Intelligence and Class Structure in American Life*. New York: Free Press.

Hetata, Sherif. 1998. "Dollarization, Fragmentation and God." In *The Cultures of Globalization*, eds, Frederic Jameson and Masao Miyoshi. Durham: Duke University Press, pp. 273–90.

Hettne, Bjorn (ed.). 1995. *International Political Economy: Understanding Global Disorder*. London: Zed.

Hilferding, Rudolf. 1910/1968. *Das Finanzkapital. Eine Studie über die jüngste Entwicklung des Kapitalismus*. Frankfurt am Main: Europäische Verlagsanstalt.

Hinsley, Fred H. 1982. "The Rise and Fall of the Modern International System." *Review of International Studies*, 8: 1–8.

Hirschman, Albert O. 1958. *The Strategy of Economic Development*. New Haven, CT: Yale University Press.

Hirst, Paul and Grahame Thompson. 1999. *Globalization in Question. The International Economy and the Possibilities of Governance*. Cambridge: Polity Press.

Hobsbawm, Eric J. 1975. *The Age of Capital, 1848–1875*. New York: Charles Scribner's Sons.

——. 1991. "Ethnicity and Nationalism in Europe Today." *Anthropology Today*, 8(1): 3–8.

Hobson, John Atkinson. 1902/1938. *Imperialism. A Study*. London: Allen & Unwin.

Hodgson, Marshall G. S. 1974. *The Venture of Islam: Conscience and History in a World Civilization: The Expansion of Islam in the Middle Periods*. Chicago: Chicago University Press.

Hodgson, Marshall G. S. 1993. *Rethinking World History: Essays on Europe, Islam and World History*, ed., Edmund Burke III. Cambridge: Cambridge University Press.

Hoffmann, Wilma and Brian McKendrick. 1990. "The Nature of Violence." In *People and Violence in South Africa*, eds, B. McKendrick and W. Hoffmann. Cape Town: Oxford University Press.

Hoggart, Richard. 1957. *The Uses of Literary: Changing Patterns in English Mass Culture*. New York: Oxford University Press.

Hollis, Martin and Steve Smith. 1991. *Explaining and Understanding International Relations*. New York, NY: Clarendon Press.

Holsti, Ole R. 1992. "Public Opinion and Foreign Policy: Challenges to the Almond-Lippmann Consensus: Mershon Series: Research Programs and Debates." *International Studies Quarterly*, 36(4): 439–66.

Holton, Gerald. 1973. *Thematic Origins of Scientific Thought*. Cambridge, MA: Harvard University Press.

———. 1987. *The Advancement of Science and its Burdens*. New York, NY: Cambridge University Press.

Hont, Istvan and Ignatieff, Michael (eds). 1983. *Wealth and Virtue: The Shaping of Political Economy in the Scottish Enlightenment*. Cambridge: Cambridge University Press.

Hopkins, Terence K. 1982. "Commentary." In *World-Systems Analysis: Theory and Methodology*, eds, T. K. Hopkins and I. Wallerstein. Beverly Hills, CA: Sage Publications, pp. 188–91.

Hopkins, Terence K. and Immanuel Wallerstein. 1982. "Preface." In *World-Systems Analysis: Theory and Methodology*. eds, T. Hopkins and I. Wallerstein. Beverly Hills, CA: Sage Publications, pp. 7–8.

Hopkins, Terence K., Immanuel Wallerstein, Robert L. Bach, Christopher Chase-Dunn, and Ramkrishna Mukherjee. 1982. "Preface." In *World-Systems Analysis: Theory and Methodology*, eds, T. Hopkins and I. Wallerstein. Beverly Hills, CA: Sage Publications.

Horkheimer, Max. 1972. "Traditional and Critical Theory." In *Critical Theory: Selected Essays*, ed., Max Horkheimer. Trans. by Herder and Herder, Inc. New York, NY: Seabury Press.

Horowitz, Donald. 1985. *Ethnic Groups in Conflict*. Berkeley: University of California Press.

Hughes, T. P. 1983. *Networks of Power: Electrification in Western Society, 1880–1930*. Baltimore: Johns Hopkins University Press.

———. 1989. *American Genesis: A Century of Invention and Technological Enthusiasm, 1870–1970*. New York, NY: Viking.

Hurwitz, Jon and Mark Peffley. 1987. "How are Foreign Policy Attitudes Structured? A Hierarchical Model." *American Political Science Review*, 81(4): 1098–120.

Hutchings, Kimberly. 1999. *International Political Theory: Rethinking Ethics in a Global Era*. London: Sage Publications.

Hutchison, Michael. 1988. *Before Adam Smith: The Emergence of Political Economy, 1662–1776*. Oxford: Basil Blackwell.

Hutton, Patrick H. 1988. "Foucault, Freud, and the Technologies of the Self." In *Technologies of the Self*, eds, L. H. Martin, H. Gutman, and P. H. Hutton. Amherst: University of Massachusetts Press, pp. 121–44.

Hymer, Stephen H. 1960/1976. *The International Operations of National Firms: A Study of Direct Foreign Investment*. Cambridge, MA and London, England: The MIT Press.

Iannaccone, Laurence R. 1993. "Heirs to the Protestant Ethic? The Economics of American Fundamentalists." In *Fundamentalisms and the State: Remaking Politics, Economies and Militance*, eds, Martin Marty and R. Scott Appleby. Chicago: University of Chicago Press, pp. 342–66.

IFO-Institut für Wirtschaftsforschung. 1994. *Der Wirtschafts- und Forschungsstandort Baden-Württemberg - Potentiale und Perspektiven*. Munich.

Ikenberry, G. John. 1992. "A World Economy Restored: Expert Consensus and the Anglo-American Postwar Settlement." *International Organization*, 46(1): 289–322.

International Institute for Labour Studies and United Nations Development Programme. 1994. *Overcoming Social Exclusion. A Contribution to the World Summit for Social Development.* Geneva: ILO/UNDP.

International Meteorological Organization (IMO). 1947. Conference of Directors, Washington, September 22–October 11, 1947. Geneva, Switzerland: World Meteorological Organization.

International Monetary Fund. Annual-a. *Balance of Payments.* Washington, DC: IMF.

——. Annual-b. *International Financial Statistics.* Washington, DC: IMF.

Irsch, Norbert. 1979. *Lohnbestimmungsmechanismen bei restringierten Substitutionsbeziehungen. Kritische Analyse grenzproduktivitätstheoretischer Verteilungsaussagen.* Aachen: Rheinisch-Westfälische Hochschule Aachen.

Irwin, Douglas A. 1996. "The United States in a New Global Economy? A Century's Perspective." *American Economic Review*, 86(2): 41–6.

Israel, Jonathan I. 1989. *Dutch Primacy in World Trade, 1585–1740.* Oxford: Clarendon.

Jacobs, Jane. 1969/1984. *Cities and the Wealth of Nations: Principles of Economic Life.* New York: Random House.

Jacobs, N. 1958. *The Origins of Modern Capitalism and Eastern Asia.* Hong Kong: Hong Kong University Press.

James, Harold. 2001. *The End of Globalization: Lessons from the Great Depression.* Cambridge: Harvard University Press.

James, Winston. 1998. *Holding Aloft the Banner of Ethiopia: Caribbean Radicalism in Early Twentieth-Century America.* London and New York: Verso.

Jameson, Fredric. 1991. *Postmodernism, or the Cultural Logic of Late Capitalism.* Durham, NC: Duke University Press.

——. 1995. *Postmodernism: or the Cultural Logic of Late Capitalism*, Durham: Duke University Press.

——. 1999. "Notes on Globalization as a Philosophical Issue." In *The Cultures of Globalization*, eds, Frederic Jameson and Masao Miyoshi. Durham: Duke University Press, pp. 54–80.

Jardine, Lisa and Jerry Brotton. 2000. *Global Interests: Renaissance Art Between East and West.* Ithaca: Cornell University Press.

Jasanoff, S. 1990. *The Fifth Branch: Science Advisers as Policymakers.* Cambridge, MA: Harvard University Press.

——. 1993. "India at the Crossroads." *Global Environmental Change*, March: 32–51.

——. 1995. *Science at the Bar: Law, Science and Technology in America.* Cambridge, MA: Harvard University Press.

——. 2001. "Image and Imagination: The Emergence of Global Environmental Conciousness." In *Changing the Atmosphere: Expert Knowledge and Global Environmental Governance*, eds, C. Miller and P. Edwards. Cambridge, MA: MIT Press.

Jasanoff, S. and Brian Wynne. 1998. "Science and Decisionmaking." *Human Choice and Climate Change*, vol. 1, *The Societal Framework*, eds, S. Rayner and E. Malone. Columbus, OH: Battelle Press.

Jasanoff, S., G. E. Markle, J. C. Peterson, T. Pinch (eds). 1996. *The Handbook of Science and Technology Studies.* Thousand Oaks, CA: Sage Publications.

Jeffries, Sheila. 2000. "Challenging the Child/Adult Distinction in Theory and Practice on Prostitution." *International Feminist Journal of Politics*, 2(3): 359–79.

Jenkins, Barbara. 1999. "The Low Politics of High Art." *Alternatives*, 24: 193–217.

Jensen, Michael C. 1987. "The Free Cash Flow Theory of Takeovers: A Financial Perspective on Mergers and Acquisitions and the Economy." In *The Merger Boom*. Proceedings of a Conference Held at Melvin Village, New Hampshire, eds, L. E. Browne and E. S. Rosengren. Boston: Federal Reserve Bank of Boston, pp. 102–43.

Jensen, Michael C. and Richard S. Ruback. 1983. "The Market for Corporate Control." *Journal of Financial Economics*, 11: 5–50.

Jenson, Jane, Elisabeth Hagen, and Ceallaigh Reddy (eds). 1988. *Feminization of the Labor Force: Paradoxes and Promises*. New York: Oxford University Press.

Josephson, Matthew. 1934. *The Robber Barons. The Great American Capitalists. 1861–1901.* New York: Harcourt, Brace and Company.

Josephy, Alvin M. 1995. *500 Nations: An Illustrated History of North American Indians*. London: Random House.

Judge, Ken, Jo-Ann Mulligan, and Michaela Benzeval. 1998. "Income Inequality and Population Health." *Social Science and Medicine* 46(4–5): 567–79.

Juergensmeyer, Mark. 1994. *The New Cold War? Religious Nationalism Confronts the Secular State.* Berkeley: University of California Press.

——. 2000. *Terror in the Mind of God. The Global Rise of Religious Violence*. Berkeley, CA: University of California Press.

Juris, Andrej (ed.). 1995. *Privatization in Slovakia: Present Problems and Questions*. Bratislava: M.E.S.A. 10 Center for Economic and Social Analysis.

Kaldor, Nicholas. 1955. "Alternative Theories of Distribution." *Review of Economic Studies*, 23(61): 83–100.

Kalecki, Michal. 1971. *Selected Essays on the Dynamics of the Capitalist Economy 1933–1970.* Cambridge: Cambridge University Press.

——. 1943a/1971. "Costs and Prices." In *Selected Essays on the Dynamics of the Capitalist Economy, 1933–1970*. Cambridge: Cambridge University Press, pp. 43–61.

——. 1943b/1990. "Political Aspects of Full Employment." In *Collected Works of Michal Kalecki*. vol. 1, *Capitalism, Business Cycle and Full Employment*, ed., J. Osiatynski. Oxford: Clarendon Press, pp. 347–56.

Kaljee, Linda M., Bonita Stanton, Izabel Ricardo, and Tony L. Whitehead. 1995. "Urban African American Adolescents and their Parents: Perceptions of Violence within and against their Communities." *Human Organization*, 54(4): 373–82.

Kandlikar, Milind and Ambuj Sagar. 1997. "Climate Science and Policy in India: Learning Some Lessons." Cambridge, MA, Environment and Natural Resources Program, Kennedy School of Government, Harvard University.

Kane, June. 1998. *Sold for Sex*. Brookfield, VT: Arena Press.

Kapferer, Bruno. 1994. "Remythologizations of Power and Identity: Nationalism and Violence in Sri Lanka." In *The Culture of Violence*, eds, Kumar Rupesinghe and Marcial Rubio C. Tokyo: United Nations University Press, pp. 59–91.

Kaplan, Abraham D. 1964. *The Conduct of Inquiry: Methodology for Behavioral Science*. San Francisco, CA: Chandler Publishing.

Kaplan, A. D. H., J. B. Dirlam, and R. F. Lanzillotti. 1958. *Pricing in Big Business. A Case Approach*. Washington, DC: The Brookings Institution.

Kapstein, Ethan B. 1994. *Governing the Global Economy: International Finance and the State*. Cambridge: Harvard University Press.

Kapur, Geeta. 1998. "Globalization and Culture: Navigating the Void." In *The Cultures of Globalization*, eds, Frederic Jameson and Masao Miyoshi. Durham: Duke University Press, pp. 191–218.

Kasozi, Abdu B. K. 1994. *The Social Origins of Violence in Uganda, 1964–1985.* Montréal, Buffalo: McGill-Queen's University Press.

Kawachi, Ichiro and Bruce P. Kennedy. 1999. "Income Inequality and Health: Pathways and Mechanisms." *Health Services Research,* 34(1): 215–27.

Kawachi, Ichiro, Bruce P. Kennedy, and Richard G. Wilkinson. 1999. "Crime: Social Disorganization and Relative Deprivation." *Social Science and Medicine,* 48(6): 719–31.

Kayatekin, Serap Aye. 1996/97. "Sharecropping and Class: A Preliminary Analysis." *Rethinking Marxism,* 9(1): 28–57.

Keane, John. 1988. "Despotism and Democracy: The Origins and Development of the Distinction Between Civil Society and the State, 1750–1850." In *Civil Society and the State,* ed., John Keane. London: Verso, pp. 35–71.

Kellner, Douglas. 1989. *Critical Theory, Marxism, and Modernity.* Baltimore, MD: Johns Hopkins University Press.

Kempadoo, Kamala and Jo Doezema. 1998. *Global Sex Workers: Rights, Resistance, and Redefinition.* New York: Routledge.

Kennedy, Bruce P., Ichiro Kawachi and Elizabeth Brainerd. 1998. "The Role of Social Capital in the Russian Mortality Crisis." *World Development,* 26(11): 2029–43.

Kennedy, Bruce P., Ichiro Kawachi, Deborah Prothrow-Stith, Kimberly Lochner, and Vanita Gupta. 1998. "Social Capital, Income Ineqality, and Firearm Violent Crime." *Social Science and Medicine,* 47(1): 7–17.

Kennedy, Paul M. 1989. *The Rise and Fall of the Great Powers: Economic Change and Military Conflict from 1500 to 2000.* New York: Vintage.

Kenney, Marvin and Richard Florida. 1988. "Beyond Mass Production: Production and the Labor Process in Japan." *Politics and Society,* 16(1): 123–58.

Kenwood, Albert G. and Alan L. Lougheed. 1971. *The Growth of the International Economy, 1820–1960. An Introductory Text.* London: Allen & Unwin.

Keohane, Robert and Joseph Nye. 2001. *Power and Interdependence.* New York, NY: Longman.

Kershaw, Ian. 1998. *Hitler, 1889–1936: Hubris.* New York: W. W. Norton.

Khidda-Makubuya, Edward. 1994. "Violence and Conflict Resolution in Uganda." In *The Culture of Violence,* eds, Kumar Rupesinghe and Marcial Rubio C. Tokyo: United Nations University Press, pp. 144–77.

Kim, Hyong Chun. 1971. "Koreas Exporterfolge 1960–1969" *Finanzierung und Entwicklung,* 8(1): 14–21.

Klodt, Henning. 1991. "Wirtschaftsförderung in den neuen Bundesländer: Qualifizierungsgutscheine als Alternative." *Weltwirtschaft,* 1: 91–103.

Knight, Alan. 1988. "Debt Bondage in Latin America." In *Slavery and Other Forms of Unfree Labour,* ed., L. J. Archer. London and New York: Routledge, pp. 102–17.

Knoedler, Janet T. 1995. "Transaction Cost Theories of Business Enterprise from Williamson and Veblen: Convergence, Divergence, and Some Evidence." *Journal of Economic Issues,* 29(2): 385–95.

Kohler, Gernot and Norman Alcock. 1976. "An Empirical Table of Structural Violence." *Journal of Peace Research,* 13(4): 343–56.

Kolata, Gina. 1997. "New View Sees Breast Cancer as Three Diseases." *New York Times,* April 1.

Konrád, György and Iván Szelényi. 1978. *Die Intelligenz auf dem Weg zur Klassenmacht.* Frankfurt am Main: Suhrkamp.

Kornai, János. 1996. "Paying the Bill for Goulash-Communism: Hungarian Development and Macro Stabilization in a Political-Economy Perspective." Collegium Budapest/ Institute for Advanced Study. Discussion Paper No. 23. March.

Kortian, Garbis. 1980. *Metacritique: The Philosophical Argument of Jurgen Habermas*. New York, NY: Cambridge University Press.

Kostiner, Joseph (ed.). 2000. *Middle East Monarchies: The Challenge of Modernity*. Boulder: Lynne Rienner.

Kramer, Samuel Noah. 1959. *History Begins At Sumer: Twenty Seven "Firsts" in Man's Recorded History*. Garden City, New York: Anchor Books.

Krieger, N., D. L. Rowley, A. A. Herman, Avery B. and M. T. Phillips. 1993. "Racism, Sexism, and Social Class: Implications for the Study of Health, Disease, and Well-Being." *American Journal of Preventive Medicine*, 9(1): 82–122.

Krishnamurty, K. and Pandit, V. 1996. "Exchange Rate, Tariff and Trade Flows: Alternative Policy Scenarios for India." *Indian Economic Review*, 31(1): 57–89.

Krugman, Paul R. 1987. "Is Free Trade Passé?" *Journal of Economic Perspectives*, 1(2): 131–44.

——. 1991. "Increasing Returns and Economic Geography." *Journal of Political Economy*, 99(3): 483–99.

——. 1993. "The Narrow and Broad Arguments for Free Trade." *American Economic Review*, 83(2): 362–6.

Kubalkova, Vendulka, Nicholas Onuf, and Paul Kowert. 1998a. "Constructing Constructivism." In *International Relations in a Constructed World*, eds, V. Kubalkova, N. Onuf, and P. Kowert. Armonk, NJ: M. E. Sharpe.

——. 1998b. *International Relations in a Constructed World*. Armonk, NJ: M.E. Sharpe.

Kuhn, Thomas. 1970. *The Structure of Scientific Revolutions*. 2nd edition. Chicago, IL: University of Chicago Press.

Laclau, Ernesto. 1971. "Feudalism and Capitalism in Latin America." *New Left Review*, 67 May–June: 19–46.

Lafay, Gérard. 1996. "Les origines internationales du chômage européen." *Revue d'Economie Politique*, 106(6): 943–63.

Laidi, Zaki. 1998. *A World Without Meaning: The Crisis of Meaning in International Politics*. New York, NY: Routledge.

Lakatos, Imre and Alan Musgrave (eds). 1970. *Criticism and the Growth of Knowledge*. New York, NY: Cambridge University Press.

Lake, David and Jeffrey A. Frieden. 1995. *International Political Economy: The Perspectives on Global Power and Wealth*. 3rd edition. London: Routledge.

Landes, David S. 1998. *The Wealth and Poverty of Nations: Why Some are so Rich and Some so Poor*. New York: W.W. Norton.

Lapid, Yosef. 1989. "The Third Debate: On the Prospects of International Theory in a Post-Positivist Era." *International Studies Quarterly*, 33(3): 235–54.

Lapid, Yosef and Friedrich Kratochwil (eds). 1996. *The Return of Culture and Identity in International Relations Theory*. Boulder, CO: L. Rienner Publishers.

Larrain, Jorge. 1989. *Theories of Development*. Cambridge: Polity Press.

Larsen, Mogens. 1967. "Old Assyrian Caravan Procedures." Istanbul: Nederlands Historisch Arceologisch Instituut te Istanbul.

——. 1976. *The Old Assyrian City-State and its Colonies*. Copenhagen: Akademish Forlag.

Lash, Scott and John Urry. 1994. *Economies of Signs and Space*. London: Sage Publications.

Latour, B. 1987. *Science in Action*. Cambridge, MA: Harvard University Press.

Lawler, Peter. 1995. *A Question of Values: Johan Galtung's Peace Research*. Boulder: Lynne Rienner.

Layder, Derek. 1997. *Modern Social Theory: Key Debates and New Directions*. London, England: University College of London Press.

Layton, E. T. 1971. *The Revolt of the Engineers: Social Responsibility and the American Engineering Profession*. Cleveland, OH: The Press of Case Western Reserve University.

Lebowitz, Michael A. 1985. "The Theoretical Status of Monopoly Capital." In *Rethinking Marxism. Struggles in Marxist Theory. Essays for Harry Magdoff & Paul Sweezy*, eds, S. Resnick and R. Wolff. Brooklyn, NY: Autonomedia, pp. 185–203.

Lefebvre, H. 1991. *The Production of Space*. Oxford: Blackwell.

Leff, Nathaniel H. 1985. "Optimal Investment Choice for Developing Countries. Rational Theory and Rational Decision-Making." *Journal of Development Economics*, 18, 4 (August): 335–60.

Lehmbruch, Gerhard. 1979. "Consociational Democracy. Class Conflict and the New Corporatism." In *Trends Toward Corporatist Intermediation*, eds, Philippe C.Schmitter and Gerhard Lehmbruch. Beverly Hills, CA: Sage Publications, pp. 53–62.

Lenel, Hans Otto. 2000. "Zu den Megafusionen in den letzten Jahren." Ordo 51: 1–32.

Lenin, Vladimir Ilyich. 1897/1951. *A Characterisation of Economic Romanticism*. Moscow: Progress Publishers.

——. 1899/1956. *The Development of Capitalism in Russia*. Moscow: Progress Publishers.

——. 1917/1964. *Imperialism. The Highest Stage of Capitalism. A Popular Outline*. Moscow: Progress Publishers.

Levene, Mark. 1999. "The Chitagong Hill Tracts: A Case Study in the Political Economy of 'Creeping' Genocide." *Third World Quarterly*, 20(2): 339–69.

Levine, Solomon B. and Makoto Ontsu. 1991. "Transplanting Japanese Labor Relations." *Annals of the American Academy of Political and Social Science*, 513 January: 102–16.

Lewis, Martin W. and Karen E. Wigen. 1997. *The Myth of Continents*. Berkeley: University of California Press.

Lewis, William Arthur. 1954. "Economic Development with Unlimited Supply of Labour." *Manchester School of Economic and Social Studies*, 22(4): 139–91.

Lichbach, Mark. 1997. "Social Theory and Comparative Politics." In *Comparative Politics: Rationality, Culture, and Structure*, eds, M. Lichbach and A. Zuckerman. New York, NY: Cambridge University Press, pp. 239–76.

Lichbach, Mark and Alan Zuckermann (eds). 1997. *Comparative Politics: Rationality, Culture, Structure*. New York, NY: Cambridge University Press.

Lijphardt, Arend. 1968. *The Politics of Accommodation: Pluralism and Democracy in the Netherlands*. Berkeley: University of California Press.

Lim, Lin Lean (ed.). 1998. *The Sex Sector: The Economic and Social Bases of Prostitution in Southeast Asia*. Geneva: International Labor Office.

Lindblom, Charles E. 1977. *Politics and Markets: The World's Political Economic Systems*. New York: Basic Books.

Linklater, Andrew. 1998. *The Transformation of Political Community: Ethical Foundations of the Post-Westphalian Era*. Columbia, SC: University of South Carolina Press.

Litfin, K. 1994. *Ozone Discourses: Science and Politics in Global Environmental Cooperation*. New York, NY: Columbia University Press.

—— (ed.). 1998. *The Greening of Sovereignty in World Politics*. Cambridge, MA: MIT Press.

Lombard, Maurice. 1975. *The Golden Age of Islam*. Amsterdam: North Holland.

London, Jack. 1957/1907. *The Iron Heel*. New York: Hill and Wang.

Loury, Glenn C. 1999. *Social Exclusion and Ethnic Groups: The Challenge to Economics*. Paper presented at the World Bank Conference on Development Economics. Washington, DC: April.

Love, John R. 1991. *Antiquity and Capitalism: Max Weber and the Sociological Foundations of Roman Civilization*. London: Routledge.

Lovelock, James. 1979. *Gaia: A New Look at Life on Earth.* Oxford: Oxford University Press.

Lubbock, Jules. 1995. *The Tyranny of Taste: The Politics of Architecture and Design in Britain, 1550–1960.* New Haven: Yale University Press.

Lucas, Robert E. 1972. "Expectations and the Neutrality of Money." *Journal of Economic Theory*, 4 (April): 103–24.

Luke, Timothy W. 1990. *Social Theory and Modernity: Critique, Dissent, and Revolution.* Newbury Park, CA: Sage Publications.

Lukes, Steven, 1986. *Marxism and Morality.* Oxford: Oxford University Press.

Luxemburg, Rosa. 1912/1923. *Die Akkumulation des Kapitals. Ein Beitrag zur ökonomischen Erklärung des Imperialismus.* Berlin: Vereinigung internationaler Verlagsanstalten.

Lyotard, Jean-Francois. 1984. *The Postmodern Condition.* Minneapolis, MN: University of Minnesota Press.

Macgregor, Felipe E. and Marcial Rubio C. 1994. "Rejoinder to the Theory of Structural Violence." In *The Culture of Violence*, eds, Kumar Rupesinghe and Marcial Rubio C. Tokyo: United Nations University Press, pp. 42–58.

Machlup, Fritz. 1946. "Marginal Analysis and Empirical Research." *American Economic Review*, 36(4): 519–54.

Magdoff, Harry. 1969. *The Age of Imperialism. The Economics of U.S. Foreign Policy.* 1st Modern Reader edition. New York: Monthly Review Press.

Malone, Thomas W. and Robert J. Laubacher. 1998. "The Dawn of the E-Lance Economy. Technology Allows Individuals and Companies to Operate in New Ways." *Harvard Business Review*, 76(5): 144–52.

Mankiw, N. Gregory. 1995. "The Growth of Nations." *Brookings Papers on Economic Activity*, 26(1): 275–326.

Mann, Michael. 1986. *The Sources of Social Power.* vol. 1, *A History of Power from the Beginning to 1760.* Cambridge: Cambridge University Press.

Manne, Henry G. 1965. "Mergers and the Market for Corporate Control." *The Journal of Political Economy*, 73(2): 110–20.

Marable, Manning, 1998. "Black Fundamentalism: Farrakhan and Conservative Black Nationalism." *Race and Class*, 39(4): 1–22.

Margalit, Avishai. 1996. *The Decent Society.* Cambridge: Harvard University Press.

Marglin, Frédérique and Stephen A. Marglin. 1996. *Decolonizing Knowledge: From Development to Dialogue.* Oxford: Clarendon Press.

Markham, J. W. 1955. "Survey of the Evidence and Findings on Mergers." In *Business Concentration and Price Policy. A Conference of the Universities-National Committee for Economic Research.* Princeton: Princeton University Press, pp. 141–190.

Markusen, James R. and Anthony J. Venables. 1998. "Multinational Firms and the New Trade Theory." *Journal of International Economics*, 28(2): 183–203.

Marshall, Alfred. 1920. *Principles of Economics. An Introductory Volume.* 8th edition. London: Macmillan.

Martin, William G. 1994. "The World-Systems Perspective in Perspective: Assessing the Attempt to Move Beyond Nineteenth-century Eurocentric Conceptions." *Review*, 17(2): 145–85.

Marty, Martin E. and R. Scott Appleby (eds). 1993. *The Fundamentalism Project*, vol. 3. *Fundamentalisms and the State: Remaking Politics, Economies, and Militance.* Chicago: University of Chicago Press.

Marx, Karl. 1867/1972. *Das Kapital.* vol 1. *MEW 23.* Berlin: Dietz.

——. 1909. *Capital. A Critique of Political Economy*. 3 vols. Chicago: Charles H. Kerr & Company.

Matthaei, Julie. 1992. "Marxist-Feminist Contributions to Radical Economics." In *Radical Economics*, eds, Bruce Roberts and Susan Feiner. Boston: Kluwer Academic Publishers, pp. 117–45.

Matustik, M. J. B. 1998. *Spectres of Liberation: Great Refusals in the New World Order*. Albany, NY: State University of New York Press.

Maurer, Rainer. 1994. "Die Exportstärke der deutschen Wirtschaft – Weltmarktspitze trotz technologischen Rückstands?." *Die Weltwirtschaft*, 3: 308–19.

Mayer, Ann Elizabeth. 1993. "The Fundamentalist Impact on Law, Politics, and Constitutions in Iran, Pakistan, and the Sudan." In *The Fundamentalism Project*, vol. 3, *Fundamentalisms and the State: Remaking Politics, Economies, and Militance*, eds, Marty, Martin E. and R. Scott Appleby. Chicago: University of Chicago Press, pp. 110–51.

Mayor, Thomas. 1968. "The Decline of the United States Capital-output Ratio." *Economic Development and Cultural Change*, 16(4): 495–516.

McCarthy, Thomas. 1987. "Introduction" to J. Habermas's *The Philosophical Discourse of Modernity*. Trans. F. Lawrence. Cambridge, MA: MIT Press.

McCloskey, D. 1990. *If You're So Smart: The Narrative of Economic Expertise*. Chicago, IL: University of Chicago Press.

McCreery, David, 1983. "Debt Servitude in Rural Guatemala 1876–1936." *Hispanic American Historical Review*, 63(4): 735–59.

McDowell, Linda and Gillian Court. 1994. "Missing Subjects: Gender, Power, and Sexuality in Merchant Banking." *Economic Geography*, 70(3): 229–51.

McGraw-Hill. Online. *DRI Database*.

McLeod, Mary. 1996. "Everyday and 'Other' Spaces." In *Architecture and Feminism*, eds, Debra Coleman, Elizabeth Danze, and Carol Henderson. New York: Princeton Architectural Press, pp. 1–37.

McMichael, Philip. 1996. *Development and Social Change: A Global Perspective*. Thousand Oaks, CA: Pine Forge Press.

McNeill, William H. 1963. *The Rise of the West: A History of the Human Community*. Chicago: University of Chicago Press.

Meiksins Wood, Ellen. 1989. "Rational Choice Marxism: Is the Game Worth the Candle?" *New Left Review*, 177 (September–October): 41–88.

——. 1995a. "The Separation of the 'Economic' and the 'Political' in Capitalism." In *Democracy Against Capitalism: Renewing Historical Materialism*. Cambridge: Cambridge University Press.

——. 1995b. "Capitalism and Human Emancipation: Race, Gender and Democracy." In *Democracy Against Capitalism: Renewing Historical Materialism*. Cambridge: Cambridge University Press.

Melvern, Linda. 2000. *A People Betrayed: The Role of the West in Rwanda's Genocide*. London: Zed.

Menocal, María Rosa. 2002. *The Ornament of the World: How Muslims, Jews, and Christians Created a Culture of Tolerance in Medieval Spain*. Boston: Little, Brown.

Mernissi, Fatima. 1992. *Islam and Democracy: Fear of the Modern World*. Trans. Mary Jo Lakeland. Reading, MA: Addison-Wesley.

Messner, Steven F. and K. Tardiff. 1986. "Economic Inequality and levels of Homicide: An Analysis of Urban Neighborhoods." *Criminology*, 24(2): 297–317.

Metcalf, Thomas. 1989. *An Imperial Vision: Indian Architecture and Britain's Raj*. Berkeley: University of California Press.

Mies, Maria. 1986. *Patriarchy and Accumulation on a World Scale: Women in the International Division of Labor.* London: Zed Books Ltd.

——. 1998/1986. *Patriarchy and Accumulation on a World Scale: Women and the International Division of Labour.* New edition with preface. London: Zed Books.

Mies, Maria, Veronika Bennholdt-Thomsen, and Claudia von Werlhof. 1988. *Women: The Last Colony.* London: Zed Books.

Milanovik, Branko. 1998. *Income, inequality, and poverty during the Transition from Planned to Market Economy.* Washington, DC: World Bank.

Miles, Robert. 1986. *Capitalism and Unfree Labour.* London: Tavistock Press.

Millennium. 1998. Special issue on Ethics. Fall.

Miller, C. A. 2000. "The Dynamics of Framing Environmental Values and Policy: Four Models of Societal Processes," *Environmental Values,* 9: 211–33.

——. 2001a. "Scientific Internationalism in American Foreign Policy: The Case of Meteorology (1947–1958)." *Changing the Atmosphere: Expert Knowledge and Environmental Governance,* eds, C. Miller and P. Edwards. Cambridge, MA: MIT Press.

——. 2001b. "Challenges to the Application of Science to Global Affairs: Contingency, Trust, and Moral Order." *Changing the Atmosphere: Expert Knowledge and Environmental Governance,* eds, C. A. Miller and P. N. Edwards. Cambridge, MA: MIT Press.

——. Forthcoming. "Climate Science and the Making of a Global Political Order." *States of Knowledge: The Coproduction of Science and Order,* ed., S. S. Jasanoff. London: Routledge.

Miller, C. A. and P. N. Edwards (eds). 2001a. *Changing the Atmosphere: Expert Knowledge and Environmental Governance.* Cambridge, MIT.

——. 2001b. "Introduction: The Globalization of Climate Science and Climate Politics." *Changing the Atmosphere: Expert Knowledge and Environmental Governance,* eds, C. Miller and P. Edwards. Cambridge, MA: MIT Press.

Miller, William I. 1993. *Humiliation. And Other Essays on Honor, Social Discomfort, and Violence.* Ithaca: Cornell University Press.

Mintzer, I. and J. A. Leonard (eds). 1993. *Negotiating Climate Change: The Inside Story of the Framework Convention.* Cambridge, UK: Cambridge University Press.

Mitchell, Mark L. and J. Harold Mulherin. 1996. "The Impact of Industry Shocks on Takeover and Restructuring Activity." *Journal of Financial Economics,* 41(2): 193–229.

Mitra, Subrata Kumar. 1999. *Culture and Personality. The Politics of Social Change in Post-Colonial India.* New Delhi: Sage.

Mittelman, James H. 1996. "The Dynamics of Globalization." In *Globalization: Critical Reflections,* ed., James H. Mittelman. Boulder: Lynne Rienner, pp. 1–19.

Mohanty, Chandra Talpade. 1997. "Women Workers and Capitalist Scripts." In *Feminist Genealogies, Colonial Legacies, Democratic Futures,* eds, M. Jacqui Alexander and Chandra Talpade Mohanty. New York: Routledge, pp. 3–45.

Morawetz, David. 1993. "The Gap between Rich and Poor Countries." In *Development–Underdevelopment. The Political Economy of Inequality,* eds, Mitchell A. Seligson and John T. Passé-Smith. Boulder: Lynne Rienner, pp. 9–14.

Morris, William. 1980. "The Worker's Share of Art." An article in *Commonweal,* 1885, reprinted in *William Morris: Selected Writings and Designs,* ed., Asa Briggs. London: Penguin, pp. 140–3.

Mouzelis, Nicos. 1992. "Book Review" of *Semiperipheral States in the World Economy,* (William G. Martin, ed., 1990). *Humboldt Journal of Social Relations,* 18(1): 247–51.

Mumford, Lewis. 1967. *The Myth of the Machine. Technics and Human Development.* New York: Harcourt, Brace & World, Inc.

——. 1970. *The Myth of the Machine. The Pentagon of Power.* New York: Harcourt, Brace Jovanovich, Inc.

Mundell, Robert A. 1963. "Capital Mobility and Stabilization Policy Under Fixed and Flexible Exchange Rates." *Canadian Journal of Economics and Political Science*, 29(4): 475–85.

Munif, Abdelrahman. 1989. *Cities of Salt*. Trans. Peter Theroux. New York: Vintage.

Murphy, Craig N. 1994. *International Organization and Industrial Change: Global Governance Since 1850*. Cambridge, UK: Polity Press.

Murphy, Craig N. and Roger Tooze (eds). 1991. *The New International Political Economy*. Boulder, CO: Lynne Rienner.

Murphy, Kevin M., Andrei Shleifer, and Robert Vishny. 1989. "Income Distribution, Market Size and industrialization." *Quarterly Journal of Economics*, 104(3): 537–64.

Myles, John. 1991. "Post-Industrialism and the Service Economy." In *The New Era of Global Competition*, eds, Daniel Drache and Meric S. Gertler. Montreal: McGill-Queen's University Press, pp. 351–66.

Narayan, Deepa, Raj Patel, Kai Schafft, Anne Rademacher, and Sarah Koch-Schulte. 2000. *Voices of the Poor. Can Anyone Hear Us?* New York, NY: World Bank and Oxford University Press.

Nardin, Terry and David Mapel (eds). 1992. *Traditions of International Ethics*. New York, NY: Cambridge University Press.

Naredo, José Manuel, 1987. *La economía en evolución: historia y perspectivas de las categorías básicas del pensamiento económico*. Madrid: Siglo XXI.

Narrasiquin, Philippe. 1995. "Croissance tirée par les exportations et politique de change: Le cas de l'île Maurice." *Revue d'Economie Politique*, 105(2): 315–31.

National Research Council (NRC). 1979. *Carbon Dioxide and Climate: A Scientific Assessment*. Washington, DC: National Academy Press.

——. 1982 *Carbon Dioxide and Climate: A Second Assessment*. Washington, DC: National Academy Press.

——. 1983. *Changing Climate: Report of the Carbon Dioxide Assessment Committee*. Washington, DC: National Academy Press.

Nelson, Ralph L. 1959. *Merger Movements in American Industry, 1895–1956*. Princeton: Princeton University Press.

Neufeld, Mark. 1995. *The Restructuring of International Relations Theory*. New York, NY: Cambridge University Press.

Nielsen, Kai and Robert Ware (eds). 1997. *Exploitation*. Atlantic Highlands, NJ: Humanities Press.

Nitzan, Jonathan. 1992. "Inflation as Restructuring. A Theoretical and Empirical Account of the US Experience." Unpublished PhD Dissertation, Department of Economics, McGill University, Montreal.

——. 1998. "Differential Accumulation: Toward a New Political Economy of Capital." *Review of International Political Economy*, 5(2): 169–217.

Nitzan, Jonathan and Shimshon Bichler. 1995. "Bringing Capital Accumulation Back In: The Weapondollar–Petrodollar Coalition – Military Contractors, Oil Companies and Middle-East 'Energy Conflicts'." *Review of International Political Economy*, 2(3): 446–515.

——. 1996. "From War Profits to Peace Dividends: The New Political Economy of Israel." *Capital and Class*, 60: 61–94.

——. 2000a. "Capital Accumulation: Breaking the Dualism of 'Economics' and 'Politics'." In *Global Political Economy: Contemporary Theories*, ed., R. Palan. New York and London: Routledge, pp. 67–88.

——. 2000b. "Inflation and Accumulation: The Case of Israel." *Science and Society*, 64(1): 274–309.

Nitzan, Jonathan and Shimshon Bichler. 2001. "Going Global: Differential Accumulation and the Great U-turn in South Africa and Israel." *Review of Radical Political Economics,* 33(1): 21–55.

Noble, D. 1977. *America by Design: Science, Technology, and the Rise of Corporate Capitalism.* New York, NY: Knopf.

Norris, Christopher. 1983. *The Deconstructive Turn: Essays in the Rhetoric of Philosophy.* New York, NY: Methuen, Inc.

——. 1997. *Against Relativism: Philosophy of Science, Deconstruction, and Critical Theory.* Malden, MA: Blackwell.

Norton, G. 1947. "Address of Welcome by Mr. Garrison Norton, Assistant Secretary of State." In WMO Conference of Directors, Washington, September 22–October 11, 1947. Geneva, Switzerland: World Meteorological Organization, pp. 372–6.

Notermans, Tom. 1993. "The Abdication from National Policy Autonomy: Why the Macroeconomic Policy Regime has become so Unfavourable to Labor." *Politics and Society,* 21(2): 133–67.

Nurkse, Ragnar. 1953. *Problems of Capital Formation in Underdeveloped Countries.* New York: Oxford University Press.

Nussbaum, Martha. 2000. *Women and Human Development: The Capabilities Approach.* Cambridge: Cambridge University Press.

O'Brien, Robert, Anne Marie Goetz, Jan Aart Scholte, and Marc Williams. 2000. *Contesting Global Governance: Multilateral Economic Institutions and Global Social Movements.* Cambridge: Cambridge University Press.

Obrinsky, Mark. 1983. *Profit Theory and Capitalism.* Philadelphia: University of Pennsylvania Press.

Ochoa, E., and M. Glick. 1992. "Competing Microeconomic Theories of Industrial Profits: An Empirical Approach." In *The Megacrop & Macrodynamics: Essays in Memory of Alfred Eichner,* ed., W. Milberg. New York: Sharpe, pp. 225–47.

Offe, Claus. 1973. "The Theory of the Capitalist State and the Problem of Policy Formation." In *Stress and Contradiction in Modern Capitalism,* eds, Leon Lindberg, Robert Alford, Colin Crouch, and Claus Offe. Lexington, MA: DC Heath.

Ohlin, Bertil. 1927. "Ist eine Modernisierung der Außenhandelstheorie erforderlich?" *Weltwirtschaftliches Archiv,* 26(1): 97–115.

Ohmae, Kenichi. 1996. *The End of the Nation-State: The Rise of Regional Economies.* New York: Free Press.

Okishio, Nobuo. 1961. "Technical Changes and the Rate of Profit." *Kobe University Economic Review,* 7: 85–90.

Oliver, Roland and John D. Fage. 1988. *A Short History of Africa.* London: Penguin.

Olson, Mancur. 1982. *The Rise and Decline of Nations: Economic Growth, Stagflation, and Social Rigidities.* New Haven: Yale University Press.

Onuf, Nicholas. 1989. *World of Our Making: Rules and Rule in Social Theory and International Relations.* Columbia, SC: University of South Carolina Press.

——. 1998a. "Preface." In *International Relations in a Constructed World,* eds, V. Kubalkova, N. Onuf, and P. Kowert. Armonk, NJ: ME Sharpe, pp. iii–xii.

——. 1998b. "Constructivism: A User's Manual." In *International Relations in a Constructed World,* eds, V. Kubalkova, N. Onuf, and P. Kowert. Armonk, NJ: ME Sharpe, pp. 58–78.

——. 1998c. *The Republican Legacy in International Thought.* New York, NY: Cambridge University Press.

O'Riordan, Timoth and Jill Jager. 1996. *Politics of Climate Change: A European Perspective.* New York, NY: Routledge.

Orwell, George. 1948. *Nineteen Eighty-Four.* London and Toronto: Secker & Warburg and SJ Reginald Saunders & Co. Ltd.

Page, John, Nancy Birdsall, Ed Campos, W. Max Corden, Chang-Shik Kim, Howard Pack, Richard Sabot, Joseph E. Stiglitz, Marilou Uy. Major contributions by Robert Cassen, William Easterly, Robert Z. Lawrence, Peter Petri, and Lant Pritchett. 1993. *The East Asian Miracle. Economic Growth and Public Policy*, ed., Lawrence MacDonald. Washington: World Bank.

Palan, Ronen. 1997a. "Ontological Consternation and the Future of International Political Economy." *Economies et Societies*, 4: 103–17.

———. 1997b. "Trying to Have your Cake and Eating it Too: How and Why the State System Created Offshore." Paper presented at the annual meeting of the International Studies Association. March.

Palan, Ronen, Jason Abbot, and Phil Deans. 1996. "The State in the Global Political Economy." In *State Strategies in the Global Political Economy*. London: Pinter, pp. 32–54.

Panitch, Leo. 1996. "Rethinking the Role of the State." In *Globalization: Critical Reflections*, ed., James H. Mittelman. Boulder: Lynne Rienner, pp. 83–113.

Paqué, Karl Heinz. 1995. "Technologie, Wissen und Wirtschafts politik – Zur Rolle des Staates in Theorien des endogenen Wachstums." *Die Weltwirtschaft*, 3: 237–53.

Park, Kyung Ae. 1994. "Women and Revolution in South and North Korea." In *Women and Revolution in Africa, Asia, and the New World*, ed., Mary Ann Tétreault. Columbia: University of South Carolina Press, pp. 161–91.

Parkin, M. and R. Bade. 1986. *Modern Macroeconomics*. 2nd edition. Scarborough, Ontario: Prentice-Hall Canada.

Parvin, Manoucher and Hashem Dezhlaakhsh. 1988. "Trade, Technology Transfer, and Hyper-Dutch Disease in OPEC: Theory and Evidence." *International Journal of Middle East Studies*, 20(4): 469–77.

Pauly, Louis. 1997. *Who Elected the Bankers? Surveillance and Control in the World Economy*. Ithaca, NY: Cornell University Press.

Pellerin, Helene. 1996. "Global Restructuring and International Migration: Consequences for the Globalization of Politics." In *Globalization: Theory and Practice*, eds, Eleonore Kofman and Gillian Youngs. London: Pinter, pp. 81–96.

Penrose, Edith Tilton. 1959. *The Theory of the Growth of the Firm*. Oxford: Blackwell.

Penvenne, Jean-Marie. 1995. *African Workers and Colonial Racism: Mozambican Strategies and Struggles in Lourenço Marques 1877–1962*. London: James Currey.

Perkins, J. H. 1997. *Geopolitics and the Green Revolution: Wheat, Genes, and the Cold War*. Oxford, UK: Oxford University Press.

Peterson, M. Jeanne. 1998. *Managing the Frozen South: The Creation and Evolution of the Antarctic Treaty System*. Berkeley, CA: University of California Press.

Peterson, V. Spike. 1997. "Commenting on Constituting IPE." In *Constituting International Political Economy*, eds, K. Burch and R. Denemark. Boulder, CO: Lynne Rienner, pp. 201–5.

———. 2003. *A Critical Rewriting of Global Political Economy: Integrating Reproductive, Productive and Virtual Economies*. London: Routledge.

Peterson, V. Spike and Anne Sisson Runyan. 1999. *Global Gender Issues*. 2nd edition. Boulder, CO: Westview Press.

Pettman, Jindy Rosa. 1996. *Worlding Women: A Feminist International Politics*. London and New York: Routledge.

Pettman, Ralph. 1997. "The Limits to a Rationalist Understanding of IPE." In *Constituting International Political Economy*, eds, K. Burch and R. Denemark. Boulder, CO: Lynne Rienner, pp. 169–85.

Phelps, E. S. 1968. "Money Wage Dynamics and Labor Market Equilibrium." *Journal of Political Economy*, 76(4, Part II): 678–711.

Pietsch, Anne-Jutta. 1978. "Der Arbeitsplatzwechsel als Konfliktmanifestation in der Sowjetunion." In *Migration und Wirtschaftsentwicklung*, ed., Hartmut Elsenhans. Frankfurt am Main/New York: Campus.

Pilling, David. 2000. "Drug Groups Wrestle with Seismic Shifts in Business Practices." *Financial Times Survey of Life Sciences & Pharmaceuticals*, April 6: I.

Pirenne, Henri. 1925. *Medieval Cities: Their Origins and the Revival of Trade*. Princeton: Princeton University Press.

———. 1939. *Mohammed and Charlemagne*. London: Allen & Unwin.

Plender, John and Victor Mallet. 2000. "A Struggle to Escape." *Financial Times* October 5: 16.

Pogge, Thomas. 1992. "Cosmopolitanism and Sovereignty" *Ethics*, 103(1): 48–75.

Polanyi, Karl. 1944. *The Great Transformation*. New York: Farrar and Rinehart.

———. 1958. *The Great Transformation*. Boston: Beacon Press.

Polanyi, Michael. 1966. *The Tacit Dimension*. New York, NY: Doubleday, Inc.

———. 1985. *Personal Knowledge: Towards a Post-Critical Philosophy*. Chicago, IL: University of Chicago Press.

Pontusson, Jonas. 1992. "At the End of the Third Road: Swedish Social Democracy in Crisis." *Politics and Society*, 20(3): 305–32.

Popkin, Samuel L. 1979. *The Rational Peasant: The Political Economy of Rural Society in Vietnam*. Berkeley, CA: University of California Press.

Porter, T. 1995. *Trust in Numbers: The Pursuit of Objectivity in Science and Public Life*. Princeton, NJ: Princeton University Press.

Poster, Mark. 1989. *Critical Theory and Poststructuralism*. Ithaca, NY: Cornell University Press.

Powlick, Philip J. 1995. "The Sources of Public Opinion for American Foreign Policy Officials." *International Studies Quarterly*, 39(4): 427–52.

Prakash, Vikramaditya. 1997. "Identity Production in Postcolonial Indian Architecture: Re-covering What We Never Had." In *Postcolonial Space(s)*, eds, G. B. Nalbantoğlu and C. T. Wong. New York: Princeton Architectural Press.

Pretzlik, Charles and William Lewis. 2000. Cross-Atlantic Consolidation Gains Pace. *Financial Times Survey of International Mergers and Acquisitions*, June 30, p.1.

Prugl, Elisabeth. 1996. "Home-Based Producers in Development Discourse." In *Homeworkers in Global Perspective*, eds, Eileen Boris and Lisa Prugl. New York: Routledge, pp. 39–59.

———. 1999. *The Global Construction of Gender: Home-Based Work in the Political Economy of the 20th Century*. New York: Columbia University Press.

Przeworski, Adam. 1980. "Material Interests, Class Compromise and the Transition to Socialism." *Politics and Society*, 10(2): 125–53.

———. 1985. *Capitalism and Social Democracy*. Cambridge: Cambridge University Press.

Putnam, Robert. 1995. "'Bowling Alone': America's Disintegrating Social Capital." *Journal of Democracy*, 6(1): 65–78.

Pyke, Karen D. 1996. "Class-Based Masculinities: The Interdependence of Gender, Class, and Interpersonal Power." *Gender & Society*, 10(5): 527–49.

Rabinow, Paul and William Sullivan (eds). 1979. *Interpretive Social Science*. Berkeley, CA: University of California Press.

Radice, Hugo. 1999. "Taking Globalization Seriously." In *Socialist Register 1999. Global Capitalism Versus Democracy*, eds, L. Panitch and C. Leys. London: Merlin Press, pp. 1–28.

Ramphele, Mamphele A. 1997. "Adolescents and Violence: 'Adults are Cruel, they Just Beat, Beat, Beat'." *Social Science and Medicine*, 45(8): 1189–97.

Randsborg, Klavs. 1991. *The First Millennium A.D. In Europe and the Mediterranean: An archaeological Essay*. Cambridge: Cambridge University Press.

Rapoport, A. 1960. *Fights, Games, and Debates*. Ann Arbor MI: University of Michigan Press.

Ravenscraft, David J. 1987. "The 1980s Merger Wave: An Industrial Organization Perspective." In *The Merger Boom*. Proceedings of a Conference Held at Melvin Village, New Hampshire, eds, L. E. Browne and E. S. Rosengren. Boston: Federal Reserve Bank of Boston, pp. 17–37.

Ravenscraft, David, J. and F. M. Scherer. 1987. *Mergers, Sell-Offs, and Economic Efficiency*. Washington, DC: The Brookings Institution.

——. 1989. "The Profitability of Mergers." *International Journal of Industrial Organization*, 7(1): 101–16.

Raynolds, Laura. 1997. "Restructuring National Agriculture, Agro-Food Trade, and Agrarian Livelihoods in the Caribbean." In *Globalising Food: Agrarian Questions and Global Restructuring*, eds, D. Goodman and M.J. Watts. London and New York: Routledge, pp. 119–32.

Rengger, Nicholas. 1995. *Political Theory, Modernity, and Postmodernity*. Cambridge, MA: Basil Blackwell, Inc.

Rey, Pierre-Philippe. 1973. *Les alliances de classes*. Paris: François Maspero.

Ricardo, David. 1817/1951. *On the Principles of Political Economy and Taxation. The Works and Correspondence of David Ricardo (1)*. Cambridge: Cambridge University Press.

Ripstein, Arthur. 1997. Responses to Humiliation. *Social Research*, 64(1)Spring: 90–112.

Rist, Gilbert. 1997. *The History of Development: From Western Origins to Global Faith*. Trans. Patrick Camiller. London: Zed Books.

Rittenberg, Libby. 1986. "Export Growth Performance of Less Developed Countries." *Journal of Development Economics*, 24(1): 167–77.

Roberts, James. 1997. "The Rational Constitution of Agents and Structures." In *Constituting International Political Economy*, eds, K. Burch and R. Denemark. Boulder, CO: Lynne Rienner, pp. 155–168.

Roberts, Marion. 1990. *Living in a Man Made World: Gender Assumptions in Housing Design*. London: Routledge.

Robertson, Roland (ed.). 1992. *Globalization: Social Theory and Global Culture*. London: Sage.

Robinson, Joan. 1953–54. "The Production Function and the Theory of Capital." *Review of Economic Studies*, 21(2): 81–106.

——. 1966. *An Essay on Marxian Economics*. 2nd edition. London: Macmillan.

Robinson, William I. and Jerry Harris. 2000. "Toward A Global Ruling Class? Globalization and the Transnational Capitalist Class." *Science & Society*, 64(1): 11–54.

Rodinson, Maxime. 1974. *Islam and Capitalism*. London: Penguin.

Rodríguez Céspedes, Ennio. 1983. "Del Crecimiento Sostenido a la Recesión: en Busca de Alternativas" *Pensamiento Iberoamericano*, 153–67.

Roemer, John E. 1979. "Continuing Controversy on the Falling Rate of Profit: Fixed Capital and Other Issues." *Cambridge Journal of Economics*, 3(4): 379–98.

Romer, Paul M. 1986. "Increasing Returns and Long-Term Growth." *Journal of Political Economy*, 94(2): 1002–37.

——. 1987. "Growth Based on Increasing Returns Due to Specialization." *American Economic Review*, 77: 56–62.

——. 1990. "Endogenous Technological Change." *Journal of Political Economy*, 98(5): 71–102.

——. 1994. "The Origins of Endogenous Growth." *Journal of Economic Perspectives*, 8(1): 3–22.

Romero, Mary. 1992. M.A.I. D. in the USA. New York: Routledge.

Rorty, Richard. 1979. *Philosophy and the Mirror of Nature*. Princeton, NJ: Princeton University Press.

Rose, Nikolas. 1992. "The Relocation of Authority in a Shrinking World." *Comparative Politics*, 24(3): 253–72.

Rose, Nikolas. 1996. "Governing 'advanced' liberal democracies." In *Foucault and Political Reason: Liberalism, Neo-liberalism and Rationalities of Government*, eds, Andrew Barry, Thomas Osborne and Nikolas Rose. London: UCL Press, pp. 37–64.

Rosenau, James N. and Mary Durfee. 1995. *Thinking Theory Thoroughly: Coherent Approaches to an Incoherent World*. Boulder, CO: Westview Press.

Rosenau, Pauline. 1992. *Post-modernism and the Social Sciences: Insights, Inroads, and Intrusions*. Princeton, NJ: Princeton University Press.

Rosenstein-Rodan, P. N. 1943. "Problems of Industrialization of Eastern and South Eastern Europe." *Economic Journal* 53(210): 202–11.

Ross, Marc H. 1993. *The Culture of Conflict. Interpretations and Interests in Comparative Perspective*. New Haven: Yale University Press.

——. 1997. "The Relevance of Culture for the Study of Political Psychology and Ethnic Conflict." *Political Psychology*, 18(2): 299–326.

Rostovtzeff, M. 1926/1957. *Social and Economic History of the Roman Empire*. Oxford: Clarendon Press.

Rostow, W. W. 1960. *The Stages of Economic Growth: A Non-Communist Manifesto*. Cambridge: Cambridge University Press.

Rowbotham, Sheila and Swasti Mitter (ed.). 1994. *Dignity and Daily Bread: New Forms of Economic Organization in the Third World and the First*. London: Routledge.

Roy, Olivier. 1994. *The Failure of Political Islam*. London: I. B. Tauris.

——. 1999. "Changing Patterns Among Radical Islamic Movements." *Brown Journal of World Affairs*, 6(1): 109–20.

——. 2001a. "Bin Laden et ses Frères." *Politique International*, 93: 67–81.

——. 2001b. "Bin Laden: An Apocalyptic Sect Severed from Political Islam." *East European Constitutional Review*, 10(4): 108–14.

Ruccio, David F. and Simon, Larry H. 1992. "Perspectives on Underdevelopment: Frank, the Modes of Production School and Amin." In *The Political Economy of Development and Underdevelopment*, 5th edition, eds, C. K. Wilber and K. P. Jameson. New York: McGraw Hill, pp. 119–48.

Rueschemeyer, D. and Theda Skocpol (eds). 1995. *States, Social Knowledge, and the Origins of Modern Social Policies*. Princeton: Princeton University Press.

Ruggie, John G. (ed.). 1993a. "Territoriality and beyond." *International Organization*, 47: 139–74.

—— (ed.). 1993b. *Multilateralism Matters: The Theory and Praxis of an Institutional Form*. New York: Columbia University Press.

——. 1998. *Constructing the World Polity*. New York: Routledge.

Runyan, Anne Sisson. 1992. "The 'State' of Nature: A Garden Unfit for Women and Other Living Things." In *Gendered States: Feminist (Re)Visions of International Relations Theory*, ed., V. Spike Peterson: *International Political Economy*, eds, Kurt Burch and Robert A. Denemark. Boulder, CO: Lynne Rienner, pp. 113–38.

Rupert, Mark. 1995. *Producing Hegemony: The Politics of Mass Production and American Global Power*. New York: Cambridge University Press.

Said, Edward. 1993. *Culture and Imperialism*. London: Chatto and Windus. Boulder, CO: Lynne Rienner Press, pp. 123–40.

Sakhnobanek, Siriphon, Boonpakdee, Nataya, Chanthathiro, Chutima. 1997. *The Traffic in Women: Human Realities of the International Sex Trade*. London: ZED Books.

Samuelson, Paul A. 1948. "International Trade and the Equalization of Factor Prices." *Economic Journal*, 58(230): 163–84.

——. 1974/1977. "World Wide Stagflation." In *Collected Scientific Papers of Paul A. Samuelson*, eds, H. Nagatani and K. Crowley. Cambridge, MA: The MIT Press, pp. 801–7.

Sanderson, Stephen K. 1994. The Transition from Feudalism to Capitalism: The Theoretical Significance of the Japanese Case." *Review*, 19(1): 15–55.

Sassen, Saskia. 1991. *The Global City: New York, London, Tokyo*. Princeton: Princeton University Press.

——. 1993. "Economic Globalization." In *Global Visions: Beyond the New World Order*. Boston: South End Press, pp. 61–6.

——. 1998. *Globalization and its Discontents*. New York: New Press.

Saul, John S. and Colin Leys. 1999. "Sub–Saharan Africa in Global Capitalism," *Monthly Review*, July–August: 13–30.

Sawchuck, Kim. 1994. Semiotics, Cybernetics, and the Ecstasy of Marketing Communications. In *Baudrillard: A Critical Reader*, ed., Douglas Kellner. Oxford: Blackwell, pp. 89–118.

Scheper-Hughes, Nancy. 1992. *Death without Weeping: the Violence of Everyday Life in Brazil*. Berkeley: University of California Press.

——. 1996. "Small Wars and Invisible Genocides." *Social Science and Medicine* 43(5): 889–900.

Scherer, F. M. and David Ross. 1990. *Industrial Market Structure and Economic Performance*. 3rd edition. Boston: Houghton Mifflin.

Schmandt-Besserat, Denise. 1992. *Before Writing, Volume One: From Counting to Cuneiform*. Austin: University of Texas Press.

Schmitt-Rink, Gerhard. 1988. "Zur Bestimmung des Hochtechnologiegehalts von Export- und Importströmen." *Jahrbuch für Sozialwissenschaft*, 39(1): 158–64.

Schmitter, Philippe C. 1974. "Still the Century of Corporatism?" In *The New Corporatism*, eds, Frederick B. Pike and Thomas Stritch. Notre Dame, In: University of Notre Dame Press, pp. 85–131.

Scholte, Jan Aart. 1996. Beyond the Buzzword: Towards a Critical Theory of Globalization. In *Globalization: Theory and Practice*, eds, Eleonore Kofman and Gillian Youngs. London: Pinter, pp. 43–57.

——. 1997. Global Trade and Finance. In *The Globalization of World Politics: An Introduction to International Relations*, eds, John Baylis and Steve Smith. Oxford: Oxford University Press, pp. 430–47.

Schorske, Carl E. 1980. *Fin-de-Siècle Vienna: Politics and Culture*. New York: Alfred A. Knopf.

Schwartz, Herman M. 2000. *States Versus Markets: History, Geography, and the Development of the International Political Economy*, 2nd edition. New York: St Martin's.

Schwebel, Milton. 1997. "Job Insecurity as Structural Violence: Implications for Destructive Intergroup Conflict." *Peace and Conflict: Journal of Peace Psychology*, 3(4): 333–51.

Schydlowsky, Daniel M. 1972. "Latin American Trade Policies in the 1970's: A Prospective Appraisal." *Quarterly Journal of Economics*, 86(2): 263–89.

Scott, James C. 1998. *Seeing Like a State: How Certain Schemes to Improve the Human Condition Have Failed*. New Haven: Yale University Press.

Screpanti, E. 1999. "Capitalist Forms and the Essence of Capitalism." *Review of International Political Economy*, 6 (1): 1–26.

Seabrook, Jeremy. 1998. *Travels in the Skin Trade*. London: Pluto Press.

Seers, Dudley. 1964. "The Mechanism of the Open Petroleum Economy." *Social and Economic Studies*, 13(2): 233–42.

Segerstrom, Paul S. 1991. "Innovation, Imitation and Economic Growth." *Journal of Political Economy*, 99(4): 807–27.

Seidman, Steven. 1983. *Liberalism and the Origins of European Social Theory*. Berkeley, CA: University of California Press.

Seligson, Mitchell A. 1993. "The Dual Gaps: An Overview of Theory and Research." In *Development–Underdevelopment. The Political Economy of Inequality*, eds, Mitchell A. Seligson and John T. Passé-Smith. Boulder: Lynne Rienner, pp. 3–8.

Sells, Michael. 1996. *The Bridge Betrayed: Religion and Genocide in Bosnia*. Berkeley: University of California Press.

Sen, Amartya Kumar. 1981. *Poverty and Famines. An Essay on Entitlement and Deprivation*. Oxford: Clarendon Press.

——. 1999. *Freedom and Development*. Oxford: Oxford University Press.

——. 2000. *Underdevelopment as Freedom*. New York: Doubleday Anchor.

Serafini, Anthony. 1989. *Linus Pauling*. New York: Paragon House.

Shackley, S. 2001. "Epistemic Lifestyles in Climate Change Modeling." *Changing the Atmosphere: Expert Knowledge and Environmental Governance*, eds, Clark Miller and P. Edwards, pp. 107–34.

Shafaeddin, Mehdi. 1995. "The Impact of Trade Liberalization on Export and GDP in Least Developed Countries." *UNCTAD Review*: 1–16.

Shannon, R. T. 1989. *An Introduction to the World-System Perspective*. Boulder, CO: Westview Press.

Shay, Jonathan. 1994. *Achilles in Vietnam: Combat Trauma and the Undoing of Character*. New York: Touchstone.

Sherman, Daniel and Irit Rogoff (ed.). 1994. *Museum Culture: Histories, Discourses, Spectacles*. Minneapolis: University of Minnesota Press.

Sherman, Howard J. 1985. "Monopoly Capital vs. the Fundamentalists." In *Rethinking Marxism. Struggles in Marxist Theory. Essays for Harry Magdoff & Paul Sweezy*, eds, S. Resnick and R. Wolff. Brooklyn, NY: Autonomedia, pp. 359–77.

Silver, Hilary. 1994. "Social Exclusion and Social Solidarity: Three Paradigms." *International Labour Review*, 133(5 – 6): 531–78.

——. 1998. "Policies to Reinforce Social Cohesion in Europe." *Social Exclusion: an ILO Perspective*, eds, J. B. Figureido and A. de Haan. Geneva: International Institute for Labour Studies.

Simons, Herbert W. and Michael Billig (ed.). 1994. *After Postmodernism: Reconstructing Ideology Critique*. Thousand Oaks, CA: Sage Publications.

Simpson, George Eaton and J. Milton Yinger. 1953. *Racial and Cultural Minorities: an Analysis of Prejudice and Discrimination*. 3rd edition. New York: Harper and Row.

Simpson, Michael A. 1993. "Bitter Waters. Effects on Children of the Stresses of Unrest and Oppression." In *International Handbook of Traumatic Stress Syndromes*, eds, J. P. Wilson and V. Raphael. New York and London: Plenum Press, pp. 601–24.

Sinclair, Timothy. 1994. "Passing Judgement: Credit Rating Processes as Regulatory Mechanisms of Governance in the Emerging World Order." *Review of International Political Economy*, 1(1): 133–59.

Sinn, Hans-Werner. 2000. "Zehn Jahre deutsche Wiedervereinigung – Ein Kommentar zur Lage der neuen Länder." *IFO-Schnelldienst* 53z9(26–7) 10–22.

Sivanandan, A. 1989. "New Circuits of Imperialism." *Race & Class*, 30(3–4): 1–20.

Sivanandan, A. and Ellen Meiksins Wood. 1997. "Capitalism, Globalization, and Epochal Shifts: An Exchange." *Monthly Review*, 48 (9): 19–32.

Sivard, Ruth Leger. 1985. *Women: A World Survey*. Washington, DC: World Priorities.

——. 1995. *Women: A World Survey*. 2nd edition. Washington, DC: World Priorities.

Skocpol, Theda. 1977. "Wallerstein's World-System: A Theoretical and Historical Critique," *American Journal of Sociology*, 82: 1075–102.

Slater, David and Taylor, Peter J. (ed.). 1999. *The American Century*. London: Routledge.

Smith, Adam. 1776/1937. *The Wealth of Nations*. New York: Random House.

———. 1776/1976. *The Wealth of Nations*. Oxford: Clarendon Press.

Smith, Anthony D. 1982. "Ethnic Identity and World Order." *Millennium*, 12: 149–61.

Smith, Joan. 1993. "The Creation of the World We Know: The World Economy and the Re-creation of Gendered Identities." In *Identity Politics and Women: Cultural Reassertions and Feminisms in International Perspective*, ed., Valentine M. Moghadam. Boulder: Westview Press.

———. Immanuel Wallerstein and Hans-Dieter Evers (ed.). 1984. *Households and the World-Economy*. Beverly Hills: Sage.

Smith, John and Immanuel Wallerstein (ed.). 1992. *Creating and Transforming Households: The Constraints of the World-Economy*. Cambridge: Cambridge University Press.

Smith, Neil. 1997. "The Satanic Geographies of Globalization: Uneven Development in the 1990s." *Public Culture*, 10(1): 169–89.

Smith, Steve. 1996. "Positivism and Beyond." In *International Theory*, eds, Steve Smith *et al.* New York: Cambridge University Press, pp. 11–44.

Smith, Woodruff D. 1984. "The Function of Commercial Centres in the Modernization of European Capitalism." *Journal of Economic History*, 44: 985–1005.

Sobel, Andrew C. 1994. *Domestic Choices, International Markets: Dismantling National Barriers and Liberalizing Securities Markets*. Ann Arbor: University of Michigan Press.

Social Research. 1992. Special Issue: "Frontiers in Social Inquiry." 59(4).

Soros, George. 2002. *George Soros on Globalization*. New York: PublicAffairs.

Speigel, Henry W. 1991. *The Growth of Economic Thought*, 3rd edition, Durham: Duke University Press.

Spencer, Jonathan. 1992. "Problems in the Analysis of Communal Violence." *Contributions to Indian Sociology*, 26(2): 261–79.

Spero, Joan and Jonathan A. Hart. 1997. *The Politics of International Economic Relations*. 5th edition. New York: St Martin's Press.

Spitz, Pierre. 1978. "Silent Violence: Famine and Inequality." *International Social Science Journal*, 30(4): 867–92.

Spivak, Gayatri. 1987. "Scattered Speculations on the Question of Value." In *In Other Worlds: Essays in Cultural Politics*. New York: Methuen.

Standing, Guy. 1989. "Global Feminization through Flexible Labor." *World Development*, 17(7): 1077–95.

Statistisches Bundesamt: *Statistisches Jahrbuch für die Bundesrepublik Deutschland* (Stuttgart: Metzler-Poeschel, various years).

Staub, Ervin. 1989. *The Roots of Evil: the Origins of Genocide and Other Group Violence*. Cambridge: Cambridge University Press.

———. 1990. "Moral Exclusion, Personal Goal Theory and Extreme Destructiveness." *Journal of Social Issues*, 46(1): 47–64.

———. 1999. "The Origins and Prevention of Genocide, Mass Killing, and Other Collective Violence." *Peace and Conflict*, 5(4): 303–48.

Stavenhagen, Rodolfo. 1990. *The Ethnic Question. Conflicts, Development, and Human Rights*. Tokyo: United Nations University Press.

Ste. Croix, G. E. M. 1981. *The Class Struggle in the Ancient Greek World*. London: Duckworth.

Stecher, Bernd. 1972. *Entwicklungsstrategien und internationale Arbeitsteilung. Die Erfahrung in Chile, Südkorea und Mexiko*. Kiel: Institut für Weltwirtschaft.

Steindl, Josef. 1952/1976. *Maturity and Stagnation in American Capitalism*. New York: Monthly Review Press.

——. 1979/1984. "Stagnation Theory and Stagnation Policy." In *The Faltering Economy. The Problem of Accumulation Under Monopoly Capitalism*, eds, J. B. Foster and H. Szlajfer. New York: Monthly Review Press, pp. 179–97.

Stern, Jessica. 2002. "Get to the Roots of Terrorism." *International Herald Tribune*, 26 April.

Stevis, Dimitris and Valerie Assetto (eds). 2001. *The International Political Economy of the Environment: Critical Perspectives*. International Political Economy Yearbook, 12. Boulder, CO: Lynne Rienner.

Stiglitz, Joseph E. 2002. *Globalization and its Discontents*. New York: Norton.

Stinchcombe, Arthur L. 1968. *Constructing Social Theories*. New York, NY: Harcourt, Brace, and World, Inc.

Stone, Lawrence. 1979. *The Family, Sex and Marriage in England, 1500–1800*. Abridged edition. New York: Harper Torchbooks.

Storey, John. 1999. *Cultural Consumption and Everyday Life*. New York: Oxford University Press and Arnold Press.

Stover, William James. 1990. "Cultural Interaction and International Change." *International Journal on World Peace*, 7(4): 55–63.

Strange, Susan. 1985. "International Political Economy: The Story So Far and the Way Ahead." In *An International Political Economy*, eds, W. Ladd Hollist and F. Lamond. Tullis. Boulder CO: Westview Press, pp. 13–25.

——. 1988. *States and Markets*. London: Pinter.

——. 1996. *The Retreat of the State*. Cambridge: Cambridge University Press.

——. 1997. *Casino Capitalism*. Manchester: Manchester University Press.

——. 1998. *Mad Money*. Manchester: Manchester University Press.

Strassmann, W. Paul. 1956. "Economic Growth and Income Distribution." *Quarterly Journal of Economics*, 70(3): 425–40.

Strauss, John. 1986. "Does Better Nutrition Raise Farm Productivity." *Journal of Political Economy*, 94(2): 297–324.

Suh, Suk Tai. 1987. "The Theory of Unequal Exchange and the Developing Countries." In *Dependency Issues in Korean Development. Comparative Perspectives*, ed., Kim Kyong Dong. Seoul: Seoul National University Press, pp. 110–31.

Sun, Lena H. 1998. "Here Comes the Russian Bride." *Washington Post National Weekly Edition*, March 16.

Sutcliffe, Bob and Andrew Glyn. 1999. "Still Underwhelmed: Indicators of Globalization and their Misinterpretations." *Review of Radical Political Economics*, 31(1): 111–31.

Sylvester, Christine. 1994. *Feminist Theory and International Relations in a Postmodern Era*. New York: Cambridge University Press.

Tabak, Faruk and Michaeline A. Crichlow (eds). 2000. *Informalization: Process and Structure*. Baltimore and London: The Johns Hopkins University Press.

Tambiah, Stanley. 1997. "Friends, Neighbors, Enemies, Strangers: Aggressor and Victim in Civilian Ethnic Rites." *Social Science & Medicine*, 45(8): 1177–88.

Tawney, R. H. 1936. *Religion and the Rise of Capitalism*. London: John Murray.

Taylor, Alan M. 1996. "International Capital Mobility in History: The Saving–Investment Relationship," NBER Working Paper No. 5943. Cambridge MA: National Bureau of Economic Research.

Taylor, Charles. 1985. *Philosophical Papers*. 2 vols. New York, NY: Cambridge University Press.

Taylor, Peter J. 1996a. *The Way the Modern World Works*. New York: Wiley.

——. 1996b. "Embedded Statism and the Social Sciences: Opening up to New Spaces." *Environment and Planning A*, 28: 1917–28.

——. 1997a. "The Crisis of Boundaries: Towards a New Heterodoxy in the Social Sciences." *Journal of Area Studies*, 11: 11–31.

——. 1997b. "Hierarchical Tendencies Amongst World Cities: a Global Research Proposal." *Cities*, 14: 323–32.

——. 1998. "The Modernity of Westphalia." Paper presented at the Annual Meeting of the International Studies Association, March, Minneapolis, MN.

——. 1999a. *Modernities: A Geohistorical Interpretation.* Minneapolis: University of Minnesota Press.

——. 1999b. *Modernities: A Geohistorical Interpretation.* Cambridge: Polity.

——. 2000. "Embedded Statism and the Social Sciences 2: Geographies (and Metageographies) in Globalization." *Environment and Planning A*: 32.

——. 2001. "Specification of the world city network." *Geographical Analysis*, (in press).

Taylor, Peter J., Michael Hoyler, David R. F. Walker, and Mark J. Szegner. 2001. "A New Mapping of the World for the New Millennium." *Geographical Journal*, 167: 213–22.

Taylor, Timothy. 1997. *Global Pop: World Music, World Markets.* New York: Routledge.

Tenkate, Adriaan. 1992. "Trade Liberalization and Economic Stabilization in Mexico: Lessons of Experience." *World Development*, 20(5) : 659–72.

Tétreault, Mary Ann. 1995. *The Kuwait Petroleum Corporation and the Economics of the New World Order.* Westport, CT: Quorum Books.

——. 1998. "Spheres of Liberty, Conflict, and Power: The Public Lives of Private Persons." *Citizenship Studies*, 2(2): 273–89.

——. 2000. *Stories of Democracy: Politics and Society in Contemporary Kuwait.* New York: Columbia University Press.

——. 2003a. "Feminist Community in Postmodern Times." In *Partial Truths and the Politics of Community*, eds, Mary Ann Tétreault and Robin L. Teske. Columbia: University of South Carolina Press, pp. 1–32.

——. 2003b. "Pleasant Dreams: The WTO as Kuwait's Holy Grail." *Critique: Critical Middle Eastern Studies*, 12(1) Spring: 75–93.

——. Forthcoming. "God, the State, and Mammon: Religious Social Movements in an Age of Globalization." In *The International Political Economy Yearbook*, vol. 13, *Guns, Gods, and Globalization: Religious Resurgence and International Political Economy*. Boulder: Lynne Rienner Publishers.

Tétreault, Mary Ann and Charles Frederick Abel (eds). 1986. *Dependency Theory and the Return of High Politics.* Westport, CT: Greenwood Press.

Tétreault, Mary Ann and Robert A. Denemark (eds). Forthcoming. *The International Political Economy Yearbook*, vol. 13. *Guns, Gods, and Globalization: Religious Resurgence and International Political Economy.* Boulder: Lynne Rienner Publishers.

Tétreault, Mary Ann and Robin L. Teske. 1997. "The Struggle to Democratize the Slovak Republic." *Current History*, March: 135–9.

Theurl, Theresia. 1999. "Globalisierung als Selektionsprozeß ordnungspolitischer Paradigmen." In *Globalisierung der Wirtschaft: Ursachen-Formen-Konsequenzen. Schriften des Vereins für Socialpolitik 263*, ed., Hartmut Berg. Berlin: Duncker & Humblot, pp. 23–50.

Thomas, Hugh. 1998. *The Slave Trade: The History of the Atlantic Slave Trade 1440–1870.* London: Papermac.

Thomas, Kenneth P. 1997. *Capital Beyond Borders: States and Firms in the Auto Industry, 1960–94.* Washington: Georgetown University Press.

Thomas, Kenneth P. 2000. *Competing for Capital: Europe and North America in a Global Era.* Washington: Georgetown University Press.

Thomas, Kenneth P. and Mary Ann Tétreault (eds). 1999. *Racing to Regionalize: Democracy, Capitalism, and Regional Political Economy.* Boulder: Lynne Rienner.

Thompson, E. P. 1965. *The Making of the English Working Class.* London: Victor Gollancz Ltd.

———. 1968. *The Making of the English Working Class.* Harmondsworth: Penguin.

Thompson, Janna. 1992. *Justice and World Order: A Philosophical Inquiry.* London: Routledge.

Thompson, John B. 1984. *Studies in the Theory of Ideology.* Cambridge, England: Polity Press.

———. 1990. *Ideology and Modern Culture: Critical Social Theory in the Era of Mass Communication.* Stanford, CA: Stanford University Press.

Thrift, Nigel. 1996. *Spatial Formations.* London: Sage Publications.

Tierney, Patrick. 2000. *Darkness in El Dorado: How Scientists and Journalists Devastated the Amazon.* New York: WW Norton.

Tilley, Virginia. 1997. "Terms of the Debate: Untangling Language on Ethnicity and Ethnic Movements." *Ethnic and Racial Studies,* 20(3): 497–522.

Tilly, Charles. 1986. "Does Modernization Breed Revolution?" In *Revolutions: Theoretical, Comparative, and Historical Studies,* ed., Jack A. Goldstone. San Diego: Harcourt, Brace, Jovanovich, pp. 47–57.

Tobin, James and William C. Brainard. 1968. "Pitfalls in Financial Model Building." *American Economic Review. Papers and Proceedings,* 58(2): 99–122.

———. 1977. "Asset Markets and the Cost of Capital." In *Economic Progress, Private Values, and Public Policy: Essays in the Honor of William Fellner,* eds, Bela Balassa and R. Nelson. Amsterdam and New York: North-Holland Publishing Co., pp. 235–62.

Tooze, Roger. 1997a. "International Political Economy in an Age of Globalization." In *The Globalization of World Politics: An Introduction to International Relations,* eds, John Baylis and Steve Smith. Oxford: Oxford University Press, pp. 213–30.

———. 1997b. "Constructive Criticism: Threats, Imperatives, and Opportunities of a Constitutive IPE." In *Constituting International Political Economy,* eds, K. Burch and R. Denemark, pp. 207–12.

Tooze, Roger and Craig N. Murphy. 1996. "The Epistemology of Poverty and the Poverty of Epistemology in IPE: Mystery, Blindness, and Invisibility." *Millennium,* 25(3): 681–707.

Toulmin, Stephen. 1972. *Human Understanding.* Princeton, NJ: Princeton University Press.

———. 1995. "Foreword." In *Rethinking Knowledge: Reflections Across the Disciplines,* eds, R. F. Goodman and W. R. Fisher. Albany, NY: State University of New York Press, p. ix.

Truong, Thanh-Dam. 1990. *Sex, Money and Morality: Prostitution and Tourism in Southeast Asia.* London and New Jersey: Zed Press.

Turner, Bryan S. 1974. *Weber and Islam.* New York: Humanities Press.

Tzannatos, P. Zafiris. 1997. *International Competitiveness in East Asian Manufacturing: Unit Labor Cost Analysis for Selected Countries.* Washington: World Bank.

Underhill, Geoffrey R. D. 1997. Transnationalizing the State in Global Financial Markets. Paper Presented at the AMEI/ISA Conference, Manzanillo, December.

United Nations. 1995. *The World's Women 1995: Trends and Statistics.* New York: United Nations.

———. 2001. *World Economic and Social Survey 2001.* New York: United Nations.

———. 2002. *World Economic Situation and Prospects 2002.* New York: United Nations.

United Nations Commission on Human Rights, Sub-Commission on Prevention of Discrimination and protection of Minorities. 1995. Draft UN Declaration on the Rights of Indigenous Peoples. *International Legal Materials,* 34 March, pp. 341–55.

United Nations Conference on Trade and Development (UNCTAD). 1992. *Measures and Incentives for Enhancing the Competitiveness of Sectors with Export Potential in Developing Countries: Evidence and Lessons from Experience.* Geneva: United Nations.

——. 1994. *World Investment Report 1994. Transnational Corporations, Employment and the Workplace.* Geneva: United Nations.

——. 1999. *World Investment Report 1999. Foreign Direct Investment and the Challenge of Development.* New York: United Nations.

——. 2000. *World Investment Report. Cross-Border Mergers and Acquisitions and Development.* New York and Geneva: United Nations.

United Nations Development Program (UNDP). 1995. *Human Development Report 1995.* New York: Oxford University Press.

——. 1997. *Human Development Report 1997.* New York: Oxford University Press.

——. 1999. *Human Development Report 1999.* New York: Oxford University Press.

——. 2001. *Human Development Report 2001: Making New Technologies Work for Human Development.* New York: Oxford University Press.

United Nations Women. 1995. *The World's Women 1995: Trends and Statistics.* New York: United Nations.

——. 2000. *The World's Women 2000: Trends and Statistics.* New York: United Nations.

United States Bureau of Labor Statistics. 1998. *News.* September 25.

US Department of Commerce. Bureau of the Census. 1975. *Historical Statistics of the United States. Colonial Times to 1970.* 2 vols. Washington, DC: Government Printing Office.

——. Annual. *Statistical Abstract of the United States.* Washington, DC: Government Printing Office.

US Internal Revenue Service. Annual. *Corporations Income Tax returns.* Washington, DC: Government Printing Office.

US President. Annual. *Economic Report of the President. Transmitted to the Congress.* Washington, DC: Government Printing Office.

Uvin, Peter. 1998. *Aiding Violence: The Development Enterprise in Rwanda.* West Hartford, CT: Kumarian Press.

——. 1999. "Mass Violence in Burundi and Rwanda: Different Paths to Similar Outcomes." *Comparative Politics*, 35(2): 253–71.

Van der Merwe, Hendrik. 1989. *Pursuing Justice and Peace in South Africa.* London: Routledge and Kegan Paul.

Van Mieghem, J. 1955a. "International Geophysical Year 1957–58, Part I: Historical Survey." *WMO Bulletin*, 4(1): 6–9.

——. 1955b. "International Geophysical Year 1957–58, Part II: The Programme." *WMO Bulletin*, 4(2): 6–9.

Van Parijs, Philippe. 1980. "The Falling Rate-of-Profit Theory of Crisis. A Rational Reconstruction by Way of Obituary." *Review of Radical Political Economics*, 12(1): 1–17.

Veblen, Thorstein. 1899/1953. *The Theory of the Leisure Class: An Economic Study of Institutions.* New York: New American Library.

——. 1904/1975. *The Theory of Business Enterprise.* Clifton, New Jersey: Augustus M. Kelley, Reprints of Economics Classics.

——. 1923/1967. *Absentee Ownership and Business Enterprise in Recent Times. The Case of America.* With an introduction by Robert Leckachman. Boston: Beacon Press.

——. 1934. *The Theory of the Leisure Class.* New edition. New York: Modern Library.

Verdier, Daniel. 1998. "Domestic Responses to Capital Market Internationalization under the Gold Standard." *International Organization*, 52(1): 1–34.

Vernon, Raymond. 1966. "International Investment and International Trade in the Product Cycle." *Quarterly Journal of Economics*, 80(1): 190–207.

Vickers, Jeanne. 1991. *Women and the World Economic Crisis.* London and New Jersey: Zed Books.

Victor, David G. 2001. *Collapse of the Kyoto Protocol and the Struggle to Slow Global Warming.* Princeton, NJ: Princeton University Press.

Vilas, Carlos M. 1997. "Inequality and the dismantling of Citizenship in Latin America." *NACLA Report on the Americas*, 31(1): 57–63.

Volkan, Vamik D. 1994. *The Need to Have Enemies and Allies. From Clinical Practice to International Relationships.* Northvale: Jason Aronson.

Waever, Ole. 1996. "The Rise and Fall of the Inter-paradigm Debate." In *International Theory: Positivism and Beyond*, eds, K. Booth Smith and Marysia Zalewski. New York: Cambridge University Press.

Walker, Michael, A. 1997. "Preface." In *The Underground Economy: Global Evidence of its Size and Impact*, eds, Owen Lippert and Michael Walker. Vancouver: The Fraser Institute, pp. vii–xiii.

Walker, R. B. J. 1993. *Inside/Outside: International Relations and Political Theory.* Cambridge: Cambridge University Press.

Wallenberg Pachaly, Andreas von. 1995. "A Group-Dynamic Understanding of Structural Violence and Psychotherapy." *Free Associations*, 5(2): 221–38.

Wallerstein, Immanuel. 1974a. "The Rise and Future Demise of the World Capitalist System: Concepts for Comparative Analysis." *Comparative Studies in Society and History*, 16(4): 387–415.

——. 1974b. *The Modern World System I: Capitalist Agriculture and the Origins of the European World-Economy in the Sixteenth Century.* New York: Academic Press.

——. 1979. *The Capitalist World-Economy.* New York: Cambridge University Press.

—— 1980. *The Modern World-System. II, Mercantilism and the Consolidation of the European World-Economy, 1600–1750.* New York: Academic Press.

——. 1982. "A Crisis As Transition." In *Dynamics of Global Crisis*, eds, Samir Amin, Arrighi, Giovanni, Frank, Andre Gunder, Wallerstein, Immanuel. New York: Monthly Review Press, pp. 14–54.

——. 1983a. "An Agenda for World-Systems Analysis." In *Contending Approaches to World System Analysis*, ed., W. Thompson. Beverly Hills, CA: Sage, pp. 299–308.

——. 1983b. *Historical Capitalism.* London, England: Verso.

——. 1987. "World-Systems Analysis." In *Social Theory Today*, eds, Anthony Giddens and J. Turner. Stanford, CA: Stanford University Press, pp. 309–24.

——. 1989. *The Modern World-System. III, The Second Era of Great Expansion of the Capitalist World-Economy 1730–1840s.* New York: Academic Press.

——. 1990. "World-Systems Analysis: The Second Phase." *Review*, XIII(2): 287–93.

——. 1991. *Geopolitics and Geopolitical Culture: Essays on the Changing World-System.* New York: Cambridge University Press.

——. 1992. "The West, Capitalism, and the Modern World-System." *Review*, XV(4): 561–619.

——. 1993. "World System versus World-Systems: A Critique." In *The World System: Five Hundred Years or Five thousand?*, eds, André Gunder Frank and Barry K. Gills. London and New York: Routledge, pp. 292–6.

——. 1995a. "The Modern World-System and Evolution." *Journal of World-System Research*, 1(19). [web: http://csf.colorado.edu/wsystems/jwsr.html]

——. 1995b. "Hold the Tiller Firm: On Method and the Unit of Analysis." In *Civilizations and World Systems. Studying World-Historical Change*, ed., Stephen K. Sanderson. Walnut Creek, CA: Altamira, pp. 239–47.

——. 1999. "Frank Proves the European Miracle," *Review*, XXII(3): 355–71.

Wallerstein, Immanuel. Editorial Board: Jean-Marie Apostolides, K. Anthony Appiah, Louis Brenner, Ngwarsungu Chiwengo, Jocelyn Dakhlia, Hans Ulrich Gumbrecht, Sandra Harding, Francoise Lionnet, Herve Moulin, Gayatri Chakravorty Spivak, V. Y. Mudimbe – editor, Bogumil Jewsiewicki – assoc. editor. 1996. *Open the Social Sciences: Report of the Gulbenkian Commission on the Restructuring of the Social Sciences*. Stanford, CA: Stanford University Press. The Gulbekian Commission: Immanuel Wallerstein, chair. Caletous Juma, Evelyn Fox Keller, Jurgen Kocka, Dominique Lecourt, V. Y. Mudimbe, Kinhide Mushakoji, Ilya Prigogine, Peter J. Taylor, Michel-Rolph Trouillot, Richard Lee (scientific secretary).

Wallich, Henry C. 1984. "Why is Net International Investment So Small?" In *International Capital Movements, Debt and Monetary System*, eds, W. Engles, A. Gutowski and H. C. Wallich. Mainz: Hase and Koehler, pp. 417–37.

Walzer, Michael. 1965. *The Revolution of the Saints: A Study in the Origins of Radical Politics*. Cambridge: Harvard University Press.

Ward, Kathryn B. (ed.). 1990. *Women Workers and Global Restructuring*. Ithaca: ILR Press of Cornell University.

Waring, Marilyn. 1988. *If Women Counted: A New Feminist Economics*. San Francisco: Harper.

Webb, James. 1979. "Women Can't Fight." *The Washingtonian*, November: 144–8, 273–7.

Weber, Cynthia. 1995. *Simulating Sovereignty: Intervention, the State and Symbolic Exchange*. Cambridge: Cambridge University Press.

Weber, Max. 1924/1976. *The Agrarian Sociology of Ancient Civilizations*. Trans. R. I. Frank. London: New Left Books.

——. 1978. *Economy and Society: An Outline of Interpretive Sociology*, eds, Guenther Roth and Claus Wittich. Berkeley: University of California Press.

Wedel, Janine R. 1998. *Collision and Collusion: The Strange Case of Western Aid to Eastern Europe, 1989–1998*. New York: St Martin's.

Weedon, Chris. 1987. *Feminist Practice and Poststructuralist Theory*. New York: Basil Blackwell.

Weeks, John. 1981. *Capital and Exploitation*. Princeton: Princeton University Press.

Weizsäcker, Carl Christoph. 1999. "Keine Angst vor Megafusionen." *Frankfurter Allgemeine Zeitung*, April 24: 15.

Weliwita, Avanda. 1998. "Cointegration Tests and The Long-Run Purchasing Power Parity: Examination of Six Currencies in Asia." *Journal of Economic Development*, 23(1): 103–13.

Wells, Miriam J. 1984. "The Resurgence of Sharecropping: Historical Anomaly or Political Strategy?" *American Journal of Sociology*, 90(1): 1–29.

Wendt, Alexander. 1999. *Social Theory of International Politics*. New York: Cambridge University Press.

Weston, J. Fred. 1987. "The Payoff in Mergers and Acquisitions." In *The Mergers and Acquisition Handbook*, ed., M. L. Rock. New York: McGraw Hill, pp. 31–47.

Weston, J. Fred, Kwang S. Chung, and Juana. Siu. 1998. *Takeovers, Restructuring and Corporate Governance*. Upper Saddle River, NJ: Prentice Hall.

Wheeler, David. 1980. "Basic Needs Fulfillment and Economic Growth: A Simultaneous Model." *Journal of Development Economics*, 7(4): 435–51.

White, Jenny B. 1994. *Money Makes Us Relatives: Women's Labor in Urban Turkey*. Austin: University of Texas Press.

White, Stephen K. 1995. "Reason, Modernity, and Democracy." In *The Cambridge Companion to Habermas*, ed., S. K. White, New York: Cambridge University Press, pp. 3–16.

Wiesenthal, Helmut. 1998. "Dimensionen und Folgen der Globalisierung. Einige Koordinaten auf unbekanntem Terrain." In *Globalisierung und Nachhaltigkeit. Zu den Chancen einer wirkungsvollen Umweltpolitik unter den Bedingungen Globalisierter Wirtschaftsbeziehungen*, ed., Ulrich Petschow. Berlin: Friedrich – Ebert – Stiftung, Forum Berlin.

Wijnbergen, Sweder van. 1984. "The 'Dutch Disease.'" *Economic Journal*, 94(373): 41–55.

Wilkinson, Richard G. 1996. *Unhealthy Societies. The Afflictions of Inequality*. London: Routledge.

——. 1997. "Health Inequalities: Relative or Absolute Material Standards." *British Medical Journal*, 314(3): 591–5.

Williams, Eric. 1944/1964. *Capitalism and Slavery*. London: André Deutsch.

Williams, Raymond. 1958. *Culture and Society*. London: Chatto & Windus.

Williamson, Jeffrey G. 1996. "Globalization, Convergence and History." *Journal of Economic History*, 56(2): 277–306.

Williamson, Oliver E. 1985. *The Economic Institutions of Capitalism: Firms, Markets, Relational Contracting*. New York and London: Free Press and Collier Macmillan.

——. 1986. "Transforming Merger Policy: The Pound of New Perspectives." *American Economic Review, Papers and Proceedings*, 76(2): 114–9.

Wills, Garry. 1990. *Under God: Religion and Politics in America*. New York: Simon and Schuster.

——. 2000. *Papal Sin: Structures of Deceit*. New York: Doubleday.

Wilson, Elizabeth. 1991. *The Sphinx in the City*. London: Virago Press.

Wilson, James. 1998. *The Earth Shall Weep: A History of Native America*. London: Picador.

Winston, Clifford. 1998. "U.S. Industry Adjustment to Economic Deregulation." *Journal of Economic Perspectives*, 12(3): 89–110.

Wisdom, J. O. 1987. *Challengeability in Modern Science*. Dorset, UK: Blackmore.

Wittgenstein, Ludwig. 1958. *Philosophical Investigations*. 3rd edition. Trans. G. E. M. Anscombe. New York: Macmillan.

Wolf, Eric R. 1982. *Europe and the People Without History*. Berkeley: University of California Press.

——. 1997. *Europe and the People Without History*. Berkeley: University of California Press.

Wolfe, Marshall. 1995. "Globalization and Social Exclusion: Some Paradoxes." *Social Exclusion: Rhetoric, Reality, Responses*, eds, G. Rodgers, C. Gore, and J. B. Figueiredo. Geneva: International Institute for Labour Studies and United Nations Development Programme.

Wolff, Edward N. 1991. "Capital Formation and Productivity Convergence Over the Long Term." *American Economic Review*, 81(3): 565–79.

Wolpe, Harold (ed.). 1980. *The Articulation of Modes of Production*. London, Boston and Henley: Routledge and Kegan Paul.

Woo, Tunoy and Shuki Tsang. 1988. "Comparative Advantage and Trade Liberalization in China." *Economy and Society*, 17(1): 21–51.

Wood, Neil, 1994. *Foundations of Political Economy: Some Early Tudor Views on State and Society*. Berkeley, Los Angeles, CA, and London: University of California Press.

Woodiwiss, Anthony. 1990. *Social Theory after Postmodernism: Rethinking Production, Law, and Class*. Winchester, MA: Pluto Press.

World Bank. 2000. *World Development Report 1999/2000. Entering the 21st Century*. New York: Oxford University Press.

——. 2001. *World Development Report 2000/2001. Attacking Poverty*. Oxford: Oxford University Press.

World Meteorological Organization (WMO). 1951a. First Congress of the World Meteorological Organization, Paris, 19 March–28 April, 1951, Final Report: Volume I, Reports. Document no. 1/I. Geneva, Switzerland: World Meteorological Organization.

——. 1951b. First Congress of the World Meteorological Organization, Paris, 19 March–28 April, 1951, Final Report: Volume II, Minutes. Document no. 1/II. Geneva, Switzerland: World Meteorological Organization.

——. 1951c. First Congress of the World Meteorological Organization, Paris, 19 March–28 April, 1951, Final Report: Volume III, Documents. Document no. 1/III. Geneva, Switzerland: World Meteorological Organization.

——. 1951d. Second Session of the Executive Committee, Lausanne, 3rd–20th October, 1951, Resolutions. Document no. 4. Geneva, Switzerland: World Meteorological Organization.

——. 1979. *World Climate Conference: Geneva, February, 1979*. Geneva, Switzerland: World Meteorological Organization.

Wright, Gwendolyn. 1991. *The Politics of Design in French Colonial Urbanism*. Chicago: Chicago University Press.

Wynne, B. 1982. *Rationality and Ritual: The Windscale Inquiry and Nuclear Decisions in Britain*. Chalfont St Giles, UK, British Society for the History of Science.

Yeatman, Anna. 1994. *Postmodern Revisionings*. New York: Routledge.

Yotopoulos, Pan A. and Lin Jenu-Yih. 1993. "Purchasing Power Parities for Taiwan: The Basic Data for 1985 and International Comparisons." *Journal of Economic Development*, 18(1): 7–52.

Young, Allyn. 1928. "Increasing Returns of and Economic Progress." *Economic Journal*, 38(152): 528–42.

Youngs, Gillian. 1997. "Globalized Lives, Bounded Identities: Rethinking Inequality in Transnational Contexts." *Development*, 40(3): 15–21.

Yuval-Davis, Nira. 1997. *Gender and Nation*. Thousand Oaks, CA: Sage.

Zeitlin, Maurice. 1974. "Corporate Ownership and Control: The Large Corporation and the Capitalist Class." *American Journal of Sociology*, 79(5): 1073–119.

Zerubavel, Eviatar. 1992. *Terra Cognita: the Mental Discovery of America* New Brunswick: Rutgers University Press.

Zimmermann, William. 1973. "Issue Area and Foreign Policy Process." *American Political Science Review*, 67(4): 1204–12.

Zuckerman, Alan. 1997. "Reformulating Explanatory Standards and Advancing Theory in Comparative Politics." In *Comparative Politics*, eds, M. Lichbach and A. Zuckerman. New York: Cambridge University Press, pp. 277–310.

Index

eBooks

eBooks – at www.eBookstore.tandf.co.uk

A library at your fingertips!

eBooks are electronic versions of printed books. You can store them on your PC/laptop or browse them online.

They have advantages for anyone needing rapid access to a wide variety of published, copyright information.

eBooks can help your research by enabling you to bookmark chapters, annotate text and use instant searches to find specific words or phrases. Several eBook files would fit on even a small laptop or PDA.

NEW: Save money by eSubscribing: cheap, online access to any eBook for as long as you need it.

Annual subscription packages

We now offer special low-cost bulk subscriptions to packages of eBooks in certain subject areas. These are available to libraries or to individuals.

For more information please contact webmaster.ebooks@tandf.co.uk

We're continually developing the eBook concept, so keep up to date by visiting the website.

www.eBookstore.tandf.co.uk